THE MANAGEMENT CONTROL PROCESS

ROBERT J. MOCKLER

St. John's University

APPLETON-CENTURY-CROFTS

Educational Division

New York   MEREDITH CORPORATION

THE MANAGEMENT CONTROL PROCESS

Other books by Robert J. Mockler

*The Business Management Process: A Situational Approach
*Business Planning and Policy Formulation
Circulation Planning and Development for the National Observer:
    A Research Study on Business Applications of Management
    Planning and Control Principles
Guide lines for More Effective Planning and Management of Franchise
    Systems (with Harrison Easop)
New Profit Opportunities in Business Publishing (editor and contributing
    author)
Putting Computers to Work More Effectively in Business Publishing
    (editor and contributing author)
*Readings in Business Planning and Policy Formulation (editor and contri-
    buting author)
*Readings in Management Control (editor and contributing author)

*published by Appleton-Century-Crofts

To Very Reverend Joseph T. Cahill, C.M.,
President, St. John's University

PREFACE

The purpose of *The Management Control Process* is to explain what management control is and how it is performed.

Management control, like most other business areas, is in a period of rapid development. The whole concept of accounting control has changed with the introduction of computerized information systems, for the computer has replaced the bookkeeper and the accountant has been called upon to perform broader management functions. The computer revolution has also brought to management's attention many operating control problems which were so often neglected in companies with accounting-oriented control systems. And new operations research tools have opened up opportunities for improved control practices. Control is thus no longer the special province of the financial or accounting officer and limited to the traditional financial control tools, but now covers a wide variety of control tools and control situations.

In spite of these developments, very little effort has been made either to develop a unifying concept of management control encompassing both new and traditional control areas or to construct an integrated approach to all kinds and levels of control situations and problems. Nor have companies moved to create specific organization units responsible for coordinating *all* the control activities that go on within the company. The result has been a somewhat haphazard approach to organizing and performing control within individual companies, fuzzy definitions of control functions which in turn lead to continuing friction among financial, systems and operating managers, and widespread frustration among company managers about how to organize the control functions within their companies. This book attempts to provide some guidelines for solving these problems.

The major thesis of this study is that management control is an integrated scientific discipline, which encompasses all control activities within a company (including financial control), and which has its own systematically organized set of principles and processes to guide the manager in handling all types of business control situations. In contrast to other control studies, this book devotes considerable attention to control situations and tools outside the financial and accounting areas, a departure deliberately designed to break the accounting and financial molds which in so many companies has stifled the development of broad-based management control operations.

Chapter 1 and 2 define the concept of management control and develop a systematic process for carrying out all types of management control action—from developing an information system for control and designing standards for it, to making control decisions and taking corrective action. The process is also applicable to all kinds and levels of control situations—from the control function performed by the individual operating manager to the overall financial control function performed for the corporation as a whole. The concept of management control, as developed in this book, thus goes beyond the controller's, accountant's and financial officer's viewpoints, and provides practical guidelines which can be used by any manager in any functional area to control his operation.

The basic steps in the management control process outlined in Chapter 2 are:

1. Diagnose the situation in order to define the control problem and the method for dealing with it.
2. Examine the control problem and review the facts in order to find the key factors affecting the problem and its solution.
3. Develop and evaluate alternative solutions.
4. Exercise control.
5. Prepare a report.

Chapter 3 through 12 examine in detail each phase of the management control process. Chapter 3 covers the preparatory steps required for management control, and chapters 4 and 5 the development and analysis of the key factors affecting the situation. Chapters 6 through 10 discuss the major types of tools used in management control and how they are developed: financial and accounting controls; individual operating and staff controls; graphic and quantitative tools used in control; and data processing systems for control. Chapter 11 concerns the problems encountered in exercising control and chapter 12 deals with selected aspects of control reporting not covered earlier in the study.

Chapters 13 and 14 present two integrated studies of actual management control situations: one, an overall corporate financial control system; the other, an operating control network in the marketing area. The conclusion to the book gives a history of the study of management control theory and practice.

The Management Control Process differs from other studies of the subject in a number of ways:

1. It views control as a broad function, only one part of which is the traditional financial accounting control area, and so treats all areas of management control within a single, integrated, conceptual framework.

2. It develops a general management control process, which parallels the basic problem-solving/decision-making process and which is applicable to all types and levels of control situations.

3. It gives greater emphasis than do other studies to some of the more difficult steps in management control, such as developing control standards and control information feedback systems, probing the meaning and significance of deviations from standard, creating networks of operating controls, using graphic and mathematical tools for operating control, and taking *positive* control action.

4. It explores in detail the application of control theory to various kinds of control situations in business, and so provides practical guidelines for management control action.

5. It covers all the basic control functions a company performs, and attempts to show how they can be organized and carried out in a more rational and co-ordinated manner.

Because of its breadth, this book can be used by anyone who wants to learn more about management control, whether he is a business executive or business student. The book is designed for use in middle management reading programs, as a main text in management control courses, or as a supplemental text in courses on management principles, systems development, operations research, and accounting and financial management. It will also serve as instructive reading for active business managers who are not now pursuing a regular study program, but who are interested in improving their management skills.

I wish to thank my editor, Eugene Jennings, and my colleagues in business for reading preliminary drafts of the book and suggesting ways to improve it. I am also indebted to my students at St. John's University for their commentaries, to my research assistant Thomas Deely, and to Mrs. Katherine Kelly for her patience in preparing many drafts of the manuscript. Finally, I want to thank my wife, without whom the book would never have come into print.

CONTENTS

THE MANAGEMENT
CONTROL PROCESS

CHAPTER 1

THE CONCEPT
OF MANAGEMENT CONTROL

Control is a basic intellectual process which each of us follows in getting any job done. For example, when a family is going to visit friends in another city by car, the driver will normally develop a plan and map out a route for driving to the destination. He will determine the expected arrival time, the time he must leave, and the speed at which he must drive to get there at that time. He will probably note the major towns along the route, if any, and the time at which they should be reached, the principal turns to be taken, and any significant landmarks by which these turns can be identified. While he is driving he will check his speedometer to be sure he is maintaining his planned speed. He will also check his time of arrival at critical points on the trip to see if he is ahead or behind schedule. If behind, he may adjust his driving speed or call ahead to say he will be late. He will also watch signs or landmarks along the way and check them against his map to verify that he is moving in the right direction.

In the same way, every business manager develops plans of action and control mechanisms, such as budgets. The first gives him the course of action to follow. The second provides him with controls through which he can check his progress against plans and, where necessary, take corrective action. This is, however, only one aspect of management control, the general control process. Management control also includes a variety of specific activities within a business.

Management control first of all involves the formal process set up by a company to develop overall financial budgets and to report on and measure company operations against these budgets. Overall financial control is the control area most often dealt with in management books—probably because it exists in all companies, deals with familiar dollar budgets, and follows widely accepted accounting and financial rules. Overall financial control differs in many ways from the control function per-

1

formed by the individual manager, because overall company control is assigned to a specific company department or executive, concentrates on financial controls and standards, and usually has a highly developed reporting and procedural system extending throughout all departments of a company.

Management control is not, however, limited to overall corporate financial control. It can be the preparation of unit sales quotas for each salesman by the marketing manager, and the corrective action he initiates when sales are not on target. It can be the control of the flow of new products by the new product manager, or the setting of a weekly output quota by the production supervisor, based on his plan. It can be quality control, manpower control, inventory control, materials control, customer complaint and service control, distribution control, or advertising control. It can be the designing of a computerized data processing system by the systems analyst for both overall financial control and operating control. It can, in short, be any of the specific jobs which must be done to maintain control of a business operation, from the development of standards and budgets, which is closely related to the planning function, to the initiating of control action, which is then carried out through the administrative function.

The purpose of this chapter is to define the concept of management control, the various levels and kinds of management control, the relation of management control to planning and the other management functions, the problems and opportunities presented by the new control technology, and the distinguishing viewpoint of management control.

THE DEFINITION OF MANAGEMENT CONTROL

Management control is a systematic effort to set performance standards consistent with planning objectives, to design information feedback systems, to compare actual performance with these predetermined standards, to determine whether there are any deviations and to measure their significance, and to take any action required to assure that all corporate resources are being used in the most effective and efficient way possible in achieving corporate objectives.

This definition is somewhat more detailed than the definition of business control given by others in the field, and places as much emphasis on setting standards, designing information control systems, determining the significance of deviations, and taking positive action as on comparing, measuring and taking corrective action. The following are some of the better-known definitions of control:

1.   Williams Travers Jerome: Executive control [is] some sort of systematic

effort to compare current performance to a predetermined plan or objective, presumably to take any immediate action required.[1]

2.   Harold Koontz and Cyril O'Donnell: The managerial function of control is the measurement and correction of the performance of subordinates in order to make sure that enterprise objectives and the plans devised to attain them are accomplished.[2]

3.   Robert Anthony: Management control is the process by which managers assure that resources are obtained and used effectively and efficiently in the accomplishment of the organization's objectives.[3]

4.   Henri Fayol: Control consists of verifying whether everything occurs in conformity with the plan adopted, the instructions issued, and principles established. It has for an object to point out weaknesses and errors in order to rectify and prevent recurrence.[4]

In all except Anthony's definition, which broadly describes the purpose of control, the emphasis in these definitions is on measuring, comparing and taking corrective action. These definitions are not incorrect, but their emphasis can be misleading. In practice the act of measuring and comparing is often the easiest control step to perform, and if a manager takes action only to correct errors he will fail to realize the benefits that come from emphasizing positive (instead of negative) control action. In contrast, other aspects of the control function not mentioned in these definitions have a much greater impact on effective control action.

The setting of standards is the most critical aspect of control. The more realistic and clear the standards are, the more meaningful will be the conclusions which can be drawn from comparing results to standards. If those using the standards participate in their creation, the meaning of deviations from the standards can be uncovered more quickly and easily and the necessity of taking "corrective" action kept to a minimum. Experience has shown that inaccurate standards are found to be the cause of a deviation almost as often as operating deficiencies.

The ability to measure and compare also depends on the accuracy and timing of the feedback of performance information. In a direct-mail

[1]William Travers Jerome III, *Executive Control—The Catalyst* (New York: John Wiley and Sons, Inc., 1961), p. 24.

[2]Harold Koontz and Cyril O'Donnell, *Principles of Management: An Analysis of Managerial Functions* (4th ed.; New York: McGraw-Hill Book Company, 1968), p. 639.

[3]Robert N. Anthony, *Planning and Control Systems: A Framework for Analysis* (Boston: Division of Research, Graduate School of Business Administration, Harvard University, 1965), p. 17.

[4]Henri Fayol, *General and Industrial Management* (New York: Pitman Corporation, 1949), pp. 107 ff. Other definitions of control can be found in Anthony, *Planning and Control Systems*, p. 129-147; Chris Luneski, "Some Aspects of the Meaning of Control," *Accounting Review*, Vol. 30, No. 3 (July 1964), pp. 591-597; and Peter F. Drucker, "Controls, Control and Management," *Management Controls: New Directions in Basic Research*, eds. Charles P. Bonini, Robert K. Jaedicke and Harvey M. Wagner (New York: McGraw-Hill Book Company, 1964), pp. 286-296.

selling operation, for example, orders are tabulated by low-paid clerks, so that when a manager is testing one price against another in a small sample, special controls are needed, since the chance of errors in reporting test results is high. In today's larger companies, control information reporting is handled mostly by complex computerized data processing systems. In these systems, in order for a manager to be certain he is getting accurate information, the manager must understand the data input processes.

In many control reports comparing and measuring are done automatically—actual figures are compared with standards and the amount of any deviation shown. In such cases the major task is not so much to find out whether there are deviations, but to determine the *meaning* and measure the *significance* of any deviations.

When corrective action is required, considerable skill is needed to take that action in a way which does not destroy initiative and creativity within a business organization. Continual emphasis on finding errors and telling people they have made mistakes can undermine confidence in a control system, and shift attention from doing things better to avoiding doing things wrong. One way to avoid this pitfall is to always examine favorable, as well as unfavorable, variances during control reviews.

In addition to measuring, comparing, and taking corrective action, therefore, there are a number of important action steps in modern management control: creating and communicating effective standards, developing information reporting systems, determining the significance of deviations from standards, and taking positive action to improve operations. The greater emphasis given to these action steps is one of the major factors which distinguishes modern management control, and the author's definition of control given at the beginning of this section, from more traditional business control concepts.

VARIOUS LEVELS AND KINDS OF MANAGEMENT CONTROL

The exact standards developed and the way in which they are developed, the kind of information system needed, the difficulties encountered in determining the significance of any deviation, and the action taken when favorable or unfavorable deviations occur, all depend on the kind and level of management control being exercised.

Control is required for the corporation as a whole. Such control is normally exercised by a corporate control executive, department or group, which translates overall corporate plans into broad quantitative financial yardsticks for use by the president, board of directors, and principal corporate officers. At this level of management control, overall corporate accounting control, budgetary control, funds flow and usage control, and legal reporting requirements are fulfilled. Financial controls are emphasized in corporate control, though as is seen in later chapters corporate managers are making increasing use of non-financial controls.

The vast majority of management control problems, however, are encountered at lower levels in a business organization. All managers exercise some form of control in carrying out their assigned responsibilities, as they translate corporate plans into action. The control process followed at these levels is the same as that followed at the corporate level, and in many instances these lower level controls are an integral part of the overall corporate financial control system. For example, the marketing manager's expense budget will be closely integrated with the corporate expense budget and his subordinate managers' expense budgets will be extensions of the department budgets.

The control situations encountered at the lower levels of an organization are quite varied, however, and extend far beyond the financial control area. For example, the marketing manager needs an entire reporting network, covering such factors as total sales, share of market, salesmen's performance, sales expense by product, new product development, service efficiency, profitability by product, advertising effectiveness, and order servicing costs, in order to compare weekly, monthly, or quarterly performance in each area against predetermined standards. This network of standards and reports is closely related to the overall corporate controls, for their purpose is to help the marketing manager reach his financial budgets. But the specific controls themselves are both financial and non-financial, and cover many areas which are outside the financial control area: for example, service efficiency may be measured by the number of complaints. The same is true in other operating areas of a business, such as manufacturing.

The managers of staff areas deal with entirely different kinds of day-to-day control situations than those faced by operating managers. For example, the personnel manager in a large corporation runs a service department, whose function is both to provide personnel services to operating managers and to plan and control overall personnel activities within the company. He has no sales against which to charge his expenses, and he uses such control standards as wage and salary guidelines, turnover and absenteeism levels, and the like. As in operating areas, his network of controls thus includes both financial and non-financial controls.

The levels of management control correspond roughly to the levels of management planning shown in Figure 1.1. As can be seen from the chart, each level of implementation planning (overall company and lower operating and staff levels) have their own budgets, and these financial controls link all company operations together. In addition to financial budgets, however, each operating area has its own network of controls designed to meet the area's specific planning requirements. For example, marketing has controls for advertising, sales, merchandising, new product development and the like, while manufacturing controls cover such areas as facilities, production output, materials, and distribution.

Figure 1.1

VARIOUS LEVELS AND KINDS OF BUSINESS PLANS

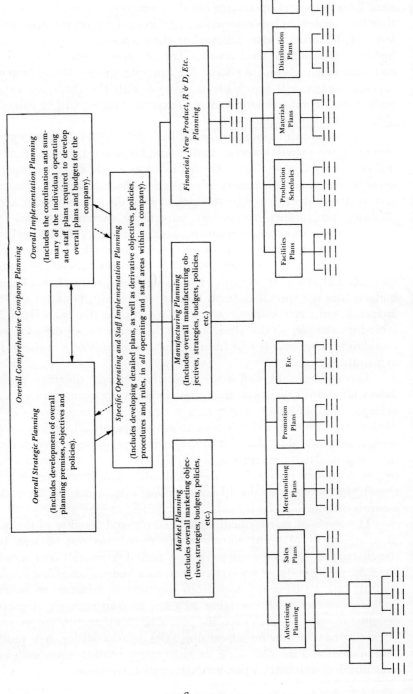

Control situations faced by managers of small business also have their own specific requirements. The scope of the operations being controlled is smaller, less staff help is available, and the situations faced are more immediate and short term. In small companies, operating controls and overall financial controls tend to be more closely integrated, because of the smaller scope of the operations.

One kind of management control, which is frequently overlooked, involves providing financial analyses for planning decisions. In making decisions, such as the type of equipment to buy, how much inventory to carry, or how to allocate production time or advertising monies, a realistic financial projection of each alternative is developed. When the effect of each alternative course of action on profits has been determined, the alternatives are then compared to each other and to some predetermined return-on-investment standard, in order to reach a decision. Control groups are very often called upon to make these financial analyses.

Besides distinguishing the level and kind of the control situation, one can also distinguish the aspect of the control process is involved in the situation. For example, the situation may involve only designing an information and control system, so that the question to be answered is "What kind of control system or tools do we need?" In another situation, the controls may already be in existence and the manager may be faced only with the problem of determining why sales are not in line with goals, and what action should be taken to raise sales.

While the focus of each type of control action is different—one involves designing a control system and the other using a control system to exercise control—the entire control process has relevance in the situation. In creating an effective system, the designer projects how managers will use it; in measuring deviations, the manager first checks to see if the standards he has and the information given him are accurate. Thus, even though the manager may be dealing specifically with only one aspect of the management control process, he will review the entire process in dealing with his specific problem.

The science of management control—its basic definition, underlying concepts, processes and principles of action—as discussed in Chapters 1 and 2 of this book, applies to all these kinds and levels of control situations and action.

MANAGEMENT CONTROL AND THE OTHER MANAGEMENT FUNCTIONS

In *Principles of Management* Koontz and O'Donnell describe the basic management functions as "planning, organizing, staffing, directing, and controlling."[5] Although other management theorists vary in their decrip-

5Koontz and O'Donnell, *Principles of Management*, p. 48.

tions of these functions, they all consider control one of the basic management functions and include some discussion of management control in their studies of general management theory and practice.

Because management is an integrated process, in which many functions are performed simultaneously, control is closely related to the other management functions. On the one hand, in order to perform management control, effective planning, organizing and staffing are needed, as are careful supervision and direction. On the other hand, management control principles are used in performing all management functions—in administrative, organization, and manpower control, and in controlling the progress of businesses toward meeting planning objectives.

Management control is not, however, synonymous with management. Success in business still depends on *planning* to exploit future opportunities, *organizing* and *staffing* to carry out plans, and *directing* effectively to get the most out of sales, production, and other personnel. The study of management control touches these areas only in the sense that management control is on the one hand a tool for performing each function and on the other hand uses tools of the other functions to carry out specific control jobs.

Management control is an extension of the corporate planning process, for a good plan will have controls built into it. A management control system thus cannot be developed, nor can management control be exercised effectively, unless the company has a specific objective and overall plan for reaching that objective. For example, in developing budgetary controls a manager needs to know the plans the company has for the coming year or for the next three, five, or even ten years, depending on how many years the budget covers.

Control standards are basically quantifications of plans, and as a result planning and control functions are performed simultaneously when establishing standards. Standards (especially in the form of budgets) are the means by which the critical aspects of a plan are translated into convenient yardsticks which can be used for measuring results against planned performance. These standards may be no more than the scheduled dates by which each phase of the plan must be completed, or they may be complex series of financial budgets designed to help the corporation maintain its gross profit and reach its planned return on investment.

Although management control is always exercised within the perspective of the overall corporate plan, the planning and control functions are distinct: the management planning process leads to the creation of a corporate plan: the management control process leads to the development of control tools and systems and controls performance within the framework of the corporate plan.

Management control is also closely related to the other management functions: directing, staffing, and organizing. The level of administrative abilities and the kind of staff affect the performance of management control. When standards are being set and control systems developed, management must deal with the attitudes of those whose actions will be controlled. Where it exists, resistance to change will have to be overcome and cooperation enlisted. When deviations occur, the way in which corrective action is handled will affect the control atmosphere throughout all the operating sections. If a negative approach is pursued too vigorously, the ability of the organization to innovate and change will be hampered.

Effective control thus depends on knowing how to manage human resources effectively—in selecting staff, in dealing with human error, in introducing organization changes, in motivating people to better efforts, and in training and guiding people. Ultimately, the success of any control system depends on the abilities of the people working within that system, for people who do not have the basic skills and psychological and emotional attitudes required for successful performance of a job will never be fully effective. It is, however, too easy to say that getting the right people solves all control problems, for qualified people need to be managed well if their potential is to be realized.

The type of company organization will also affect control systems and practices. Controls should be built into a company's organization structure as part of the responsibilities and authorities of every key position. Sometimes, the organization of control systems will be tailored to the organization being controlled. At other times, especially where computer systems are being introduced, the system study can lead to modifications in a company's organization structure to accommodate the data processing systems needed for control. As Arnold Emch has put it, "organization and control are inseparable when there is effective management; they cannot function properly without each other."[6]

In spite of its close relation to the other functions, management control is none the less a distinct management science—a systematically organized set of principles to guide the manager in handling all types of business control situations. The science of management control has its own distinct definitions, underlying concepts, processes, principles of action, techniques and tools. And considerable study, training and experience are needed to acquire the knowledge, skill, and judgment required for putting management control theory to work in an actual business situation. The purpose of this book is to outline, examine, and develop this science of management control.

MANAGEMENT CONTROL AND NEW TECHNOLOGY

Management control draws upon many areas of management science in dealing with control situations. These areas include systems theory, PERT/CPM, operations research, forecasting, and electronic data processing.

[6]Arnold F. Emch, "Control Means Action," *Harvard Business Review* (July-August, 1954), p. 95.

Systems theory guides the development of data processing and information systems for control; PERT (Program Evaluation and Review Techniques) and CPM (Critical Path Method) aid both the planning and control of specific programs and projects; decision theory and operations research provide tools which can be applied to situations ranging from inventory and shipping control, to production, manpower and resource control; forecasting provides the means of translating plans into specific sales and output forecasts, which can in turn be used as control standards; electronic data processing provides more elaborate and economical means of storing and processing control information.

Admittedly, no manager could be expected to fully master all these highly technical fields. It is, however, possible to learn enough about these areas to understand their role in management control and so put these tools to work in developing better business controls and exercising control more effectively.

THE VIEWPOINT OF MANAGEMENT CONTROL

While management control has characteristics common to all forms of control in life, it also has a number of distinguishing characteristics.

First, management control refers specifically to the control functions within a business enterprise. Second, it involves executive action. Third, it is control designed to help a business enterprise reach its overall objectives, and it is always viewed as an extension of a company's long-range plan. In other words, management control is another means that managers have to achieve corporate objectives more effectively, whether it be at the overall company or operational level, whether the controls are used to protect assets or to stimulate creative use of those assets, and whether the controls are used to maintain production efficiency or to make equipment purchasing decisions.

In solving management control problems and exercising management control, therefore, the perspective is always that of a decision-making business manager. Such a manager looks at how and why controls are developed, the reasoning behind a control system, the ways to use the control tools to manage better, and other management implications of the control question at hand. Although he needs some knowledge of basic control tools, such as operations research, information systems, automated data processing, accounting and finance, economics and statistics, the manager does not limit himself to developing the tools needed to solve the control problems.

Management control requires looking behind the tools at such factors as the purpose of a system, the objectives of a corporation, the basis of standards, the assumptions behind figures, and the methods used in collecting and disseminating information. If presented with figures, an alert manager is skeptical. He never assumes that accountants, statisticians, economists, operations researchers or systems analysts will present solutions designed specifically for his control purposes. In short, he examines the entire control problem and reviews all the steps in the control process, and does not limit himself to the more immediate aspects of the control situation.

In subsequently exercising control, an effective manager does not confine himself to merely maintaining compliance. He also looks at the many constructive ways in which the control tool or system can be employed to improve the use of corporate resources.

CONCLUSION

Management control is a complex function, involving more than just comparing, measuring, and taking corrective action. It requires carefully developed control tools and systems, considerable energy to uncover hidden meanings and judgment to determine their significance, and skillful execution to avoid negative backlash. The concept of management control presented in this chapter attempts to encompass the complexities of the control process at work.

Within each company there are a variety of possible control situations, ranging from overall corporate financial control to individual operating control and quantitative analyses of planning alternatives. The kind of control action involved in the situation can also vary, from developing a control system to using it for control. The management control process presented in this study is applicable to all these levels and kinds of control problems and situations.

Management control draws upon many areas for its tools. Some of these, such as accounting and finance, are widely known and used. Others, such as operations research, systems theory, and economic forecasting, are highly technical and difficult to master. They are, none the less, important in management control and so are an integral part of this study.

Because of the variety of management control tasks, situations, decisions, and tools, there has been a tendency in the past to approach both the study and the practice of control piecemeal, as a series of only loosely related subjects and events. Business planning at one time was approached in the same way, but work during the 1960's by both business managers and consultants has evolved a consistent approach to planning, as well as guidelines for carrying out that approach which are now fairly widely accepted and practiced in business.

The management control concepts and process presented in Chapters 1 and 2 of this book, and their amplifications presented in later chapters, are intended to provide such an integrated framework for the control function. Admittedly, the control process given here needs additional refinement. It does, however, have value, for the process is not a theoretical ideal. It has been developed from the experiences of active business executives, and has been tested and used in a variety of control situations. It is a working model applicable to a wide range of control problems and situations. As they now stand, therefore, the control concepts given in this study provide an integrating force for bringing into perspective the varied and sometimes seemingly incompatible aspects of management control.

Knowledge of theory, principles, and tools is, however, only a beginning. Being able to put this knowledge into practice is the key to success in management control. This study thus devotes considerable attention to the ways in which management control concepts, principles, and tools can be applied to specific business control problems.

Although still in its early stages of development, management control is a scientific discipline. The concept can be defined, as can its unique viewpoint and its distinctions from other management sciences. It is also possible to outline a detailed, systematic approach to performing management control. This approach is discussed in the next chapter.

DISCUSSION QUESTIONS

1. What is the author's definition of management control? Why do you think the definition emphasizes such areas as establishing standards, developing control information systems, determining the causes of deviations, and taking positive control action?
2. What are the major differences between the definition of management control given in this book and those given by Jerome and Anthony?
3. Outline and discuss the various levels and kinds of control problems and situations. In what ways are they related to planning levels? How is control analysis used to support planning decisions?
4. Discuss the different kinds of control action which can be taken. Why are the development of controls and the use of control always so closely related?
5. Why do you think that men like Koontz and O'Donnell have divided the management job into five functions: planning, control, administration, organization, and staffing? Are these divisions valid?
6. Discuss the ways in which control is related to the planning function.
7. Discuss the relation of control to the other management functions.
8. Name some of the scientific tools employed in management control, and discuss the ways in which they are used for control.
9. Outline and discuss the distinguishing characteristics of management control.
10. What distinguishes management control from other types of control outside the business area? In what ways is business control similar to control in other areas?

CHAPTER 2

THE STEPS
IN THE MANAGEMENT
CONTROL PROCESS

In order to understand how control decisions are made and how business operations are controlled in achieving company objectives, it is necessary to examine in detail the management control process.

The process is a comprehensive one, covering both the approach to setting up a system for effective control and the approach to exercising control once the system has been developed. Even though in any given situation a manager may be dealing with only one aspect of management control, both areas are important: one needs to know the control decisions that are to be made using a system before he can create a truly effective system; one needs to review the accuracy of his data and standards before determining the significance of any deviation and taking action.

The process is also applicable to a wide variety of control situations, although it must be adapted to the requirements of each situation—for example, overall corporate control has different requirements from those encountered in operating control situations. No matter what the situation, however, each management level works within the overall management control perspective. The subordinate manager has to be familiar with the network of corporate planning, controls, and information systems to exercise control effectively at his level; the corporate controller needs to understand the impact of his control network on individual operating areas, if his control system is to be useful.

This chapter outlines the management control process, its basis, and some of the problems encountered in using the process.

THE BASIC PROBLEM-SOLVING/DECISION-MAKING PROCESS

The management control process closely parallels the problem-solving/ decision-making process. The basic steps in the problem-solving/decision-making process are:[1]

1. Diagnose the situation and review all of the facts in order to find and define the problem.
2. Examine the problem and review the facts in order to find the key factors affecting the problem and its solution. This step is sometimes referred to as premising.
3. Develop alternative solutions to the problem.
4. Test and evaluate the alternatives to determine the best solution.
5. Construct a clear statement of the solution selected, and convert the decision into a plan of action.

The apparent simplicity of this statement of the problem-solving/ decision-making process is deceptive. The statement of the process is in reality no more than a descriptive model, an artificial breakdown of the process into its component activities. The process describes the areas which must be covered to solve a business problem and the order in which they should be covered in coming to a final solution. While the breakdown is useful for understanding business decision making and provides a guideline for organizing one's thoughts, it is not a description of the actual process one goes through while solving an actual business problem.

Rather than being an orderly and sequential series of steps, the actual process involves much overlapping and back-and-forth movement among the different parts of the outline, many of which must be performed simultaneously.[2] For example, while one is searching for the key factors or

[1]These steps are given in Peter Drucker, *The Practice of Management* (New York: Harper and Row, 1954), pp. 351-359, H. Igor Ansoff, *Corporate Strategy* (New York: McGraw-Hill Book Company, 1965), pp. 1-11, and C. William Emory and Powell Niland, *Making Management Decisions* (Boston: Houghton Mifflin Company. 1968), p. 9. For other discussions of problem-solving/decision-making theory see C. T. Hardwick and B. F. Landuyt, *Administrative Strategy and Decision-Making* (2nd ed.; Cincinnati, Ohio: South-Western Publishing Company, 1966); Manley Howe Jones, *Executive Decision-Making* (Rev. ed.; Homewood, Illinois: Richard D. Irwin, Inc., 1962), Charles H. Kepner and Benjamin B. Tregoe, *The Rational Manager: A Systematic Approach to Problem Solving and Decision-Making* (New York: McGraw-Hill Book Company, 1965); Charles E. Summer, Jr. and Jeremiah J. O'Connell, *The Managerial Mind: Science and Theory in Policy Decisions* (Homewood, Illinois: Richard D. Irwin, Inc., 1964); and Max D. Richards and Paul S. Greenlaw, *Management Decision-Making* (Homewood, Illinois: Richard D. Irwin, Inc., 1966).

[2]Manley Howe Jones, *Executive Decision-Making* (Rev. ed.; Homewood, Illinois: Richard D. Irwin, Inc., 1962); Charles H. Kepner and Benjamin B. Tregoe, *The Rational Manager: A Systematic Approach to Problem Solving and Decision-Making* (New York: McGraw-Hill Book Company, 1965). Only a few writers have attempted to describe the intellectual process involved in solving a problem and in making a decision. One of the best descriptions of this subject is Jones's book, which provides additional insight into the complexities of solving a management control problem.

Jones traces how one searches for the key factors or premises affecting a decision. While searching one is constantly developing tentative courses of action. As one sub-premises affecting a decision, he is simultaneously developing alternative solutions built on these premises. A manager works this way instinctively. He simply does not wait until all the factors are analyzed before he begins thinking about solutions. Nor does he wait to develop all the alternatives before evaluating them, but usually evaluates alternatives as they are developed.

This back-and-forth process continues in all stages of the process. For example, when one begins to evaluate alternative solutions in a more orderly way, one frequently uncovers key factors which have an important bearing on the decision but were not found in the earlier analysis.

In addition to recognizing the complexities of the problem-solving/ decision-making process at work, one should also be aware of the difficulties involved in applying the process in specific situations. Each situation may have its own distinct characteristics and so may require a different approach. For example, the situation may be a problem; that is, something that has gone wrong—for instance, the defect rate rises sharply on a manufactured product one morning. In this situation, the decision-maker's attention may be devoted mainly to finding the cause of the problem, and the actual decision may be fairly simple: eliminate the cause of the defective work once the cause is found. In another situation, the emphasis may be on making a decision, rather than solving a problem — for instance, deciding on what new products to add to the company's present product line. In this situation, much greater emphasis would be given to steps three and four in the process, for the decision maker would spend considerable time evaluating market opportunities, as well as alternative products available to the company, in deciding on what new avenues to pursue. The focus of the situation thus may range from solving and correcting a problem, to choosing among a number of alternative courses of action, to some combination of the two.

Because the outline is a simplified statement, the average executive or business student is initially a little skeptical that the process is valid and useful. First, therefore, he should reconstruct how he solved a recent problem or made a recent decision. Gradually he will come to realize that this was the process he followed, but only in a very general way. Second, he should try to solve some actual business problems, using the problem-solving/decision-making process. It is usually only after wrestling with several of them that he begins to get some feeling for how the process is

---

sequently evaluates alternatives, he frequently uncovers key factors which have an important bearing on the decision but which he failed to recognize in the earlier analysis. The intellectual interplay which Jones describes parallels very closely that involved in developing solutions to management control problems. As a result, in the management control process (as in the problem-solving process) the key factors (or premises) are always stated in their clearest form only after the control system or controls (or solution) have been developed.

applied in practice and can help him make better decisions by providing him with systematic approach to problem solving and decision making.

The outline of the process also gives no hint of the difficulties involved in finding and creating solutions. While logic and experience are important in making decisions, they are frequently not enough. Experience helps develop judgment and provides a useful starting point in solving many problems, but just as often experience can be a wall blocking progress. Creative persons attempt to break through this wall and cut the inhibiting limitations imposed by experience. Creative persons also break patterns of logic in finding unusual associations and linking factors in new ways. For these reasons, creative energies can be disruptive, unless harnessed and directed towards constructive, profitable business solutions. Creative energies are needed, however, if a business is to change with its environment, so that while they should be controlled, they should not be suppressed.

Some authorities have attempted to reconstruct the creative process, in order to develop a structured approach to creative problem solving for business[3] and so help others learn how to take a more creative approach to business decision making. Others have developed simplified tests for identifying creativity.[4] In general, however, creativity cannot be taught, but only stimulated; it is hard to identify and even harder to harness and put to work in a business organization.

What seems at the outset to be a simple approach to making business decisions and solving business problems is in reality, therefore, a very complex process. Three aspects of this complexity have been identified here:

1. The outline of the process is only a guideline for organizing one's thoughts about a business problem, systematically comparing alternatives and arriving at a clear statement of the basis and justification of the decision. The actual intellectual activity is much more complex, and not a simple step-by-step procedure.
2. The process is very difficult to apply successfully and consistently in practice.
3. Considerable creative ingenuity is needed to solve complex business problems.

This list is by no means complete. But it does give some idea of the difficulties that are encountered in applying the process to actual business situations.

The importance of the decision-making process in management today cannot be over-emphasized. The process is the core of all the management

---

[3]M. O. Edwards, "Solving Problems Creatively," *Systems and Procedures Journal*, January-February, 1966, pp. 16-24.

[4]"Test your Creativity," *Nation's Business*, June, 1965, pp. 80-83.

[5]Robert J. Mockler, *Business Planning and Policy Formulation* (New York: Appleton-Century-Crofts, 1971), Chapter One; Merwin M. Hargrove, *Behavioral Science Implications* (Rev. ed.; Homewood, Illinois: Richard D. Irwin, Inc., 1966), pp. 1-6.

functions, and in his daily work the manager is deeply involved in business problem solving and decision making. As has been pointed out elsewhere at some length, the process of management planning and the process of carrying out the administrative and organization functions, like the process of management control, have their foundations in the problem-solving/decision-making process.[5]

The problem-solving/decision-making process is in essence the integrating force which brings together all the disparate aspects of management. As Richards and Greenlaw point out in *Management Decision-Making*, "decision-making represents the focus of activity performed by managers."[6] Simon goes even further and calls managing and decision making "synonymous."[7]

THE MANAGEMENT CONTROL PROCESS

The approach to dealing with management control situations, outlined below, closely parallels the problem-solving/decision-making process:

1. *Diagnose the situation in order to define the control problem and the method for dealing with it.* This investigation should result in definitions (i.e., simple statements) of:
   a. The specific kind and level of control situation that is being dealt with.
   b. The objective and scope of the control effort.
   c. The method to be used in solving the problem.
   d. The organization of the control effort.

2. *Examine the control problem and review the facts in order to find the key factors affecting the problem and its solution.* The principal areas of investigation would be:
   a. Corporate planning factors, such as important planning premises, the the company's objectives and major policies, its implementation plans, and other factors related to company planning at all levels.
   b. The specific characteristics of the operation or decision for which the control tools or control system are being created. For example, the situation could involve the entire corporate operation, a capital equipment acquisition, or a production, inventory or other operational control problem. This step would include a description of all corporate activities affected by the control problem.
   c. The purpose for which the controls or control system are being developed, including who will be using the system and the kinds of decisions which will be made based on the system.
   d. The nature of the controls or control system desired.

[6]Max D. Richards and Paul S. Greenlaw, *Management Decision Making* (Homewood, Illinois: Richard D. Irwin, Inc., 1966), p. vii.

[7]Herbert A. Simon, *The New Science of Management Decision* (New York: Harper & Row, Publishers, Inc., 1960), p. 1.

   e.   The nature of the standards or criteria against which performance will
        be measured.
   f.   Additional factors affecting the exercise of control.
3. *Develop and evaluate alternative controls.* The areas covered would be:
   a.   Developing alternatives. This covers:
       1.   Designing the controls. This phase might involve: an overall fin-
            ancial budgetary system, a cost accounting controls, specific op-
            erating department controls, or a company-wide information
            system for control; the specific standards to be used for measuring
            and the form in which they will be presented; the reporting forms
            needed and the feedback information wanted on these forms; and
            the mathematical and analytical models which will be used, if any.
            Where one is dealing with existing controls, the present controls
            would be included as one of the alternatives, and would be des-
            cribed in detail.
       2.   Implementation. The way to put the new solution, if one is
            proposed, into operation.
   b.   Testing and evaluating these alternatives to determine the best control
        tools, techniques or system, and how they can best be put into operation.
4. *Exercise control.* Where the controls or control system are automatic, this
    step would be included as part of the system design. Where they are not, the
    manager performs the control. This involves comparing actual performance
    against standards, determining the significance of any deviation (including
    checking the accuracy of standards and performance data), and taking action.
    In many instances a written report would also be needed.
5. *Prepare a report.* This step involves preparing a written statement of the
    solution selected in all major areas, and of the ways to carry it out.

Like the problem-solving/decision-making process, the above outline
organizes into a systematic process the steps followed by successful executives in exercising control. It is not a hypothetical ideal but an attempt to
develop a working model for showing others how successful executives
work.

THE COMPLEXITIES OF THE CONTROL PROCESS AT WORK

Like the problem-solving/decision-making process, the management control process in practice is not a simple, step-by-step procedure that can be
mechanically and rigidly applied to every control situation. For example,
contrary to what is implied by the outline of the process, the "developing
alternatives" phase is never completed once and for all at step three in
the process. This phase is stated prior to the "exercise of control" phase
merely because in theory the system must be in operation before one can
use it to make control decisions.
   The actual intellectual activity is quite different from the outline.
During the preliminary review of the situation, the executive solving the

control problem is likely to form some vague and generalized ideas of what his system will be. For example, he may think he needs a system which will use an IBM 360 computer but may not be at all sure how much it will be able to do, whether it will be worth the cost, and what all the available alternatives are.

As the analysis of the situation proceeds, he develops tentative alternative solutions to assist in evaluating the feasibility of certain courses of action. For example, he may first examine the various alternative computerized systems. Then he may look at how they will be used to determine how effective each is in aiding the exercise of control. After investigating each of the alternatives in this way he may come to the conclusion that any kind of computerized information and control system is too costly for his operation and that a combined manual and punched card processing system will be best. At this point he would develop additional alternatives.

As the analysis progresses further, therefore, new alternatives and revised solutions are usually developed. This is the phase during which the executive has the opportunity to correct, adjust or confirm the earlier solutions in the light of subsequent analysis and evaluation.

Lastly, he develops final solutions. This is the stage during which the solutions are stated in the formal written plan presented to management, where such a report is required.

This same process is at work in step two of the management control process, when the executive is seeking, defining, and quantifying the key factors affecting his solution. For example, while the executive may form a preliminary idea of the general kinds of standards that will fulfil the purpose of the control system, he will uncover many additional factors in developing the specific standards and the format in which they will be presented. Questions are raised about how those using the standards will respond to them and use them, the cost of collecting certain information, and the like, and sometimes these questions lead to the establishment of different kinds of standards or a modified purpose for the system. Constant probing, testing and hypothesizing are, therefore, necessary before a clear definition of the most relevant key factors can be formulated.

The process is repeated again when developing plans for putting the new system into operation, for example, when thinking of ways to get operating managers to accept a new control system. And nothing can be done to by-pass or simplify this continual process of investigation and evaluation so necessary for successful management control.

Since very few control situations are identical, applying the process in a specific situation is also not a simple task. All the steps in the control process are not given the same emphasis in each control situation. If the objective of the control effort is to develop a new control system, for example, step three will receive the greatest emphasis. If the objective is to take corrective action—for example bring costs or sales into line with budget—step four will receive the greatest emphasis. In addition, each situation has its own peculiar set of requirements—for example, corporate budgetary control is closely linked with overall long-term planning and requires heavy use of financial controls, while operating control requires a variety of financial and non-financial controls and is closely linked to short-term operational plans. And no two people initiate and carry out action in the same way, so that the exercise of control depends in large measure on the administrative abilities of the managers involved.

As in the problem-solving/decision-making process, considerable creativity is needed to devise solutions to control problems and develop alternative courses of action. Exercising control involves more than just sitting back and "correcting" a deviation. Such steps as uncovering the exact cause of a deviation and devising the most economical information system are demanding and challenging tasks, and essential to effective management control.

There are also many practical roadblocks encountered in putting control theory into practice in a company. There is *never* enough time or manpower to do the control job right, so that compromises are inevitable. The intellectual limitations of some managers will also contribute to errors, false starts, and poor control practices. Policies, no matter how clearly stated, will be misinterpreted by some workers, leading to further confusion and problems. And on occasions, an executive may deliberately undermine a control effort for personal reasons.

Another area in which practical problems arise is in establishing and administering the control department in larger corporations. While this is only one of the specialized areas of management control, it is a crucial one, since it is normally the mechanism through which overall corporate control is administered.

In the past, the control process has all too often been depicted as a relatively simple process. Figure 2.1 gives a typical diagrammatic representation of the process.[8] The diagram is not incorrect. What bothers business managers about such a diagram is that it oversimplifies the control process. The management control process outlined and discussed in this book attempts to capture more fully the complexities and difficulties of control in action.

The existence of these many practical difficulties and complexities does not mean that management control is not a science, for underlying the back-and-forth movements described in this section are the familiar steps of problem definition, premising, and developing, testing, and implementing the solution. What the complexities do mean is that knowing management control theory is only a small beginning. Adapting that

[8]Earl P. Strong and Robert D. Smith, *Management Control Models* (New York: Holt, Rinehart and Winston, 1968), p. 6.

Figure 2.1

A SIMPLIFIED TRADITIONAL DIAGRAM OF THE
MANAGEMENT CONTROL PROCESS

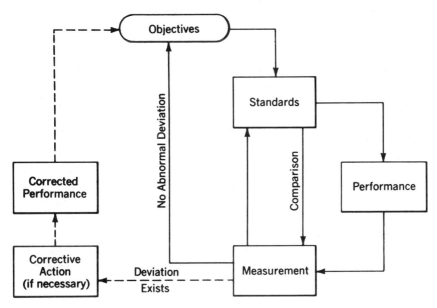

theory to solving the problem at hand is the art of management control, which complements the science. It is an art that is critical to the successful application of the science of management control in a business situation. It is an art that requires considerable experience and judgment and so is learned principally by doing.

CONCLUSION: THE CONTROL PROCESS AS AN INTEGRATING FORCE

The management control process, which clearly parallels the problem-solving/decision-making process, is applicable to both operating and overall corporate control, makes use of a wide range of tools, and covers both taking corrective action and developing controls.

In the past, control has all too frequently been associated solely with financial or accounting control. As operating managers quickly learn, however, for the most part financial controls monitor results, not activities. Activity control is the operating manager's main daily concern, for it is through controlling the activities going on daily within his operation that the operating manager controls financial results.

In controlling activities, the manager makes use of information systems, EDP, mathematical and graphic tools, and behavioral science and other administrative tools, as well as individual controls he develops for his operation. While this network of controls are ultimately related to overall company financial control, these operating controls are distinct from overall financial controls.

Many of the different aspects of control discussed in Chapter 1 and 2 have been studied by other writers in separate works. Very little attention has been paid, however, to developing a unified science of management control, whose underlying principles of action and processes are comprehensive enough and sufficiently detailed to provide a consistent approach to all management control areas. The control process outlined in this chapter attempts to present a practical, unified approach to all types of business control situations.

Because the process covers all the control functions within a company, not all the steps in the process are given the same emphasis in every control situation. For example, the purpose of the control effort may be to take corrective action. In this situation, step four—the exercise of control— will receive the greatest emphasis, while step three will be used mainly to check the adequacy of the control information upon which the action will be based. In another situation, the manager's objective may be to develop new production controls. In this case, emphasis would be on step three in the process. Nor is the process applied in the same way at each management level, for the lower level operating and staff managers' key factors, control standards and tools, and control action can differ greatly from those of the corporate controller.

The overall process is none the less helpful in each situation, as has been proven in practice. For example, if a manager is concerned with taking corrective action, the process helps remind him that he first should check the accuracy of his standards and result information before exercising control. The process also helps remind the over-zealous controller that his function is only one aspect of control, that his profit and loss or cost figures are only one kind of control standard, and that the operating manager's network of controls extends beyond financial controls and is equally important to effective control of company operations. In short, the process gives both top company managers and lower level operating and staff managers a more sophisticated and effective approach to handling their control jobs, and a better grasp of how to use the wide range of control tools available to them.

The statement of the process is only a first step, however, towards an understanding of the process. Management control, like all of the management functions, is an applied science, so that it is never fully understood until its practical applications are explored in detail, the tools needed to carry it out are specified, and guidelines for action established. The remaining parts of this study attempt to do this.

DISCUSSION QUESTIONS

1. Describe the way you made a recent decision. How was it similar to or different from the process described in this chapter?

2. Why do you think the problem-solving/decision-making process is so complex in practice? Are there any ways it could be simplified?

3. List the steps in the management control process and discuss the difference in the approach used in solving operational and overall corporate control problems.

4. There are major differences between "creating" a control system and "using" a control system, even though the two are closely related. List and discuss these differences.

5. Why is it so important to specify the objective of the control effort before proceeding with the control study?

6. Discuss some of the areas which should be considered in examining key factors. How would those studied in an operational control situation differ from those studied in a corporate control situation?

7. List and discuss the various categories of control systems and tools which a manager may be called upon to develop.

8. What are the major questions answered in evaluating alternative systems?

9. Discuss the various ways in which control can be exercised.

10. What kinds of control reports are discussed in this chapter?

11. In what ways does the management control process function as an integrating force?

12. Discuss the ways in which the process model given by the author differs from that given in Figure 2.1. In what ways is the author's a more effective guideline for action?

13. Management control is a developing science which needs refinement and further study. Discuss ways in which you feel the management control problem-solving/decision-making process could be improved.

CHAPTER 3

STEP ONE: DEFINING THE CONTROL SITUATION AND DEVELOPING AN APPROACH TO IT

During the early phases of a situation diagnosis, the nature of the control situation is identified, the objective and scope of the control effort defined, an approach developed for dealing with the situation, and the control effort organized. This chapter covers all these phases of the first step in the management control process.

DIAGNOSING THE SITUATION

Finding the basic problem in a business situation is considered by many to be the most difficult step in any management process.

A common pitfall in management is to mistake a symptom for a problem. For example, the fact that sales are 7% under budget is not a marketing manager's real problem. His problem is determining the cause of the deviation in sales from budget: poorly conceived advertising, or special competitor promotions, or changing competitor new product or marketing strategy, or misdirected sales efforts, or a recession, or maybe even an unrealistically high budget. Sometimes finding the cause of a business problem is easy; more often it is a complex and challenging job. Because of the difficulties often encountered in uncovering the true cause of a problem, a thorough diagnosis of all the facts affecting a business problem is needed to insure correct problem identification.

The diagnosis of a control situation begins with collecting the facts of the situation. Except in simple control situations, extensive probing is usually needed to gather all the pertinent information affecting the situation under study. While collecting this information, the manager will be mentally reviewing the entire management control process—developing alternatives, testing and refining them, rejecting some, and exploring new alternatives. One works this way instinctively. The main thrust at this point is still, however, simply to get the facts assembled.

Next, the facts are organized in some orderly fashion. For those readers who have worked with Harvard Business School case studies either at school or in executive training programs, this phase should be easy to visualize. It is the job the case writer performs in preparing a case, the main difference being that in an actual business situation the manager usually does not go through the formal process of preparing a written case. The manager should, however, organize his facts informally into logical groupings, much as is done in a formal case study.

Once this exploratory diagnosis is complete, one can begin to formulate a statement of the control problem or control situation being dealt with.

THE NATURE OF THE CONTROL SITUATION AND PROBLEM

Based on this preliminary investigation of the facts, the exact nature of the control situation or problem under study is identified. This phase would involve answering such questions as:

1. Is there really a problem to be dealt with, or a decision to be made, or an action to be taken? If there is, define it and summarize it in a single sentence, or continue to diagnose the situation until you can.
2. What operating or staff areas, departments, and levels of corporate operations are involved in the situation?

The answer to these questions can usually be summarized in a single sentence: "The company needs better cost control for the marketing or production operation," or "The corporate budgetary system is inadequate," or "Projections of the financial implications of alternative capital investments are needed to help make a planning decision," or "The problem is to find out why sales are below budget or why production costs are over budget."

There are a variety of control situations and control problems to which the business manager might be exposed. At the overall corporate level he may be concerned, for example, with improving the control organization or the overall company budgetary control system. At the operational level, the manager may be faced with the need for better control of advertising or the lack of integration between operating controls and overall corporate accounting controls. The situation may involve overspending on materials, or defective finished goods in an automobile assembly plant, or falling circulation at a national publication. It may

involve a feasibility study on converting to a new computerized information system to be used by both the corporate controller and line managers
in making planning and control decisions. It may involve the study of
two new alternative equipment purchase proposals. In short, it may be any
one of the thousands of different situations involving control in business.

In many of the above instances, the manager may be assigned the task
and so be told what the situation and problem are—for example, he may
be assigned by his superior to study the problem of inadequate operating
controls in the personnel area or to find out why a certain deviation occurred and if anything need be done to correct it. In other situations, the
manager may initiate his own investigation—for example, he may see
there are problems with the present data processing system and assign someone to investigate the situation. Whatever the circumstances, the level and
kind of control situation and the nature of the control problem must be
determined before the objective and scope of the control effort can be
defined.

THE OBJECTIVE AND SCOPE OF THE CONTROL EFFORT

It is not enough to merely identify the problem and say that the objective
of the control effort is to solve that problem. A manager goes further and
define in *precise terms* both what the control effort is to accomplish (its
objective) and how far it should extend (its scope).

A major question to be answered at this point is "What kind of control
action is required in this situation?" Basically, there are two types of
control action: developing controls (step three in the management control
process) and exercising control (step four in the control process). The objective of the control effort will, therefore, be either the first or the second
or both. If one were developing controls or a control system, a general statement such as "the objective is to develop _____ controls for _____
operation" might be formulated at this point; if one were exercising control, the statement might read "the objective is to determine the cause of
_____ deviation and correct it."

If the objective of the control effort is to develop a new control
system, the emphasis will be on the early steps in the process, for even
though one has to project the problems which will be encountered in
exercising control and using the system in order to develop a good system,
no control is actually exercised in such a situation. The job, in other words,
would be only to create the system (step three), not use it (step four). By
contrast, in most corporate control situations the major thrust of the
control effort is to use the control system to actually make control decisions
and take some sort of corrective action. In these situations, step three in
the control process serves merely as review of the present system to double-
check its adequacy and to determine if improvements in the system are

warranted or needed. In some situations, more of a balance is struck as in *The National Observer* study described in Chapter 14 where the operating manager was given the job not only of devising the system itself, but also of using it to keep operations on target.

The question of how extensive the control effort should be is also answered during this phase. Is the manager to only recommend action, or is he to take the action? Is the study to be only a cursory one, requiring just a verbal report? Or is it to be an in-depth study requiring an extensive written report?

The determination of the objective and scope of the control effort leads the manager to probe many aspects of the control situation, asking such diverse questions as:

1. If a new control system is being explored, who will be using it, and what kinds of decisions will be made based on the information supplied? How important are these decisions? Do they justify a major control effort?
2. How much will it cost to develop and maintain the new system? Do the benefits of the new versus the old system justify the cost? If not, should the objective and scope of the control study be narrowed?
3. Is management prepared to commit the money and manpower needed to develop and maintain the new system? If not, should the purpose of the control effort be more narrowly defined?
4. If deviations are being examined, what additional information will be needed to determine the true causes of problems? Can this information be obtained in time and at a justifiable cost? If not, should the objective of the control effort be redefined?
5. Are the performance figures really accurate and are the standards good measures of performance? Or must they be questioned? If they should, the scope of the control effort should be expanded.
6. If corrective action is required, who will actually be taking and administering the action? Is it within my areas of responsibility, or should it be handled by another executive?
7. If the situation involves financial analysis, is the job merely to present quantitative analyses on which a decision by someone else will be based, or should a recommendation for action be made?
8. Is a report required and, if it is, to whom will it be made and how extensive should it be?

These and other questions affecting the objective and scope of the control effort need answering before one can determine finally exactly what is to be accomplished by the control effort, how extensive it will be, how many people and how much time and money it will require, and how effectively it can be carried out with available resources.

DEVELOPING AN APPROACH

Once the objective and scope of the control effort have been identified, a manager would determine the specific ways in which the control process can be put to work in the situation. The following is a summary of how the process was adapted in three typical situations: operational (production) control; overall corporate control; and resource allocation analysis. These examples are not designed to show that the process works nor do they give detailed guidance in applying the process. Rather, they are intended to show how an approach to a specific control situation is developed from the management control process to meet the individual needs of the situation. More extensive discussions of how the process is carried out in specific control situations are found in the later chapters of this study.

Operational Control.

In a recent study, a small specialty valve manufacturer was considering the possiblity of creating a new cost control system for one of its valve production divisions. This division had five production sections. The same cost standards were presently used for all five sections. However, since all valves did not go through all five sections, and since overhead costs varied considerably by section, the company wanted a system based on section cost standards (rather than division cost standards), so that product pricing and costing would be more accurate. The objective of the study was to develop such a system.

The major factors affecting the situation were then analyzed. Since the company was small, it competed on the basis of price. As a result, the company needed tight control of costs and accurate pricing. Management had raised the control question because one valve (Valve A), which sold very well, seemed underpriced. This valve, which accounted for one third of the company's volume, passed through only two sections of the production division under study. It was decided, therefore, to develop a system to give more accurate cost information. The system would be based on five sectional cost center standards, rather than on overall cost standards for the division as a whole. Since neither the production supervisor nor the sales manager felt that any change was needed, they would naturally resist any change in the present control system and so probably lessen the effectiveness of any new system developed.

Following step three in the management control process, an alternative control system was developed. The new system (based on section cost standards) revealed that in fact Valve A was underpriced, and that it was impossible to make accurate pricing decisions based on the old system. The new system required additional work in collecting weekly figures and reporting on them, but it was feasible and appeared worth the added cost.

Because of the additional work involved in collecting information, the production supervisor resisted changing to the new system. The sales manager also argued against the new system, since it might lead to raising the price of his largest-selling valve. Unfortunately, neither executive was involved in the initial development of the new system, and so did not really understand its implications.

Instead of simply overruling the production supervisor and the sales manager and putting the new system into operation, the company was advised to spend the time needed to let each executive study why the change was made and to propose alternatives. These executives were made part of a committee appointed to evaluate the new system and to study how a new system would be put into operation. In the process, more efficient methods were developed for collecting and reporting information. At the same time, the sales manager was reassured that the purpose of the new system was only to get a true picture of costs, and that the pricing would be a separate decision which would take into account such factors as market competition.

Following this alternative in implementing the new system paved the way for smoother exercise of control once the system was in operation. If the new system had been forced through over the objections of key people, considerable difficulties might have been encountered at a later date in exercising control—for example, when evaluating production costs and recommending more realistic prices.

Because this situation was a relatively simple one, the application of the management control problem-solving process is easy to see. The problem, and its scope and implications, were first defined. Next, key factors affecting the problem and its solution were isolated. Third, an alternative solution was developed, both for the new system itself and for the method of putting it into operation. The new solution was then tested and refined, and then evaluated against the old system. A decision was made to adopt the new system, a method for implementing it was developed, and the new system was finally put into operation. In this assignment the fourth step in the control process was not emphasized as much as step three, since the objective of the control effort was to develop a new control system and the consultant did not become involved in actually exercising control or making control decisions once the system was in operation. Because the company was small and the system covered only a small department, the report on the new system was a brief one.

Overall Corporate Control.

More recently, a medium-sized electronics company asked for a review of the overall financial control system used to control the operating results of its seven divisions. The scope of this study was quite broad, for the system was designed to give accurate profit and loss information for each division and for the entire corporation, and was to be used by the president and board of directors in making major corporate planning decisions.

Once the objective of the study had been defined, the key factors affecting the situation were examined. The company's businesses ranged from production-line electronics products (such as medium-priced radar simulators and high speed electronic checkweighers) and systems-engineered products (such as coordinated electronic systems using a variety of machines) to the sale of research and development consulting services. The company had ambitious plans for expansion into a variety of products and services related to the three areas of their business, but had limited capital resources. Company management decided that the purpose of the new control system would be to give the board of directors the information it would need both to evaluate divisional operating efficiency and to make major decisions on the allocation of resources for research and development purposes and for facility expansion. Management further agreed that the system would need different standards for each of the company's three major business areas: production-line products, system-engineered products, and consulting services. As for the exercise of control under the present system, there was a major problem: management rarely took corrective action when variations occurred, except to adjust standards. As a result, lower level managers paid little attention to variations from standards.

Next, alternative solutions were studied. First, the design of the present system was examined. The present system used common information classifications, standards, timing and review procedures for all products, and so failed to recognize the needs of the different types of businesses in which the company was engaged.

A new control system was developed to replace the old one. The new system had three parts, one for each of the company's three business areas. In the production-line area, strict cost controls and more frequent reviews were instituted; and when cost and scheduling standards were not met, firm corrective action was taken. The systems-engineered products area, which required longer lead times, was also subjected to a variety of new controls: precise lead times and critical control points were identified and PERT schedules developed, a new pricing system was instituted, a system of less frequent reviews than in the production-line area was established, and special reporting forms were developed. Separate controls and control reports were also developed for the operations that sold research and development services. Under the new system, the research and development expenses related to internal product development were segregated from those related to services sold to customers. Schedules for spending money on internal projects were developed and became critical control points, and at those times when additional commitments had to be made, management reevaluated the potential profitability of the project.

Implementing the new system was relatively easy, as everyone had been dissatisfied with the existing control system. The changeover was handled in a way similar to that used successfully at other companies: all involved personnel were brought into the development and institution of the new system. As in most situations of this kind, the new system was developed, instituted and maintained by the corporate control department.

In this study, the fourth step in the management control process was important, for major changes were also introduced in the way in which the control system was used. Control review meetings were held regularly (but at different intervals for each product line), explanations were required for deviations from standards, and changes were introduced in operations based on these analyses. Under the old control system, the practice had been to revise standards (not operations) when deviations occurred.

The report recommending the new system was extensive, since the entire company operation was covered. A three-page summary was, however, given at the beginning of the report, which covered the highlights and basis of the new system.

The same basic management control process was followed in this situation, as in the operating situation described above: the overall objective and scope of the control effort were first defined; key factors were then analyzed; alternative solutions were developed and evaluated and a new system put into operation; control was exercised using the new system; a report was prepared explaining the new system. However, at the same time the process still had to be adapted somewhat to the needs of the situation— overall company control: overall company factors, instead of operating department factors, were given greatest emphasis; the system developed was much more complex, but the method of implementing it was easier; procedures for the exercise of control were outlined in greater detail, because the system was a three-part system, and greater emphasis was given to the way in which control was exercised; the report on the system was longer, reflecting the greater complexity of the control problem.

Specific Resource Allocation Problems.

The management control process is also useful in providing guidance for developing control information needed to solve planning problems. At the outset, a clear distinction must be drawn between the planning function and control function: the control group or analyst provides only the background analysis and quantitative bases for the decision; the manager making the decision must then weigh these factors with other factors in order to come to a decision. This second decision-making step is not necessarily within the control function.

A few years ago, a public transportation company had decided to replace its old equipment with either gas buses or a combined system of electric buses and gas buses. The controller's department was asked to recommend what type of equipment to use, based on financial considerations.

Key factors affecting the problem were examined. The company's main business was defined as providing transportation services to the public, so that the new equipment would be judged as much on its ability to provide better customer service and so increase customer use of the transportation facilities, as on its cost savings. The community served by the company was a fast growing one, that included both industrial and residential areas. Public service factors were important, since the company was regulated by the local government, which responded to voter complaints about such things as noise and air pollution. The performance characteristics of each type of vehicle were also spelled out at this point. The purpose of the control system was defined: to provide a quantitative basis for evaluating the new equipment alternatives. The tools used would be comparative investment calculations and *pro-forma* incremental profit statements. The standard used was a minimum return on investment established by management.

The third step in the process was slightly different in this situation than in the others, since it concerned determining what analytical tools would be used in evaluating the alternative investments. The control department had prepared statements of operating and investment costs for each alternative, but these statements were clearly insufficient and so a new approach was developed. First, an expanded form for calculating the cost basis for each alternative was established. Since the life span of each type of transportation equipment and its supporting power and servicing facilities was different, it was decided to use the present value of the alternative investments over a thirty-year period. Second, an expanded form for calculating the anticipated differences in operating costs of the alternatives was developed and their present value determined. Third, a form for calculating revenues and returns on investment from each alternative was prepared. Next, categories for determining service capabilities were established. These included seating capacity, speed, mobility in traffic, flexibility to meet anticipated population shifts, acceleration, and effect on air pollution. Each of these factors was then given a weighted quantitative value. In this way a systematic approach for reaching a decision was developed by the control department. Before putting the tools to work and making calculations, the members of the Board and top management who were to make the decision reviewed the proposal thoroughly and agreed that these tools would provide a valid basis upon which to base their decision.

During step four, the exercise of control, financial projections were made for each alternative using the tools or forms developed during step three. The information generated by the controller showed that the combined system of trackless trolleys and gas buses gave a somewhat better return on investment, but that the all-gas bus system gave better service and provided the flexibility to meet changing population needs. Since both types of equipment systems were superior to the present one, and since the all-gas bus system would probably increase revenues, top management and the Board decided to adopt the all-bus system.

While at first glance it might not have been apparent that the management control process could be applied in solving this kind of problem, closer review shows how the process was applicable. The overall control problem and the objective of the control effort were first defined: to provide a quantitative, systematically organized basis for making a planning decision. Next, key factors such as the nature of the company's business, the requirements for success in its business, performance characteristics of the equipment, the purpose of the controls, and the kinds of control tools and standards to be used were isolated. Third, alternative control tools were developed and agreement reached with all the decision makers that these tools should be used. Fourth, control was exercised using the system: financial projections were made using the newly developed control tools, the relative profitability of each alternative was determined, and the alternatives were compared on the basis of which best met predetermined standards. Finally, a report *recommendation* was made by the control analyst as to which alternative appeared most profitable.

The control function ended here, for the final decision as to which type of equipment to buy was made by top management based on both financial and non-financial considerations—thus clearly distinguishing between the control and planning decision areas in the situation.

The description of these three studies—operating control, overall corporate control, and financial analysis for planning—is designed to show that while the same basic control process is used in different situations, at the same time the process needs to be adapted in developing an approach to each individual situation. The discussions were deliberately oversimplified, in order to focus on how the management control process is adapted to meet the requirements of specific control situations. The later chapters of this study give detailed descriptions of how each step is carried out.

ORGANIZATION OF THE CONTROL EFFORT

Responsibility for developing controls and for exercising control varies by company and by control situation. The following are some of the departments which would most often become involved in control administration: finance; accounting; control; systems and data processing; management sciences; planning; and any operational or staff department which will be using the controls. The following discussion covers the major jobs performed in each of these control areas, and the alternative ways in which these control jobs might be organized.

Finance.

The finance function involves obtaining funds and monitoring the use of company funds and other assets. Performance of the finance function requires extensive financial analysis of operations, especially through the use of such tools as financial ratios and return on investment analysis. These financial tools are used widely in overall corporate control.

Accounting.

The accounting function is in concept limited to bookkeeping, credit and collections, tax reporting, cost control, payroll, and sometimes budgeting. All these functions are important in control. In most companies the accounting function has tended to expand into a broader control function and includes responsibility for developing accounting and financial control reporting systems, overall company budgeting and profit planning, analyzing performance figures in relation to budget, reporting on deviations, and recommending action. Where a company's accounting department performs these expanded functions plus the basic accounting functions and financial analysis, it is in fact a corporate "Control" department.

Control.

While many companies have chosen to expand the accounting department into a broader control department, other companies have created separate departments called "Control" departments. Ideally, not only would such a department perform the functions listed in the preceding paragraph, but also be responsible for coordinating all types of controls within the operating areas—accounting and financial reporting systems, as well as the individual non-financial controls in each operating area. Few companies, however, see control as such a broad function, requiring the coordination of all types of control. For this reason, control outside the accounting and financial area is normally a piecemeal, fragmented, and frustrating affair in most companies.

EDP Systems Development and Administration.

Control requires information, and company data processing systems provide much of this information. In many companies data processing groups have grown considerably in size, because of the growth in computer usage, and now represent a major department. Systems analysts are needed to conduct feasibility and systems studies, programmers to translate systems designs into machine language, equipment operators to operate the data processing equipment, typists to prepare input documents, and EDP managers to administer the operation. Because of the size of EDP systems and their impact on all aspects of a company's operation, more and more companies are creating a top officer job of information systems manager, who reports directly to the chief executive. Because of the position of the systems department, it performs major control functions, especially in the overall accounting area and in the operating area, where it designs and administers many of the specific control systems used.

Management Sciences.

The functions of this department are generally designated by the title "Operations Research". Operations research tools are most useful in operational planning and in developing control standards based on plans. Where operating departments, such as production, use operations research extensively, the management sciences department would be under the appropriate operations area. In other instances, companies put the management sciences department under the systems department, since operations research often requires extensive use of computers and is used extensively in systems development work.

Individual Operating and Staff Areas.

Each area manager within a company will invariably have his own network of controls designed to meet the specific needs of his operation. Many operating controls are linked with the overall accounting and finance control system. Many others, however, are non-financial controls. These other controls may be developed by the company's systems department and be part of overall company information systems, or they may be developed and maintained within the individual department.

Planning.

In more and more companies, intermediate and long-term planning has become a separate function, which is most concerned with long-term strategic planning and sometimes also handles diversification through mergers and acquisitions. Industry and economic analyses would also be performed in this area. This function is closely coordinated with the budgeting function and provides basic control directions, but is distinct from the control function.

As can be seen from the above discussion, there are a variety of ways in which companies organize for control. At the Frost Company described in Chapter 13, for example, all of the control functions were under the "Finance" department, except for management sciences, which were under the manufacturing area. This was done because the company's control system was heavily finance and accounting oriented. At a large mail-order company, which is described later in this book, the finance, accounting, and budgeting functions were grouped within a "Control" department, while the systems and management sciences departments were separate departments under the executive vice president.

While there is no overall formula for organizing for management control which can be applied to all companies, some guidelines can be established for organizing the control functions. "Control" seems to be the logical departmental grouping for the accounting, budgeting, profit planning and financial analysis functions, since they are all major control systems, and some companies have set up "Control" departments to handle these functions. The "Control" department might include the systems development function, but only where the control function was very broadly defined and where the "Control" department was not accounting oriented. EDP systems development and management should not be part of an accounting department at any time. Subordinating the systems department to accounting is no more justified than is putting it under manufacturing or marketing. Since management sciences are used for more than just control, they too should normally be kept distinct from the control group (though closely coordinated with it). Since short-term considerations usually dominate control thinking, strategic planning should not be performed within a control department but in a separate department. The funds management functions in the finance area are also distinct enough to be handled by a separate department.

Obviously much of what has been said thus far does not apply to a small company and certain specialized industries such as computer leasing companies. And in these situations the organization of control functions must be tailored to the individual company operations. The general functions to be performed, however, still remain the same.

The question of who performs control and how the various control sections will interact in a given situation depends to a large degree on the level and kind of control which is performed. The corporate president will rely heavily on the overall company accounting and financial control department to assist him in overall control of company operations. In this regard a corporate control department acts as the control watchdog of corporate operations for the president.

At lower management levels, the staff control groups (such as the systems, management sciences, and accounting departments) participate in control as asked or needed. Where the systems department is studying the computerization of control reporting within a company, the systems group performs the work. Operating managers, such as the marketing manager, can advise, suggest, and complain, but the systems group will usually have a major voice in what will be computerized and the design of the final system. The budgetary and accounting control groups require certain information at certain times, and operating managers must provide the required data at the times needed so that these control responsibilities can be fulfilled. The budgetary and accounting control groups thus generally work with the operating managers in developing and administering financial controls for each operating area. In other situations, the operating manager will be concerned with developing his own non-financial controls. In these instances, he may sometimes be assisted by corporate staff groups, though most often he must develop these controls himself or have his department personnel do it.

Each level of control and each control situation thus has its own organizational requirements. Various examples of the different approaches to organizing for control in individual situations have been given above and additional examples are given throughout the following chapters. In all these examples, one principle prevails—the manager using the controls and control systems must have considerable voice in the structure of them and the procedures developed for using them. Otherwise, he cannot exercise control effectively.

BREAKING THE ACCOUNTING AND FINANCE MOLD IN ORGANIZING FOR CONTROL

Overall control cannot be maintained without a network of financial controls that extend into every operating and staff area of a business. These controls help monitor costs, profits, and the use of assets and are essential to corporate survival. Because of the importance of this aspect of management control, the accounting and finance departments have traditionally been the locus of the control function within business enterprises.

While financial controls are important, the concept of management control is much broader. The definition of control given in Chapter 1 outlines a functional process which make use of a variety of control tools, not just accounting and financial tools, and which operates in many different kinds of situations and at all levels of a company, not just for overall profit control.

The marketing manager, for example, will always have his overall expense budgets, which are derived from and closely related to the corporate expense budget and profit plan. And financial controls will always be a major aspect of the network of marketing controls. Most often, however, financial controls do not provide control of specific critical marketing activities which affect results. To achieve desired financial results, the marketing manager must control such activities as salesmen's use of time, advertising commitments, customer service, market penetration, new product development, and the like—all areas not directly surveyed by financial controls. Operating managers thus have always found it necessary to develop a variety of additional non-financial controls.

Non-financial operating controls are those controls designed to monitor critical activities in the operating area under study—the number of calls and sales made by each salesman, delivery of the product, new product testing, answering customer complaints, advertising efficiency, manpower usage, production schedules and the like— in short, all the activities which affect performance efficiency, and ultimately profits, in the operating areas. Developing and maintaining controls for these activities is as important to corporate success as any financial control network. And from an operating manager's viewpoint they are far more relevant and immediately useful controls.

In developing his network of non-financial operating controls, the operating manager is often not able to get the corporate staff assistance needed from the financially-oriented control groups. This is to be expected, since these groups are not always trained in non-financial control areas, nor are they given responsibility for doing that kind of work. The operating manager has thus had to either create his own network of operating controls or to turn to other staff groups for help.

As a result of the expanded control requirements of today's corporations, many staff departments (in addition to the accounting and finance departments) now provide assistance in developing operating controls. These include: economic planners and forecasters, who can assist in developing control standards; data processing systems specialists, who develop control information gathering, storage and reporting systems; management scientists (operations researchers), who quantify decision criteria; and behavioral scientists, who provide tools for the exercise of control.

Often in large companies the systems department is the most helpful staff area in developing operating controls. The systems specialist is not trapped by the financial control mold. He is trained to examine total information networks for control, of which financial controls are only one aspect. More and more, therefore, the systems analyst fills the gap in staff control assistance and provides professional aid to the operating manager in developing a network of operating controls. The systems analyst is equipped to examine operating control needs broadly and to objectively evaluate the economics of providing the needed control reports with available data processing equipment. In short, he can do the actual footwork involved in developing a system. Because of this, accounting and finance departments have gradually lost many of their control functions to the systems department by default.

A major problem in organizing a company's control functions has been the accounting and financial mold into which control has been cast in so many companies. What is needed is to break this mold and to develop an entirely new concept in control organization, along the lines of that shown in Figure 3.1. This concept of a redefined control function in business is not new. In 1965 Joseph Littlefield studied the evolution of the control organization in business and came to the conclusion that the accounting department as it was commonly set up would eventually dis-

Figure 3.1

ORGANIZATION OF CONTROL FUNCTIONS AND
CONTROL-RELATED FUNCTIONS

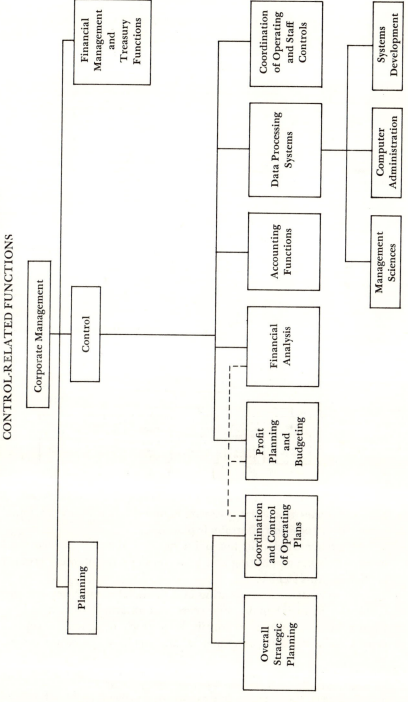

Figure 3.2

THE CONTROLLER'S AND TREASURER'S ORGANIZATION[2]

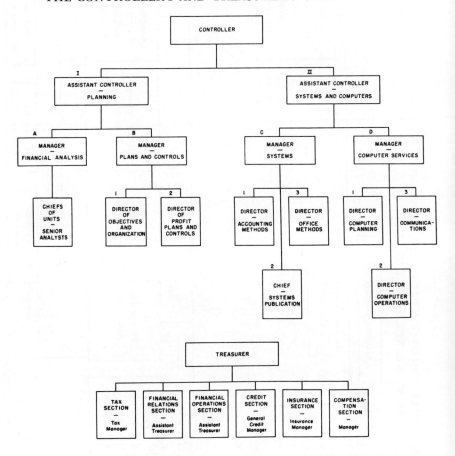

appear.[1] His concept of a modern control organization is given in Figure 3.2,[2] and varies from that given in Figure 3.1 mainly in the importance given to, and position of, strategic planning.

What his article did not point out was that the change would not occur if existing accounting and financial departments were given the job of effecting this change.

All too often the accounting and financial mentalities are unable to break the financial mold. For years accountants have trained to work within strictly limited accounting traditions designed to report costs, profits, and asset usage, and financial analysts have been trained to identify

[1]W. Joseph Littlefield, "Developments in Financial Organizations, 1915-1965," *Financial Executive — Supplement*, September 1965, pp. 3-20.

[2]Littlefield, "Developments in Financial Organizations," pp. 14 and 16.

variations from budgeted standards—that is, to highlight the symptoms and financial results of problems. And the operating manager has grown to resent the nagging reminders that he is over or under budget, mainly because he feels it does not take great intelligence to spot such deviations in final costs. The heart of the operating manager's control problem is how to develop controls for the individual activities that effect final profit—that is, controls that are more direct and current. The operating manager's viewpoint is operational, not financial, control—that is, activity control, plus result control in terms of units, or output, or percent, or dollars, or whatever measure is appropriate to the activity being controlled. This is the viewpoint that dominates the new concept of control. To achieve this viewpoint the financial and accounting control mold must be broken—a very difficult task for the trained accountant or financial analyst.

Control is a broad function, which covers many control situations and levels of control, and makes use of diverse control tools. A company's organization for control must recognize the breadth and complexity of the management control function, both in the definition of responsibilities and in the assignment of personnel, if a true "Management Control" department is to be created. Otherwise, the company may end up with just a disguised accounting and finance department, fashioned out of old and outdated molds.

CONCLUSION

Step one in the management control process involves diagnosing the control situation to determine the specific kind and level of control situation being dealt with, the objective and scope of the control effort, the approach to the situation, and the organization of the control effort. This chapter has explained how each of these steps is carried out, and how a sound basis is developed for performing the subsequent steps in the management control process.

In defining the control situation, the facts of the situation are first diagnosed; and based on this diagnosis a statement is formulated of the nature of the control situation or problem. The statement is brief and in very general terms, since it is designed only to give focus to the study.

Defining the objective and scope of the control effort is the second phase of step one in the control process. The statement of objective is also brief, and designed only to give direction to the control effort and help prevent wasted time and effort. The definition of the scope of the control effort reinforces and clarifies the objective. In determining the scope of the control effort, the manager would ask himself such questions as: On what aspects of the process should I concentrate, the development of controls or the exercise of control? How broad is the control area under study and what aspects of it are critical? What kind of control tools and system are needed? How complete should the solution be? Are there major roadblocks to implementing the solution and will implementation be a major area of consideration? What categories of key factors will I need to examine? How important are overall company planning factors to my particular task? Is the evaluation complex or simple? Is a report on the solution required? How extensive a report on the action to be taken is needed? How far into the administrative area should the solution go?

The manager next develops the approach to be followed in dealing with the control situation at hand. Basically, this approach is the management control process. However, as was seen from the discussion of company studies in this chapter, that process needs to be adapted to suit the specific requirements of each control problem.

The last phase in step one of the control process is organizing the control effort. The discussion of this phase concentrated mainly on what the control functions are and how they interrelate, especially in the operating area, and how companies organize the control functions. In general, it has been found that the control function is not organized effectively in most companies surveyed, insufficient consideration is given to the development of an integrated network of operating controls, and all too often the control organization is dominated by restrictive accounting and financial viewpoints.

DISCUSSION QUESTIONS

1. Discuss the various kinds and levels of control problems to which the business manager might be exposed.
2. What are the major factors to be considered in defining the objective and scope of the control effort?
3. How does the fact that the control situation involves only developing a new system affect the use of the control process? How is the control process adapted in situations involving the exercise of control?
4. When one has to take corrective action, in what ways is he involved in the early steps in the control process? When one is concerned with developing a control system, in what ways is he still involved in the later steps in the control process?
5. In what ways does the approach to operational control problems differ from that used at the corporate level?
6. What are the special requirements which must be met in dealing with a resource allocation problem?
7. What are the special problems faced by the small business manager in using the management control process?
8. Describe some of the different ways in which control was exercised in each of the control situations described in this chapter.

9. What are the various control functions which are performed within a large company? What are the different ways in which these functions are departmentalized and organized?

10. Give some guidelines for organizing the control functions. How will the organization vary by size of company and type of company?

11. What is the relation between individual operating controls and overall corporate controls? In what ways can they be better integrated?

12. Why is it so important to understand the distinction between the operating manager's network of controls and the network of overall corporate financial controls?

CHAPTER 4

STEP TWO: IDENTIFYING KEY FACTORS AFFECTING THE CONTROL SITUATION — PLANNING CONSIDERATIONS

Once the general directions of the control effort have been defined, the major factors affecting the control situation are specified. Six critical areas are covered in this discussion of the second step in the control process: planning considerations; specific characteristics of the control situation; the purpose of the controls needed; the nature of the controls to be used; the nature of the control standards; and special factors affecting the exercise of control. This chapter concerns the first of these six: the overall planning factors.

MANAGEMENT CONTROL AND THE PLANNING PROCESS

Planning and control are almost inseparable in practice. As can be seen from the outline of the planning process below, control is an integral part of the planning process. Controls are an indispensable aid to the manager in carrying out plans and achieving planned objectives. Planning is, therefore, where control begins and the principal base upon which controls are built.

The steps in the planning process are:[1]

1. Planning and organizing the planning effort.
2. Defining industry and company planning premises.

[1]Robert J. Mockler, *Business Planning and Policy Formulation* (New York: Appleton-Century-Crofts, 1971).

3. Determining the objective.
4. Developing and stating policies.
5. Developing and stating implementation plans.
6. Coordinating and controlling planning.
7. Organization planning.
8. Review.

The following discussion covers those aspects of the planning process which are important to management control; environmental planning premises, including market forecasts; company planning premises, including sales forecasts; overall planning directions, including objectives and policies; and implementation planning factors.

EXTERNAL PLANNING PREMISES: DEVELOPING MEANINGFUL INFORMATION ABOUT THE ENVIRONMENT

All planning is done within the context of external planning premises— that is, specific, stated assumptions about factors within the economy, society, politics, industry, or market that will affect the company's future profitability. This is true no matter what level of planning is being done, for all corporate activities focus on the movement of goods or services at a profit to some area of the company's environment.

In all cases, therefore, planning involves an evaluation of the external environment within which the company is or will be operating.[2] Sometimes the external planning premises are general prose statements of possible or likely events and general trends that will materially affect planning. In other instances they are forecasts or predictions which quantify trends, risks, or the impact of likely events.

In scanning the environment to develop these quantitative and non-quantitative planning premises, the planner finds that not all of the future events in the social, political, economic and market environment will affect every company, nor will they affect each company in the same way. Therefore, what corporate management requires is economic, industry and market information related to their company's specific product and marketing needs. This is a challenging area, since in most cases economic forecast information is not compiled in a way *directly* related to the corporation's business.

A comparison of the approaches of a major oil company, American Machine and Foundry, Lockheed, American Airlines, and A-D-M Company shows that although each began by studying external factors that would affect their futures, there was considerable variation in the kind of information developed. None of the solutions were the same, and none of the solutions were simple or perfect.

[2]Murray L. Weidenbaum, "The Role of Economics in Business Planning," *Business Topics*, Summer, 1962, p. 47.

For example, a major oil company had long used a limited number of market forecasts, which upon review were found to be inadequate as planning tools. As a result of this review, the company developed much more detailed forecasts of environmental and competitive factors related specifically to its own marketing problems. Under the new system, ten-year projections by state or trading area were made of car registrations, population and new road construction—all major factors influencing the sale of petroleum products. Internal factors influencing planning were also examined more carefully, and specific performance standards—such as market share by state, sales and profit contribution by product, and capital budgets by district—were developed in much greater detail, thus giving management critical control yardsticks by which performance could be measured periodically against plans, and through which corrective action could be more effectively initiated where warranted. Figure 4.1 below illustrates the kinds of planning premises and related control standards initially formulated, and those developed when the company's planning became more sophisticated.[3]

In its attempt to improve corporate planning, American Machine and Foundry developed even more specific market and industry information and forecasts in their planning premises. The degree of detail developed in AMF's planning effort can be seen from the following checklist of some of the environmental information gathered and forecasts made for planning by the company:[4]

1.   The market.
   a.   Present major product lines and proposed new major product lines.
   b.   Total industry volume and unit sales volume in each.
2.   The competition.
   a.   Present major product lines and proposed new major product lines.
   b.   Total industry volume and unit sales volume in each.
3.   Factors affecting unit performance.
   a.   Future price structure for products.
   b.   Direct and indirect labor costs.
   c.   Market strategy.
   d.   Trends within the industry.
   e.   Technological changes affecting product cost and use.
   f.   Market penetration (percent and dollar volume).

Broader economic, political, and social premises are used by such companies as Lockheed and American Airlines. The future of Lockheed depends heavily on international, as well as domestic, political and eco-

---

[3]D. R. Daniel, "Management Information Crisis," *Harvard Business Review*, September-October, 1961, p. 118.

[4]Stewart Thompson, "Planning at American Machine and Foundry Company," in *Long-range Planning for Management*, ed. David W. Ewing (Rev. ed.; New York: Harper & Row, Publishers, 1964), pp. 266-272.

Figure 4.1

COMPARATIVE ANALYSIS OF MARKETING PLANNING
INFORMATION NEEDED BY A MAJOR OIL COMPANY

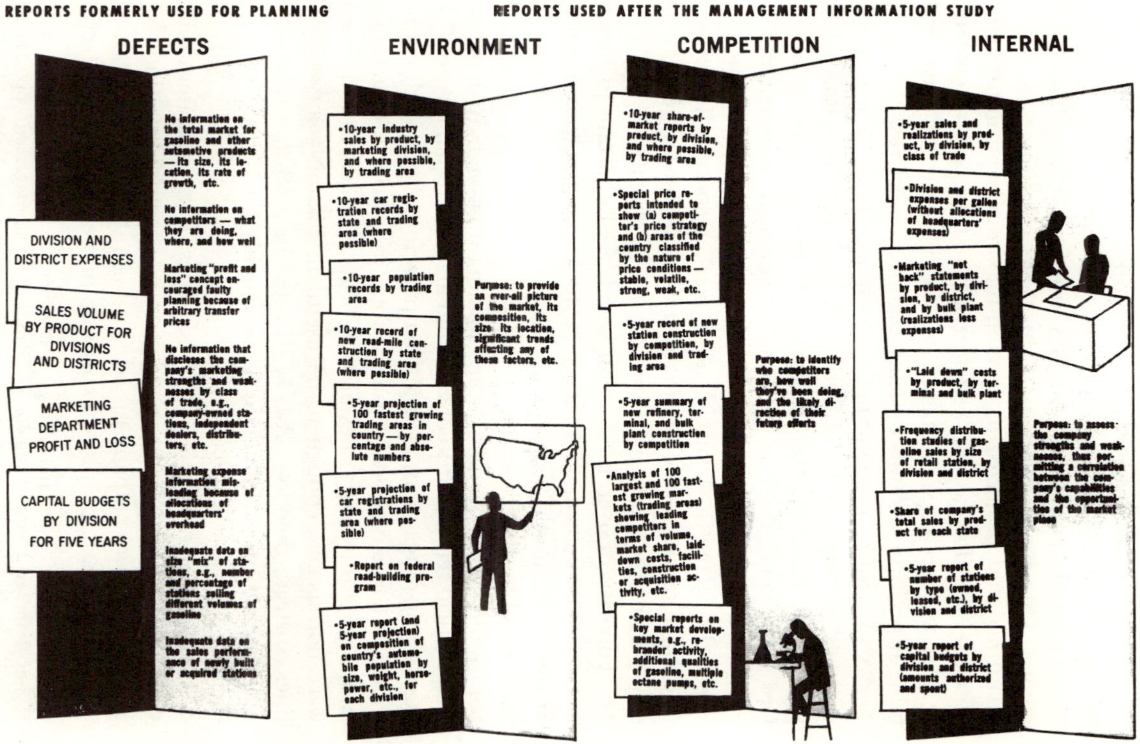

nomic factors since its major customers are government agencies and government-regulated airlines. In addition to projections of general domestic economic and market conditions, therefore, Lockheed includes in its planning premises such factors as the international political situation and projected Cold War conditions, the United States government's attitudes towards power and missiles, and possible technological developments. The effects of changes in these conditions on sales are then quantified and projected to develop maximum and minimum long-range potential sales forecasts.[5] These forecasts in turn become control yardsticks against which company operations are subsequently measured to determine if performance was meeting planned objectives.

A forecast of the external environment is the first step in American Airlines' planning. Unlike Lockheed, however, American Airlines begins with projections of overall factors in the domestic economy, such as Gross National Product, disposable personal income, and population growth, and then isolates those additional economic indicators which affect the domestic transportation market specifically, in order to develop a forecast of the domestic travel market in general and the air transport market (passenger and cargo) in particular.[6]

Forecasts of overall economic trends are important to a large company or to a company whose business is related very closely to major movements in the political and economic environment. This is not true for the vast majority of businesses, however. As Clarence Danielson of A-D-M Company points out, "few companies are fortunate enough to have well-defined arithmetical relationships of sales and major external factors."[7] In developing its long-range plans, A-D-M Company found that such major economic trends as Gross National Product, total industrial production, and population growth affected sales of each of its products in a different way and were not specific enough to be useful in planning for A-D-M's product lines. Instead, therefore, A-D-M directed its attention to isolating specific industry indices which might be reasonably related to its specific product lines.[8]

In smaller companies and industries, it is sometimes difficult to develop very much relevant industry and market information. For example, a leading paper company for which this author worked wanted planning information for a proposed expansion into envelope manufacturing. Since

[5]L. Eugene Root and George A. Steiner, "The Lockheed Aircraft Corporation Master Plan," in Ewing, *Long-Range Planning for Management*, pp. 239-259.

[6]C. N. Oursler, "Long-Range Planning at American Airlines, Inc.," in *Managerial Long-Range Planning*, ed. George A. Steiner (New York: McGraw-Hill Book Company, 1963), pp 115-126. For an evaluation of the approach used by TWA, see John J. Clark and Pieter T. Elgers, "Evaluating the Sales Forecast," *Michigan Business Review*, May, 1968, pp. 14-19.

[7]Clarence A. Danielson, "How We Took Hold of Long-Range Planning at A-D-M," in Ewing, *Long-Range Planning for Management*, p. 259.

[8]Danielson, "How We Took Hold of Long-Range Planning at A-D-M," pp. 259-266.

at the time most envelope manufacturing companies were privately held, practically no information was available on the size or composition of the market or on the competition within it. Neither envelope or paper associations nor government statistical sources had much information related to the specific type of expansion proposed—even though the envelope group is a sizeable segment of the paper industry. An extended, round-about search of diverse information sources, such as banks, suppliers, and company financial reports, yielded the semblance of background information upon which decisions could be made. Although this information on past and future trends was hardly an adequate basis for a major investment decision, it was all the information that could be found and a major decision was made on the basis of it—evidently a fairly common business practice.

More recently, the author was involved in planning for a mail-order marketing operation. Total retail sales had some relevance in developing a long-range plan for the operation, as did trends and forecasts of population, disposable income and selected product-group sales. But none of these were directly related to mail-order sales and so were of no real help when developing detailed product and marketing plans. Since there were few adequate specific breakdowns of sales trends within the mail-order industry, plans had to be based largely on premises other than forecasts, such as probable developments in postal rates and service, in marketing concepts and media, in consumer attitudes and mail-order buying habits, and the like.

Many sources are used to obtain information about a company's environment. Among the most common, according to a recent study,[9] are:

1. Personal Experience
2. Journals
3. Reports
4. Books
5. Professional Meetings
6. Industrial Conferences and Association Publications
7. Colleagues
8. Board Members
9. Friends
10. Employees
11. Suppliers and Customers
12. Other Sources

According to the same survey, the kind of information most often sought is:[10]

Category	General Content
1. Market potential	Supply and demand considerations for market areas of current or potential interest: for example, capacity, consumption, imports, exports.

[9]Francis F. Aguilar, *Scanning the Business Environment* (New York: The Macmillan Company, 1968).

[10]Aguilar, *Scanning the Business Environment*, p. 40.

2. Structural change	Mergers, acquisitions, and joint ventures involving competitors; new entries into the industry.
3. Competitors and industry	General information about a competitor, industry policy, concerted actions in the industry, and so forth.
4. Pricing	Effective and proposed prices for products of current and potential interest.
5. Sales negotiations	Information relating to a specific current or potential sale or contract for the firm.
6. Customers	General information about current or near-potential customers, their markets, their problems.
7. Leads for mergers, joint ventures, or acquisitions	Information concerning possibilities for the manager's own company.
8. Suppliers and raw materials	Purchasing considerations for products of current or potential interest.
9. New products, processes, and technology	Technical information relatively new and unknown to the company.
10. Product problems	Problems involving existing products.
11. Costs	Costs for processing, operations, and so forth for current and potential competitors, suppliers and customers, and for proposed company activities.
12. Licensing and patents	Products and processes.
13. General conditions	Events of a general nature: political, demographic, national, and so forth.
14. Government actions and policies	Governmental decisions affecting the industry.
15. Resources available	Persons, land, and other resources possibly available for the company.
16. Miscellaneous	Items not elsewhere classified.

Not all companies, nor all levels or types of managers, need the same kind of information nor obtain it from the same sources.[11] For example, small companies and lower level managers tend to use more personal, less

[11]Aguilar, *Scanning the Business Environment, passim.*, especially Chapters Five and Six.

formal sources for obtaining information, while large companies and higher level managers tend to use more formal sources. On the one hand, marketing managers will most often seek out industry and market information; on the other hand, financial managers are more interested in broader economic information. And lower level managers tend to get more unsolicited information, whereas higher level managers tend to solicit and seek out environmental information more aggressively. In brief, each company and each manager must determine particular information needs, the specific sources that will provide this information, and the best way to get it.

Obtaining information about competitors is one of the most perplexing problems facing a manager. In the author's experience, a company's suppliers and customers have proved to be the most accurate and current source of information on competitors. This is especially true for smaller companies.

While larger companies tend to be more fully integrated and so are more likely to do exploratory work internally, smaller companies are not, and so need to consult and use suppliers more heavily when exploring new products and services. Since suppliers serve many customers, they tend to be channels of information about new projects being considered. Smaller companies are also forced to use outside market research and testing facilities more than larger companies, for smaller companies are less likely to have internal testing and research facilities, thus making these outside facilities an independent source of information on new developments. Information on the new operations of fully integrated companies is harder to come by during the early stages of development, except through direct hiring of competitor personnel or through corporate espionage.

Specific information on competitor profitability and efficiency by product line is practically impossible to acquire, except in a very general way.

ECONOMIC AND MARKET FORECASTS AND FORECASTING TECHNIQUES

Economic and market forecasts are the external planning premises most directly related to management control, since the sales forecast is partially derived from economic and market forecasts and many control standards are derived in turn from the sales forecast.

Such forecasting may start with overall economic forecasts—projections of what will happen in the overall economy. Wherever possible, forecasts are then made of trends within the industry and market served by the company, including what the total market for the company's products will be and what share of that market the company can realistically expect to obtain. These forecasts are then combined with internal company factors to come up with a sales forecast.

Some of the more commonly used long-term economic forecasts are:[12] projections of the Gross National Product; projections of disposable personal income; full employment models; and long-term economic series. Some of the more commonly used short-term economic forecasts are:[13] short-range forecasts of the GNP; industrial production models; leading, coincident, and lagging series; and econometric models of the economy.

These forecasts of the economic environment form the background within which industry and market forecasts are made in areas more closely related to a company's business. In the majority of companies, these specific industry and market forecasts (where they can be developed) are the ones which have the most relevance to planning and control. An example of how market forecasts were developed and used to build company sales forecasts at a large telephone company is given below. Before describing this study, however, the following sections review some of the statistical techniques used in forecasting.

Various statistical techniques can be used in forecasting. Three of the major ones—time series analysis (including trend development), regression analysis, and adaptive forecasting— as well as the data formulation process, are discussed here.

The Data Formulation Process.

Before a forecast or prediction can be made, the data must first be formulated, that is, it must be collected, analyzed, interpreted and presented.

In the *collection* phase, data can be obtained from existing published or unpublished sources, such as government agencies, trade associations, research bureaus, magazines, newspapers, individual research workers, and others. In addition to these data sources, the investigator may find it necessary to collect his own information by physically going to the originating sources and compiling it. Although a person may never have to collect data, it is essential that he have a working knowledge of the processes of collection and be able to evaluate the reliability of data he uses.

In the *analysis* phase, data must be classified into useful and logical categories. The four important bases of classification of statistical data

[12]Carl A. Dauten, *Business Cycles and Forecasting* (2nd ed.; Cincinnati, South-Western Publishing Company, 1961), pp. 353-358; Adolph G. Abramson, "Techniques of Forecasting," in *Business Forecasting in Practice*, ed. by Adolph G. Abramson and Russell H. Mack (New York: John Wiley and Sons, Inc., 1956), p. 75; Harry Deane Wolfe, *Business Forecasting Methods* (New York: Holt, Rinehart and Winston, 1966), p. 133.

[13]Elmer Clark Bratt, *Business Cycles and Forecasting* (5th ed.; Homewood, Illinois: Richard D. Irwin, Inc., 1961), p. 408, 438-439; Dauten, *Business Cycles and Forecasting*, pp. 388-415; Geoffrey H. Moore, *Business Cycles Indicators* (Princeton, New Jersey: Princeton University Press, 1960), Vol. 1; Norman N. Barish, *Economic Analysis for Engineering and Managerial Decision-Making* (New York: McGraw-Hill Book Company, 1962), p. 561.

are: 1) qualitative, 2) quantitative, 3) chronological, and 4) geographical.[14] For example, in doing a forecast of telephone usage, classifying telephones as rotary or touchtone gives a qualitative differentiation, for the distinction is one of a kind rather than of amount. When items vary in respect to some measurable characteristic, a quantitative classification is appropriate. For example, families may be classified according to the number of children, and individuals may be classified according to the amount of income tax they pay. Chronological data, or time series classification, shows information about continuing series of events at various specified times. For example, one may chart daily stock prices over a period of months or years. Geographical classifications present data arranged by geographical region. For example, one can show the number and kinds of telephone users for each of the counties in New York City.

The *interpretation* phase of the data formulation process consists of drawing conclusions based on the analysis. In doing this step, the limitations of the original data must be studied carefully, so that the investigator can discover and clarify all the useful and applicable meanings present in his data.

Finally, the data must be *presented* in some suitable form either for one's own use or for the use of others. Usually the figures are arranged in a table or represented by various graphic devices.

The four-step procedure for formulating data is a prerequisite to developing a significant forecast.

Time Series Analysis.

The first major forecasting technique to be discussed in this section is time series analysis. All data reported at regular intervals of time are referred to as time series. This includes data reported daily, weekly, monthly, annually or at some other relevant time interval.

There are four kinds of movements which can be examined in any time series: trend, cyclical, seasonal, and irregular. In order to study the influences that affect a particular series, it is necessary to isolate these four factors.

1. *Trend* is the basic tendency of an activity to either increase or decrease over a long period of time. The Gross National Product is in a rising trend. A declining trend is found in the number of candlestick manufacturers. It is important to describe the trend of a series for a number of reasons. First, this description gives one an idea of the general direction of the activity being studied, and avoids the confusion which may be introduced by random fluctuations. Second, once an historical trend has been established, it helps one to project the future behavior of the trend. Third, trend development enables the planner to compare one trend against another more easily—

[14]Frederick E. Croxton and Dudley J. Cowden, *Applied General Statistics* (Englewood Cliffs, New Jersey: Prentice-Hall, Inc., 1965), p. 326.

for example, the trend of his company's sales against the sales of the industry in general.

The simplest method of developing a trend graphically is by inspection. If the trend is a straight line, or linear, it may be drawn with a straight edge (see Figure 4.2). If the trend is non-linear, it may be drawn freehand or with a curvilinear ruler (see Figure 4.3). The straight line is the simplest type of trend line. For short periods of time a straight line may provide a reasonably good description of the trend of a series, but for longer periods a curved or non-linear line may be called for. It is also possible to represent trends by mathematical formulas.[15]

2.   *Cyclical* movements are successive phases of expansion and contraction above and below the trend. Turning points occur with little advance warning and usually for different reasons. Recession and recovery in overall business conditions are the primary causes of cyclical movements.

3.   *Seasonal* variations are distinct from cyclical ones, because they recur regularly and last one year or less. A seasonal pattern could be man made, or it could be the result of weather conditions, holidays or other recurring developments.

4.   *Irregular* movements are those fluctuations caused by such unusual events as strikes, storms, assassinations, and the like.

Isolating the various kinds of movements within a time series and going beyond merely looking at the trend of the series enables one to pro-

[15]Croxton and Cowden, *Applied General Statistics*, Chapter 14.

Figure 4.2

MAGAZINE ADVERTISING IN THE U.S.
1915-1971

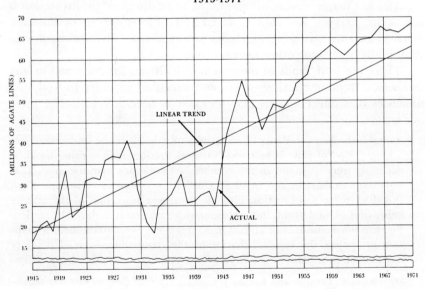

Figure 4.3

PRODUCTION OF ASPHALT FROM PETROLEUM
1941-1971

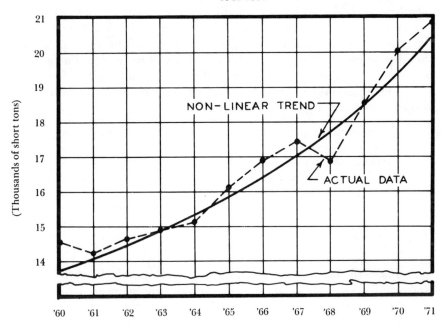

ject into the future the variations which can be expected within a trend over a short term. In addition, when several time series are being studied, it may be possible to compare movements in one trend with those in another series and establish a lead-lag relationship. For example, a comparison of movements within the time series of new factory orders and of factory production might indicate that an upturn in the former will usually precede the latter by a fixed number of months. The usefulness of such leading indicators is, however, very limited, since only in rare instances are they highly reliable.[16]

The time series method is not recommended for long-term projections. It is best suited for one-year or two-year month-to-month forecasts.[17]

Regression Analysis.

The econometrician's standard analytical tool in business cycle research is regression and correlation analysis.[18] The regression and cor-

16Wolfe, *Business Forecasting Methods*, pp. 48-51.

17"New Horizons in Telephone Forecasting," *Telephony*, November 7, 1964, p. 60.

18William F. Butler and Robert A. Kavish, *How Business Economists Forecast* (Englewood Cliffs, New Jersey: Prentice-Hall, Inc., 1966), p. 8.

relation approach is based on the fact that elements of the economy are interrelated and that many of these inter-relationships are relatively constant. If two variables are related, then a knowledge of one, the independent variable, will make possible an estimate of the other, the dependent variable. For example, if one can predict the number of marriages that will occur over the coming years, one can predict the number of new houses or apartments which will be needed during those years, since marriages normally create the need for new homes.

There are three measurements which must be made in conjunction with simple *linear regression analysis*.

1.   A mathematical regression equation which describes the relationship between the two variables.
2.   A measure of the possible divergence of the actual values of the dependent variable from their estimated or computed values. For example, if one projects a GNP of $1300 billion for 1974, one must also specify how much the actual results might vary from the projections. This measure is called the standard error of estimate.
3.   A measure of the degree of relationship or correlation (r) between the variables.[19]

The term linear describes those relationships which when plotted, independent variable vs. dependent variable, approximate a linear relationship. For example, if one were to plot temperature on the X-axis and cricket chirps per minute on the Y-axis one would find scatter points lying on an almost straight line, since cricket chirping increases with the temperature. By determining the regression equation, it would then be possible to forecast the dependent variable, chirps per minute, if one could forecast the temperature, the independent variable.

An example of the use of regression analysis in business might be to determine if there is a relationship between furniture sales and personal income. If the relationship is signficant enough, it might then be possible to forecast one event, furniture sales, knowing the value of the other, personal income.

The statistical term used for measuring the degree of relationship between two factors is correlation. The correlation coefficient is a figure which measures the degree to which two variables correlate. It is usually accepted that an 80 percent correlation coefficient is significant.

Exactly the same principles are involved in *multiple linear regression analysis* as in simple linear regression analysis. The procedure for computing measures of relationship is also essentially the same, although it is more laborious in multiple linear regression analysis, since there is more than one independent variable.

[19]Croxton and Cowden, *Applied General Statistics*, pp. 454-455.

Adaptive Forecasting.

Adaptive or exponential forecasting deals with forecasting of individual products for inventory control and for production scheduling.[20] The need for adaptive forecasts of individual product lines most frequently arises when a company has an inventory control system or a production scheduling system with predetermined decision rules that specify when to produce or order more of a particular item. These decision rules are based in part on a prediction of sales or usage of each item in the near future.

Certain desirable characteristics of these forecasts are implied by their use: they must be made quickly, cheaply, easily, and in such a manner that they can be followed routinely. In its simplest form, the adaptive or exponential forecasting system produces a forecast of expected sales in the next period by a weighted average of sales in the current period and the forecast of sales for the current period made during the previous period.[21] Such a method has the characteristics desired in a prediction method: current sales information is easily introduced, the forecast calculation is fast, and only a limited amount of information need be maintained. For products with stable sales rates and little seasonal fluctuations, this simple exponential model proves quite satisfactory.

It is usually worthwhile to extend the adaptive forecasting system to take into account long-range trends and seasonal effects. While more information is required with this more complete model, the accuracy of prediction is also substantially increased for most kinds of products.

A STUDY IN MARKET AND SALES FORECASTING

A major telephone company recently completed a study of ways to improve forecasting of new telephone demand, which illustrates how forecasting techniques are used for planning and control. The technique used in the study was multiple regression, a technique which is commonly used in economic and business forecasting.

The purpose of the study was to develop a way to forecast telephone usage a year in advance, so that the company could develop manufacturing and service facilities to make, install, and maintain new telephones. The study was confined to one geographical area.

Two methods are used in making a multiple regression analysis. First is the graphic method, which involves developing scatter diagrams, regression lines, and regression estimates. The second is the mathematical approach. Graphic methods involve manually drawing regression lines

[20]Peter R. Winters, "Forecasting Sales by Exponentially Weighted Moving Averages," *Management Science*, April, 1960, pp. 324-342.

[21]H. Theil and S. Wage, "Some Observations on Adaptive Forecasting," *Management Science*, January, 1964, p. 198.

through scatter points. This can cause significant errors, especially when the lines must be drawn free hand. The mathematical approach yields a more accurate forecast because the judgment error is eliminated. Because of the availability of a time-sharing computer, which virtually eliminates the need for manual calculations, the analysis in this study was confined to the mathematical approach.

It was first necessary to examine the factors that appeared to affect station or telephone demand, which in this case was the dependent variable. Two factors were initially examined: live births and marriage licenses issued. These factors were selected because marriages create households, which are potential new telephone users, and these marriages can be shown to be the result of births 22 years earlier.

The lead time of 22 years was determined through a computer program. The number of marriages was shown to relate very closely to births 22 years earlier, which in statistical terms meant there was an extremely high index of determination.

The problem was then to forecast marriages, using births as the controlling independent variable. A computer was used to perform the many mathematical calculations although longhand or manual methods could have been used.

Once a projection of the marriages expected each year was made, then information was developed on the housing that would be available to accomodate these potential telephone users. Since in the area being studied it usually took one full year from the issuance of the permit to the completion of a building, data from the F. W. Dodge Corporation regarding building permits issued and building contracts awarded was analyzed. The data was then projected one year to provide meaningful forecast information. This information was then compared with the projections of marriage licenses to be issued and station demand, in order to determine the degree of correlation, if any, that existed among the three variables.

A computer program was used to perform the multiple linear regression of these three variables. This program fits the linear regression equation $Y = A + B (X_1) + C (X_2)$, where Y = station demand, X_1 = marriage licenses issued, X_2 = building contracts awarded, and A, B and C were the regression coefficients. The index of determination was 0.998776, indicating an extremely close fit among the variables. The forecast equation was readily obtained by using the coefficients from the computer program and substituting them for the variables A, B, and C.

The forecasts proved to be very accurate. For example, for the coming year the company had previously forecast 51,000 installations. In contrast, the new forecasting method predicted 48,700. The actual figure proved to be 47,000.

This case is a very simple example of how forecasting techniques can be used to predict events within a company's environment, and so help develop more precise external planning premises. A simple example was selected in order to illustrate the basic approach to doing market forecasting. Since the telephone company in this case was the only one serving the market, the company proceeded to develop sales forecasts and plans to produce and service the new telephones expected to be sold.

This is an exceptional situation, however, for normally more than one company competes in a market. If the market had been served by more than one telephone company, subsequent studies would have been needed to determine the expected share of the market for each company before a sales forecast could be made.

Under normal circumstances, therefore, once the economic forecaster has studied the environmental factors and established what the overall market for a company's product line will be, he must predict the share of the market his company might expect to achieve profitably. This he can do partially through analysis of historical industry, economic, and company data. These ideal projections must then be studied in the light of the company's available resources and the sales the operating managers feel can be achieved through these resources.[22]

HOW ACCURATE SHOULD FORECASTS BE?

In many ways economic forecasts are not much different from non-quantitative or qualitative planning premises, since they are basically refined estimates, translated into numbers, of probable future circumstances. The definition of probable events through forecasts only gives the planner a more precise, quantitative framework within which to work.

Since forecasts are basically estimates and so can never be considered 100% accurate, it is important in planning to know the possible range of deviations of actual performance from forecast, the probability of their occurrence, and the magnitude of the effect of such deviations on corporate operations in quantitative terms. What management needs to know is what margin of error in the forecast he should plan for. The manager's job is then to create alternative operational plans to meet and exploit possible future occurrences. The sooner a manager knows that performance could possibly deviate by 2% or 10% or 50% from forecast, the sooner he can develop alternative operational plans to meet these possible future circumstances.

For example, in a retail sales operation, it is impossible to predict exactly how much of each product will be sold. The astute merchandiser, therefore, develops outlets through which he can dispose of a specific amount of excess inventory, or arranges with the manufacturer to carry back-up inventory for him, or spaces his promotions in such a way as to limit his risk and his investment in inventory. The planning information

22Wolfe, *Business Forecasting Methods*, Chapters Seven and Eight.

the merchandiser needs is a forecast of the maximum and minimum amount of merchandise that he is likely to have to dispose of in this way, or how much he must ask the manufacturer to provide in back-up inventory of the product, or the degree to which he should stagger his promotions.

The manager can never expect to have exact predictions or forecasts of future events, and the forecaster is not expected to produce them. The most a manager will ever know is the likelihood and probable range of future events, their impact on his operation, and the risks involved in the various courses of action. This is the information the forecaster should provide. With this information in hand, the planner can prepare to meet each probable turn of events.

COMPANY PLANNING PREMISES

The information developed during the economic analysis stage only tells the manager what sales he might reasonably expect under various circumstances. Whatever conclusions are drawn from an analysis of external factors, these conclusions must be tempered by what the company can realistically do and the owners want to do. Normally, a company's planning is influenced as much by internal company factors as it is by environmental factors.

Company planning premises are all the internal corporate factors that must be taken into account when developing corporate plans. Company planning premises may concern the amount of available financing, manpower, and facilities; the areas in which the company has experience (including marketing expertise, present product line, and production knowhow); and the kind and sophistication of internal, automated information and control systems. These premises may also concern the internal "character" of the organization, and how much and how soon it can be adapted to growth and change. And they may include the needs and desires of company stockholders and the aspirations, values, and prejudices of company managers.

An intense corporate self-appraisal is needed to determine the relevance of internal strengths and weaknesses to planning and control. The expansion of facilities will always be limited by the availability of funds and management resources. Entry into new markets will always be helped or hindered by the strengths and weaknesses of a company's production and marketing experience: if the company has a strong distribution system for selling toiletries in drug stores, for example, it can expand most easily by adding new products that can be sold through the same channels.

In some instances, as David Ewing has pointed out, a study of internal corporate resources (especially in the area of marketing and production experience) has caused management to go against conclusions drawn from a study of industry opportunities, and to choose to concentrate on seemingly less dynamic portions of a market.[23] For example, both Franklin Life Insurance Company in the 1940's and AMP Inc. in the 1950's successfully used this approach. By concentrating on their areas of expertise, they were able to build very strong businesses in face of what appeared to be unfavorable market indicators. In contrast, Joseph E. Seagrams and Sons, Inc. used the "market opportunity" approach. They foresaw expanding markets for a wider range of expensive beverages and expanded their product line. Unfortunately, the same approach was used by competitors, and severe competition resulted.

What were the lessons learned from these experiences? First, success depends on doing a job better than the competition, so that companies are *sometimes* better off concentrating on what they know how to do best, in spite of perceived potential market opportunities in new fields. Second, while forecasts of market potential are useful, they have their limitations. No matter how clairvoyant an economic forecaster may be, there is no way of fully anticipating what the competition will do.

Successful past experience in a functional area does not, however, always guarantee success. For example, Famous Schools, a leader in the correspondence school field, had been extremely successful in starting art and writing schools and had the industry's most highly developed field-sales system. In the early 1960's management decided to introduce a photography school, which they felt would be successfully marketed in the same way as the art and writing schools, and they proceeded to follow the same marketing and product patterns for the photography school that they had used in their art and writing schools. Unfortunately, the photographers' market was distinct enough from the writers' and artists' market to require different marketing techniques, a different price for the product, and different student services, so that many changes had to be made after the product was introduced, and much time and money was needlessly lost. In the end, the photography school failed to live up to management expectations and at best seemed destined to make only a marginal contribution to company profits.

Dow Jones had a similar experience with their new publication, *The National Observer*. When Dow Jones introduced the new publication, a weekly newspaper, they used the marketing techniques they had used in marketing *The Wall Street Journal*, a daily business and financial paper, which was highly successful. As is shown in the discussion of *The National Observer* in Chapter 14 this marketing experience was not transferable and so was not a sound basis upon which to build a marketing program for the new publication.

[23]David W. Ewing, "Corporate Planning at the Crossroads," *Harvard Business Review*, July-August, 1967, pp. 83-85.

The lack of adequate automated information and control systems is another limiting factor which is having an ever-increasing impact on planning today. For example, one major corporation in the entertainment field has been forced to wait indefinitely to develop a $25,000,000 business because, even though marketing plans and programs are tested and ready and adequate financial resources are available, the company's computerized order servicing operation and its manpower resources are inadequate to handle even current business.

The effect of the personal biases and the desires of chief executives or major stockholders on a company's planning is well known. Ideally, emotional and personal biases should be eliminated in planning for a business. In practice, however, they cannot be, and they frequently have a major impact on the ultimate choice of what direction a company follows or how the company plans to get there.

THE SALES FORECAST AND CONTROL STANDARDS

The sales forecast is the basis of most company plans and their related controls. Marketing, production, manpower, financial, and other plans are based on this forecast, as in overall corporate profit planning.

Wherever possible, external economic forecasts are first made to arrive at an estimate of the sales the company should achieve under ideal circumstances. These forecasts are then adjusted on the basis of information gathered from operation managers and other sources,[24] as well as information on the limitations set by company planning premises.

For example, in the oil company case described earlier in this chapter, economic forecasts of total demand and of the company's potential share of that demand were first made. Internal factors were then examined to determine what proportion of these potential sales the company could get with its present and planned facilities and manpower, before a final sales forecast was made. The initial forecasts were then adjusted on the basis of executive judgment and on information gathered from the operating managers on the plans of major customers and on other local market factors affecting major segments of the company's sales.

In larger companies overall industry and market forecasts can have a major impact on company sales forecasting: first, a large company normally has a significant share of the market, so that changes in its sales are more likely to coincide with changes in total industry sales; second, large companies are more likely to have adequate resources to meet major increases in demand, so that they do not necessarily have to adjust sales forecasts downward because of limited resources. The smaller the company, the

---

[24]Wolfe, *Business Forecasting Methods*, Chapters Seven and Eight, describes the various methods used to make sales forecasts for a company.

more important internal company factors and specific market factors are likely to be in developing the sales forecast, since the company's share of market is smaller and its resources are more limited.

Overall sales forecasts are always refined and broken down into major product and market categories. These specific sales forecasts in turn are used as quantified marketing goals for each marketing division. Marketing, manpower, production, and financing plans are next developed, along with budgets and controls to meet these sales goals. Overall profit and expense goals are also developed as part of this process, thus producing a whole fabric of sub-objectives, implementation plans and control standards for all the operating and staff areas in a company. Economic, market, and sales forecasts are thus extremely important to business planning and control, for they are the origin of sub-objectives, implementation plans, and performance standards for each profit center segment of a company's operation.

As can be seen from the above discussion, developing company sales forecasts is not a simple process of economic analysis. The market can be studied and the ideal share of that market a company should reasonably expect to achieve can be determined. But normally a company's business is influenced by special market factors and its resources limited, so that except in very large companies ideal forecasts of sales and profits must always be tempered by what the operating managers feel can be achieved with their available resources in the light of special market factors, and a balance must be struck between the ideal economic and pragmatic operating points of view.

Sometimes it may be necessary to insist that an operating manager set higher goals for his operation, when he appears to be overly conservative or merely trying to make his job a little easier. At the same time, an economic forecaster is not omniscient, so that his projection may be unrealistically high and must be tempered. Considerable executive judgment is needed to reconcile these two points of view.

Presumably, the two points of view act as controls on each other, and temper any shortcomings or excesses at either the operating management or economic analysis level. Having these two points of view does not, of course, guarantee that one will come up with an accurate sales forecast, but they do help the manager come closer to the right answer.

The sales forecast, then, is in a sense the catalyst through which the effects of internal and external planning premises are reconciled. The sales forecast is also a means by which planning goals are translated into control standards, for it is both the basis upon which overall company budgets are developed, as well as the basis for establishing sales and output goals for each operation within a company, from which specific operation control standards are developed.

OVERALL PLANNING DIRECTIONS: OBJECTIVES AND POLICIES

The overall corporate objective defines the kind of business the owners, usually through their representatives, the Board of Directors, want their company to be. It states the overall direction which when followed should most profitably put the company's resources to work in exploiting available market opportunities over the long term.

Many objectives are established within a company. Marketing will have sales goals, market mix goals and market penetration goals. Finance will have return-on-investment goals, and personnel will have manpower and staffing goals. In other words, all the functional activities within a business enterprise have their own objectives and goals.

Such goals are, however, only sub-goals within the larger context of the overall corporate plan. These sub-goals are intermediate goals. They support and further overall objectives, and are the means of achieving an overall objective—making maximum profits within a well-defined area of business activity and within certain limitations established by the owners or their representatives, the Board of Directors. It is through these sub-objectives and goals, therefore, that overall company objectives are translated into specific performance standards against which performance can be measured through the management control process. And it is because these sub-objectives and department goals are so closely related to overall company directions that successful management control requires the study of company objectives.

In almost all instances, companies have found that the simple statement of an objective does not give adequate guidance, and that some amplification is needed. These amplifications can include statements of corporate philosophy, principles of action, and company strategy. Where such statements have been developed, they should be reviewed at this phase in the management control process, for they are part of the objective and so also condition control development.

Overall policies also give direction to corporate activities, for they are designed to give guidance in achieving corporate objectives. In that they give specific direction to operations, they provide guidance as to where control efforts should be concentrated.

The company organization structure is also important, since controls are often structured around the existing organization patterns. For example, the structure of the marketing division will dictate to some degree the kinds of controls needed to keep the organization functioning smoothly. As is seen below in Chapter 9, however, organization patterns can change, as control systems are developed and new reporting relationships are established.

In addition to the company factors identified during the planning premises phase of planning, therefore, one should also identify both overall and individual operating company objectives and policies. They indicate the kind of company for which the controls or control system are being created, specify company strengths and weaknesses, define the company organization structure, give guidelines within which control must be exercised, and establish a network of major control goals and standards which are closely related to corporate objectives.

IMPLEMENTATION PLANNING FACTORS

Once overall company directions have been spelled out, detailed plans must be drawn up for reaching corporate objectives and carrying out corporate strategy. Since these plans are designed to carry out or "implement", they are usually called implementation plans. A detailed diagram of the network of implementation plans normally found within a company is given in Figure 1.1 in Chapter 1.

The network of company implementation plans, their sales goals and their budgets, are the basis for the control network within a company. These implementation plans are what the controls are designed to help carry out. Implementation sales goals are the major quantitative standards within a control system, as well as the basis for many derivative standards designed to see that operations function to meet sales goals. Implementation budgets are developed as part of the planning and control processes, as plans are translated into quantitative operating standards and useful control reporting formats.

CONCLUSION

Obviously, when writing up a control study one does not rewrite or redo the entire company plan. A brief summary of key planning factors is all that is usually included in a control study. The relatively small amount of space that is given to planning factors in control studies should not be mistaken for a measure of their importance to control. The importance of planning factors in control is enormous, and planning affects all phases of a control effort.

If controls are to function effectively to help a company reach a goal and carry out a plan, then one must know where the company wants to go (objectives and policies) and how the company hopes to get there (implementation plans). Or, a manager will not be able to build an effective control system.

The basis of company planning is the planning premise. It is here that key external economic industry and market factors are indentified, and market forecasts developed. It is here that company factors influencing performance are identified, and overall sales forecasts are developed. It is here, therefore, that one finds the basis for major control standards.

As implementation plans are formulated, budgetary controls must be

developed to quantify them, and so give more specific guidance to operations and establish standards by which to judge operating performance.
These budgets, in turn, are the basis of many other performance standards within each operating division. The development of controls and
control systems thus begins with the planning process.

Too much emphasis cannot be given to the importance of studying
planning factors before undertaking any management control. For the
plans give direction to all subsequent steps in the control process—both in
development of controls and control systems, as well as in exercising control
and taking corrective action.

DISCUSSION QUESTIONS

1. What are the major steps in the planning process? What is the function of
    management control within the planning process?
2. What is the role of forecasting in the planning process?
3. Harry Deane Wolfe, in *Business Forecasting Methods* (Chapters 7 and 8),
    lists the many ways in which a company's sales goal can be developed. Starting
    with a forecast of the economy, the industry and the market, the economic
    forecaster can use historical information to predict the percentage of that
    market (and the total sales) that the company should attain. This must be
    balanced with internally generated information from the operating person-
    nel. Discuss the problems which may be encountered in reconciling these
    two points of view.
4. Once overall company sales have been predicted, it is necessary to predict
    sales by product category. This is extremely difficult in the case, for example,
    of a department store, which carries many thousands of items. Discuss the
    methods you would use to arrive at detailed foecasts by product. How much
    weight would you give to a buyer's estimate of volume for the next six months
    in the refrigerator and stove department, for example? What economic in-
    dicators might you use as a cross check against the buyer's forecast?
5. Discuss the ways in which economic forecasting is important to setting goals
    for a toy manufacturer's marketing department. What overall economic
    trends would affect this department's sales? How important are seasonal
    variations in forecasting these sales?
6. In a circulation marketing department at a large national publication, what
    economic indicators might be helpful in predicting new subscription sales
    and circulation growth? Do you feel the economic forecaster can be of much
    help? Or, do you feel the forecast depends almost entirely on the money avail-
    able for advertising and the advertising cost of obtaining new subscribers?
7. In what way are forecasting and forecast related to management control?
8. Discuss the ways in which other company planning premises, overall com-
    pany directions (objectives and policies), and implementation plans are re-
    lated to management control.
9. Why is the study of planning factors so important to all subsequent steps
    in the management control process?

CHAPTER 5

STEP TWO: IDENTIFYING KEY FACTORS AFFECTING THE CONTROL SITUATION — OTHER CONSIDERATIONS

This chapter continues the discussion of the second step in the management control process begun in Chapter 4. The discussion covers the additional key factors affecting the control situation which must be identified in step two: the specific characteristics of the control situation; the purpose of the control system and tools needed; the kinds of controls to be used; the nature of their standards; and special factors affecting the exercise of control and the implementation of changes in controls.

SPECIFIC CHARACTERISTICS OF THE CONTROL SITUATION

In step one in the management control process the nature of the control situation is identified in very general terms: overall budgetary control in a large or small company; operating control for a circulation marketing department; cost control in a valve manufacturing department; a decision about what type of equipment to purchase. While in each instance there was some consideration of the details of the situation, the main thrust in step one was merely to identify the general nature of the situation or problem, in order to give focus to the control effort. During step two of the control process a manager pinpoints in more detail the significant characteristics of the situation or problem.

The following discussion explores how one identifies significant characteristics in some of the more commonly encountered control situations: overall financial budgetary control in a large company; company-wide information needs for control; operating control in the marketing and production areas; control for a staff area, such as personnel; financial analysis for alternative equipment decisions; and overall control in a small company.

A manager may, for example, be assigned to review and improve wherever possible a company's overall financial budgetary control. Since the situation in this instance involves the entire company's operation, redefinitions would thus be needed of:

1. The flow of business. How are orders generated, and how do they move from sales to manufacturing to customer service to collections? How are products manufactured and delivered?
2. The organization of the company's operation. What does the organization chart look like?
3. The interaction among the components of a company's organization. What exchanges of information among divisions are needed?
4. The major decision areas affecting success. What critical aspects of the particular operation under study, such as cost per order, inventory turnover, length of production runs, etc., significantly affect sales and profits and so will give a quick indication of how well the business is doing?
5. The place of the systems and control departments in the company organization. To whom do the controller and systems manager report to and what are their responsibilities?
6. Any other similarly pertinent factors which will affect the development of controls.

The answers to these questions would be specific and most often written out in detail—if one expected to make a careful evaluation of the control system. For example, in evaluating overall budgetary control at a large electric company, the Frost Electric Company, a considerable amount of information about the company was gathered during this phase of the study.[1] First, major planning factors were examined to determine the nature of the company, its market, and its objectives. Next, a description was drawn up of the organization of the company, the responsibility of each major organizational unit, and the way they worked together: the company's production department was responsible for industrial and plant engineering, tool engineering, plant management and procurement, transportation and warehousing; the research and development department, which employed over 200 persons, was organized around the company's three major product lines (power tools, builder's supplies, and electric motors), and worked closely with both production and marketing; the marketing operation had a sales manager for each product line, and departments for advertising and sales promotion, customer service, market

---

[1]Robert H. Deming, *Characteristics of an Effective Management Control System in an Industrial Organization* (Boston: Division of Research, Graduate School of Business Administration, Harvard University, 1968), Chapters One and Two.

research, and forecasting and inventory control (which coordinated sales plans with production plans); the finance department was responsible for general accounting, credit and collections, data processing and payroll, cost accounting, and overall budgetary control; in addition, a number of committees were designated to handle overall coordination of corporate operations and assured that adequate information was flowing between operating and staff divisions. Such an extensive discussion of all facets of the company's operation was required in the Frost study since the control system being analyzed and evaluated spanned the entire corporate operation. In other words, the whole company was the control situation.

An extensive background study of company operations is also needed in the situation where one is developing a company-wide computerized data processing system, since such a system touches every aspect of a company's operation. For example, when developing an information processing system for a mail-order company recently, the systems study group developed complete statements of company objectives and policies, a flow chart of all company operations, and a definition of the responsibilities and decision-making needs of each major division.

Such extensive studies of all company operations are not, however, needed in a majority of control situations. For example, in a study of *The National Observer's* circulation operation,[2] the major focus of this phase of the study was to define the specific characteristics of the *circulation* operation, since the purpose of the control effort was to create controls that would help the circulation manager effectively get and keep circulation. An organization and flow chart of the operation was drawn up and a description made of the major responsibilities of the circulation manager and how he carried them out. The critical aspects of his operation were also identified: subscription selling costs, total subscription and newsstand sales, weekly increases and decreases in circulation, and the like. The entire circulation marketing operation was then restructured, and a new marketing plan developed as part of the study before any controls were developed. While overall company factors were an important general framework within which management controls were developed, they did not directly control that development, and so did not receive as much attention as they would have in an overall corporate situation.

Specific operating conditions were also the primary concern in the valve manufacturer study described in Chapter 3. In that study, while the production operation instead of the marketing operation was studied,

[2]Robert J. Mockler, *Circulation Planning and Development for The National Observer: A Research Study on Business Applications of Management Planning and Control Principles* ("Research Paper No. 39;" Atlanta, Georgia; Bureau of Business and Economic Research, School of Business Administration, Georgia State College, October 1967), and, "How Systematic Management Planning Helped a New Product Succeed," *University of Washington Business Review* (October 1966).

the pattern was the same. The production department's operation was charted, as was the flow of products through its five sections; the significant characteristics of Valve A were described, as was its production process through two of the production sections. Since the problem was cost control, the cost characteristics of the operation were defined (the overhead costs were significantly different in each of the five production sections). Overall company planning factors were studied briefly to provide background guidance, but the major thrust of the investigation was to outline the major characteristics of the production process and of the kinds of costs incurred in that operation.

A description of a staff control situation, in personnel for example, would follow the same pattern. In such a situation, the specific characteristics of the operation under study would be defined, including such factors as: the type and kind of personnel required, the reporting requirements of management, competitive wage rates, local availability of manpower, and other critical factors which affected the success of the personnel operation.

In a situation involving the evaluation of alternative investment opportunities, at this phase in the management control process the manager would go beyond simply defining the nature of the decision to be made, for example, a choice between two types of transportation equipment. He would investigate the cost and performance characteristics of the alternatives: for example, he would list the costs, life span, seating capacity, speed, and other performance characteristics of the two types of transportation equipment being considered. He would also specify any other aspects of the decision which he felt were important, such as company objectives and policies, local market conditions, government regulations, and availability of capital.

A control situation involving establishing overall controls for a small company presents an entirely different kind of problem. On one level, the situation is similar to the kind encountered in the Frost Electric Company study, for all company operations need to be analyzed and their major characteristics spelled out in some sort of organized, systematic way. On another level, if the company is very small the situation resembles an operational control problem in the amount of detailed description needed and the immediacy of the control problems. A small company also faces many more limitations than a large company, including lack of manpower, time, and money for developing and maintaining elaborate controls.

The above discussion by no means exhausts the variety of situations in which this phase of the management control process may deal. Companies come in all sizes; each operational area has its own peculiar characteristics and requirements; each decision maker's needs are different; and in each decision the interaction of various factors differs. What is important at this point is to describe in detail the characteristics of the control situation or problem under study—before going on to serious consideration of the subsequent phases of step two in the control process.

THE PURPOSE OF THE CONTROL TOOLS AND SYSTEMS

The purpose of the control tools or system next also needs definition, for the kind of system or tool which will be developed, or kind of control exercised, will depend not only on the specific characteristics of the control situation, but also on the use to which the tool or system is to be put, and who will be using it.

During the first step in the management control process, some preliminary questions relevant to this phase should have been raised, such as "Who will be using the system?" and "What kinds of decisions will he be making?" During step two in the management control process, the manager defines specifically all of the uses to which the control tools or system will be put. In most companies analyzed, this investigation usually uncovers more uses than were initially designated during the preliminary study. For example, in the valve company study careful investigation showed that the new production cost control system might be used for more than just estimating product costs, for these cost figures in turn would be used to judge worker efficiency, institute production quality changes, and alter prices and product lines. In *The National Observer* study the circulation manager, among other things, used the control system to pick advertising media, change the size of promotion efforts, raise or lower product prices, and schedule promotions. While in each situation the analysis of the decisions to be made did not affect the general kind of control system which was to be used, it did affect the specific design of the system and tools, as well as the standards used within the system in each situation studied.

In almost every situation analyzed, the investigation during this phase uncovered the fact that no single control reporting system could efficiently serve all the purposes initially designated for the control system. For example, in a mail-order operation the accounting department is concerned with cost information on an accrued basis: for instance, advertising costs are assigned to a sale which is usually made many months after the advertisement is run and paid for. This is necessary to fulfill accounting purposes—reporting sales along with related expenses to show true profits. The advertising manager, however, needs different kinds of reports on advertising to control his operation: for instance, the number of inquiries received from each ad, the cost for each inquiry, the orders subsequently received from the inquirers, and so on. While the same basic information sources may be used in both accounting and operating control reports, different kinds of reports are needed to serve the control needs of the accounting manager and of the advertising manager.

It is because it affects all subsequent stages in the management control process that the purpose of the tools or system—the uses to which it will be put, the decisions to be made based on the information generated—are spelled out before going on.

THE NATURE OF THE CONTROL TOOLS AND SYSTEMS

In all control situations some kind of mechanism (that is, tool or system) is needed to collect and organize data, feed it back to the decision maker, and facilitate comparisons with predetermined standards. This mechanism can range from a simple mathematical formula (model) or accounting form to a complex computerized information system. The kind of control mechanism used depends on many factors—the requirements of the situation, the control function to be filled, the kind of decision to be made, and the like. The following discussion covers some of the more widely used control tools and systems: accounting systems; financial analysis tools; operating and staff controls; graphic and mathematical control tools; and data processing systems.

Since a company's major concern is making money from the use of its resources, traditionally accounting has always provided one of the basic control systems within a company. Accounting (like any other business area) has distinct functions to fulfill no matter what the size of the company. At a minimum, accounting is responsible for balance sheet control, overall income statement control, credit and collections control, payroll control, manufacturing cost control, profit center control, and usually (though not always) budgetary control through its basic account record keeping systems. In small companies, the accounting system usually also stores and records all the basic data needed for control. In large companies with computerized data processing systems, the use of accounting tools in control is more limited, for the data processing system will perform the functions of storing and recording data and generating control reports.

Financial controls, which are closely related to accounting controls, are another group of traditional control tools. Financial analysis ratios are used to examine the way a company's assets are being used, as well as to compare performance figures against budgeted figures.

In those situations involving the evaluation of alternative investments, the tools of financial analysis were used extensively to analyse and compare projected investment costs, savings, and return on investment. In such situations, during this phase of the control process, a manager would identify the type of financial tools which he would use in analyzing the alternative types of equipment.

Each operation and staff area, as well as each individual manager, will have additional control systems. These may or may not be part of the company-wide accounting and financial control systems. These individual operating systems may be like the one described at *The National Observer*, which was created principally for control of circulation marketing operation, but which was administered by the corporate data processing system and was linked closely with corporate accounting control. Or, they may be like the production control system in the small valve manufacturer studied in Chapter 3, which was closely linked to the company's cost accounting system. Or, they may be designed for staff operations, such as the personnel department or office administration. Production quality control systems, controls for research and development, production manpower controls, and similar operating or staff unit controls are all non-financial operating controls.

Another major group of control tools which the manager may have occasion to use are graphic and mathematical. Decision theory, queuing or waiting line techniques, linear programming and other operations research tools are used to control inventory, schedule production and distribution, and monitor many other company operations. PERT/CPM is one of the newer graphic techniques used for project planning and control. And there is a host of more traditional graphic control devices, such as Gantt charts, bar charts, schedule boards and the like, which are particularly useful in the production area.

Data processing and information systems are basic to the control function in every area of a company, for all control areas need data to compare standards and results, isolate deviations, and take corrective action. These systems may be manual, electromechanical (punched card), or computerized. Computerized data processing systems have been developed in most large corporations. A manager in these companies must know the concept behind these systems and how they can be used, for the majority of other systems within these companies in one way or another depend upon the basic computer data processing system to store and generate data for manual reports, to produce control reports, to make comparisons, to generate corrective action, or to perform complex mathematical computations.

During this phase of step two in the management control process, therefore, the manager designates the general outlines of the controls (or combination of them) he will use—that is, the controls which will best meet the needs of the situation with which he is dealing, and which best fulfills the purpose the controls will serve. The major ones discussed here were:

1. Accounting and financial tools
2. Specific operating and staff department control systems
3. Graphic and mathematical control tools
4. Data processing and information systems

These tools and systems are reviewed at length in Chapters 6 through 10, in the discussion of step three in the management control process. It is during step three that the manager works out the details of his control system.

NATURE OF CONTROL STANDARDS

During the second step in the management control process, the manager also defines the kind of standards needed to meet the requirements of the situation. For the most part, standards in business control are quantified, such as dollars of expenses, units of sale, number of customers served, production hours, and percentage relationships. These standards are the criteria against which performance is measured. No control system, in fact no control, can exist without standards.

Many basic control standards are developed from the sales forecast. The sales forecast, which was discussed in the last chapter, initially establishes a goal or target that management feels might reasonably be achieved. Once the sales forecast has been adjusted to a level which management feels can and should be met, it becomes a base from which short-term company plans are developed. Production schedules are devised to meet sales goals, sales and promotion efforts are planned to produce the sales, financial plans are made to generate the funds needed to support the sales effort, and the like. The specific budgets and goals developed as part of this implementation planning become standards by which performance is subsequently judged and controlled.

Generally, this network of standards based on quantified plans is coordinated through the budgetary process, which is always part of the overall company control system. Budgetary standards are probably the most familiar kind of standards to the reader: profit as a percentage of sales, standard unit costs, expenses as a percentage of sales, budgeted expense levels, and the like. Related financial goals are equally familiar: return on investment, capital budgets, liquidity ratios, asset and funds turnover, and the like.

Individual operating and staff managers will invariably extend the network of standards even further, as they determine critical areas of concern to their operation. If well conceived, these standards will be closely integrated with overall company plans and budgets. In the marketing area, share of market, number of customer complaints, salesmen goals, and the like, are all standards designed to monitor those aspects of the marketing operation which are critical to meeting sales forecasts and expense budgets. In manufacturing, quality control standards, machine usage ratios, unit labor standards, and the like, are all part of the manager's network of operating standards needed to produce the desired volume at the desired cost, while maintaining desired quality levels. In personnel, turnover ratios, levels of absences, grievances, injuries, and the like, are designed to see that manpower utilization is within planned performance goals. All these standards are peculiar to each operating area, and are different from the financial budgetary standards used in the overall company financial control system.

Standards are frequently presented in graphic form, through such techniques as PERT/CPM and Gantt and other kinds of control charts. And operations research provides tools for establishing quantitative standards for control of such areas as inventory, distribution, and production.

Wherever possible, standards are built into the information system used for management control and are part of the control reporting framework. The purpose of standards is to signal points at which performance is not conforming to plans. The sooner this information on deviations is reported, therefore, the faster corrective action can be taken. For this reason, wherever possible comparative control reports are used, for these reports enable quick comparison of actual and budgeted results and easy identification of deviations.

Standards are important in all phases of life, for they provide a common frame of reference for understanding and evaluation. Communication, for example, is based on more or less standard meanings of words and symbols. And every time we use the word good or bad we are implying that something is good or bad in relation to a pre-established norm or standard.

Standards are often developed from tradition, past performance or experience in business and in life. For example, a company's budget for the next year is often built on the basis of a reasonable increase over the current year's sales and profits. The manager may justifiably point out that the size of this year's performance automatically sets limits on what can be expected to happen next year, and so it is reasonable to set a standard of "a little more" and "a little better" than this year.

While this concept is correct as far as it goes, using only an historical basis in setting standards may stifle progress where higher standards should have been set. It may also lead to unwarranted disappointments and unfair criticism, where management should have anticipated that results would be lower because of external events (such as a recession) which were beyond their control.

Standards need not always be quantitative, though most standards can ultimately be quantified. For example, a manager may tell his office staff that they will be promoted on the basis of their ability to generate new ideas and anticipate problems. Obviously, performance will not be judged on the number but on the quality of ideas originated and the importance of problems anticipated. Eventually, as sales are realized from an idea, a measure of its value can be quantified—and a standard can eventually be developed from experience. Initially, however, the standard is highly judgmental.

Standards will not only vary according to the operation being controlled; they may also change over a period of time for the same operation, as innovations are introduced and operational requirements change. For example, when a computer system is introduced,[3] its value will be judged against the performance of the old system—usually a punched card system. Later, various applications of a computer are compared to each other, that is, which function—payroll, simulation, or market analysis—does the computer perform most efficiently? Next, the theoretical limits of the computer become the standard for judging performance, that is, are all the computer's information storage capacity and computational capabilities being used, and are there additional problem-solving areas for which the computer could be used? Last, the original computer system is compared to new innovations, which become the ideal standard for judging its efficiency in accomplishing work. At present, real-time computer use is spreading and its capabilities are highlighting the limitations of ordinary computers.

While standards are necessary, not all standards are good. For example, in a production operation, workers (especially unionized workers) tend to limit their output to the standards set. When one company sets a lower output standard than its competitor, the company can be costed out of business, or forced to make major adjustments in facilities.[4]

Standards are to some degree arbitrary. This must be clearly understood by all persons using them. For this reason, it is important that the individual managers working within the control system know the *intent* of the standards, since the actual standards themselves are merely specific restatements of overall objectives. In this way, much of the confusion which may have been introduced when translating planning objectives into standards can be eliminated.

As a matter of principle it is not good to change standards too often or haphazardly. In the multi-division electronic company study discussed in Chapter 3, the control situation degenerated to the point where every time performance deviated from standard, the standard was changed. Such frequent changes hurt control. But a periodic reevaluation of standards is good. Conditions change, better standards are developed, or people may simply need a new kind of challenge or stimulus. Every control system, therefore, should allow for such review of standards.

Even though standards are not always as precise as one would like them to be, and can cause more harm than good on occasion, they are essential to comparing and measuring for control. For this reason, no matter what the imperfections, standards must be established before control systems can be developed and control tools can be put to work.

IDENTIFYING CRITICAL CONTROL AREAS AND INDICATORS

Standards are not formulated for every aspect of every business operation, but only those areas critical to success. Without this selectivity, a manager

[3]Herbert G. Hicks and Frederick Goronzy, "Notes on the Nature of Standards," *Academy of Management Journal*, December 1966, pp. 284-288.

[4]Hicks and Goronzy, "Notes on the Nature of Standards," pp. 291-293.

would be inundated with information and be unable to focus on the most important aspects of his operation.

In developing standards, therefore, it is important to identify those areas critical to successful operations. For example, in an overall company control situation, Paul Stokes has isolated eight key performance areas in which standards are needed:[5]

1. Financial condition
2. Operations
3. Productivity
4. Market position
5. Service or customer relations
6. Public, customer, and government relations
7. Employee relations and development
8. Ownership or membership relations

Within each critical area identified, a manager would go further and pinpoint key indicators of performance within that area. For example, in an oil refining (production) operation a key indicator might be the cost of refining a barrel of oil. A specific standard would then be established in cents per barrel. Or, in the finance area, one key indicator of performance would be net profit as a percentage of return on investment. The actual standard here might be 10 percent.

The following is an example of the pertinent key performance areas and indicators which might be needed at a retail supply organization, where the purpose of the control system was to monitor overall company operations:[6]

1. Financial Condition
   a. Ratio of gross sales to net margin
   b. Ratio of operating expense to gross sales
   c. Ratio of current assets to current liabilities
   d. Cash position compared with standard
   e. Capital expenditures compared with budget
   f. Days credit outstanding compared with budget
   g. Total book inventory compared with actual count
   h. Ratio of overtime hours to straight time
   i. Receipts from routes per day
   j. Processing costs per unit
   k. Delivery costs compared with standard
2. Operations
   Purchasing and Procurement
   a. Cost of sales to total sales
   b. Percentage of products for resale

[5]Paul M. Stokes, *A Total Systems Approach to Management Control* (New York: American Management Association, 1968), p. 33.
   [6]Adapted from Stokes, *A Total Systems Approach to Management Control*, pp. 149-151.

    c.   Quantities ordered from mills and processing plants, in dollars
    d.   Number of acres contracted
    e.   Purchases vs. requirements

Manufacturing and Processing

    a.   Total products processed by classification: feed, seed, fertilizer, grain, and so on

Sales

    a.   Budgeted sales vs. quotas
    b.   Volume figures by product
    c.   Sales targets vs. results
    d.   Dollars allocated to advertising of point-of-sale merchandise/total advertising budget

Distribution

    a.   Percentage of farm to market
    b.   Percentage of market served
    c.   Customer acceptance of products or services

3.   Employee Relations

    a.   Percentage of turnover
    b.   Employee performance compared with job standards
    c.   Ratio of employees available for promotions to total employees
    d.   Ratio of hours spent in training and development to total hours on job
    e.   Accident frequency and days lost
    f.   Employee attitudes toward company compared with attitudes of employees in other companies

4.   Productivity

    a.   Ratio of total product purchased to product sold
    b.   Production units compared with man-hours
    c.   Units produced per equipment unit
    d.   Maintenance cost per mile
    e.   Units delivered per mile, per man, per truck, per customer
    f.   Ratio of equipment operating time to down time

5.   Market Position

    a.   Percentage of total market served
    b.   Percentage of total market desired compared with market served
    c.   Net increases or decreases compared with total customers or units
    d.   Type of customer desired compared with those available
    e.   Sales, advertising, promotion dollars compared with market increase desired
    f.   Percentage of market penetration
    g.   Discounts compared with regular prices

6.   Public Relations

    a.   Attitudes of inspectors and other public servants toward the organization compared with what is desired
    b.   Respect of key citizens for the organization compared with opposition of others
    c.   Attitudes of civic and public organizations toward company compared with what is desired
    d.   Image of the organization in community compared with image deserved

    e.   Leadership in civic, community, social, religious, educational institutions or other projects compared with nonparticipation

    f.   Degree of legal support when needed (laws, restrictions, ordinances, and so on

7.   Customer Relations

    a.   Number and type of communications per customer

    b.   Number and types of decisions referred to customers compared with number and types of decisions made

    c.   Awareness of customers regarding key operating problems

    d.   Degree of customer identification with business

    e.   Degree of customer support for management decisions

    f.   Teamwork compared with member ownership

    g.   Attitudes of customers compared with attitudes of operating management

8.   Service Leadership

    a.   Types and kinds of complaints per customer area, and so on

    b.   Frequency of service per day, per week, or deliveries per customer

    c.   Services offered to customers compared with possible services

    d.   Special deliveries compared with regular deliveries

    e.   Ratio of adjustments to products sold

    f.   Special discounts compared with special groups

The above example is a good illustration of how control standards are developed from a study of the specific operation being controlled, for the nature and needs of the business were first analyzed and from this analysis a decision was made as to what aspects of the operation were most critical to success. Once these areas were isolated, specific standards were created to monitor results in each area, as part of step three in the management control process. The above example is also good illustration of how controls in a company (both overall corporate and lower-level operating and staff controls) are not limited to financial and accounting controls. Additional examples of how critical areas are identified and standards developed in a variety of control situations is given in the following chapters.

Naturally, where the purpose of the control system is narrower, for example to provide control over a circulation marketing operation, the critical areas and indicators will also be more limited, the control tools used different, and the standards adapted to meet the dictates of the situation, the purpose of the controls, and the kind of controls to be used. The general steps followed in creating control standards will be the same, however, no matter what kind or level of control problem is being dealt with.

SPECIAL FACTORS AFFECTING CONTROL ACTION

If they have not already been identified during the analysis of the specific characteristics of the control situation, those factors which will directly affect the implementation of any changes in control systems and the exercise of control should be identified here.

For example, in *The National Observer* study such factors as the attitudes of corporate managers and lower level managers and the personality of the circulation manager were factors which did not affect the development of the control system, but which did affect the way control could be exercised. They had to be identified early in the study, therefore, because they would have an important influence on the control action taken. In the valve company study the resistance of the production supervisor and the sales manager to the new system were major factors affecting both the implementation of the new system and the use of it later. These factors would, therefore, be identified during this phase of the process.

In a situation involving the evaluation of alternative investments, at this phase in the management control process one would specify the type of control to be exercised—that is, the nature and extent of the decision. There are two distinct levels of decision-making in these situations: first, the use of these tools in making a quantitative analysis (for example, in the transportation company study examining the costs, savings and return on investments of each alternative) and reaching a decision based on the financial data; and second, the weighing of these quantitative factors against other planning considerations (for example, in the transportation company study evaluating the flexibility, safety, speed, seating capacity, maneuverability in traffic, and the like, of each type of equipment in meeting market demands), in order to reach a final planning decision. A recommendation based on the quantitative analysis is usually all that is asked for from the financial analyst, although the analyst may extend the study into the area of "other considerations" and make a further recommendation based on this broad-based study, if he has the time and information needed to do a broader study. Evaluating these "other considerations" is technically beyond the scope of management control, but in many situations the planning information is available to the control analyst, so he may include it in his report. This was done, for example, in the transportation company study described in Chapter 3, because management asked for it.

In contrast, in *The National Observer* study the manager did more than just *recommend* a course of action. In that situation specific procedures for taking action were needed, specific operating decisions were made, and corrective action was taken. In the *Observer* situation, therefore, it was also necessary to make use of administrative tools. The tools of behavioral science are important in any management control situation where people are involved in the required action. By pinpointing motivational and leadership problem areas, and specifying the kinds of behavioral science tools which might help overcome these problems, the effectiveness of control action can be improved.

The importance of this last phase of step two in the management control process will depend on the objective of the control effort. On the one hand, where the objective of the control effort is to develop a new computerized information system, manager attitudes and other factors affecting the exercise of control, while relevant, are secondary to considerations concerning the mechanics and effectiveness of the system itself. On the other hand, in a situation involving direct control action, such as checking quality control charts and visiting the plant when rejects are above the norm, factors which affect finding the cause of a deviation and correcting it are of primary importance and so are spelled out in some detail at this point in the control process.

During this last phase of step two in the management control process, therefore, the manager might cover a number of areas, depending on the control situation. These could include specifying the kind of control action required, the additional key factors which will affect the control action, and any specific types of administrative tools and techniques which will be used to take control action.

CONCLUSION

The second step in the management control process is necessary to identify those factors which will have a significant impact on the development of controls and on the exercise of control.

Since the basis of all management control is found in a company's plans, the planning area is analyzed first. The next step is to spell out the requirements of the situation under study, since the controls and control standards must meet these requirements. Since direction is needed for the control development work, the purpose of the controls is also defined. The manager then designates the kind of control tools or system which best fulfills that purpose and the requirements of the control situation, and defines the nature of the standards to be used within the system. Those factors influencing the exercise of control, if any is required in the situation, are also identified.

While the same phases are gone through in every kind of control situation, the process is applied in a different way in each situation. In practice, no two control situations are identical, or will be handled in exactly the same way. The nature of the control situation in the transportation company study was quite distinct from that in *The National Observer* study. Both were different from the control situation encountered at the valve company and at the Frost Electric Company. In all instances, however, the same phases were gone through in dealing with the control situation—whether dealing with an operational or corporate control situation, and whether the objective of the control effort is to develop a new computerized information system, or to examine deviations from standard and take corrective action.

This second step is the base upon which the actual controls or control system are built and the framework within which control is exercised.

DISCUSSION QUESTIONS

1. Outline the six phases in the second step of the management control process covered in Chapters 4 and 5, and describe the function of each.
2. Describe the different kinds of control situations discussed in this chapter.
3. Discuss the similarities and differences in the way in which this second step in the management control process is applied in each type of situation.
4. Name and discuss the kinds of control systems and tools which are most frequently used in management control. In what kinds of situations is each kind used?
5. Why are standards so important to management control?
6. Discuss the different kinds of standards which can be used in control.
7. How valid and accurate are control standards and how often should they be adjusted?
8. What kinds of factors will affect the exercise of control? How does their importance vary by type of control situation?
9. Describe a control situation which you have dealt with at work or one which you have read about in depth. Discuss the ways in which the second step in the control process can be applied to the situation.
10. Why do you think this second step is so important? In what specific ways does it provide a base for the next steps in the management control process?

STEP THREE: DEVELOPING CONTROL TOOLS AND SYSTEMS

The discussion of step three in the management control process is divided into five chapters. Chapter 6 is an introductory chapter: it outlines the general approach followed in carrying out step three and discusses how the importance of this step will vary in different control situations. The next four chapters, 7 through 10, discuss in detail four specific areas of control tools and systems: accounting and financial controls; controls in major operating and staff areas; mathematical and graphic tools used in management control; and information processing systems used for control.

THE VARYING IMPORTANCE AND COMPLEXITY OF THIS STEP

The importance and complexity of step three in the management control process depends on the objective of the control effort and the nature of the control situation.

Where the objective of the control effort is to monitor performance and take corrective action, emphasis is naturally given to step four in the process, exercising control, and step three is of secondary importance. Even in these situations, however, step three is a necessary one. For example, many managers automatically assume in an operational situation that they are getting accurate information, the standards are correct, and the system is the best one for their control purposes. And they will take action based on apparent deviations, *without first examining and evaluating the control tool or system they are using*. This is a mistake.

Every time a manager is involved in exercising control he should ask himself three questions:

1. Is the result information accurate?
2. Are the standards against which I am comparing results valid?

3.   Is the reporting system the most accurate, efficient, and economical one possible?

A manager does not need to be a control expert to explore the answers to these questions. If the financial department gives him comparative costs of two alternative types of equipment, he has an obligation to question the basis of these cost figures. If the systems department gives him information on sales, he has an obligation to question the nature of the input information and the original source documents used. If he receives comparisons of actual and budgeted expenses, he has an obligation to question what the accounting department includes within "costs" to see if it conforms to what he understands costs to be.

In other words, even though the objective of the control effort may be to make a control decision or take some kind of control action, the manager should first review (even if only briefly in his mind) the control tools he is using to see if he has an adequate basis upon which to make his decision or to take action.

The importance of step three is, of course, greatest (and its place in the control process clearest) in those situations where the objective is to develop a new control system. In these situations the manager's attention will focus almost exclusively on the concept and mechanics of the system, and on the ways in which he can develop a system which will effectively meet the requirements of those who will be using the system to exercise control.

Where the control situation involves developing a company-wide control system, step three can be extremely complex. For example, a corporate control system recently developed for a major mail-order company took four analysts two years to develop. Top management, as well as all major operating managers, were involved in the development and all levels of management spent considerable time working on the project. The majority of control development situations are, however, much more limited in scope.

Every manager, no matter what his level, becomes involved in situations requiring him to develop some sort of control tool or system. The situation may be a very simple one, for example a manager controlling his own work schedule. Or, it may be a more involved situation, for example controlling office administrative procedures, product scheduling, manpower allocation, advertising expenditures by media, customer service calls, and the like. Ideally, there should be staff control specialists—that is, a department to which a manager can turn for assistance in solving all his more important control problems. Unfortunately, no company has such a department. Instead, the operating manager must draw upon a variety of staff departments (such as data systems, accounting and finance or operations research) or go it alone, using his own resources to develop many of the tools and systems he needs to maintain control over his operations.

The importance and complexity of step three in the control process will thus vary considerably, depending on what the control effort is supposed to accomplish and the level and kind of control situation. No matter what the situation or objective, however, step three is a vital link in effectively performing management control and so cannot be bypassed.

CONTROL TOOLS AND SYSTEMS

Control tools and systems have been defined as the mechanisms used to collect and organize data, feed it back to the decision maker, and facilitate comparisons with predetermined standards.

During step two in the management control process, the kind of controls needed in a situation is identified in very general terms, as are the kinds of standards to be used in these systems. Various areas of controls were covered in the discussion of step two: accounting and financial; specific operating and staff; graphic and mathematical; and data processing and information systems.

During step three in the control process the actual controls (and their standards) are developed. Two criteria guide the development of controls: first, they must fulfill the purpose designated for the control mechanism; and second, they must suit the requirements of the control situation.

Financial budgetary control systems are the most common control systems found in business, and financial cost, profit and sales figures the most common control standards. They are basically extensions of accounting systems. These systems are designed to fulfill a specific control purpose, overall company financial control. They are important to the operating manager, for they give overall focus to the controls in his area and they link his operating controls with overall financial controls. But these financial controls are only one part of the network of operating controls he needs and uses to maintain control over his operation.

Each operating and staff area within a business has it own control requirements. Marketing is concerned with selling the company's products. Marketing's primary requirement, therefore, is for controls which measure the effectiveness of those operations which stimulate and create sales: salesmen's efforts, customer service, delivery and stocking, advertising coverage, and the like. While marketing is responsible for selling products at a reasonable cost, cost considerations are of secondary importance in the marketing area. Manufacturing, on the other hand, is more concerned with cost efficiency, since a considerable amount of capital is often tied up in the manufacturing operation and manufacturing costs are more easily subjected to direct control. Cost accounting has thus developed into a major manufacturing control system. Since manufacturing is responsible for effectively servicing the marketing effort within specific cost standards, additional manufacturing controls are needed in such areas as production scheduling, storage, delivery, product quality, order fulfillment, and the like.

Staff areas, such as personnel, have yet another set of requirements. Because personnel control involves control of individual behavior, its needs cannot be fully met by the objective, quantitative controls used in other areas. And because it is a staff area, it cannot be monitored by the same productivity controls used in the marketing and manufacturing areas. Like the other areas discussed, therefore, the personnel area uses many controls designed specifically to meet its individual needs.

In developing controls, operating and staff managers use many graphic and mathematical tools, in addition to financial control tools. Charts, schedule boards, queuing theory, linear programming, and the like are all useful in varying degrees to getting the control job done, so that the manager must be as familiar with this area of control tools as with financial budgetary control tools.

Basic to this entire network of operating and overall financial controls is a company's data processing system. Data is required in every control situation before any action can be taken. In years past, much of this data was supplied by a company's accounting system or department. Today in business, the function is more and more being assumed by information systems specialists and departments. Because information is generated and needed at all critical points in an operation, systems analysts generally become involved in all an operating manager's control problems—as they attempt to fulfill his information requirements economically, help him select the information most critically needed to control his operation, and develop an efficient and convenient reporting system.

In selecting the most appropriate controls and standards in each of these four major control areas, continual reference is made to the purpose of the controls and the requirements of the operation (and its manager) which will be using the tool or system. The specific steps followed in developing and selecting controls and control standards are covered in the next four chapters which discuss what control tools and systems are available to the manager, in what situations they can best be used, and what principal control purposes they can best fulfill. Before going on to this discussion of specific control tools and systems available to the manager, however, some consideration is needed of how alternative controls are developed and evaluated.

DEVELOPING ALTERNATIVES

Before any decision concerning developing and implementing controls can be made, one must first develop the alternative tools and systems which might possibly meet the requirements of the situation. The following discussion covers the general approach used in developing alternative courses of action, evaluating them, and coming to a decision.[1]

The search for viable alternatives will usually begin with the manager's review of his experience, to see if he can find a quick solution to the problem at hand. Where the situation is similar to ones he has encountered before, he may settle on following past experience. Where the situation is not related to ones he has encountered before, he will next focus on courses of action under his control. For example, if his problem is improving output in his department, he will first concentrate on actions within his department—improving worker morale, rearranging work assignments or equipment, adding new workers, and the like—all factors which he can manipulate. If this fails, he will seek solutions outside his department or area of control, which may involve other departments and less immediate (longer-term) courses of action.

A manager works in this way instinctively, starting with the easiest, most immediate, most controllable solutions. Sometimes this can be a trap, for the manager's search may stop when an expedient solution is found, and better courses of action may never be investigated. The management control process attempts to broaden the manager's problem-solving perspective and open up new opportunities and new courses of action—by first focusing on the total situation and its broadest implications in steps one and two in the process.

Other roadblocks to an effective search are a limited information base and the manager's work habits. It is axiomatic that the larger the information base, the more alternative courses of action and outcomes of alternatives one is likely to think of. A manager can thus improve his control decision making by opening up (and keeping open) channels of communication in areas critical to his operation. Ways to expand the manager's information base were reviewed in Chapters 4 and 5, where the information gathering steps of the management control process was discussed.

Creative managers usually develop an environment conducive to creative thinking—a favourite desk, room or mode of writing—and set aside specific times of the day for doing this thinking—usually their most productive hours. Setting a quota for new ideas and a timetable for generating them also helps creative thinking, as does the habit of taking notes on ideas—a device for helping shape an idea into a usable form and allowing time for it to incubate in a systematic way.

Probably the most common roadblock to creative thinking is the difficulty of breaking existing patterns of action. In many situations, the

[1]Excellent discussions of how alternatives are developed and evaluated are found in Manley Howe Jones, *Executive Decision Making* (Rev. ed.; Homewood, Illinois: Richard D. Irwin, Inc., 1962); Charles H. Kepner and Benjamin B. Tregoe, *The Rational Manager* (New York: McGraw-Hill Book Company, 1965); Kenneth E. Schnelle, *Case Analysis and Business Problem Solving* (New York: McGraw-Hill Book Company, 1967); and C. William Emory and Powell Niland, *Making Management Decisions* (Boston: Houghton Mifflin Company, 1968).

first available alternative will be the existing control system. Except in a new company, some form of financial budgetary control system and some form of data processing system will be in existence. These and any other relevant existing systems are examined during the earlier steps in the management control process, for they give a good indication of control purposes and control requirements. At step three in the control process, the specific characteristics of existing systems are drawn up where such systems could possibly meet the needs of the control situation under study.

Where there is an existing system which is not adequate or which could be improved upon, alternatives to it would then be proposed. Where the situation is a new one, alternative ways to meet the control requirements of the situation are developed.

All too often in creating and finding alternative controls, a manager's perspective is limited by the restraints of an existing system. It is very difficult to break through these restraints and come up with innovations. For example, many medium-size companies are today faced with the problem of converting their existing data systems to computers or of upgrading their computerized systems. A typical situation is one in which the old system is a punched-card or first-generation computer system and in which various alternative new computerized systems are being considered.[2] The most effective solution in these situations is found by going beyond analyzing the old system (punched-card or first-generation computer) and the most obvious alternative (an IBM 360, for example), and taking a hard look at the key factors in the situation. In other words, one must break the mold and go beyond the limitations of existing systems and obvious alternatives and begin with a fundamental analysis of the requirements of the situation. This approach will lead to a wide-ranging review of all possible systems or tools which might be used, presuming the manager could have any type of tool or system he wanted.

Breaking through these barriers is one of the keys to successful creative decision-making. The following example illustrates the point. There is a familiar puzzle question which most of us have encountered. One is given nine dots arranged in a box format.

· · ·

· · ·

· · ·

2Robert J. Mockler, ed., *Putting Computers to Work More Effectively in Business Publishing* (New York: American Business Press Association, 1969).

The problem is to connect all nine dots with four straight lines without going through the same dot twice and without drawing over a line already drawn. One line can, however, cross over another line. Most people work within the confines of the box.

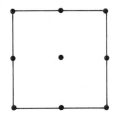

As most readers probably know, the solution is impossible without breaking the mold of conventional thinking and going beyond the obvious limits of the problem, for the solution looks like this:

In the same way, when developing alternative control tools and systems one should go beyond the obvious. The management control process attempts to help achieve this, by taking the focus off the existing solution and putting it where it belongs—on the requirements of the situation, the needs of the company, and the purpose which the control system or tool is designed to serve.

The more traditional the control area, the more difficult it is to break the mold. This problem is encountered most frequently in the accounting and finance areas, probably because their systems and tools have been in use longer and specific legal requirements govern reporting for accounting purposes. Creative energies in this area, therefore, are most often directed towards modifications of existing systems, rather than towards developing dramatically new approaches.

In those operating areas where the control situation does not involve accounting and finance systems, the possibility for exercising creative ingenuity in developing new controls and new applications of existing tools and systems is considerably less limited. The same is true in the operations research area, since this is a relatively new area.

A number of methods have been developed to stimulate creative problem-solving. These techniques generally fall into two categories: free association techniques and structured techniques. In practice the two types of techniques are generally used together.

The essence of the free association approach is to think about ways to deal with a problem or situation in an unstructured way—without judging the value of the solutions. The search has a minimum amount of structure in order to allow the association of any and all ideas that come to mind. The decision maker makes a conscious effort to manipulate, combine, and recombine any new ideas that come to mind in attempting to come up with a solution to his problem.

Brainstorming is probably the best known free association technique. A brainstorming session is designed to achieve one purpose—to generate large numbers of ideas by a free-flowing exchange of ideas among members of a panel. Alex Osborne, who originally developed and popularized the idea, gives in his book *Applied Imagination* the groundrules which should be followed if a brainstorming session is to be successful.[3]

Structured techniques are helpful in making the search more systematic and comprehensive, and less haphazard. Some managers use checklists, such as the list of questions given in steps one and two of the management control process. Others use process models, such as the basic problem-solving/decision-making process outlined in Chapter 2. Most successful managers have also developed from experience their own individual structured approaches to finding alternative solutions to problems, which supplement or adapt those they have read about or learned in school. This study endeavors to provide a structured approach to management control problem solving, which can be used in combination with unstructured techniques to develop alternative control tools and systems.

In developing alternative controls using these structured and unstructured techniques, one works within the general limits set in step two of the control process, where the kind of tool or system was specified. This limitation is, however, a very broad one—budgetary control system, operation control system, mathematical models, automated data processing system—which is designed merely to give focus to control development, not restrict it.

Within each of the general control areas discussed in the following chapters—accounting and financial, operating and staff, graphic and mathematical and data processing systems—alternatives are needed for standards, forms, scope of information included, reporting procedures, timing, source of information generation, methods of comparison, mathematical models, graphic presentation, and the like. In other words, alternatives are created for all aspects of the control tool or system being developed. The discussion in this section has given only the general approach to developing

---

[3]Alex F. Osborn, *Applied Imagination* (New York: Charles Scribner's Sons, 1953).

these alternatives. The discussion in Chapters 7 through 10 are designed to review the various ways in which specific alternatives are developed in major areas of control tools and systems.

EVALUATING ALTERNATIVES

The following is the procedure followed in evaluating and refining alternatives:

1. State all the required background factors affecting the evaluation.
2. Develop a wide range of alternatives, including extremes which might at first seem impractical.
3. Classify and segregate alternatives.
4. List the advantages and disadvantages of each alternative, based on the key background factors developed in step one.
5. Determine the true significance or outcome of each advantage and disadvantage, and quantify each where possible.
6. Determine the certainty of occurrence of the advantages and disadvantages.
7. Narrow the number of alternatives, and compare again the advantages and disadvantages of each.
8. Select the best alternative, and test it whenever possible.
9. Develop plans for implementing the alternative and refine the alternative.
10. Implement the alternative, and compare expected results with actual results.

The evaluation and selection of alternative controls proceeds along the same lines. In developing a new computerized information system, for example, steps one and two of the management control process are used to develop key background factors. In studying alternatives, various types of equipment alternatives and information systems of varying complexity will be studied. One of these alternatives will be the existing system. The costs are then calculated for each alternative. The ability of each system to meet decision-making needs is weighed against costs—usually through a series of studies by a systems department, working with operating managers who would be using the system, so that the full impact of each system on his operations will be known. The alternatives are then narrowed to the two or three best ones, and a decision is then normally made by higher management.

The same evaluation procedure is followed in other control situations. Care must be taken, however, to recognize the complexities of the evaluation process in practice.

In such areas as company-wide information systems and overall financial control systems many different operating areas in a company will be involved. Predicting all the major outcomes in each operating area and reconciling competing operating needs in finding a solution that produces greatest overall company profits can thus be a complex job.

In many control situations, it is also difficult to determine the true significance and certainty of the outcomes of each alternative, since operating managers tend to exaggerate advantages and minimize disadvantages when fighting for new services which are needed in their operation. There are a number of mathematical tools which are useful in quantifying the analysis of alternatives and which can lead to more scientific evaluation of outcomes. There tools are discussed in Chapter 9.

Like the decision-making and management control processes given in Chapter 2, the evaluation process is thus not a description of the mental activities followed by an individual in thinking about a problem. Rather, it is a way to organize one's thoughts, give them focus, systematically compare alternatives, and arrive at a clear statement of the basis or justification of the decision.

IMPLEMENTING THE TOOL OR SYSTEM

Once a decision has been reached as to what tool or system is best, alternative ways to implement it may also have to be developed and evaluated. Such alternatives will normally be required in all control situations where the system is a complex one involving many managers, or where a change is major enough to affect a significant part of an organization. The development and evaluation procedure followed during this phase of the management control process is the same as that described above.

Instituting change always involves dealing with people. In the valve company discussed earlier in this book, for example, both the sales manager and production supervisor resisted change. Since the new system was developed by the owner's son, one alternative was simply to order the change to be made. Another more effective alternative was, however, developed. The sales manager and production supervisor were asked to participate in the development of the new system, in order to solicit their ideas on it, to help them understand it better, and to possibly increase their receptivity to the change.

The manner in which change is instituted has a major impact on the way in which control is expected. Attitudes towards the system are formed by operating personnel during its implementation and information on the nature and purpose of the system is communicated. If negative attitudes are formed or if there is a poor understanding of how a system works or what it is supposed to achieve, then the effectiveness of the system will be impaired.

Because this phase of the control process is so closely related to the exercise of control, it is discussed further in Chapter 11, the chapter on the exercise of control.

CONCLUSION

The importance and complexities of step three in the management control process will vary in each control situation. Sometimes the objective of the control effort is to develop controls, and step three consumes most of the manager's attention. At other times, the focus is on the exercise of control, and step three only serves to verify that the manager has a sound basis upon which to make a decision. Whatever the relative importance of step three in the situation, however, this step is a necessary one.

This chaper has given general guidelines for developing and evaluating alternative controls. The process of searching for alternatives may seem wasteful to many managers, especially those who feel that good managers should find the right solution quickly. It is true that much time is consumed examining alternatives that are later rejected, but it is a necessary step to insure the best available solution is found. It is also true that some managers have the mental capabilities to perform the search and evaluation more quickly than others. This does not mean, however, that they bypass the search and evaluation process, for a comprehensive, well-rounded solution cannot be found without carefully exploring many "blind alleys" and going through the painful process of weighing all the predictable consequences of each alternative.

The discussion in this chapter did not, however, go into the specifics of control development. Many control systems are used within a company. Accounting statements and accounting record-keeping process have traditionally been a major management control system within a company. And most companies have a system of financial controls, based on tools of financial analysis and accounting budgetary process, which monitors the use of resources in specified areas. Accounting and financial control systems must be integrated within the company's overall computerized data processing information systems, for accounting and financial controls make use of the information processed by these systems and these systems can handle much of the mechanical work involved in report preparation.

Each operating and staff group needs controls and control systems that enable managers to monitor performance. Sometimes these controls are extensions of accounting and financial control systems, and sometimes these controls are created to meet specific operating requirements. The company's overall information processing system will usually provide much of the information needed for these specialized control areas, so that individual operating and staff controls are generally (though not always) developed within the framework of a company's overall data processing systems.

Operating managers also make use of many specialized control tools in the graphic and mathematical areas. Operations research and PERT/CPM are thus important areas to be considered in developing control tools and systems.

Some form of information processing system is needed in all kinds of management control, in order to process and store the data required for control and to feed back actual or projected performance information. In larger corporations these systems are frequently computerized and cover a wide range of company activities. In some instances, these systems are capable of comparing performance against standards and initiating action.

The discussions in Chapters 7 through 10 cover the actual development of specific controls within the four major control areas, under the following headings: accounting and financial controls; control requirements in major operating and staff areas; mathematical and graphic tools used in management control; and data and information processing systems.

Before going on to these individual discussions, it should be noted that management control depends on the effective integration and interaction of many control areas. While each will be discussed separately in the following chapters of this book, in practice they are often inseparable. Management Control is a single function. In performing it, the manager draws upon many information sources and is aided by many control tools. The final pattern in which these tools will intereact and be used will depend on the control needs of the situation under study.

DISCUSSION QUESTIONS

1. Explain why the third step in the management control process is important in all types of control situations.
2. In what ways does the importance of this step vary when the objective of the control effort is to exercise control and when it is to develop a control system?
3. List the major categories of control tools and systems. In what ways are they distinct from each other?
4. What is the relation of company-wide financial budgetary controls to the network of controls needed by an operating manager?
5. In what ways can an operating manager make use of graphic and mathematical tools in performing control?
6. Why are data processing and information systems important to all kinds and levels of control? Why is the information system specialist in such a unique position to deal with such a wide range of control problem?
7. Discuss the major considerations in developing alternative control tools and systems. Why do managers so often have a problem developing innovative solutions?
8. Why is the job of creating and finding alternatives so complex and challenging? What are some basic ways to insure more creative problem solving?
9. Outline and discuss the procedure followed in evaluating alternative tools and systems.
10. Under what circumstances do alternatives ways of implementing a new system need to be developed?
11. Why is implementing controls so closely related to exercising control?

CHAPTER 7

STEP THREE: ACCOUNTING AND FINANCE CONTROLS

The most familiar management control tools are drawn from the accounting and finance areas. This chapter discusses those aspects of the accounting and finance functions which are important in management control: basic accounting functions and reporting systems; comparative analysis in accounting reports; budgeting; cost accounting; basic finance functions; cash forecasting; financial analysis through financial ratios; capital budgeting; and return-on-investment analysis.

THE BASIC ACCOUNTING FUNCTION

The American Institute of Certified Public Accountants defines accounting as "the art of recording, classifying and summarizing in a significant manner and in terms of money, transactions and events which are, in part at least, of a financial character, and interpreting the results thereof."[1] The accounting function is basically the process of keeping a company's "books" and reporting historical financial data on operating results.

This aspect of accounting has been called by some "financial accounting," in order to distinguish it from "management accounting."[2] Management accounting involves making financial estimates of future performance, that is, budgeting, and then later analyzing actual performance in relation to these financial budgets or estimates.

Since the accounting department, prior to the introduction of EDP systems, normally kept the only complete records on a company's operating results, it was often called upon to produce control reports for other departments. This sometimes led to confusion in performing control, since

[1]American Institute of Certified Public Accountants, Committee on Terminology, *Accounting Terminology Bulletin Number 1, Review and Resume* (New York: The Institute, 1953), p. 9.

[2]Robert N. Anthony, *Management Accounting Principles* (Homewood, Illinois: Richard D. Irwin, Inc., 1965), pp. 185-187 and 243-245.

the accountant was trained to keep financial records and produce reports for accounting purposes.

This situation no longer exists in most larger companies. The central EDP department is now the record-keeping and information-processing department. The systems analysts are the experts who work with each of the functional areas—such as accounting, finance, marketing, manufacturing or personnel—to help develop and coordinate control reporting for each area. Accounting is now only another area whose control needs must be served by the central record keeping and information processing department. This is a major conceptual change, which is altering the basic nature of the accounting function in business today.[3]

This shift in emphasis has led to greater emphasis on management analysis, and less on record keeping, in the accounting area. This extension of the accounting function into management analysis is called management accounting. It includes such functions as budgeting, budgetary analysis, and sometimes financial analysis and many management control functions.

As can be seen from the diagram of an accounting department's expanded functions in Figure 7.1[4] below, accounting has a major impact on control in business. The department provides control of assets and liabilities, reports on income and expenses, sees to it that employees are paid, provides cost controls, and usually coordinates preparation of annual budgets. The accounting department also prepares statements for tax purposes, although the treasurer's department sometimes handles tax reporting. An accounting department can thus be an important control nerve center for many aspects of a business's operation.

There are certain basic principles or concepts that guide accounting procedures and so are fundamental to an understanding of accounting as a control tool. The first basic accounting concept is the money measurement concept: in accounting, records are made only of what can be expressed in monetary terms. The second basic accounting concept is the business entity concept: in keeping accounting records, each transaction is viewed from the standpoint of the business itself, not from the position of the owners of the business or any particular person associated with the business. A third accounting concept, the going concern concept, is the assumption that the business will continue to operate for an indefinite period of time, and will not be liquidated or sold in the near future. A fourth accounting concept, the cost concept, is that assets (tangible and intangible properties) of a company are ordinarily entered in accounting records at the price paid to acquire them, that is, at their cost.

[3]W. Joseph Littlefield, "Developments in Financial Organizations, 1915-1965," *Financial Executive* (September 1965), Special Supplement.

[4]William H. Childs, *Accounting for Management Control* (New York: Simmons-Boardman, 1960), p. 11.

Figure 7.1

MAJOR ACCOUNTING FUNCTIONS[4]

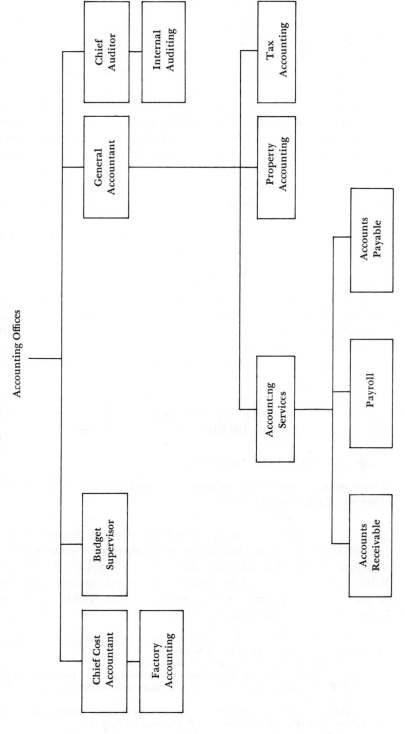

A fifth basic accounting concept is the dual aspect concept. On the one hand, the resources owned by a business are called "assets;" on the other hand, the claims of various parties against these assets are called "equities." There are two types of equities: 1) liabilities, which are the claims of creditors, that is, everyone other than the owners of a business; and 2) owners' equity, which is the claim of the owners of the business. In accounting, total assets must equal total equities. A simplified balance sheet shown in Table 7.1 below illustrates this equality. As a result, every event that is recorded affects at least two accounting records. For example, if XYZ Company paid off $10,000 of its long-term debt, this would reduce total assets by a $10,000 decrease in cash and at the same time reduce total equities through a $10,000 decrease in long-term debt. Thus accounting is properly called a "double-entry" system.[5]

A sixth concept in accounting is the accrual concept. This is the procedure whereby revenue is recognized when earned regardless of when collected, and expense is matched to the revenue regardless of when the expense is actually paid.[6] Fundamental to the accrual accounting process is the matching of revenue with the related costs over some specific period of time, called the "accounting period." This period may be a month, a year, or some other interval. After revenue has been identified for the accounting period, the costs which are casually related to that revenue are charged against the revenue of the same period.[7] In this way, income earned by the company during the accounting period can be determined.

These basic concepts underlie all accounting systems, and so are fundamental to understanding how management maintains overall control of a business's assets, liabilities, income, and expenses.

BASIC ACCOUNTING REPORTS

The two basic accounting reports most used in control are the balance sheet and the income statement.

A balance sheet is a statement of a company's financial position at a given time. It does not attempt to express what has happened over any particular period of time, but rather shows where a company is at a certain moment.[8] On the balance sheet the assets are listed on the left and the liabilities and equities on the right. Each group is broken into categories or account classifications, as can be seen from examining the sample balance sheet shown in Table 7.1.

[5]Robert N. Anthony, *Management Accounting: Text and Cases* (3rd ed.; Homewood, Illinois: Richard D. Irwin, Inc., 1964), p. 37.

[6]Childs, *Accounting for Management Control*, p. 47.

[7]Homer A. Black, John E. Champion and R. Gene Brown, *Accounting in Business Decisions: Theory, Method and Use* (2nd ed.; Englewood Cliffs, New Jersey: Prentice-Hall, Inc., 1967), p. 13.

[8]Ralph F. Lewis, *Management Uses of Accounting: Planning and Control for Profit* (New York: Harper and Brothers, Publishers, 1961), p. 16.

Current assets are cash and other assets that are convertible into cash within the near future, usually not more than a year from the date of the balance sheet. Besides cash, current assets would include checks, money orders, letters of credit, marketable securities, accounts receivable (less

Table 7.1

XYZ COMPANY BALANCE SHEET
DECEMBER 31, 1970

Assets			*Liabilities and Equity*		
Current Assets:			Current Liabilities:		
Cash		$ 50,000	Accounts Payable	$ 50,000	
Marketable Securities		$20,000	Wages & Salaries	10,000	
Accounts Receivable	$60,000		Payable		
Less: Allowance for			Taxes Payable	10,000	
Bad Debts	10,000		Accrued Expenses	5,000	
		50,000	Total Current		
Inventory (at lower		100,000	Liabilities		$ 75,000
of cost or market value)			Long-Term Liabilities:		
Prepaid expenses		5,000	Long-Term Bonds	50,000	
Total Current Assets		$225,000	Total Long-Term		50,000
			Bonds		
Long-Term Assets:			Total Liabilities		$125,000
Building & Equip-	60,000		Equity:		
ment			Capital Stock	60,000	
Less: Allowance for	10,000		Retained Earnings	125,000	
Depreciation					
	50,000		Total Equity		185,000
Investments	30,000		Total Liabilities and		$325,000
Total Long-Term		80,000	Equity		
Assets					
Intangible Assets:					
Patents	2,500				
Leases	2,500				
Total Intangible		5,000			
Assets					
Total Assets		$325,000			

an estimate of bad debts), inventory and prepaid expenses and deferred charges. *Long-term assets* are those assets that are expected to be owned by the company for a long period of time, usually for more than one year. These include fixed assets (less depreciation), such as land, buildings, and equipment; long-term investments in securities; and intangible assets, such as goodwill, patents, copyrights, leases, licenses, franchises, and similar valuable but nonphysical things owned by the company.

Current liabilities are obligations which are payable in a short time, usually within a year.[9] Current liabilities include both accounts and notes

[9]Lawrence L. Vance and Russell Taussig, *Accounting Principles and Control* (Rev. ed.; New York: Holt, Rinehart and Winston, 1966), p. 21.

payable, which represent the claims of creditors and others, and other categories, such as wages and salaries payable, taxes payable and accrued expenses. *Long-term liabilities* are claims of creditors that do not fall due within one year, such as long-term bond issues. *Owners' equity* is the claim of the owners of the company, or the stockholders in the case of a corporation. The owners' equity section of the balance sheet also shows what part of earnings have been retained by the company.

The balance sheet is a basic management control tool. It shows what kind of assets the business has, and the dollar amount of each. It shows what amounts are owed and whether or not the amounts owed are due during the current year or over a longer period. It shows the sources from which funds used to operate the business have been obtained (liabilities and owners' equity) and the types of property and property rights in which these funds are invested (assets). Management, investors, and creditors look to the balance sheet for an indication of the company's resources, the amount of claims against it, and the general financial condition of the company.

The income statement describes in summary form the transactions that have made a profit or loss for the business over a specified period.[10] It covers the revenue items, the expense items, and the difference between them (the net income or loss) for an accounting period. The income statement reports the results of operations and indicates reasons for the firm's profitability or lack thereof. Table 7.2 presents one company's income statement for 1970.

The following is a brief description of the sections found in most income statements:

Revenue.   The revenue in most companies comes from sales. The sales total represents the amount charged to customers for goods or services.

Cost of Goods Sold.   This section shows the cost to the business of the merchandise delivered to customers. Cost of goods sold is an expense, that is, something that must be deducted from revenue to calculate net income.

Selling Expenses.   These are the expenses incurred in selling the goods or services for the period. They include the expenses of soliciting sales and waiting on customers, and of storing and delivering merchandise.

General and Administrative Expenses.   These are the expenses of conducting other business activities. They include the cost of accounting services, salaries of general officers, legal expenses, office rent, and the like.

Other Income.   Other income is that which is not derived from the main operations of the business. This includes such items as interest on investments, rent from company owned property, and so on.

Other Expenses.   This section includes expenses not incurred in connection with the main operations of the business, for example, interest paid on borrowed money.

[10]Lewis, *Management Uses of Accounting*, p. 20.

The income statement, like the balance sheet, provides basic historical information about a company's operations, which can be used for comparative control studies.[11]

The information on the balance sheet and income statement is based on data collected and recorded through the accounting data processing system. This system starts with the recording of all transactions in the company's *journal*, a chronological record of transactions showing the names of accounts that are to be debited or credited, the amounts of the debits and credits, and any useful supplementary information about the transaction.[12] These transactions are then recorded or "posted" in the company's *ledger*, which contains a separate account for each item on the balance sheet and income statement.[13] At the end of an accounting period,

Table 7.2

XYZ COMPANY
INCOME STATEMENT
FOR THE YEAR ENDING DECEMBER 31, 1970

Sales:			$700,000
Less: Cost of Goods Sold			350,000
Gross Margin on Sales			$350,000
Operating Expenses:			
Selling Expenses:			
Salesmen's Salaries	$70,000		
Advertising	30,000		
Delivery Expense	10,000		
Total Selling Expenses		$110,000	
General & Administrative Expense:			
General Salaries	$25,000		
Rent of Office	5,000		
Total General & Administrative Expenses		$ 30,000	
Total Operating Expenses			$140,000
Gross Operating Profit			$210,000
Less: Depreciation			5,000
Net Operating Profit			$205,000
Other Income:			
Rent			20,000
Gross Income			$225,000
Other Expenses:			
Interest			5,000
Profit before Income Taxes			$220,000
Provision for Income Taxes			110,000
Net Income			$110,000

11Vance and Taussig, *Accounting Principles and Control*, p. 60.
12Anthony, *Management Accounting: Text and Cases*, p. 98.
13Vance and Taussig, *Accounting Principles and Control*, p. 16.

Table 7.3

XYZ COMPANY
COMPARATIVE INCOME STATEMENT

For the Year Ending December 31, 1970

	Amount		Percent of Net Sales		Dollar Increase (Decrease)	Percent Increase (Decrease)
	1970	1969	1970	1969		
Sales	$700,000	$500,000	100	100	$200,000	40
Less: Cost of Goods Sold	350,000	290,000	50	58	60,000	21
Gross Margin on Sales	350,000	210,000	50	42	140,000	66
Operating Expenses						
Selling Expenses						
Salesmen's Salaries	70,000	60,000	10	12	10,000	17
Advertising	30,000	20,000	4	4	10,000	50
Delivery Expense	10,000	8,000	1	2	2,000	25
Total Selling Expenses	110,000	88,000	15	18	22,000	25
General and Administrative Expense						
General Salaries	25,000	25,000	4	5	-	-
Rent of Office	5,000	5,000	1	1	-	-
Total General and Administrative Expense	30,000	30,000	5	6	-	-
Total Operating Expenses	140,000	118,000	20	24	22,000	19
Gross Operating Profit	210,000	92,000	30	18	118,000	128
Less: Depreciation	5,000	5,000	1	1	-	-
Net Operating Profit	205,000	87,000	29	17	118,000	136
Other Income: Rent	20,000	-	3	-	20,000	-
Gross Income	225,000	87,000	32	17	138,000	159
Other Expenses: Interest	5,000	5,000	1	1	-	-
Profit before Income Taxes	220,000	82,000	31	16	138,000	168
Provision for Income Taxes	110,000	36,000	15.7	7	74,000	206
Net Income	$110,000	$46,000	15.7	9	$ 64,000	139

some adjusting entries must be made and certain accounts closed, in order to bring the accounts up to date, so that accurate statements may be prepared.[14] A trial balance is run,[15] preliminary income statement and balance sheet work sheets are developed, and the final statements are prepared. Supervision and administration of this data collection and preparation process is one of the most important jobs performed by the accountant, and one in which he works closely with the computer systems department in large companies, since computer systems handle most of the data collection and recording there.

[14]Vance and Taussig, *Accounting Principles and Control*, p. 79, and Anthony, *Management Accounting: Text and Cases*, p. 102.
[15]Anthony, *Management Accounting Principles*, p. 70.

COMPARATIVE ACCOUNTING AND CONTROL REPORTS

The above introductory sections concentrated on the accounting record keeping systems and reports used to give historical performance results. In order to exercise control these results must be compared to some standard.

The most familiar kind of comparison is found in company annual reports—comparisons to prior years' performance. These comparative statements usually present both a horizontal and a vertical analysis. Table 7.3 gives a simple example of such a comparison. The vertical analysis translates the figures for any given year into percentages and gives the relative importance of each item. The horizontal analysis provides information on trends from period to period, by showing both the dollar amount of change and the relative increase or decrease in importance of the item. Both horizontal and vertical analysis, as well as percent and dollar variances, are used in all types of control reports. Control reports, however, rarely use historical standards as the sole yardstick against which to measure performance.

In management control the focus is not on comparing historical figures with each other. It is instead on comparing performance against a planning standard—that is, a figure based on planned expectations of what management feels should happen. Budgets are the most familiar kinds of planning standards, for budgets are quantifications of plans.

Budgets can be made for all aspects of an operation. Those budgets prepared for overall income and asset control are called *proforma* income and expense statements and balance sheets, and take the form of projections of the accounts in these statements for as many years into the future as desired. An example of a comparative control report based on a *proforma* balance sheet is given in Table 7.4. In this report horizontal analysis is used to study the variances of performance results from control standards. Budgets are not, however, limited to financial accounting statements. As is seen later in this chapter, *proforma* cash flow statements are needed, along with supporting capital outlay budgets, for the finance area, and, as is seen in the next chapter, each operating area has its own individual budgetary areas, which are integrated with but distinct from overall corporate financial budgets.

Multiple comparisons are favored by many managers. These combined control reports contain three sets of figures, showing current period results, the results of a comparable prior period, and budgeted results. Such comparison are very helpful, for the manager not only has two standards against which to compare performance, but he also has a standard against which to judge the reliability of the budget. For example, if the current year's results are 10% above last year's results but 10% below budget, the manager would be just as likely to question the reliability of the budget as he would to question performance.

Table 7.4

ABC COMPANY
BALANCE SHEET
JANUARY 31, 1972[16]

ASSETS:	*Actual*	*Budget*	*Over (Under)*
Current assets:			
Cash on hand and in banks	$229,340	$ 245,360	($16,020)
Accounts receivable	358,300	373,000	(14,700)
Allowance for doubtful accounts	(21,788)	(22,400)	612
Inventories at standard cost:			
Direct materials	238,600	219,000	19,600
Finished parts	100,400	100,400	
Work in process	54,400	54,400	
Finished product	559,870	544,200	15,670
Prepaid expenses and deferred charges:			
Insurance			
Excess of standard cost in finished product inventory over current standard	3,150	3,500	(350)
Deferred advertising	4,500	4,500	
Total current assets	$1,526,772	$1,521,960	$ 4,812
Mixed assets:			
Machinery and equipment	$1,000,000	$1,000,000	
Depreciation taken to date	(210,000)	(210,000)	
Buildings	800,000	800,000	
Depreciation taken to date	(102,000)	(102,000)	
Land	100,000	100,000	
Total fixed assets	$1,588,000	$1,588,000	
Total assets	$3,114,772	$3,109,960	$ 4,812
LIABILITIES:			
Current liabilities:			
Accounts payable	$ 287,500	$ 271,500	$16,000
Dividends payable			
Accrued sales commissions	17,682	18,600	(918)
Federal income tax accrued	227,995	233,130	(5,135)
Real estate taxes accrued	21,300	21,300	
Accrued interest on mortgage	5,000	5,000	
Mortgage payable, current installment	12,000	12,000	
Accrued interest on demand note			
Note payable			
Total current liabilities	$ 571,477	$ 561,530	$ 9,947
Long-term debt, mortgage payable	$ 228,000	$ 228,000	
Total liabilities	$ 799,477	$ 789,530	$ 9,947

[16]Adapted from Herman C. Heiser, *Budgeting: Principles and Practice* (New York: The Ronald Press Company, 1959), p. 116.

CAPITAL:

Capital stock, 20,000 shares, common, par $100	$2,000,000	$2,000,000	
Retained earnings	315,295	320,430	($ 5,135)
Total capital	$2,315,295	$2,320,430	($ 5,135)
Total liabilities and capital	$3,114,772	$3,109,960	$ 4,812

BUDGETARY CONTROL

The term "budget" has been the source of much confusion in business planning and control. A budget is a statement of expected results expressed in numerical terms. It is a quantification of a plan. As a result, a budget is only as good as the plans upon which it is based and should not be mistaken for the plan itself.

Budgeting is important to the success of a company, for the budget and the process of budgeting assist management in fulfilling its functions of planning, coordinating, and controlling enterprise activities.[17] Through a budget, management can state its plans quantitatively for a given time period, usually a year, and so guide actions during that period. Thus a budget can be thought of as a blueprint for action, through which each area of corporate operations knows what is expected and what must be accomplished. A budget also provides a very important standard for the evaluation of performance. Since the budget is a quantitative blueprint for action, it functions as a "yardstick" against which actual performance can be measured to determine if corporate results are in line with predetermined performance expectations, and if corrective action is necessary.

Developing Budgetary Standards.

A financial budget must be prepared for each major operational and staff area of a company for a specified time period, usually one year. These financial budgets, which are usually prepared along with plans under the direction of the operating managers, are then reviewed by the control executive or his staff, who bring together the financial budgets of all the areas of the company—both operating and staff—and develop the overall financial corporate budget.

The sales budget is generally considered to be one of the most important budgets formulated, since other company planning is predicated to a large extent on sales plans. Once the sales forecast is fixed, budgets can be prepared for other activities within a business. There are overall income and expense budgets and balance sheet budgets, which normally are in the same format as the company's standard accounting statements. There are

[17]Ernest I. Hanson, "The Budgetary Control Function," *Accounting Review* (April 1966), p. 239.

capital outlay budgets, and budgets for cash receipts and expenditures, which are discussed in the following sections of this chapter. In addition, there are a variety of budgets for operating and staff sections of a company, many of which are discussed in the next chapter. Each operation within a company normally has an expense and manpower budget. Marketing divisions have both unit and dollar sales budgets, and manufacturing divisions have product output and machine utilization budgets. There can be budgets for distribution, administration, and overhead. Many of these budgets are expressed in physical terms, such as the budgets for direct-labor hours, machine hours, units of material, square feet allocated, and units produced—where the situation requires them. Most of these budgets, however, are expressed in financial terms.

In developing budgets, it is necessary to have a clear definition of each manager's responsibility, accountability and authority. An individual should not be accountable for achieving certain budget objectives unless he has the operational responsibility and authority to reach the goals.[18] The operating responsibility of each manager should, therefore, be stated in writing in unequivocal terms, and his authority for action should be clearly delineated. And the budget should be constructed to differentiate clearly between costs that are controllable and non-controllable by the responsible manager.

The human elements must be recognized in budgetary control. As Chris Argyris has stated, budgets are accounting techniques designed to control performance through people.[19] As a result, the impact of budgets is felt by everyone in the organization. Those who will have the responsibility for the achievement of budget goals should, therefore, be involved in the setting of goals and the establishing of budgets.

In preparing the budget, there must be a balance between setting goals that are too easily attainable, and those that are too difficult to achieve. If budget standards are not reasonably attainable, there may be much inefficiency and frustrated employee performance. On the other hand, budget standards that are too easily attainable are also inefficient, since they can lead to lower performance than might otherwise be possible. Both these extremes cause the budget to lose much of its effectiveness as a control tool. In order to obtain efficient and productive performance, budget goals should be attainable and yet challenging.[20]

One method for achieving this balance is the use of a flexible budget. Under a fixed budget, goals become meaningless as soon as the operating level varies from the one assumed. A flexible budget is intended to provide

---

[18]James L. Peirce, "Budgeting Accounting and Its Prospects," *Financial Executive* (February 1968), p. 68.

[19]Chris Argyris, "Human Problems with Budgets," *Harvard Business Review* (January-February 1953), p. 97.

[20]Hanson, "The Budgetary Control Function," p. 242.

attainable goals regardless of the operating level, by fixing different budget figures for different levels of operation. For example, a department would establish budget figures for operations at 100% of capacity, 95% of capacity, 90% of capacity and so on. Table 7.5 gives in summary form a flexible budget of manufacturing costs for the XYZ Company under different levels of productivity.

Table 7.5

XYZ COMPANY
MANUFACTURING COST BUDGET

Number of items produced	100,000	150,000	175,000	200,000
Manufacturing Costs:				
Materials	$ 50,000	$ 75,000	$ 87,500	$100,000
Direct Labor	25,000	37,500	43,750	50,000
Supervision	10,000	12,000	14,000	16,000
Maintenance	5,000	6,000	6,500	7,000
Depreciation	20,000	20,000	20,000	20,000
Other Overhead	10,000	10,000	12,000	13,000
Total Manufacturing Costs	$120,000	$160,000	$183,750	$206,000
Cost per item produced	$1.20	$1.07	$1.05	$1.03

Budgetary review practices vary from company to company. Budgets for individual operations may be reviewed quarterly, monthly or even weekly, but whatever the time period, budget revision must be kept at a minimum, for frequent changes in standards undercut their validity and create the feeling that all company standards are poorly conceived and so are valueless criteria for measuring performance. At the electronics company described in Chapter 3 monthly reviews were made, and when deviations from budget occurred, the budget was changed. As a result, the operating causes of deviations were never examined thoroughly, and operational deficiencies were never corrected. In contrast, at *The National Observer* overall budgets were prepared for the coming year, reviewed quarterly, but revised only at mid-year.

Budgetary practices should be reexamined periodically, for it is possible that continual variances from budget may be caused by poor budgeting, rather than by below standard operating performance. Such was the case at the electronics company described in Chapter 3. Over the years, the president had continually set unrealistically high budgets, so that eventually they ceased to have any meaning for the operating managers.

While there are these general groundrules for budget preparation, no two companies seem to develop their overall financial budgets in the same way. In many large companies major departments and divisions are asked to submit five-year plans, with financial budgets, to a control section every year. The control section normally provides managers with the information needed to prepare these budgets, such as anticipated economic and market changes, overall sales forecasts, restrictions on spending, and overall corporate objectives and policies. There is usually considerable interaction between the control section and the various planning managers concerning major factors affecting the budget-plan, and many adjustments are made on the basis of this exchange of information.

This first developmental stage results in a budget-plan which the department or division manager believes is reasonable and which he believes the managers above him will believe is reasonable. Then another round of development occurs, as pressures come from higher management to reach for higher sales goals, cut costs, or change the direction of a unit's efforts. This process continues until a final budget-plan is agreed upon.

There are many variations in this process. In some companies the control section and higher management develop plans and the related financial budgets in more detail for sub-managers, and sub-managers are given less freedom to do their planning. In general this practice will hurt planning, but it may be justified by the particular corporation's circumstances. Many companies ask for one-year instead of five-year plans, others revise current plans quarterly and five-year plans annually, and still others vary the requirements by level of management.

Whatever budgetary process is followed, it is important that there be an interaction in the planning stage between the manager who is responsible for developing and carrying out a plan, and the economic or financial expert who translates these plans into a realistic estimate of their profitability. Through this interaction, the profitability of plans can be tested and greater reality can be given to the budgets based on them.

Some Case Histories.

Pennsalt Chemicals Corporation has rigorous financial budgetary program (called the Program for Profit Control), which has been a very successful management control tool.[21]

Their budgetary process begins each fall when the company's profit analysis group prepares and provides all company departments with an economic forecast for the coming year. This forecast is tailored to the market served by each department. Sales projections are next prepared by each division sales manager in conjunction with his salesman and then assembled by the accounting department. A coordinated sales forecast is in this way developed, which becomes the basis of all budgeting. Manufacturing groups are given sales forecasts and they develop cost estimates

21J. D. Baxter, "Budget Guides Profit Growth," *The Iron Age* (October 28, 1965), pp. 44-46.

based on volume estimates. Staff groups also prepare financial budgets for their operations.

In December, top management reviews these budgets, and usually revises them to bring them into line with corporate objectives. After the top-level review, budgets go back to departments and divisions for review and discussion. The final budget is set in January.

At Pennsalt, each manager is given responsibility, and is held accountable, for meeting the budget for the year. Once set, the budget is never changed during the year. Each month each department and division reports actual results, and these are reviewed against budget by the president himself.

The key elements in the success of the Pennsalt budget, according to the president, are:

1. Full backing of the budget by top management.
2. Participation in budget preparation by all managers and key employees who must live by the budget.
3. Coverage by budget of every activity of company on a coordinated and integrated basis.
4. No changing of budget during year once it is set.
5. Monthly review of budget performance by middle and top management.
6. Thorough checking of all deviations from budget during year.
7. Integration of a single-year budget with longer-term plan.
8. Indoctrination of all employees in corporate objective of budget as well as individual objectives.
9. Inclusion of top managers' accounts in budget.

The National Observer study described in Chapter 14 provides another example of budget preparation and use. At The Observer, expense and sales budgets for the circulation operation were prepared by the operating manager, working with corporate management and the controller's department. These budgets were presented in a format consistent with other operating control reports used in the circulation area. The National Observer's circulation and subscription sales budget and the paper's monthly report comparing sales with budget standards are given in Chapther 14, Tables 14.4 and 14.5. At The Observer operating management was given considerable leeway in developing budget standards, and there was a minimum of management pressure to adjust standards upward. Management placed considerable emphasis on the planning and budgeting process as a means of controlling circulation growth.

The financial budgetary procedure at a mail-order company studied by the author was somewhat different. Each year the company's president was required to make a formal budget presentation to the president of the parent company. The first part of the meeting was devoted to reviewing the prior year's results, and the second half to outlining plans and the budget for coming year.

In preparing for this presentation in years past, the president asked each operating manager to draw up a general financial budget and plan for his department. The reference point for most of these budgets was the prior year's results. The department heads were provided with some sketchy economic forecasts, and the controller's staff was available to answer any questions the department heads might have. Once the preliminary department financial budgets were finished, the control section reviewed and refined them. Assumptions as to sales and costs were rechecked, and final figures were developed by the controller.

Unfortunately, in this process figures were often distorted and arbitrary changes were made, since management was committed to satisfying certain profit goals of the parent company. Because of this, the budgets lost much of their impact. Operating management devoted less and less time to preparing them, and felt little obligation to meet budget goals.

Unlike *The National Observer* and Pennsalt, this mail-order company did not have strong budgetary procedures, nor did it exercise tight control of operations. Emotion, instead of reason, dominated much of the decision making. And operating results reflected this lack of planning and control, for profits fell while those of competitors rose, unprofitable ventures were started, sales growth slowed, and a general lack of enthusiasm could be sensed among the staff.

Guidelines.

The following are some useful guidelines for budget preparation and use which are developed from the above studies, as well as from other studies made by the author:

1. A budget is both a planning tool and a control tool, for it is both a quantification of a plan and a yardstick against which performance is measured.
2. All managers should be indoctrinated in overall corporate planning objectives, and have clearly defined individual department objectives. Preliminary plans should be developed before budgets are formulated.
3. Top management must give their full backing to planning and budgeting.
4. Plans and their budgets should be prepared for overall corporate operations, as well as for all divisions, departments and individual operations within the corporation.
5. The budgetary process should provide for thorough analysis of deviations from actual results, preferably on a monthly basis. A follow-up procedure for correction of undesirable conditions should be incorporated in the budget plan.
6. A budget that is built upon wishful thinking invites frustration and loss of confidence in the value of budgeting. If a budget's goals are designed to be surpassed with minimum effort on the part of the organization, a below-standard performance can be expected.
7. Operating responsibilities for achieving budgeted goals must be clearly de-

fined. Those who are responsible for achieving budget goals should participate in the setting of these goals.

8. Individual managers must participate in the preparation of plans and budgets
   for their operations.
9. Individual plans and budgets should be integrated within an overall corporate budget, and longer-term corporate plans.
10. Normal and abnormal expenditure should be separated. as should control-
    lable and non-controllable expenses, in order that deviations from the norm
    can be accounted for.
11. Along with a summary type of budget, it is a good idea to set up a variable
    expense budget indicating precisely what the direct expense will be for each
    budget item at the various possible levels of activity.
12. Provision must be made for revising budgets, but only at specific periods or
    when there are major changes in company operations or the company's
    market.

The budget is an important management control tool. It provides
standards and goals against which actual performance can be measured.
When information on actual results is fed back, it can be compared with
budgeted results, thus enabling management to take corrective steps to
bring operations more in line with predetermined performance, and so
exercise control.

BUDGETS AND PEOPLE

In the 1950's Chris Argyris conducted a pioneer study of budgetary planning, which pinpointed many of the problems that can arise from neglect-
ing human considerations in this phase of control.[22]

Argyris studied four plants of a large corporation. At each, top management used financial budgets to motivate, "pressure," and evaluate
factory supervisors. In carrying out their jobs, the budget personnel placed
emphasis on finding things that were "sour," and when they did, they
reported errors immediately to top management—not to the factory supervisor involved. This was only natural, because it was the easiest way for
budget personnel to look good, to stand out, to get raises.

To the factory personnel, budgets had become symbols which aroused
fear, resentment, hostility and aggression. The factory personnel objected
that the budgets showed only that something was wrong, that if met, budgets would only be raised, and that the use of budgets implied a lack of
motivation in factory personnel. They felt that the budget personnel were
not flexible enough to understand the daily problems at the factory level,
emphasized past history too much, and were generally too remote from the
actual working situation. Factory personnel described the budget personnel as "sarcastic," with "over-exalted" opinions of their positions.

[22]Chris Argyris, *The Impact of Budgets on People* (New York: Controllership
Foundation, Inc., 1952).

The executives interviewed by Argyris generally felt that accountants, controllers and budget supervisors needed more training in human relations. Some typical comments were: "They're technicians, they don't know how to handle people"; "they have a narrow breadth of view"; "the better the accountant, the poorer he is in human relations"; "they are too figure conscious."

The study concluded that this kind of budget pressure tended to unite the employees against management and place factory supervisors under tension that could lead to inefficiency, aggression, or even a complete breakdown on the part of the supervisor. Instead of focusing on the entire plant or company outlook, this kind of budget pressure tended to make each party defensive: the factory supervisor concentrated on his own department's problems, and the budget supervisor looked for more and more "errors" in order to increase his impact on the organization.

To make matters worse, there was very little supervisor participation in goal setting. While most controllers interviewed held review meetings and paid lip service to factory supervisors' participation in budgeting, the supervisors were in reality asked to accept, reject, or modify the controller's budget—not to help create their *own* budgets. In his study, Argyris applied human relations techniques in developing a method for obtaining truly active participation by supervisors in the budget planning process. The new method involved the following participative approach:

1. The executive first determines if the factory supervisors really see the need for changes in the budget or for a new budget. He then determines how ready the supervisors are for a change.
2. The executive encourages and supports the supervisors in building up a picture of what they can get out of the new budget. He has the supervisors list the advantages and disadvantages, while he makes contributions.
3. The executive helps the group make a step-by-step plan of the best way to introduce the new budget plan or system.
4. The executive then helps the group membership list the resources they feel they have or could obtain as individuals or as a group to meet the budget.
5. Finally, the executive creates a feeling on the part of all the group members that they are responsible for active participation.

The participative approach does not necessarily diminish the manager's control of his operation. As Arnold Tannenbaum points out in *Control in Organizations*,[23] use of the participative approach, greater concern for the individual, and increased control of his own operations by the worker can lead to more efficient operations. Involving the individual in the budgetary process actually increases his commitment to goals and standards, and places greater obligations on him to achieve these goals and standards. The planning and control system can, of course, break down, if

[23]Arnold S. Tannenbaum, *Control in Organization* (New York: McGraw-Hill Book Company, 1968).

the leadership is weak and the manager fails to maintain his final decision-making authority. But the studies made under Tannenbaum's direction show that given strong leadership, increased individual participation in the budgetary process leads to increased effectiveness.

The budgetary area is not the only management control area in which behavioral science tools are useful. In developing other kinds of controls and control standards, greater attention to human factors can also make a substantial contribution to more effective control. And throughout the exercise of conrol, these tools can help improve performance. Because of their importance in step four of the management control process, behavioral science tools are explored in detail in Chapter 11, which concerns the exercise of control.

THE NATURE OF COSTS

In constructing financial budgets for planning and control, the manager needs to understand the various categories or kinds of expenses with which he is dealing. For accounting purposes, expenses are classified as variable, semi-variable, and fixed or assigned. Variable costs are those costs which are "sales-made", that is, are made to service sales and so vary directly with sales or production. Fixed or assigned costs are established by management, and so do not vary with sales or production (although management can vary them as sales move up or down). Advertising costs, factory rent, and facility depreciation are fixed costs. Semivariable costs vary partially with sales or production.

Costs must be *allocated* or *assigned* to objects—products, territories, or customers. Variable costs are *allocated* to objects, either on a direct or apportioned basis: drivers' salaries are direct variable costs, when they can be charged directly to distribution expenses; apportioned variable costs, for example electricity, require a basis of distribution, such as machine hours used or horsepower ratings of each machine. Fixed costs are *assigned* to objects, also either on a direct or apportioned basis: advertising costs, for example, may be assigned directly to the product advertised; on the other hand, a sales manager's salary may be apportioned to the various sales territories under him on the basis of the number of salesmen in each territory. (For example, if there are 10 salesmen in Territory A, 20 in B, and 30 in C, and the sales manager's salary is $30,000 a year, $5,000 would be assigned to Territory A, $10,000 to B and $15,000 to C).

The point to note is that certain costs, variable or fixed, may be direct for one object and apportioned for another. Some fixed costs may be measured directly for a productive department, but must be apportioned when attached to units of product. For example, in the situation where a salesman in Territory A solicits orders for three products, his salary would be assigned directly to the territory expenses but apportioned to the sales expense of the three products. Or, the depreciation of a machine may be assigned directly to productive department expenses but must be apportioned when calculating unit costs.

The above distinctions need to be clearly understood when establishing budget standards. For example, a manager might at first think that advertising is a variable expense, since it can be changed at relatively short intervals. This is true, but only before the advertising is placed. Once the cost is incurred, it becomes a fixed cost, which must then be assigned to products subsequently sold on the basis of the advertisement.

These concepts are particularly important when establishing standards for cost accounting and manufacturing cost control.

COST ACCOUNTING

One specialized accounting area important in management control is cost accounting. Cost accounting is concerned with the proper recording, reporting, and analysis of the various costs incurred in the operation of an enterprise.[24] The purpose of cost accounting, which is part of the financial accounting system of a business concern, is to inform management promptly of the cost of producing or selling an article or rendering a particular service.[25]

Cost accounting was first developed and used in finding the unit manufacturing costs of products. The principal aim was to get inventory values for presentation of financial accounting statements. This is still an important aim, for accurate inventory valuation depends on finding a valid unit cost for each type of product. In addition, however, unit costs are important in budgeting, in pricing, and in other management decision areas, so that the techniques of unit costing are used in calculating costs in many operating areas.

Cost accounting can be divided into *actual* and *standard* cost systems. One deals with costs that have actually been incurred, and the other deals with costs that should have been incurred.

There are two basic *actual* cost accounting systems, job-order costing and process costing. Job-order costing suits industries that manufacture products according to the specifications of individual customers, whereas process costing suits industries that manufacture uniform products.[26] The job-order cost system, where each job represents different manufacturing specifications, involves the accumulation and attachment of costs to jobs or batches of products. The process cost system, where uniform products are manufactured, involves the collection of production costs for a specified

24James M. Fremgen, *Managerial Cost Analysis* (Homewood, Illinois: Richard D. Irwin, Inc., 1966), p. 7.

25John J. W. Neuner, *Cost Accounting: Principles and Practice* (6th ed.; Homewood, Illinois: Richard D. Irwin, Inc., 1962), p. 3.

26I. Wayne Keller and William L. Ferrara, *Management Accounting for Profit Control* (2nd ed.; New York: McGraw-Hill Book Company, 1966), p. 131.

period of time, by the departments, processes, or cost centers through which products flow.[27]

The elements that enter into the cost of manufacturing a particular product are direct materials, direct labor, and manufacturing overhead. Direct material costs are those which can be identified with a specific unit of production. Direct labor costs refer to the wages paid for work done on a specific unit of production. Manufacturing overhead costs are the indirect or apportioned manufacturing costs, such as the cost of heating and light, foremen's salaries and machine repairs, which cannot be identified with specific units of production.

Under the job-order cost system, costs are collected on a job cost sheet, which contains spaces to record the material, labor, and overhead costs charged to the job. These costs are recorded as the job moves through the various departments in the company. Figure 7.2 gives a simplified example of a job cost sheet for one of the products produced at the XYZ Company.

Figure 7.2

XYZ Company
Job Cost Sheet

Job No. 101   Customer Acme
Item Machine Tool A   Quantity 1
Date Begun 6/4/68   Date Completed 6/6/68

Materials			Labor Time			Overhead			
Date	Req. No.	Amt.	Date	Ticket	Amt.	Date	Dept.	Rate	Amt.
6/4	1006	$22.60	6/4	10687	$ 8.00	6/4	Assembly	125%	$10.00
			6/5	10705	9.00	6/5	"	125%	11.25
	Total	$22.60		Total	$17.00		Total		$21.25

When each job is completed, the costs are totalled. The total on the job cost sheet is the basis for the entry transferring the product from goods in process to finished goods inventory, and when the product is sold, this same cost is the basis for the entry transferring the product from finished goods inventory to cost of goods sold.[28] At the end of each accounting period, all the material, labor and estimated overhead costs charged to all the jobs worked on during an accounting period are totalled. These costs are the basis for the entries debiting goods in process, and crediting raw material inventory, wages, and overhead accounts at the end of the period.

In a process cost accounting system emphasis is placed on production for a given period, a day, a week or a month. This period of time is comparable to the job or lot in a job-order cost system.[29] Material, labor, and

[27]Morton Backer and Lyle E. Jacobsen, *Cost Accounting: A Managerial Approach* (New York: McGraw-Hill Book Company, 1964), p. 184.

[28]Anthony, *Management Accounting Principles*, p. 285.

[29]Neuner, *Cost Accounting*, p. 337.

manufacturing overhead costs are accumulated and recorded by departments or processes on a time basis, not a job basis. At the end of the given
period of time all costs are totaled, and this total is divided by the number
of units produced to arrive at the cost per unit. This cost is the basis for
valuing units transferred to the finished goods inventory, and later on, for
transferring units from finished goods inventory to cost of goods sold.

In an *actual* job-order and process system, product units are charged
with the actual costs incurred in their production. Some cost accounting
systems, in addition, also calculate the cost of product units that should
have been incurred. Such systems are called *standard* cost systems and are
used for budgetary control comparisons.

Under a standard cost system, standard or estimated costs are established in advance of actual production for such items as direct materials,
direct labor, and manufacturing overhead. These standard costs are usually
established by the cost accounting department working with operating
managers, and are based on historical costs and known future events, such
as rises in wage rates and material costs. Both the standard cost and the
actual cost of production, as well as any variances between them, are recorded in the cost accounts. The difference between standard and actual
costs is called a variance. Table 7.6 illustrates the recording of standard and
actual costs, and the variances.

Table 7.6

COMPARATIVE COST ANALYSIS[30]
OF PRODUCT A
(STANDARD QUANTITY: 100)

Cost Components	Standard Cost	Actual Cost	Variation
Materials:			
50 lbs. @$0.32	$ 16.00		
52 lbs. @$0.30		$ 15.60	$ 0.40*
Labor:			
Operation No. 1:			
18 hrs. @$2.50	45.00		
16 hrs. @$2.45		39.20	5.80*
Operation No. 2:			
20 hrs. @$2.40	48.00		
24 hrs. @$2.42		58.08	10.08#
Operation No. 3:			
10 hrs. @$2.60	26.00		
15 hrs. @$2.55		38.25	12.25#
Manufacturing overhead:			
48 hrs. @$0.70	33.60		
55 hrs. @$0.70		38.50	4.90#
Totals	$168.60	$189.63	$21.03#

*Under standard   #Over standard

[30]Neuner, *Cost Accounting*, p. 614.

By examining the variances between standard and actual costs and isolating the significant variances, management can determine where inefficiency and waste may exist or where standards might be changed. The process through which the causes of deviations are investigated is discussed in Chapter 11, which concerns the exercise of control.

A standard cost system has a number of advantages.[31] Cost standards can be important in evaluating performance and in stimulating individuals to perform more effectively. Variances from standard can focus management's attention on problem areas and lead to management cost reduction programs. In short, establishing a standard cost system enables the manager to exercise control more easily.

Cost accounting is an important tool of management control, for it enables a company to determine immediately, instead of at the end of a fiscal period, the cost of producing and selling an article or rendering a service. It also gives management the breakdown of costs of materials, labor and manufacturing overhead for *specific* jobs, departments or processes, and so enables management to analyze costs in the hope of reducing them immediately. While cost accounting mainly provides a guide for evaluating and controlling production performance, its tools are also used in other operating areas, such as marketing, and so provides a major basis for developing budgets for all company operating areas.

RESPONSIBILITY ACCOUNTING

Responsibility accounting is basically a method of relating expenditures to the people responsible for incurring the expenses. To establish these relationships, accounting reports and budget reports are divided into units of responsibility that correspond to the control centers and profit centers for which individual managers have spending responsibility.[32] In these reports controllable and non-controllable expenses are normally segregated. In each company there is an hierarchical structure of authority and responsibility, around which controls are developed.[33] Responsibility accounting is structured around the areas of responsibility specified by a firm's organization structure.[34] It is based on the theory that the official who exercised the highest authority at each level of the organization should be accountable for the expenses which are under his control.[35]

[31]Backer and Jacobsen, *Cost Accounting*, p. 277.

[32]Paul Friedman, "Effective Control through Responsibility Reporting," *Systems and Procedures Journal* (November-December 1967), pp. 24-26.

[33]Charles E. Bowen, Jr., "Expense Control Must Focus on Responsibility," *N.A.A. Bulletin* (November 1964), p. 46.

[34]William L. Ferrara, "Responsibility Accounting—A Basic Control Concept," *N.A.A. Bulletin* (September 1964), p. 11.

[35]Jose Manuel Pintado, "Responsibility Accounting," *Management Services* (March-April 1965), p. 35.

As a control tool, responsibility accounting serves two important functions.[36] First, it provides a feedback of information to the responsible manager, showing him the effects of his past decisions and the important areas for future consideration and attention. It thus directs the information to the manager who can take action, the one who has authority and responsibility in the area affected. Second, it enables higher management to better evaluate individual performance and take action more quickly, if any situation gets out of hand.

THE BASIC FINANCE FUNCTIONS

The finance function involves obtaining the funds needed to run a business and seeing to it that all funds are used in the most efficient and effective way possible. In the sense that all company resources represent past, present, and future investments of funds, the financial officer is concerned with the most basic of all management decisions—the efficient allocation of resources.

Since the efficient management of capital is the basic purpose of any business, the financial function has always been an important one, usually handled by a firm's president or an officer working closely with him. As J. Fred Weston and Eugene Brigham have put it:

> The financial manager plays a key role in the guidance of the firm. He has a central responsibility in analysis, planning and control which guide the firm's resources into the most profitable lines. . . .
>
> The importance of the financial manager is recognized by his place at the top levels in the organization structure of the firm. Financial decisions are crucial for the well being of a firm, because they determine the ability of the company to obtain plant and equipment when needed, to carry the requisite amount of inventories and receivables, to avoid burdensome fixed charges when sales and profits fall, and to prevent loss of effective control of the company.[37]

The finance function can be viewed as two separate but equally important tasks. First, financial management must provide the funds which the business needs to achieve its objectives, at the most reasonable available terms. Second, financial management is concerned with the effective use of funds within the business.[38] The process and tools used in this second task, financial analysis, are of greatest concern to management control.

The finance function can be broken down into four activities:

1. Determining the financial resources required to meet the company's objectives and operating requirements.

[36]Robert Beyer, *Profitability Accounting for Planning and Control* (New York: The Ronald Press Company, 1963), p. 35.

[37]J. Fred Weston and Eugene F. Brigham, *Managerial Finance* (2nd ed.; New York: Holt, Rinehart and Winston, 1962), p. 15.

[38]Pearson Hunt, Charles M. Williams, and Gordon Donaldson, *Basic Business Finance: Text and Cases* (3rd ed.; Homewood, Illinois: Richard D. Irwin, Inc., 1966), p. 4.

2. Forecasting how much of these requirements will be met by generation of funds within the company and how much will have to be obtained outside the company.

3. Developing the best ways to obtain the funds needed from external sources, or where there are excess funds, the best ways to invest excess capital.

4. Establishing and maintaining a system of financial controls governing the allocation and use of funds within the company.[39]

The average business must maintain a substantial investment in inventory, credits to customers (receivables), cash, plant and equipment, and research and development, in order to operate effectively and achieve its objectives. The financial manager must examine all these areas and determine both what funds will be needed to enable the business to operate profitably, and what additional capital projects should be undertaken to achieve the company's long-term goals, if funds can be obtained for them.

Once a preliminary forecast of funds needed has been made, the financial manager must determine where funds can be obtained, if they are needed. Internally generated funds—funds arising from profitable sales—will usually meet some of these requirements. External financing, both long-term and short-term, must be used to meet any remaining funds needs. Long-term financing can be done either through debt financing (principally the issuance of bonds) or through equity financing (principally the issuance of common or preferred stock), depending on the needs, financial condition and objectives of the company. Some sources of short-term financing are trade credits, bank loans, commercial paper, factoring of accounts receivable, and leasing. In those rare instances where excess funds are available, the financial officer would study ways to invest these funds.

Since there is never an unlimited supply of funds, the typical company has a wide range of alternatives competing for the use of its funds. Financial management is responsible for guiding the selection of the uses to which available funds will be put, and for insuring that funds are obtained and used in the most efficient manner possible. There are two basic criteria controlling funds allocations: first, the allocation of funds should be guided by the principle of the maximization of return on investment; and second, funds should be used to help the company attain its strategic objectives.

The general availability of funds in the economy, the cost at which they are available, inflationary pressures on the economy, and government spending policies also affect financial decision making. During periods such as mid -1969, for example, when interest rates on long-term debt securities were relatively high, many companies were forced to seek alternative means of financing. The tax environment in which a business oper-

[39]Jerome B. Cohen and Sidney M. Robbins, *The Financial Manager: Basic Aspects of Financial Administration* (New York: Harper and Row, Publishers, 1966), p. 5.

ates also has a major impact on funds management. In many cases, the success of a company rests on how it adjusts to its tax environment. Planning for finance thus requires the study of federal, state and local tax environment, as well as the economic environment to determine its impact on company operations.

Once the funds have been put to work in a business, the financial manager is responsible for monitoring how the funds are being used. Cash flow statements, financial analysis through financial ratios, capital budgeting, and return-on-investment analysis are the major control tools he uses to perform this control job.

CASH FLOW STATEMENTS

Before plans to obtain funds can be made, it is necessary to forecast cash requirements for some future period. Once plans are agreed upon and programs are under way, the forecasted levels of cash in turn serve as check points against which actual results can be compared for control purposes.[40]

The basic method of predicting the amount and timing of future funds needs is through the preparation of a *cash flow forecast* or a *cash budget.* The cash flow forecast is a prediction of when and in what quantity cash receipts will come into the company, and of when and in what quantity cash payments will be made.

Anticipated cash receipts would include such items as cash from the sale of securities and fixed assets, as well as cash from sales and the collection of accounts receivable. Cash disbursement would include such non-routine disbursements as outlays for equipment, as well as routine payment of wages, accounts payable, taxes, dividends, and so on. Table 7.7 gives a simplified cash flow budget for the XYZ Company for the six months January to June 1971.

Table 7.7

SCHEDULE OF ESTIMATED CASH FLOWS
XYZ COMPANY—JANUARY TO JUNE 1971
(IN THOUSANDS)

	Jan.	Feb.	March	April	May	June	Total
Total Net Receipts	$25.5	$59.5	$65	$55	$80	$85	$370
Total Net Payments	40	60	62	65	75	78	380
Net Inflow or (Outflow)	($14.5)	($ .5)	$ 3	($10)	$ 5	$ 7	($ 10)
Cumulative Inflow or (Outflow)	($14.5)	($15)	($12)	($22)	($17)	($10)	($ 10)

[40]Hunt, Williams and Donaldson, *Basic Business Finance,* p. 153.

The cash budget allows management of the XYZ Company to determine approximately how much cash will flow into the company and out of the company for the first six months of the year. For the months in which there will be a net outflow of cash, management can take action to secure needed funds from outside sources. In the months in which there will be a net inflow of cash, management can consider using the excess funds for investment or the purchase of additional capital assets. Through the cash budget, management is made aware of possible problem areas in funds flow.

The cash budget also serves as a standard or yardstick of performance. Management can compare the budget cash inflow and outflow with the actual inflow and outflow. If actual cash flows have deviated significantly from budgeted flows, management can determine the reasons for this deviation and either take action to eliminate the problems in order to bring actual flows more in line with the budget, or revise the cash budget to make it more realistic.

In order to make this budget comparison, the financial manager needs to have statements of the flow of funds—the sources from which cash was obtained and the ways in which the money was applied or spent.[41] Table 7.8 gives an example of such a cash flow statement. Accounting records and reports—the balance sheet, income statement, and their detailed back-up figures—provide the basic data for the flow statement.

Using this information the financial manager would then compare actual cash flow with budgeted cash flow to control overall funds movement within the company. For example, a comparison of the figures in Table 7.8 and those in Table 7.7 shows that the movement of funds in the XYZ Company in January were exactly on budget.

FINANCIAL ANALYSIS THROUGH FINANCIAL RATIOS

A major technique used to study the financial health of a company and the efficiency of its use of capital is financial analysis through financial ratios. These financial ratios are generally grouped in four fundamental categories and are used in conjunction with both historical and budget reports:

1. *Liquidity ratios*, which are designed to measure the ability of the firm to meet its maturing short-term obligations.
2. *Leverage ratios*, which measure the contribution of owners as compared with the financing provided by the firm's creditors.
3. *Activity ratios*, which measure how effectively the firm is employing its resources.
4. *Profitability ratios*, which measure management's effectiveness as shown by the returns generated on sales and investment.[42]

[41]Weston and Brigham, *Managerial Finance*, pp. 89-92.
[42]Weston and Brigham, *Managerial Finance*, pp. 67-68.

Table 7.8

XYZ COMPANY

Statement of Cash Flow
January 1971

```
Cash Provided by:
  Operations
    Net Income for period                                        $11,000
    Charges to Income Not Affecting Cash
      Depreciation of Plant and Equipment        $1,000
      Amortization of Deferred Charges              500            1,500
    Total provided by Operations                                  12,500
  Reduction of Accounts Receivable                                 8,000
  Sale of Investments                                              5,000
Total Cash Provided                                              $25,500

Cash Applied to:
  Purchase of Equipment                                          $20,000
  Increase of Inventories                                         11,000
  Reduction of Accounts Payable                                    4,000
  Payment of Dividends                                             5,000
Total Cash Applied                                              $40,000

Reduction in Cash Balance                                       $14,500

Cash Balance January 1,  1971                                   $50,000
Cash Balance January 31, 1971                                   $35,500
```

These ratios provide a means for measuring a company's performance. As an illustration of how management control is exercised using these ratios, the financial ratios of the XYZ Company, a manufacturer of machine tools, are analyzed below and compared to the average ratios for the machine tool industry, where industry figures are available,[43] as well as to standards established by the company from past experience. The statements presented in Tables 7.1 and 7.2 earlier in this chapter are the basis of the following discussion of financial ratio analysis.

Liquidity Ratios.

Liquidity analysis, which is designed to measure a firm's ability to meet its maturing obligations, uses such ratios as current assets to current liabilities, cash or readily negotiable securities to current liabilities, and inventory to working capital.

1. *Current Ratio.* The current ratio is determined by dividing current liabilities into current assets. The current ratio is the generally accepted measure

[43]The average machine tool manufacturing industry ratios are taken from Weston and Brigham, *Managerial Finance*, p. 814.

of short-term solvency, as it indicates the extent to which the claims of short-term creditors are covered by assets that are expected to be converted into cash at an early date. The accepted norm is that current assets should be at least twice as great as current liabilities, though this figure varies from industry to industry and company to company. The XYZ Company's current ratio is 3.0 ($225,000 ÷ $75,000) as compared to the machine tool industry average of 2.5. XYZ thus has an above average current ratio.

2. *Quick Ratio.* The quick ratio is calculated by deducting inventories from current assets and dividing the result by current liabilities. The quick ratio measures the firm's ability to pay off short-term obligations without relying on the sale of inventories. The XYZ Company's quick ratio is 1.67 ($225,000— $100,000 ÷ $75,000). Thus XYZ could pay off its current liabilities without relying on sale of its inventory, and so is in a very solvent position.

3. *Inventory to Working Capital Ratio.* This ratio is determined by dividing working capital (current assets minus current liabilities) into inventory. It indicates the proportion of net current assets tied up in inventory. The XYZ Company's ratio of inventory to working capital is 0.67 ($100,000 ÷ $225,000 — $75,000). Thus XYZ has tied up about two-thirds of its current assets in inventory, which is about the level they had been maintaining for the past five years.

Leverage Ratios.

Leverage analysis, which measures the contribution of owners as compared with financing provided by creditors, uses the following ratios:

1. *Debt to Total Assets.* This ratio, determined by dividing total assets into debt, measures the firm's obligation to creditors in relation to all funds that have been provided. The lower this ratio, the safer the company's position. The XYZ Company's debt to total assets ratio is 38% ($125,000 ÷ $325,000), as compared to the average industry ratio of 10%, indicating that the company must proceed cautiously with any further debt financing.

2. *Times Interest Earned.* This ratio is determined by dividing earnings before interest and taxes by interest charges. It measures the extent to which earnings could decline before the firm would be unable to meet interest charges. The XYZ Company has a ratio of 45 ($225,000 ÷ $5,000), which is a very safe position, since earnings would have to drop considerably before XYZ could have a problem meeting its interest payments.

3. *Fixed-Charge Coverage.* The number of times fixed charges are covered is determined by dividing profit before fixed charges by the total fixed charges (interest, lease payments, sinking fund requirements, and the tax related to sinking fund payments). The XYZ Company's fixed charge ratio is 23 ($230,000 ÷ $10,000), again a very safe position.

4. *Current Liabilities to Net Worth.* By dividing current liabilities by net worth, it is possible to measure the amount of funds supplied by owners against the amount raised by current debt. The XYZ Company's ratio of 41% ($75,000 ÷ $185,000) is very close to the industry ratio of 38%, and shows that the company is making ample use of short-term credit to finance operations.

5. *Fixed Assets to Net Worth.*   This ratio, which is determined by dividing net worth into fixed assets, shows the extent to which ownership funds are invested in assets with relatively low turnover. The XYZ Company's ratio of 43% ($80,000 ÷ $185,000) is good, since it indicates that management has tied up less than half of its ownership funds in long-term assets.

Activity Ratios.

Activity analysis, which measures how effectively a company is using its resources, employs the following ratios:

1. *Cash Velocity.*   This ratio is calculated by dividing Cash and Cash equivalents (short-term negotiable securities) into yearly sales. It indicates the number of times cash has been turned over during the year. The XYZ Company's ratio is a relatively high 10 times ($700,000 ÷ $70,000), indicating that XYZ is using its cash effectively.

2. *Inventory Turnover.*   Inventory turnover is calculated by dividing inventory into sales. Since sales are at market price, inventories should be valued at the same market price in making this calculation. If inventories are carried at cost, costs of goods sold should be used in place of sales. Sales occur over the entire year, but inventory figures are for one point in the year. To compensate for this, an average figure should be used, computed by adding the beginning and end of the year inventories and dividing by two. In the case of the XYZ Company, data is provided for only the end of the year, so no average can be calculated. Using the ending inventory only, the inventory turnover ratio is 7 ($70,000 ÷ $100,000), as compared to the average ratio of 4.6 in the machine tool industry.

3. *Fixed Assets Turnover.*   This ratio, calculated by dividing fixed assets into sales, measures the turnover of capital assets. The higher the ratio, the better a company is using its fixed assets. The XYZ Company's fixed assets turnover ratio of 8.8 ($7000,000 ÷ $80,000) shows that the company is making good use of its fixed assets.

4. *Average Collection Period.*   This ratio measures the turnover of accounts receivable. First, the annual sales are divided by 360 to get the average daily sales. Second, daily sale are divided into accounts receivable to find the number of days' sales that are tied up in receivables. Compared to the industry average of 46 days, the XYZ Company's average collection period of 26 days ($50,000 ÷ $700,000 — 360) shows that the company is being paid at a faster rate than the industry as a whole.

5. *Total Assets Turnover.*   This ratio is determined by dividing yearly sales by total assets. The higher the ratio, the better use a company is making of its assets. The XYZ Company's ratio of 2.2 ($700,000 ÷ $325,000), as compared to the industry ratio of 1.6, shows that XYZ is making better use of its assets than the industry as a whole.

Profitability Ratios.

Profitability analysis, which measures a company's overall effectiveness as shown by the returns generated on sales and investment, uses the following ratios:

1. *Gross Operating Margin.* This ratio is calculated by dividing sales into gross operating profit. It indicates the degree to which unit selling prices may decline without resulting in a loss from operations. The XYZ Company's ratio is 30% ($210,000 ÷ $700,000), which is a comfortable margin.

2. *Net Operating Margin.* This ratio, calculated by dividing net operating profit by sales, indicates the degree to which unit selling prices may decline without losses resulting on an accrued rather than a cash basis. Again the XYZ Company has a comfortable margin, with a ratio of 29% ($205,000 ÷ $700,000).

3. *Sales Margin.* This ratio, determined by dividing net income by sales, indicates the profitability of overall sales. The XYZ Company's ratio of 16% ($110,000 ÷ $700,000), is four times as high as the average industry figure of 4%.

4. *Productivity of Assets.* This ratio is calculated by dividing the sum of net profits after taxes, plus interest expenses, by total assets. It measures the rate of return on a company's total resources. Compared to the industry average of 6.3%, the XYZ Company has a ratio of 35% ($115,000 ÷ $325,000), showing that XYZ has made very good use of its assets.

5. *Return on Net Worth.* The ratio of net profit after taxes to net worth measures the productivity of the resources the owners of the company have committed to the operation of the business. The XYZ Company's ratio of 60% ($110,000 ÷ $185,00) is extremely good, since it is more than six times greater than the machine tool industry average of 9.7%.

In order to use financial ratios for control, their behavior should be examined over a period of time. By examining the same ratios over a period of months or years, management can get a picture of whether or not the company's position is improving, for the trend can be determined and the effect of seasonal factors and extraordinary events can be eliminated from the analysis.

Ratios should also be compared with those of other companies and with industry averages. Through such comparisons it is possible to determine just how well a company is doing within its industry, and to better judge relative efficiency, profitability, and potential earning power.

CAPITAL BUDGETING

Capital budgeting involves planning and controlling the acquisition, allocation, and expenditure of long-term investments funds. The capital budget specifies the projects selected by management which will require capital investment, together with the estimated cost of and return on each project. Since capital budgets forecast requirements for funds, they enable management to plan in advance to secure whatever additional funds may be needed to finance potentially profitable projects. Capital budgets, like other budgets, can also be used to monitor the spending on capital projects and the efficiency of capital spending.

Capital budgeting may be viewed as a four phase process:

1. Determining the amount of money available within the company itself that can be used for capital investments.
2. Examining each possible capital project to determine its cost in relation to its potential return on investment.
3. Selecting those projects which appear to be the most profitable, and determining the total amount of money that will be needed for capital expenditures in the coming time period.
4. Determining how much money will have to be raised externally for capital expenditures and selecting methods of external financing.

The first step in the capital budgeting process is the determination of what internal company funds can be used to finance capital investments. This step facilitates the appraisal of potential capital projects, for it gives management an approximate idea of the company's capacity to undertake capital projects and sets very general limits on what can and cannot realistically be done.

The heart of the capital budgeting process is the examination of potential capital investments to determine their possible profitability to the company. The process is complex, since capital expenditures involve spending of sums of money in the present, and then waiting for a period of years to receive the benefits resulting from those expenditures.[44]

In general, a capital expenditure should not be made if the investment will return less than what the firm has to pay on the funds necessary to finance the project. [45] In other words, a project's return must be sufficient to pay the interest on the debt invested in the project and/or the cost of equity (stock) capital used to finance the project. In addition, under normal circumstances a company would also plan to earn a profit on the investment. This does not mean that a company may not occasionally use other investment criteria. For example, if a firm's main plant burns down, the company may rebuild it immediately simply to stay in business. Such instances are the exception, however, and not the rule.

The combined cost of debt (percentage of interest) capital and equity capital (earnings as a percentage of equity) used to finance a project is known as the *cost of capital*.[46] It is based on a weighted average of the different types of funds needed. The cost of capital is usually calculated on the basis of after-tax figures.

The cost of debt capital is basically the interest that must be paid each year after taxes. If corporations are in the 48% income tax bracket, they receive a credit to taxes equivalent to 48% of the interest.[47] Thus if the

[44]C. G. Edge, "Capital Budgeting: Principles and Projection," *Financial Executive* (September 1965), p. 50.

[45]Alexander A. Robichek and John G. McDonald, "The Cost of Capital Concept: Potential Use and Misuse," *Financial Executive* (June 1965), p. 21.

[46]Edge, "Capital Budgeting," p. 52.

[47]"Financial Decision Tools," A Presentation by A. J. Magee at the 1967 Controller's Conference of Airco Corporation, p. 3.

XYZ Company must pay 6% interest on borrowed funds before taxes, it would only pay 52% of the 6% interest, or 3.12%, after calculating tax credits.

The cost of equity capital is that rate of return which stock-holders require before they will invest their funds. For example, at the XYZ Company, stockholders require a 10% rate of return on their money.

In order to calculate the cost of capital for XYZ it is necessary to find the weighted average of the cost of both types of capital. At the end of 1969, XYZ's long-term debt was $50,000 and its total equity was $185,000. The sum of these two (called total invested capital) is $235,000, of which 21% (called the debt ratio) is debt and 79% (called the equity ratio) is equity. In order to obtain the cost of total invested capital, 3.12% (the cost of debt capital) is multiplied by 21% and 10% (the cost of equity capital) is multiplied by 79%:

$$3.12\% \times 21\% = .66\%$$
$$10\% \times 79\% = \underline{7.9 \%}$$
$$8.56\%$$

The sum of these two, 8.56%, is the total cost of capital for the XYZ Company.

Some allowance for profit to the company must then be added to this figure. For example, the XYZ Company may feel that 5% profit is adequate. This 5% is added to the 8.56% to give 13.56%, which represents the minimum acceptable return on capital investment required by the company.

Next, each proposed project is studied and its expected return on investment (ROI) is calculated. For example, the XYZ Company might consider introducing a new product line which requires new machinery. The company expects to make 17% on the investment, based on reasonably conservative assumptions about price and volume. (Methods used to calculate this return on investment are discussed in detail in the next section of this chapter). This 17% is comfortably above the 13.56% minimum, and so the project would be acceptable, provided that capital could be obtained and that it met planning objectives.

Once the total investment for all the capital projects considered worthwhile has been calculated and the timing of the money needs has been forecast, the company must determine where the funds will be obtained. The initial funds flow forecast would indicate the amount of money available from operations. Any capital requirements in excess of this amount would have to be obtained from outside sources. For example, if XYZ's total capital expenditure requirements are $200,000, and it has $50,000 from operations available for capital investments, it must raise $150,000 from outside sources.

If funds are needed from outside sources, the company must next select the method or methods of external financing it will use. Funds can be raised externally through debt financing (principally the issuing of bonds), or through equity financing (the issuing of common or preferred stock), or through some combination or variation of the two. For example, Ling-Temco, which has been very imaginative (though not always successful) in its approach to financing, has made a number of combined equity debt offerings with unusual conversion terms.[48] The exact solution will depend on the requirements of the particular company.

Capital budgeting is another useful tool which management can use for controlling and maximizing company profitability. Through capital budgeting, management is able to plan and control the long-term use of company funds. It enables management to analyze potential capital investments more thoroughly, to select those investments which will maximize return on investment and to finance these projects in a controlled manner. The capital budget also provides a yardstick or guideline for controlling the progress of capital expenditures, as can be seen from the status report given in Table 7.9.[49]

RETURN ON INVESTMENT ANALYSIS

Return on investment (ROI) can be used to measure the effectiveness of past decisions or to predict the profitability of future capital investments.

Profitability ratios which measure return on investment were discussed in the section on financial ratios above. Through profitability ratios, such as return on net worth and return on assets, management can judge how effectively the company is using its resources to earn money.

Return on investment analysis can also be used to judge the profitability of potential capital investments. Through this technique management can calculate the dollars that have been invested, the dollars that will be earned, and the ROI percentage. This percentage can then be compared with a company's minimum acceptable return on investment— 13.56% for the XYZ Company, for example—to determine whether the proposed capital project is worthwhile.

A number of methods are used to evaluate an investment in capital projects. Among the most common are the payback method, the accounting method and the discounted cash flow method.[50]

Payback Method.

The payback method involves calculating the number of years required to return the original investment. The payback is computed by

[48]Jim Hyatt, "LTV's New Capitalization Plan Intrigues, Impresses Many Analysts and Investors," *The Wall Street Journal* (March 11, 1968), p. 6.

[49]Adapted from J. Brooks Heckert and James D. Willson, *Business Budgeting and Control* (3rd ed.; New York: The Ronald Press Company, 1967), p. 472.

[50]Richard F. Perdunn, "Capital Investment and Large Projects," *Financial Executive* (June 1965), p. 15.

Table 7.9

MONROE MANUFACTURING COMPANY[49]

Capital Spending Status Report
As of August 31, 1971

Appropriation No.	Description	Work Order No.	Actual Completion Date	Original Budget	Outstanding Commitments	Actual Expenditures to Date	Estimated Cost to Complete	Indicated Total Cost	(Over) or Under Original Budget
24	OTTAWA AVENUE PLANT.								
	Buildings and Equipment.............	241		$670,796.52	286,672.84	384,123.68	–	670,796.52	$ –
	Site Clearance.................	242		13,552.86	–	13,552.86	–	13,552.86	–
	Total Appropriation 24.............			684,349.38	286,672.81	397,676.54	–	684,349.38	–
25	MODIFICATIONS OF OVERHEAD CONVEYOR.	251							
	Installation Y Building.................			28,353.00	14,533.05	236.39	13,583.56	28,353.00	(1,655.55)
	Others Completed as of 7/31/			2,990.00	–	4,645.55	–	4,645.55	1,655.55
	Total Appropriation 25.............			31,343.00	14,533.05	4,881.94	13,583.56	32,998.55	(1,655.55)
26	MISCELLANEOUS IMPROVEMENTS........								
	Magnesium Pilot Line.............	261	7/31	8,910.00	–	8,551.48	–	8,551.48	358.52
	Wrapping Equipment.............	262	2/28	16,900.00	6.50	14,122.52	–	14,129.02	2,770.98
	Roll Mill—Design and Install—A.C. Plant....	263		11,680.00	8,944.00	154.00	2,582.00	11,680.00	–
	Intercommunication System...........	264		24,974.00	4,794.57	20,179.43	–	24,974.00	–
	Move Hydraulic Press and Install in Y Building.	265	5/31	1,155.50	79.15	926.68	–	1,005.83	149.67
	Design and Install Air Conditioning Unit in Y Building.	266		9,725.00	750.00	8,626.84	348.16	9,725.00	–
	Changes and Modifications in Paint Room.....	267	5/31	30,115.00	29.89	26,664.06	–	26,693.95	3,421.05
	Buggy Scales.................	268		11,275.00	212.20	10,158.39	904.41	11,275.00	–
	Tote Boxes—A.C. Plant...........	269	7/31	7,700.00	340.57	3,198.86	–	3,539.43	57.57
	Prepare Annealing Oven for Production Use.....	270		7,700.00	1,290.03	6,202.29	207.68	7,700.00	–
	Move Electric Furnaces to A.C. Plant.....	271		3,585.00	2,989.20	–	595.80	3,585.00	–
	Lift truck with Exide batteries and Battery Charger..	272		30,486.00	21,670.19	2,737.83	6,077.98	30,486.00	–
	Purchase and Install 100 HP motor in Y Building....	273	7/31	4,692.00	424.00	3,701.97	–	4,125.97	566.03
	Others Completed as of 7/31/			3,701.00	–	2,482.18	–	2,482.18	1,218.82
	Total Appropriation 26.............			168,495.50	41,530.30	107,706.53	10,716.03	159,952.86	8,542.64
29	ALUMINUM EXPERIMENTAL UNIT........	291							
	Construction of Unit.............			50,000.00	5,533.34	15,385.04	29,081.62	50,000.00	–
	Total Appropriation 29.............			50,000.00	5,533.34	15,385.04	29,081.62	50,000.00	–
	Grand Total.............			$934,187.88	348,269.53	525,650.05	53,381.21	927,300.79	$ 6,887.09

Issued by Accounting Department—September 5, 1971

calculating the estimated annual *after-tax* savings or funds inflow and determining the point at which the investment has been recovered.

For example, the XYZ Company is considering a capital investment project costing $100,000. The project has an estimated life of five years. Funds inflow from the project will be as follows:

Year	Amount of Funds Inflow
1	$20,000
2	30,000
3	30,000
4	20,000
5	20,000

Since the investment will be recovered by the end of the fourth year, the payback period is four years. The principal objection to the payback method is that it measures only return of investment, not profitability. Simply measuring how long it will take to recover the initial investment does not measure the earning power of a project.[51]

Accounting Method.

The accounting method involves calculating the percentage of income it is anticipated a project will earn on the original investment. This can be done in a number of ways. The simplest way is to divide average annual income by the total investment. Another way is to use average investment instead of total investment, because the total investment gradually decreases over the life of the project and is fully recovered by the end of the project's useful life. In general, since the average investment is roughly half the total investment, the return on the average investment is roughly double that on the total investment.

The example, if the XYZ Company spends $100,000 for a machine that *earns a profit* (after taxes and depreciation) of $5,000 a year over a life of five years, the return on total investment would be:

$$\frac{\$5,000 \times 100}{\$100,000} = 5\%$$

The return on average investment would be:

$$\frac{\$5,000 \times 100}{\$100,000 \div 2} = \frac{\$5,000 \times 100}{\$50,000} = 10\%$$

Discounted Cash Flow Method.

The discounted cash flow method, unlike the first two methods of evaluating capital investments, takes into consideration the fact that money received over a period of years is not worth as much as money received today.

[51]Alfred Rappaport, "The Discounted Payback Period," *Management Services* (July-August 1965), p. 31.

The discounted cash flow method is based on the premise that tomorrow's money is worth less than today's. Over a given period of time, the sooner an investor can obtain funds, the earlier he can reinvest them and start earning interest on them. For example, if a person will receive one dollar 10 years from now, that dollar is worth only 56¢ to him today, since by investing 56¢ today at 6% his money will earn 44¢ over 10 years. At the same 6% interest rate, one dollar received 5 years from now is worth only 75¢ today, and a dollar received next year has a present value of only about 94¢. At a lower interest rate, say 5%, one dollar received today would be worth a little more, approximately 95¢. Inflation is another factor which lessens the value of future dollars, and can be taken into account through the discounted cash flow method.

The present value of money that is to be received in the future thus depends both on the interest rate used and the length of time over which the money is to be returned. The greater the interest rate and the longer the time period over which the money is to be received, the smaller the present value of the money.

The following is a simplified example of the use of the discounted cash flow method of determining return on investment. The XYZ Company is considering investing in a capital project costing $100,000. The project has a useful life of 5 years. The amount of cash inflow from the project will be: first year, $20,000; second year, $30,000; third year, $30,000; fourth year, $20,000; and fifth year, $20,000.

As was computed in the previous section, XYZ's minimum acceptable rate of return on capital investments is 13.56%, or for simlicity's sake, 14%. Thus, the capital investment of $100,000 will have to return at least 14% or it will not be accepted.

Tables that list the present value of one dollar at different percentages for each future year can be found in most accounting and finance textbooks.[52] Using these charts, one can develop the following analysis of the $100,000 investment proposed for the XYZ Company:

End of Year[53]	Present Value of $1 Discounted at 14%	Unadjusted Annual Cash-Flow	Present Value of Annual Cash Flow
1—Return cash flow	.877	$ 20,000	$17,540
2—Return cash flow	.769	30,000	23,070
3—Return cash flow	.675	30,000	20,250
4—Return cash flow	.592	20,000	11,840
5—Return cash flow	.519	20,000	10,380
Total Return Cash Flow		$120,000	$83,080
Gain (or loss) where $100,000 is invested		$ 20,000	($16,920)

[52]For example, Robert N. Anthony, *Management Accounting Principles* (Homewood, Illinois: Richard D. Irwin, Inc., 1965), p. 428.
[53]*Ibid.*

The investment of $100,000 in this capital project will not give the desired minimum acceptable return on investment over the five year life of the investment, since when the cash inflows are discounted at the rate of 14% (the nearest round figure to the 13.56% minimum return on investment desired by the XYZ Company), the present value of all cash inflows from year 1 to year 5 is only $83,080, or $16,920 less than the initial outflow or investment of $100,000. Since the present of the cash inflow does not equal or exceed the present value of the cash outflow, this investment would not be undertaken.

Discounted cash flow thus presents a realistic picture of what tomorrow's earning are worth today, and enables management to develop a single standard, the value of a dollar today, for comparing all types of capital projects, no matter how long the payback period.

These methods of evaluating investments and calculating ROI are tools for controlling capital expenditures, since they give management a simple dollar standard for comparing alternative capital investments. As such, ROI analysis is a most useful management planning and control tool in the area of capital funds management.

CONCLUSION

Accounting provides the historical information on assets, revenues, profits and expenses needed to meet overall financial reporting requirements in a company. This aspect of accounting is called financial accounting. Accounting in today's business is also concerned with management analysis, through such tools as budgetary control and cost accounting. This aspect of accounting is referred to as management accounting. Since accounting reports use monetary measures, they are part of the financial control area.

The basic accounting statements are the income and expense statement and the balance sheet. Historical financial data is collected within this framework. In these historical financial reports vertical and horizontal comparisons are frequently made of current results with prior years' results, in order to provide a measure of historical progress. Vertical and horizontal analysis is used in all types of control reports.

Historical standards, however, are not adequate control yardsticks. Control requires standards related to plans. Planning standards in the management accounting area are most often in the form of financial budgets.

This chapter has reviewed in detail the budgetary control process at the corporate level. Budgets extend into every area of a business's operations and are an important part of the network of financial controls within each operating area, since all operating and staff controls are ultimately designed to control profits and return on investment.

Finance is concerned with the efficient management of company funds, and financial analysis tools are used to control the overall use of funds within a company. The funds flow statement and budget facilitate control of the overall inflow and outflow of funds, as well as control of funds requirements. Capital budgets subject planned expenditures to the acid test, the ROI test—what will they earn on the invested money? Financial analysis through financial ratios facilitates control of four basic aspects of a company's operation:

1. Profitability: how much are we earning on sales and on assets?
2. Liquidity: do we have adequate funds with which to run the business?
3. Efficiency of asset usage: how hard are the company's money and its other assets working?
4. General financial condition: do we owe too much money?

Accounting and finance tools, such as comparative statement analysis, the budgetary process, cost accounting, responsibility accounting, financial ratios, cash flow and capital budgets, and ROI analysis, are all used for management control. Since the purpose of these accounting and financial control tools is principally to monitor and report on revenue, costs, profits, and the status and use of assets—all areas of concern to a company's *overall* success—overall company control is largely concerned with financial controls. These tools can provide answers to such questions as: How are overall company sales, expenses and profits doing in comparison to expectations? What is the status of company assets? Are assets being used as efficiently as they could be?

Overall financial controls affect every operating and staff manager, for each area has control reports which are an integral part of a company's overall financial control system. For example, in the marketing area a marketing manager will have an overall expense, sales, and profit budget, which is an extension of the company's overall profit and expense control budgets.

Financial controls are, however, only one part of an operating or staff manager's network of control. While the most important controls in an operating area may be accounting and financial (since they control overall expenses and profit), the largest number of controls, and the bulk of the control job, is most often outside the scope of financial controls.

The following chapter discusses a variety of specific control tools and systems found within three operating and staff areas. The discussion covers both financial tools which extend the overall financial controls discussed in this chapter, as well as non-financial controls which are developed to meet the specific needs of the individual operations.

DISCUSSION QUESTIONS

1. Define and discuss the difference between the finance and accounting functions. In what ways are they related?

2. Discuss the differences between financial accounting and management accounting. In what ways are both related to management control?

3. It has been said that in a very small business the accounting control system is the management control system. Explain and discuss.

4. Of what use are horizontal and vertical statement analysis?

5. Outline the major accounting control tools and systems discussed in this chapter.

6. What is the role of sales and expense budgets in control? Why are they called "quantified" plans?

7. What are the various classifications of costs, and how is cost accounting used to determine which person, operation, or product incurred these costs?

8. Why is it so impotant to management control to break down cost reports and budgets into responsibility units?

9. Give the basic definition of the finance function, and outline the major tools used in financial analysis and control.

10. Discuss the importance of cash flow statements and budgets in management control.

11. What are the major types of financial ratios, and of what value are they in management control?

12. What techniques are used to aid in determining and controlling the investment of a company's capital?

13. In what way is return on investment the basic standard by which all manager performance is measured? Why do you think many managers say that the ROI concept is probably the one most important management control concept? What specific control purposes does each ROI technique serve?

14. Why are the accounting and finance control tools discussed in this chapter called "financial" controls? Why are they so closely related to overall corporate control? In what ways are they related to individual area operating controls?

CHAPTER 8

STEP THREE: OPERATING AND STAFF CONTROLS

This chapter discusses some of the controls commonly developed in three important operating and staff areas: marketing, manufacturing, and personnel. The network of controls in each area is closely linked to the overall financial controls discussed in the last chapter, and employs similar analytical techniques such as horizontal and vertical comparative analysis. These networks of controls, however, also go considerably beyond accounting and finance controls, since operating and staff controls often concentrate on non-financial aspects of the business operation and use more than just dollars as a yardstick for measuring. Both kinds of controls—financial and non-financial—are covered in each section of this chapter.

In discussing these broad networks of controls, the chapter concentrates on describing and showing the tools themselves, how they are set up, the kinds of situations in which they are used, and the use to which they can be put. Illustrations of how a manager uses the tools to exercise control are not covered here, because this chapter concerns only the development of tools and systems—step three in the management control process. The exercise of control is covered in Chapters 11, 13 and 14. Nor are the more advanced graphic, mathematical, and computer techniques used in operating control discussed in detail here, since they are covered in Chapters 9 and 10.

MARKETING

Since sales are what set in motion all company operations, the sales forecast and overall marketing plans are normally the first operating plans developed. At the same time, corresponding controls are needed to monitor the progress of the marketing operation towards reaching planned objectives. Development of marketing control tools and systems thus starts with market planning and its related sales forecasts. Overall corporate financial controls also provide a framework within which marketing controls are developed.

While the exact areas covered by marketing controls will depend on the marketing activities of the company, they will always include some (if not all) of the following: marketing profit planning, sales management, advertising, market research, product management, and marketing services. The managers of each of these activities would be the ones using the controls, and so are the ones who are responsible for seeing to it that they have adequate and suitable controls. The majority of the actual work involved in developing these controls, however, would probably be done by the company systems department and accounting and financial department.

The purpose of the marketing controls is to monitor marketing performance in the major marketing areas. Table 8.1 gives a checklist of controls used in each of the major marketing operating areas.[1] The kinds of controls listed in Table 8.1 include some which merely extend overall financial controls: sales, profits, overall expenses, and product costs. Others are designed to meet specific marketing operating requirements: customer accounts, pricing, finished goods inventory, order backlog, customer service, credit, advertising, market research, product, and personnel. While these controls are important to achieving budgeted company profits, they are somewhat different from the basic corporate financial controls, and they are controls which are for the most part unique to the marketing area.

An analysis of the list thus illustrates a major thesis of this study: developing operating controls requires creating an integrated network of controls made up of both financial operating controls (related directly to overall financial controls) and other controls designed to meet individual operating requirements.

As can be seen from Table 8.1, the critical aspects of each marketing area are first isolated in developing marketing controls. For example, under customer service, control information is gathered on complaints, warranty claims and adjustments, exchanges and refunds, and service calls—each of which presumably provides a specific measure of the adequacy of customer service. Next, standards, measures of variance, and reporting systems are created.

The standards against which performance is measured vary according to the requirements of each area. The dollar and unit sales forecast is the standard used for sales control and the expense budget for expense control —both financial control standards. Planned performance is the standard

---

[1]Victor P. Buell, *Marketing Management in Action* (New York: McGraw-Hill Book Company, 1966), pp. 171-173.

Table 8.1

MARKETING MANAGEMENT CONTROL CHECKLIST[1]

Performance Information	Report frequency	Year-to-date	Standard	Variance shown by:	Marketing mgr.	Sales mgr.	Advertising mgr.	Marketing research mgr.	Product mgr.	Marketing services mgr.
					— Managers receiving reports · C = For control purposes · I = For information purposes					
1. Sales										
a. Total dollars	Daily or weekly	Yes	Forecast	Dollars and %	C	C	C	I	C	I
b. Units and dollars:										
(1) By product line	Weekly or monthly	"	"	Units, dollars and %	C	C	C	I	C	I
(2) By region	"	"	"	"	C	C	C	I	C	I
(3) By district	"	"	"	"	C	C	C	I	C	I
(4) By territory	"	"	"	"		C			C	
(5) By major accounts	Monthly	"	"	"	C	C		I	I	
2. Profits										
a. Net for company	"	"	"	Dollars and %	C					
b. Company return on investment	Quarterly	"	"	"	C					
c. Gross profit or marginal return:*										
(1) By product line	Monthly	"	"	"	C	I	I	I	C	I
(2) By region	"	"	"	"	C	C	I	I	C	I
(3) By district	"	"	"	"	C	C	I		I	
(4) By territory	"	"	"	"		C			I	
(5) By major accounts	"	"	"	"	C	C		I	I	
3. Expenses										
a. Total marketing	"	"	Budget	Dollars and %	C					
b. Each department	"	"	"	"	C	For control — receive report for own department only				
c. By region, district and territory	"	"	"	"		C				C
d. Administrative and rental for each branch office	"	"	"	"	C					C
e. Operating expense by field warehouse	"	"	"	"	C					C
f. Auto and truck	"	"	"	"	C					C
g. Product transportation	"	"	"	"	C				I	C
4. Production costs										
By product	"	"	"	"	I				I	I
5. Customer accounts										
a. Number added by region	"	"	Plan	Number		C				
b. Number lost by region	"	"	"	"		C				
c. Net change by region and total	"	"	"	"	I	C	I	I	I	I
6. Pricing										
Amount of variance from planned prices by product, region, and district	Weekly	Yes	Plan	Dollars and %	C	C	I	I	C	I
7. Inventory of finished goods										
a. By product:										
(1) Units	"	No	"	Units and %	C	C			C	C
(2) Number of days of supply	"	"	"	Number	C	C			C	C
b. By plant and warehouse:										
(1) Product by units	"	"	"	Units and %	C	C			C	C
(2) Product by number of days of supply	"	"	"	Number	C	C			C	C
8. Order backlog by product										
a. Number of orders in excess of standard time allowed to fill:										
(1) By plant	"	"	o	–	I	I			I	I
(2) By distribution point	"	"	o	–	C	I			I	C
b. Anticipated date will become current:										
(1) By plant	"	"	–	–	I	I			I	I
(2) By distribution point	"	"	–	–	C	I			I	C
9. Customer service										
a. Number of complaints by product and by type of complaint	Monthly	Yes	Acceptable ratio to units delivered	%	C	I	I	I	C	I
b. Number of warranty claims and adjustments	"	"	"	"	C	I			I	C
c. Number of exchanges and refunds	"	"	"	"	C	I			I	C
d. Number of technical service calls	"	"	Plan	Number and %	C	I			I	C
10. Credit										
a. Number of accounts and dollar amounts outstanding:										
(1) Over 10 days	"	No	Goal	Number, $, and %	C	C			I	C
(2) Over 30 days	"	"	"	"	C	C			I	C
(3) Over 60 days	"	"	"	"	C	C			I	C
b. Names of accounts with amounts over 60 days	"	"	–	–	C	C			I	C
11. Advertising										
a. Dollars spent by:										
(1) Media	"	Yes	Budget	Dollars and %	C	I	C		I	
(2) Sales promotion	"	"	"	"	C	I	C		I	
(3) Co-op	"	"	"	"	C	I	C		I	
b. Exceptions to schedules	"	No	Plan	–	C	I	C		C	
c. Status report on degree of readiness for trade shows and exhibits	"	"	"	–			C			
d. Status report on scheduled functions such as label design, signs, bulletins, product literature	"	"	"	–			C			C
e. Market awareness of, and preference for, company and products	Semi-annually	No	Goal	%	C	I	C	I	I	I
12. Marketing research										
a. Projects completed and projects pending, with expected completion dates	Monthly	No	Plan	Projects and % complete	C				C	I
b. Share of market:										
(1) By product line	Quarterly	"	Goal	"	C	C	C	I	C	I
(2) By region and district	"	"	"	"	C	C	C	I	C	I
13. Product planning										
a. Status of each product and packaging project with estimated completion date; new projects begun or scheduled	Monthly	"	Plan	Number of Weeks	C	I	I	I	C	I
b. Schedule of each project showing assignments for each department and estimated completion dates for each	"	"	"	"					C	
14. Marketing personnel										
a. Manning: Number of unfilled positions by type, number of weeks unfilled; and those for which candidates are being sought	"	"	–	–	C	For control—receive report for own department only				
b. Training:										
(1) Number and type of courses in process and completed	Quarterly	Yes	Plan	Statement of variance	C	"			"	
(2) Number and classifications of personnel attending and completed	"	"	"	"	C	"			"	

*Marginal return may be used by those companies using marginal income accounting.
NOTE: Information submitted to product manager normally will cover his assigned product lines only.

used for customer account control and an acceptable ratio to units delivered for customer service—both non-financial controls. The measure of deviation also varies with each control factor: expense deviations are measured in dollars and percents; sales deviations in units, dollars and percents; customer account deviations in numbers; product planning schedule deviations in days; and customer service deviations in percents.

The period covered and report frequency also vary according to each area's individual control requirements, from daily to semi-annually. And since not all marketing managers are involved in each control area, not all managers receive all the control reports.

A careful review of the checklist is important to an understanding of the nature of operating controls and the way in which these controls are developed. It presents a capsule summary of the network of controls used within a typical marketing operation. Under normal circumstances, the reporting system required to support these controls would be created by the systems development department. If the marketing manager is lucky, the systems department would also assist him in creating the original checklist and coordinating it with the overall accounting and finance department requirements. Whatever the corporate organization, however, every marketing manager should have a similar checklist for his operation—even if he has to prepare it himself.

There is considerable variation in the control reporting systems used in individual marketing operations. The following discussion examines specific examples of different kinds of control reports used in major marketing areas.

Management first needs an overall control report on actual and budgeted sales, its major responsibility. Table 8.2 illustrates a sales analysis report which shows actual and budgeted sales by product line.[2] In the first column major product lines are listed, the second column shows the budgeted sales in dollars by month for each product line, the third actual sales, and the fourth the dollar deviations in actual sales from budget. The next three columns show the same figures for the year to date. Other types of marketing operations may require different breakdowns of information: weekly instead of monthly figures; an additional column showing last year's results during the same periods; other kinds of product categories. While the actual form of the marketing sales analysis report may vary by company and type of marketing operation, the pattern of the report is the same: breakdown of information into critical control points; comparative columns; and a measure of deviations.

Detailed information on marketing expenses is also important to an evaluation of a company's marketing effort. An example of a marketing

---

[2]Adapted from J. Brooks Heckert and James D. Willson, *Controllership* (2nd ed.; New York: The Ronald Press Company, 1962), p. 198.

Table 8.2

ABC MANUFACTURING COMPANY[2]

Monthly Comparative Sales Analysis Report

Product	Month			Year to Date		
	Budgeted Sales	Actual Sales	Over or (Under) Budget	Budgeted Sales	Actual Sales	Over or (Under) Budget
COATING COMPOUNDS						
Alkyds............	$ 50,000	$ 52,315	$ 2,315	$ 190,000	$ 201,325	$ 11,325
Hard Resins.......	20,000	17,819	(2,181)	85,000	82,300	(2,700)
Ureas.............	320,000	321,510	1,510	1,410,000	1,520,000	110,000
Total...........	390,000	391,644	1,644	1,685,000	1,803,625	118,625
MOLDING COMPOUNDS						
Alkyds...........	190,000	197,410	7,410	860,000	812,520	(47,480)
Ureas............	25,000	22,820	(2,180)	82,000	71,900	(10,100)
Melamines........	415,000	472,320	57,320	1,560,000	1,611,000	51,000
Total...........	630,000	692,550	62,550	2,502,000	2,495,420	(6,580)
Grand Total.....	$1,020,000	$1,084,194	$64,194	$4,187,000	$4,299,045	$112,045
% of Budget......			106.3			102.7

Remarks:

139

expense control report is given in Table 8.3.[3] The report lists all the major expense categories in the left hand column. The next columns show the actual total expenses in each category. The remaining columns break total expenses down by type of market. The report is thus designed to help monitor expenses both in relation to type of expense and type of market. The line across the bottom identifies the percent of marketing expense to total sales, a control figure which is important in controlling overall company expenses and profits and which directly links this report with overall financial controls. The amount of variations were not identified in this report for two reasons: first, because it would have made the report too complex and so cumbersome to read; second, the size of variations can be read easily by inspection. As can be seen from an examination of this report, the marketing expense analysis report can be broken down by product, product line, or type of market, depending on the particular needs of the company. And the analysis can be shown in both dollars and percentages.

A company's marketing success depends to a great extent on its salesmen meeting their budgeted sales quotas. In comparing the actual sales of each salesman to budgeted sales, the salesman analysis report can either report on all salesmen or on an exception basis, that is, only on those salesment who did not meet their budgeted sales figure by more than a certain percentage. An example of an exception control report is given in Table 8.4.[4]

The left hand column of this report identifies the salesmen in the Pittsburgh district (and their number) who are under budget by a significant amount. Not all variations are significant in control, and each manager must determine what level of variation will generate action. In this report management estimated that any variation under 5% was part of normal operating variations and so not a cause for control action. This report differs in many ways from others examined. While total actual sales are shown, total budgeted sales are not shown—mainly because they are not as important as the variances that are shown. The total budgets could be eliminated from this report because it is a variance report, designed only to monitor salesman performance relative to budget standards. The reports shown earlier served a dual purpose, monitoring as they do both total sales and expenses by major category, and deviations of actual from budgeted performance.

A major problem with this type of control report is that it fails to identify those salesmen who exceeded budget and who may provide management with ways to improve overall performance. Wherever possible a control report should show favorable as well as unfavorable variances.

[3]Adapted from Buell, *Marketing Management in Action*, p. 180.
[4]Adapted from J. Brooks Heckert and James D. Willson, *Business Budgeting and Control* (3rd ed.; New York: The Ronald Press Company, 1967), p. 211.

Table 8.3

MONTHLY EVALUATION OF MARKETING EXPENSES BY
TYPE OF MARKET[3]

	Total		Regular Commercial		Direct Mail		International	
	Actual	Budget	Actual	Budget	Actual	Budget	Actual	Budget
Gross sales:								
Regular commercial	$38,000	$41,000	$38,000	$41,000				
Direct mail	10,000	9,500			$10,000	$ 9,500		
International	6,000	6,500					$ 6,000	$ 6,500
Total	54,000	57,000	38,000	41,000	10,000	9,500	$ 6,000	$ 6,500
Expenses:								
Discounts and Allowances	3,000	3,400	2,700	3,000	200	300	100	100
Per cent	6%	6%	7%	7%	2%	3.1%	2%	1.6%
Direct selling	600	700	600	700	--	--	--	--
All other selling:								
Central Sales Office	1,500	1,600	1,200	1,300	100	100	200	200
Regional Offices	100	100	100	100	--	--	--	--
Special Products	200	200	150	150	50	50	--	--
Total all other selling	1,800	1,900	1,450	1,550	150	150	200	200
Per cent	3%	3.3%	4%	3.8%	2%	2%	3%	3.1%
Market research	50	50	50	50	--	--	--	--
Advertising and sales promotion:								
General advertising	2,000	2,000	1,800	1,800	200	200	--	--
Special advertising	150	400	150	400	--	--	--	--
Sales promotion	600	600	600	600	--	--	--	--
Sales programs	300	400	300	400	--	--	--	--
Total	3,050	3,600	2,850	3,200	200	200	--	--
Per cent	6%	6.3%	8%	8%	2%	2.2%	--	--
Warehouse and delivery:								
Central Distribution	1,000	1,000	750	750	130	130	120	120
Regional Warehosing	400	400	400	400	--	--	--	--
Special Order Finished Goods	100	100	70	70	10	10	20	20
Total	1,500	1,500	1,220	1,220	110	110	110	110
Per cent	3%	2.6%	3%	3%	1%	1.5%	2%	2.1%
Total marketing	$10,000	$11,150	$ 8,870	$ 9,720	$ 690	$ 790	$ 410	$ 410
Per cent of sales	19%	19.6%	24.4%	24%	7%	8.3%	7%	6.8%

141

Table 8.4

ABC COMPANY[4]

Sales Analysis Report

Salesman Under Budget 5 Per Cent or More Year to Date

District Pittsburgh

Current Month and Year to Date

Description	Salesman No.	Current Month			Year to Date		
		Actual Sales	Under or Over Budget* Amount	%	Actual Sales	Under or Over Budget* Amount	%
PERFORMANCE SATISFACTORY		$ 827,432	$112,610 *	15.8 *	$4,623,096	$497,830 *	12.1 *
UNDER BUDGET PERFORMANCE:							
Abernathy	2609	32,016	1,760	5.2	102,600	6,300	5.8
Bristol	2671	17,433	1,390	7.4	61,080	4,270	6.5
Caldwell	2685	19,811	1,320	6.2	70,100	4,600	6.2
Fischer	2716	24,033	1,470	5.8	84,390	5,090	5.7
Gordon	2804	8,995	480	5.1	31,600	1,810	5.4
Inch	2827	27,666	1,820	6.2	97,010	5,930	5.8
Long	2982	4,277	600	12.3	15,020	900	5.7
Mather	3007	39,474	3,800	8.8	138,400	8,540	5.8
Owens	5066	43,189	4,400	9.6	151,800	9,080	5.6
Subtotal		216,894	17,040	7.3	752,000	46,520	5.8
District Total		$1,044,326	$ 95,570 *	10.1 *	$5,375,096	$451,310 *	9.2 *

* Figures marked with an asterisk are over budget; all others are under budget.

Management also needs control information on advertising and sales promotion effectiveness. Such reports basically deal with advertising and sales promotion costs by media classifications, although this information is sometimes also broken down by product. Table 8.5 gives an example of an advertising and promotion expense report that shows management how much money has been spent on advertising and sales promotion, how actual costs compare with budgeted costs, how much money will be spent on advertising and sales promotion in the future, and how much actual expenses for the period will be over or under budget.[5]

This control report differs from the ones examined thus far because of the nature of advertising expenses and the purpose of the control report. The report deals with a specific project or campaign, and so is limited to the expenses for that project. Commitments for advertising can be made many months before an advertisement actually appears and is paid for, so that a regular accounting report on how much advertising dollars have been spent is not a useful control tool. Instead a control report was developed specifically for advertising to show *commitments* (which are equivalent to expenses actually incurred) and *estimates* of remaining expenses, in order to arrive at an over or under budget figure. Such a report enables a manager to take action in using funds many months before he otherwise would be able to if he used a standard accounting expense control report which showed only actual expenditures to date.

This report typifies a problem faced by many operating managers. His primary objective is to maintain profits and sales, and to control sales expenses—major financial control areas. But the control tool or system he uses is not necessarily a standard financial control report. While the report in Table 8.5 uses dollars as a measure (as do financial reports) and so looks like a financial report on the surface, it is not a financial accounting report —for it does not report actual expenses, but commitments and estimates. Since commitments are usually not recognized as expenses by accounting control until a purchase order is issued and since estimates are a kind of reforecast, this is a mixed control report only partially within the financial control mold.

Generally, every manager has a whole network of controls which do not fit precisely into the accounting and finance mold, and he needs staff assistance in developing these controls. Where the overall company control department is too accounting oriented, it often lacks the perspective needed to provide this assistance. A systems department is, however, equipped to provide assistance in this situation and in situations involving non-financial controls. It is for this reason that control coordination is gradually passing into the hands of the system analyst and systems department in large companies.

[5]Heckert and Willson, *Business Budgeting and Control*, p. 344.

Table 8.5

ABC COMPANY

Monthly Status Report—Advertising and Sales Promotion Budget
(In Thousands of Dollars)

Category	Project Budget	Actual to 4/30/— Expenditures	Commitments	Total	Estimated Cost To Complete	Indicated Total Cost	Balance Available for Use or Transfer
Broadcast Media:							
Television							
National	$ 800	$270	$390	$ 660	$120	$ 780	$ 20
Local Spots	200	40	60	100	100	200	–
Total	1,000	310	450	760	220	980	20
Radio—Local	100	20	10	30	40	70	30
Total Broadcast	1,100	330	460	790	260	1,050	50
Printed Media:							
Consumer Magazines	140	70	20	90	40	130	10
Newspapers	90	20	10	30	20	50	40
Business Publications	40	30	10	40	–	40	–
Total	270	120	40	160	60	220	50
Direct Mail	180	110	60	170	20	190	(10)
Catalogs	70	60	10	70	–	70	–
Displays and Exhibits	80	–	70	70	30	100	(20)
Total Printed Media	600	290	180	470	110	580	20
Advertising Administration	300	100	–	100	200	300	–
GRAND TOTAL	$2,000	$720	$640	$1,360	$570	$1,930	$ 70

Management is also interested in the company's share of market. Such information enables management to determine how a company's products stand in relation to the rest of its industry.[6] An example of such a report for the XYZ Company's products is given in Table 8.6.

Table 8.6

XYZ COMPANY
SHARE OF TOTAL MARKET BY PRODUCT
QUARTERLY REPORT

Product	Estimated Share	Actual Share	Variance Actual—Estimated
A	13.6%	14.0%	+ .4%
B	8.5%	8.3%	− .2%
C	7.5%	6.5%	−1.0%
D	3.7%	3.9%	+ .2%
E	10.4%	11.5%	+1.1%
F	11.2%	11.2%	—

This report provides a horizontal analysis of variations by product. It is a variance report, and deals with a single measure of variance, the variation in percent of market.

The above sample control reports have been chosen to illustrate a wide variety of control tools and techniques in the marketing area. The reports show how each control report must be designed to meet the specific needs of the situation and the decision maker. They illustrate the various situations under which vertical analysis is used, where different kinds of deviation measurements are used, and how different critical control points are identified. And they show the degree to which overall financial controls influence and are tied in with the development of a network of controls in one operating area, marketing.

The control reports described above by no means cover all types of marketing control reports, for each company's operations will require different types and forms of reports and standards. Detailed examples of how one company handled control reporting on marketing operations are given in the discussion of *The National Observer* study in Chapter 14. There the company needs were well defined—mail-order marketing control —and the marketing control reports were structured to meet this need. However, that reporting system could not be transferred to another company in another industry. While reporting needs are generally the same in all marketing areas, therefore, the specific reports used will vary from company to company. Another example of control reports in the marketing area are found in the Frost Company study in Chapter 13.

---

[6]For a detailed discussion of share of market see Martin M. Eigen, "The Share of Market: A Focal Point for Financial Reporting," *N.A.A. Management Accounting*, July 1967, pp. 51-55.

Table 8.7

THE GENERAL CORPORATION
AIRCRAFT DIVISION

Monthly Manufacturing Expense Budget

Department __Fabrication__ Department Head __Carson__

Year ____ Normal Activity 85,000 hours Base ____ Standard labor hours

	Per Cent of Normal Activity							
	60%	70%	80%	90%	100%	110%	120%	136%
Salaries								
General Foremen	$ 700	$ 700	$ 700	$ 700	$ 700	$ 700	$ 700	$ 700
Foremen	1,900	1,900	1,900	2,200	2,200	2,200	2,600	2,600
Clerks, etc.	700	700	950	950	950	950	950	1,200
Subtotal:	3,300	3,300	3,550	3,850	3,850	3,850	4,250	4,500
Hourly Labor—Indirect	1,500	1,750	2,000	2,250	2,500	2,750	3,000	3,250
Fuel	360	400	440	480	520	560	600	640
Power	2,620	3,020	3,430	3,870	4,300	4,740	5,140	5,320
Water	210	220	230	240	250	260	270	280
Maintenance and Repairs	1,630	1,875	2,050	2,500	2,500	2,790	3,070	3,300
Supplies	270	315	360	405	450	495	540	585
Traveling	70	70	100	100	100	100	120	120
Telephone and Telegraph	70	80	90	100	100	100	120	120
Cartons and Containers	150	175	200	225	250	275	300	325
Recreation and Welfare	30	40	50	50	50	60	60	60
Miscellaneous	120	130	150	160	175	190	200	210
Subtotal:	10,330	11,375	12,650	14,230	15,045	16,170	17,670	18,710
Depreciation—Building	900	900	900	900	900	900	900	900
Depreciation—Machinery and Equipment	1,800	1,800	1,800	1,800	1,800	1,800	1,800	1,800
Property Taxes	1,200	1,200	1,200	1,200	1,200	1,200	1,200	1,200
Insurance	350	350	400	400	400	400	400	450
TOTAL	$14,580	$15,625	$16,950	$18,530	$19,345	$20,470	$21,970	$23,060

146

The pattern followed in all cases is the same, however: the control reports show actual results, performance standards, and some measure of deviation in those areas considered critical to success of the particular marketing operation under study; the forms of the control tools are tailored to meet the requirements of the situation and the purpose which the controls are designed to serve.

MANUFACTURING

Marketing does not operate in a vacuum. Its success is tied closely to the cost, quality and availability of the product sold. Manufacturing deals with all operations that are connected with producing a company's products.

As in marketing, control in manufacturing begins with the study of company plans: overall corporate plans, marketing plans and sales forecasts, and manufacturing plans. Within this planning framework, critical areas affecting operations are identified. These would include such areas as manufacturing expenses, production scheduling, manpower, physical plant and machinery, materials, and quality.[7] Manufacturing controls would be developed in all these critical areas.

Expense control in the manufacturing area is linked directly with overall company control through cost accounting, which was discussed in the last chapter. As in other control areas, expense control starts with establishing some form of standard or budget. Table 8.7 gives an example of a flexible manufacturing expense budget.[8] In this budget, standards are established by major expense area at different levels of operation and fixed and variable expenses are segregated. Cost accountants are usually responsible for developing these budgets, working with manufacturing management. Such a budget is flexible only in the sense that it varies with level of operations. For the level of operations attained, the budget is a fixed standard for monitoring performance efficiency. Such a flexible budget is needed for the manufacturing area because of the requirements of the manufacturing area: to produce the units required by marketing (whatever level that may be) at an economical cost.

The reports in which actual expense results are compared with budget will vary according to the requirements of the situation. Normally, there is an overall plant or facility control report. Table 8.8 gives a sample of such a report. In this report, variable and fixed expenses are segregated and the budgeted and actual figures (and the variances between them)

---

[7]Franklin G. Moore, *Manufacturing Management* (5th ed.; Homewood, Illinois; Richard D. Irwin, Inc., 1969); Richard J. Hopeman, *Production Concepts and Controls* (Columbus, Ohio: Charles E. Merrill Books, Inc., 1965).

[8]Elwood S. Buffa, *Modern Production Management* (3rd ed.; New York: John Wiley and Sons, Inc., 1969), p. 690.

Table 8.8

SUMMARY OF PLANT COSTS AND EXPENSES[9]
SAMPLE MONTH

	Fixed Costs			Variable Costs		
	Forecast	Actual	Deviation	Standard	Actual	Variance
Salaries	15,000	14,500	500			
Salaries O.T.	350	400	(50)			
Labor	40,000	36,700	3,300			
Labor O.T. Prem.	1,500	2,700	(1,200)			
Welfare—Salary	1,900	1,750	150			
Welfare—Wageroll	8,000	7,340	660			
Travel	100	—	100			
Supplies	6,500	8,250	(1,750)			
Sundries	150	1,200	(1,050)			
Chemicals	1,070	775	295	41,500	42,684	(1,184)
Catalyst Amortization	1,640	1,500	140			
Tel. & Tel.	900	1,150	(250)			
Fuel Gas	9,000	9,000	—	121,200	120,000	1,200
Material X				165,750	163,500	2,250
Purchased Electricity	28,385	28,385	—			
Purchased Water	2,400	3,000	(600)			
Royalty				500	500	—
Maintenance	50,000	50,000	—			
Feedwater				1,524	1,874	(350)
Electricity	32,150	32,150	—	56,500	57,927	(1,427)
Steam	8,000	9,250	(1,250)	47,100	46,959	141
Well Water	200	175	25	150	166	(16)
Mine Water	575	650	(75)			
Cooling Water	6,250	6,350	(100)	14,600	15,650	(1,050)
TOTAL	214,070	215,225	(1,155)	448,824	449,260	(436)

are given for all major categories of expenses. The report covers only those items under the control of the plant manager, so that depreciation, taxes, and insurance are not covered. In this report, labor expenses are fixed, because of the technical nature of the operation. In other types of manufacturing operations, such as dress manufacturing, labor would be variable with output—another illustration of how the exact form of the control tool will vary to meet the requirements of the manufacturing operation.

In most manufacturing situations, control of manufacturing operations is broken down by department and by product. Table 8.9 identifies expenses by department.[10] This report covers not only those areas under the control of the department, but also depreciation allocated to the department. It thus can be used both as a measure of department efficiency, by

[9]Richard E. Williams, "Converting to a Direct Costing System," N.A.A. Management Accounting, January 1968, p. 33.

[10]Adapted from I, Wayne Keller and William L. Ferrara, Management Accounting for Profit Control (2nd ed.; New York: McGraw-Hill Book Company, 1966), p. 250.

Table 8.9

MONTHLY DEPARTMENTAL COST REPORT[10]
DEPARTMENT M

	Budget	Actual	Variance
Direct materials...............	$10,500	$10,200	$(300) *
Direct labor....................	18,400	18,800	400
Indirect labor..................	2,800	2,900	100
Idle time......................	500	550	50
Supplies.......................	340	325	(15)*
Stationery.....................	110	106	(4)*
Salaries—department head........	1,200	1,200	
Salaries—staff.................	800	750	(50)*
Depreciation—equipment.........	4,800	4,800	
Depreciation—building..........	2,200	2,200	
Payroll taxes...................	810	870	60
Insurance.....................	220	220	
Total......................	$42,680	$42,921	$ 241

* Favorable.

ignoring the fixed items and examining only the variances in items under the department manager's control, as well as a measure of the department's position relative to the entire manufacturing operation. If the department is not processing adequate volume to justify the amount of depreciation assigned to it, either the assignment is inaccurate, the department occupies too much plant space or has too much machinery, or volume is abnormally low for the period. It is fairly common in a business to have control reports which serve dual purposes, in order to economize on data collection and reporting. There is nothing wrong with this practice, providing both purposes can effectively be served by the report.

A third kind of manufacturing expense control report is by product. Table 8.10 shows such a report. This report makes use of standard costs, that is, the amount it should have cost to make a product. These standard costs are developed by cost accounting, and the process by which they are developed was explained in the last chapter. These standard costs are then adjusted on the basis of variations in inventory valuation and current market prices, actual factory overhead expenses, and material purchase and usage variances, to arrive at an actual cost of sales by product. In this report the standard cost system enables allocation of manufacturing expenses to individual products and so the control of individual product costs. The standard cost system also facilitates the general control of certain overhead,

Table 8.10

ABC COMPANY[11]

MONTHLY SALES AND COST OF SALES

| | January | | | |
	Actual	Budget	Over (Under)	Per Cent of Change
Sales volume in units:				
Product A	1,800	2,000	(200)	(10.00)
Product B	2,100	2,000	100	5.00
Product C	7,600	8,000	(400)	(5.00)
Sales, cost of sales, and				
gross margin:				
Product A:				
Sales	$144,000	$160,000	($16,000)	(10.00)
Standard cost of sales	95,040	105,600	(10,560)	(10.00)
Standard gross margin	$ 48,960	$ 54,400	($ 5,440)	(10.00)
Product B:				
Sales	$187,000	$180,000	$ 7,000	3.89
Standard cost of sales	135,450	129,000	6,450	5.00
Standard gross margin	$ 51,550	51,000	$ 550	1.08
Product C:				
Sales	$258,400	$280,000	$21,600)	(7.71)
Standard cost of sales	219,640	231,200	(11,560)	(5.00)
Standard gross margin	$ 38,760	$ 48,800	($10,040)	(20.57)
Total sales	$589,400	$620,000	($30,600)	(4.94)
Total standard cost of				
sales	$450,130	$465,800	($15,670)	(3.36)
Adjustments:				
Variations in standards				
in opening inventory				
sales				
1,000 of Product A	800	800		
2,100 of Product B	(7,350)	(7,000)	(350)	(5.00)
6,000 of Product C	3,000	3,000		
Overabsorption of factory				
burden	7,000	7,200	(200)	(2.78)
Purchase variance—				
direct materials				
(Material A-1)	4,000		4,000	$4,000
Material usage variance,				
direct materials				
(Material B-2)	(400)		(400)	($ 400)
Cost of sales, actual	$443,080	$461,800	($18,720)	(4.05)
Gross margin, actual	$146,320	$158,200	($11,880)	(7.51)
Gross margin, standard	$139,270	$154,200	($14,930)	(9.68)

[11]Adapted from Herman C. Heiser, *Budgeting: Principles and Practices* (New York: The Ronald Press Company, 1959), p. 119.

material, and inventory items by showing the variances in these items of actual costs from budgeted standard costs. Variances in these reports are shown both in dollars and percentages, in order to show both the absolute and the relative value of each variance.

Table 8.11

WEEKLY FACTORY LABOR EXPENSE COMPARISONS[12]

Dept. A

	Week			Month to date		
	Incurred cost	Budget allow.	* Deviation	Incurred cost	Budget allow.	Deviation
Earned hours	1,382			1,382		
Standard labor	3,904	3,708	196 *	3,904	3,708	196
Sub-std. labor	352	216	136 *	352	216	136
Total direct labor	4,256	3,924	332 *	4,256	3,924	332
Tot. wait time	165	139	26 *	165	139	26
Empl. welfare & srv.	9		*	9		
Union activities	6		*	6		
Tot. employee act.	15	37	—22 *	15	37	—22
Tot. training	88	10	78 *	88	10	78
Overtime	105	55	50 *	105	55	50
Setup-reg. prod.	1,317		*	1,317		
Setup-tool trouble	616		*	616		
Tot. setup	1,933	1,793	140 *	1,933	1,793	140
8200	—3		*	—3		
Salv.-operating	161		*	161		
Salv.-other	3		*	3		
Tot. salvage	161	67	94 *	161	67	94
Group leaders	924		*	924		
Clerical	59		*	59		
Tot. dept. admin.	983	804	179 *	983	804	179
Stockmen	397		*	397		
Tot. stock handling	397	442	—45 *	397	442	—45
Lunch & washup	81		*	81		
Night shift bonus	261		*	261		
Tot. premiums	342	340	2 *	342	340	2
Prod. lab. not std.	79	121	—42 *	79	121	—42
Maint. lab-mach. eqp.	7		*	7		
Tot. tool rpr. maint.	7	16	— 9 *	7	16	— 9
Tot. repair & rebld.		1	— 1 *		1	— 1
Crib attendants	92	191	—99 *	92	191	—99
Missing labor	59		*	59		
Experimental work	73		*	73		
General ind. labor	69		*	69		
8406	13		*	13		
Tot. misc. labor	214	32	182 *	214	32	182
Total burden labor	4,581	4,048	533 *	4,581	4,048	533
Total all labor	8,837	7,972	865 *	8,837	7,972	865
SM. tools & gauges	243		*	243		

12A. J. Diedrich and D. A. Dinker, "Flexible Budgeting—A Proven Computer Application," N.A.A. Management Accounting, August 1966, p. 23.

Labor can be a major expense item in the manufacturing operation. Table 8.11 shows a factory labor expense control report. In this report direct labor and indirect (or burden) labor are segregated and the figures shown for both the current week and for the month to date. Direct and indirect labor are segregated because the first is related to output and the second is not, and as a result each expense is controlled by different kinds of administrative action.

The sample expense control reports given above are designed only to give some indication of the general areas covered in manufacturing reports. Additional breakdowns are needed in all areas. For example, control reports are usually developed for overhead expenses. An example of such a report is given in Table 8.12.

As can be seen from the above discussion of manufacturing expense control reports, their final form will depend on the type of manufacturing operation and the purpose (or purposes) that the expense control report is designed to serve. While not all types of expense control reports have been covered, the discussion shows some of the major expense control areas and the financial tools and techniques used in manufacturing expense control.

Expense controls are given greater emphasis in manufacturing controls, because manufacturing is almost entirely a "cost" operation and is more easily subjectable to financial accounting control. In the manufacturing area, money is spent to produce tangible items, to which the manufacturing expenses can be affixed. In most manufacturing operations the movement from money expended to the production of a finished item can be traced with a high degree of accuracy, and so costed and controlled more objectively.

In contrast, money is spent in marketing to generate sales. In retrospect, the cost of getting these sales can be accounted for. But the process by which the sales are produced is less measurable, mainly because many factors affecting sales, such as consumer behavior and economic trends, cannot be predicted as easily as factors affecting manufacturing processes, nor can they be controlled as directly as segments of the manufacturing process.

The inherent differences between the manufacturing and market processes account for the differences in the network of controls in each area and for the greater emphasis given to financial controls in the manufacturing area. While the network of manufacturing controls is more financially oriented, however, other types of controls are also needed in the manufacturing area.

Production scheduling control is basically the control of the operations and elements required to produce a company's products. The simplest forms of output controls are the schedule boards and charts which give visual control of the amounts and dates of production. These controls are used mainly for short-term production scheduling and are used instead of control reports where they are easier to keep current than written reports. Control reports comparing output with standards are generally used more for larger operations and for more extended reporting periods.

Table 8.12

C. F. CHURCH MFG. CO.[13]
HOLYOKE
ANALYSIS OF OVERHEAD EXPENSES

Department #3   *Month June*

		Budget	Actual Expense	Over or Under Actual
INDIRECT LABOR				
01	Supervision	775.00	756.00	19.00
04	Truck Drivers & Helpers			
06	Shipping			
08	General Labor	440.00	417.69	22.31
09	Repair and Rework			
10	Idle and Lost Time			
11	Guaranteed Rate Cost	263.00	50.14	212.86
16	Overtime Bonus	80.00	36.96	43.04
19	Repairs & Maint. & Mchy. & Equip.	160.00	34.79	125.21
17	Vacations			
21	Paid Holidays			
	Total	1,718.00	1,295.58	422.42
INDIRECT SUPPLIES				
31	Repairs & Maint. & Mchy. & Equip.	20.00	175.53	(155.53)
33	Repairs & Maint. Trucks			
35	Acetone & Isotone	1,140.00	1,030.78	109.22
36	Buffing Compounds & Buffs			
37	Sandpaper & Sandbelts	8.00	4.80	3.20
39	Labels, Tape, etc. Glue & Cement	540.00	181.67	358.33
40	Shipping Cartons			
41	Consumable Supplies	88.00	47.94	40.06
42	Loose & Hand Tools	35.00	9.86	25.14
46	Miscellaneous	10.00	9.20	80
	Total	1,841.00	1,459.78	381.22
OTHER OVERHEAD expenses				
Insurance, power, taxes ⎱				
Social security, depreciation ⎰		1,910.22	1,835.81	74.41
Group insurance, & pension				
DEFECTIVE WORK		600.00	593.83	6.17
DIRECT LABOR		6,562.00	6,598.01	(36.01)

[13]*C. F. Church Manufacturing Company*, A case prepared for the Harvard Graduate School of Business Administration, 1964, p. 22.

The most complex kinds of production scheduling control involve the use of computers. For example, Hazeltine Corporation uses computer simulation for control of its complex job-shop scheduling.[14] A "simulated" model of the job-shop is programmed. First, priority rules are established for dispatching orders. A large number of different factors are taken into account in calculating priorities, including estimated processing time, order due date, amount of work remaining after current operations, and the value of the order. Once such priority rules have been established, the scheduling of orders on hand and anticipated orders is simulated on the computer using the priority rules. The simulated results are then examined: some orders have been finished on time, others have not; work-in-process inventory averaged some given level; and machine and labor capacity were utilized at a given rate. If the decisions made with the simulated model are satisfactory, the same simulated sequence is used in the shop and becomes the control standard for monitoring production. If not, corrective steps can be taken, such as modifying the priority rules or adjusting overtime work, until a satisfactory schedule is developed. Additional examples of the use of the computer and operations research models in establishing inventory, distribution, and production control standards are given in Chapters 9 and 10.

The purpose of this section is not, however, to anticipate the description of the graphic, mathematical, and computer tools discussed in Chapters 9 and 10. Rather, this section concentrates on the basic control needs in the manufacturing area and the characteristics of the reporting tools used to meet these control needs.

Production control involves more than merely the control of production schedules—that is, the quantities and timing of production through graphic controls, mathematical programming, and control reports. The utilization of manpower, machines and material in meeting production requirements also needs to be controlled. Table 8.13 illustrates one way in which manpower utilization is controlled. In this report, actual and expected production are listed, as are the actual and expected production hours and the variances from expected hours, by operator. The hourly figures are broken down into five minute (one twelfth of an hour) segments. This report is sufficiently detailed to enable determining by operator where operator efficiency is below budgeted expectations.

Considerable care is needed in using these types of reports, because of the time involved in preparing them. In this instance, labor represented a significant enough cost element to justify elaborate manual controls.

The report shown in Table 8.13 illustrates how the network of operating controls is at the same time different from overall financial controls,

[14]M. J. Kantrowitz, *Dynamic Priorities* (Little Neck, New Jersey: Hazeltine Corporation, September 1968).

Table 8.13

GILLETTE SAFETY RAZOR COMPANY 15
DAILY REPORT OF PRODUCTION BY OPERATORS

DATE   490 BUFFING DEPARTMENT

	Total Expected Hours	181 9
"	Productive Hours Not Measured	48 6
	Lost Hours	13 3
	Gained Hours	5
	Nonproductive Hours Charged to This Dept.	50 4
"	" Not Charged to This Dept.	2
	Loaned Hours	48
	Total Actual Hours Worked incl. Loaned	343 10

	Name	Operation Number	Acct.	Total Actual	Expected per Hour	Expected	Actual	Diff Red-Loss R	Bl.-Gain B	Operation Number	Acct.	Total Actual	Expected per Hour	Expected	Actual	Diff Red-Loss R	Bl.-Gain B
4126	MOORE, STELLA	195 D 20	502	2800	375	7	6	8	6								
4126	MOORE, STELLA																
4127	MACCAREY, ELEANOR	1001 DG 25	502	2800	-		7										
4127	MACCAREY, ELEANOR	195 DG 25	502	400	400	1	1										
4128	MURPHY, ELLEN	1005 R 200	502	200			1 9			195 D 20	502	450	375	1 2	1 6	4	
4128	MURPHY, ELLEN	1005 RG 26	502	100			6			194 H 20	522	600	300	2 3	3	1 3	
4129	LEIGH, VIRGINIA	139 B 204	502	20000	2250	8 11	8	11									
4129	LEIGH, VIRGINIA																
4130	FILLIPETTI, RUTH	195 D 20	502	2100	375	5 7	7 10	2 3									
4130	FILLIPETTI, RUTH																
4131	LURRELLO, HELEN	139 B 24	502	14000	1750	8	8										
4131	LURRELLO, HELEN																
4132	CONRAD, HORTENSE	Loaned					8										
4132	CONRAD, HORTENSE																
4133	O'LEARY, KATHARINE	1005 AG 210	502	76			3										
4133	O'LEARY, KATHARINE	195 D 20	502	2275	375	6 1	7 9	1 8									
4134	WOODROW, ESTHER	139 B 206	502	20000	2250	8 11	8	11									
4134	WOODROW, ESTHER																
4135	ROVETA, MILDRED	195 C 24	502	12000	1750	6 10	8	1 2									
4135	ROVETA, MILDRED																
4136	CAPRA, JOSEPHINE	1004 A 20	522	500		3 5											
4136	CAPRA, JOSEPHINE	195 D 20	502	1600	375	4 3	4 7	4									
4137	CASSIDY, ELINOR	195 D 20	502	2400	375	6 5	8	1 7									
4137	CASSIDY, ELINOR																
4138	LOVITT, MARION	Group															
4138	LOVITT, MARION																
4139	LESLIE, ALTHEA	1004 A 20	522	1100			8										
4139	LESLIE, ALTHEA																
4140	SMITH, MARY	139 B 29	502	14000	1750	8	8										
4140	SMITH, MARY																
4141	GRADY, ANNE	Loaned															
4141	GRADY, ANNE																
4142	LAMB, ELIZABETH	1001 D 211	502	23000	3500	6 7	8	1 5									
4142	LAMB, ELIZABETH																

yet closely related to them. Financial controls are concerned with the dollar cost of each item produced, and part of that cost is labor. While the financial control reports may show when labor costs are or are not in line with budgeted costs, they cannot be used to actually control those costs at the operating level. Labor costs by product are a function of the time a worker spends on each unit of production, so that operating control in-

Table 8.14

ABC COMPANY

Weekly Summary of Idle Machine Hours

Department	Available Hours	Operating Hours	Lost Hours	% Available Hours Utilized	REASON FOR LOST HOURS				COST OF IDLE TIME			
					Lack of Material	Lack of Orders	Operating Down Time	Other Unsort. For	Out of Pocket	Total Dept. Cost	Lost Pounds	Lost Profit
PHENOLIC SYSTEM												
51 Mixing	304	304	–	100.0	–	–	–	–	$ –	$ –	–	$ –
52 Milling	456	456	–	100.0	–	–	–	–	–	–	–	–
53 Grinding	1,872	1,870	2	99.9	–	–	2	–	5	12	624	115
54 Granulating—1	48	45	3	93.7	–	–	3	–	16	43	1,437	376
55 Screening	864	864	–	100.0	–	–	–	–	–	–	–	–
56 Granulating—2	144	144	–	100.0	–	–	–	–	–	–	–	–
Total or Average	3,688	3,683	5	99.9	–	–	5	–	$ 21	$ 55		$ 491
MELAMINE RESIN SYSTEM												
21 Mixing	240	120	120	50.0	–	120	–	–	$ –	$ 738	135,451	12,466
22 Milling—5	120	46	74	38.3	–	–	–	74	548	1,907	191,257	16,352
23 Milling—7	240	164	76	68.3	–	–	–	76	293	521	53,387	4,565
24 Grinding	120	115	5	95.8	–	–	–	5	19	45	5,647	523
27 Granulating—3	120	96	24	80.0	–	–	–	24	56	118	6,228	532
31 Granulating—4	120	118	2	98.3	–	–	2	–	35	100	2,381	204
Total or Average	960	659	301	68.6	–	120	2	179	$ 951	$3,429		$34,642
INDUSTRIAL RESINS SYSTEM												
106 Drying	120	111	9	92.5	–	–	9	–	$ 72	$ 257	6,390	353
111 Blending	240	111	129	46.3	–	129	1	–	260	1,486	124,227	6,870
112 Liquid Resins	120	119	1	99.2	–	–	1	–	2	12	766	14
114 "200" Series	120	111	9	92.5	–	9	–	–	55	118	3,402	154
Total or Average	600	452	148	75.3	–	138	10	–	$ 389	$1,873		$ 7,391
Grand Total	5,248	4,794	454	91.3	–	258	17	179	$1,361	$5,357		$42,524

volves monitoring time a worker spends on a unit. Given this type of operation, the control report was designed around labor minutes and hours in relation to units produced—that is, the control tool was designed to suit the operation being controlled. It functions to control labor costs, but uses non-financial forms of measurement.

Table 8.14, which gives a control report on machine usage, is another example of a control in the manufacturing area which is basically non-financial but which is also closely tied to financial control.[16] In this report, machine utilization is calculated for each department by percent. The number of hours "lost" or under standard (available hours) are also shown, as are the reasons for underutilization where possible. The dollar cost of the underutilization is also given as a measure of its impact on overall manufacturing expenses and profits, thus giving this report an added financial control dimension. The report facilitates easy control of how efficiently factory machinery is being used by department and by product line.

Materials control is another major aspect of manufacturing control. Materials controls cover such areas as the cost of raw materials, inventory levels, and reordering. Tables 8.15,[17] 8.16, 8.17[19] give examples of control reports in each of these areas. The first covers the overall cost of materials purchased, broken down into supplier and product categories. Both the budgeted and actual unit and total costs are shown, as well as the amount of variance by item and by date. The second report covers total inventory levels and inventory usage. As in the first report, variances are shown in dollar amounts. This report is also an extension of the financial control system. The third report is a simple inventory reorder control report, and is a non-financial control used to maintain inventory at levels needed to maintain production schedules. This report shows on-hand inventory, orders placed, and reorder points for all items whose inventory is below minimum standards. As can be seen from the report, orders were placed when inventories fell below the reorder point. The quantity ordered is set by a predetermined reorder standard (the last column). Based on this report, orders need to be placed for the last two items.

Control reports are needed in all areas of manufacturing to assist management in monitoring performance. As in the marketing area, the controls are developed for the critical areas of the operation, and their form and standards are dictated by the operation being controlled and the

15Robert N. Anthony, *Management Accounting: Text and Cases* (3rd ed.; Homewood, Illinois: Richard D. Irwin, Inc., 1964), pp. 382-383.

16Heckert and Willson, *Business Budgeting and Control*, p. 477.

17Adapted from William H. Childs, *Accounting for Management Control* (New York: Simmons-Boardman, 1960), p. 657.

19Arnold P. McIlwain, "Utilizing EDP for Stock Material Inventory Transactions," *N.A.A. Management Accounting*, August 1967, p. 31.

Table 8.15

MONTHLY RAW MATERIALS PURCHASES REPORT

Lumber			Budget			Actual			Variances (Over)/Under		
Date	Supplier	Voucher No.	Quantity	Price	Amount	Quantity	Price	Amount	Price	Quantity	Net
	Budgeted		6,473 M	$200	$1,294,600						
1/2	Jamestown Mills	865				500 M	$210	$ 105,000	($ 5,000)		
1/8	Ralston and Co.	886				2,000 M	195	390,000	10,000		
1/12	Jamestown Mills	897				3,000 M	220	660,000	(60,000)		
	Variance from budget quantity at standard price									$194,600	
	Totals—Lumber		6,473 M	$200	$1,294,600	5,500 M	$210 (Average)	$1,155,000	($55,000)	$194,600	$139,600
Hardware											
Date											
	Budgeted		1,024,800	$.50	$ 512,400						
1/2	Townley Copper and Brass	866				200,000	$.50	$ 100,000	$ 0		
1/5	Old Lyme Reproductions, Inc.	875				300,000	.40	120,000	30,000		
1/10	Revere Hardware Co.	892				700,000	.44	308,000	42,000		
	Variance from budget quantity at standard price									($87,600)	
	Totals—Hardware		1,024,800	$.50	$ 512,400	1,200,000	$.44 (Average)	$ 528,000	$72,000	($87,600)	($15,600)
	Totals—Raw Materials				$1,807,000			$1,683,000			$124,000

158

Table 8.16

MONTHLY INVENTORY ANALYSIS REPORT[18]

Division Summary

Raw Materials

Product Plant	Total Inventory	Surplus Items	Net Inventory	Allowable Stock	Inventory Excess
A	$ 580,000	$ 76,000	$ 504,000	$ 466,000	$38,000
B	670,500	55,500	615,000	606,000	9,000
C	178,700	—	178,700	207,000	(28,300)
D	619,000	20,000	599,000	585,000	14,000
Total	$2,048,200	$151,500	$1,896,700	$1,864,000	$32,700
August	$2,062,600	$158,000	$1,904,600	$1,843,000	$61,600
July	2,048,100	165,000	1,883,100	1,795,400	87,700
June	2,020,200	140,000	1,880,200	1,850,500	29,700

Finished & In-Process

Product Plant	Total Inventory	Surplus Items	Net Inventory	Allowable Stock	Inventory Excess
A	$ 570,000	$ 25,000	$ 545,000	$ 517,000	$28,000
B	577,000	—	577,000	535,000	42,000
C	380,000	—	380,000	373,000	7,000
D	1,090,000	75,000	1,015,000	1,075,000	(60,000)
Total	$2,617,000	$100,000	$2,517,000	$2,500,000	$17,000
August	$2,640,500	$110,000	$2,530,500	$2,495,000	$35,500
July	2,563,000	118,000	2,445,000	2,420,000	25,000
June	2,544,000	109,000	2,435,000	2,390,000	45,000

Note: 1. Total inventory figures are before any deductions for balance-sheet reserves.
2. Excess inventory represents amount the net inventory is over the budget stocks for going rate of sales and production.

purpose the controls are designed to serve. This discussion, like that on marketing controls, by no means covers all areas of manufacturing control, nor all types of control tools used in manufacturing. Computers are used extensively in manufacturing control, as are many graphic and mathematical tools. Examples of the use of these tools in manufacturing and other business areas are discussed in Chapters 9 and 10. The discussion in this section does, however, give an idea of the range of control requirements in the manufacturing area, and of some of the most widely used kinds of manufacturing control reports.

[18]Charles H. Gleason, "Inventory Control through Budgeted Turnover," *N.A.A. Bulletin*, December 1953, p. 540.

Table 8.17

UPDATING OF INVENTORY
MONTHLY STOCK REORDER REPORT[19]

Inventory Code	Description	On Hand	On Order	P.O. Number	Reserved	Reorder Point	Quantity Needed
2-044-440	Bolt sq hd machine nut 3/4 x 12	14	100	M00636		50	100
2-044-496	Bolt sq hd machine nut 7/8 x 3-3/4	292	675	M00630		300	675
2-212-064	Nut-Flexloc cad plat 1/2	3	25	M00637		5	25
2-312-004	Cotter pin brass 1/16 x 2	468	1,000	M00638		500	1,000
2-436-076	Screw hx bd cap plt 1/4 x 1-1/2	246	600	M00639		300	600
6-386-096	Terminal tube tem br 4 F 3/4 FO 34	23				30	60
38-760-192	Pipe stl std galv T & C 2 in	69		R.I.		550	2,730

PERSONNEL

The personnel function, like many other staff functions, reaches into many areas of a business' operations. Like the operating areas discussed above, the personnel area has it own peculiar requirements, which must be met in developing controls. While there are these individual requirements, however, the same steps in the management control process guide the development of personnel controls: the control problem is defined; key factors, such as the planning base, the requirements of the situation, and the purpose of the controls, are isolated; control systems and tools are developed within the limitations set by the key factors.

Personnel planning is closely related to overall corporate planning. In the same way that a company must take steps to have the buildings and machines needed to meet sales growth objectives, it must also have trained management and labor resources. Personnel controls are closely related to overall corporate controls, because the personnel department monitors the cost, as well as the use, of people working within a company.

Personnel planning standards extended into most areas of a company's operation, and monitor not only manning levels, but also wage and salary levels and the efficiency of the use of personnel. The controls designed to aid personnel management in achieving planned objectives and maintaining overall company cost control thus cover such areas as: manning levels; manpower and skills inventories, job specifications, wage and salary administration, employee benefits, recruiting, appraisals, turnover, absenteeism, grievances and injuries. Unlike marketing and manufacturing, personnel is not an operating function. As a result, greater emphasis is given to non-financial controls in this area.

A very simple management manpower plan translated into a report format useful as a control standard is shown in Table 8.18. The footnote gives in capsule form the figures which must be met in order to have sufficient management personnel to meet future yearly requirements. If not met, these control standards should generate increased hiring and training activity.

The personnel department or manager is responsible for maintaining the basic records of all employees. These records provide the raw data for many personnel control reports. Depending on the size of the company, these records may be kept either manually or by computer systems. Such records normally show the employees past experience and education, as well as his work record, wage or salary, and additional education after joining the company.

In most larger companies, electronic data processing systems are used to maintain employee records. Such a system enables the gathering, storing and reporting of vast amounts of control information on various aspects of the personnel operation—number of employees by job or salary classifi-

Table 8.18

FIVE-YEAR MANAGEMENT REPLACEMENT PLAN[20]

Position	No. of Positions	Quits	Normal Retire.	Death & Early Retire.	Total	Cumul. Promotions
President..............	1	..	1	..	1	1
Executive staff..........	13	..	4	..	4	5
General staff............	39	..	11	5	16	21
4th level...............	115	6	40	14	60	81
5th level...............	162	2	36	19	57	138
	330	8	92	38	138	246

*Briefly, we must be prepared to: (1) produce at least 1 new top executive; (2) produce 2 department managers per year; (3) upgrade 22 people per year at the middle management level; (4) hire and retain annually 14 young people with good management potential.

cation, their qualifications, turnover, injury and absenteeism levels and rates, recruiting performance, and the like.[21] The computer is a great aid in personnel control, for it enables faster, more complete and more extensive control reporting on a company's work force.[22]

In more advanced computerized personnel record-keeping systems, these records function as a skills inventory—that is, a systematically organized inventory of the skills and past job experience of each employee, which can be reviewed and drawn from when job openings need to be filled elsewhere in the company. Such a system enables control of the allocation of available manpower resources within the company.

In order to control personnel levels and expenses, all the jobs within a company must first be described and classified. Individual job specifications cover such elements as:

1.   Job title or titles.
2.   Number of employees on the job.
3.   Number of immediate supervisors.
4.   Equipment used or worked with.
5.   Hours of work and wage levels.
6.   Educational and experience requirements.
7.   Skills, aptitudes, and abilities required.
8.   Description of actual work performed.

[20]Adapted from Michael J. Jucius, *Personnel Management* (5th ed.; Homewood, Illinois: Richard D. Irwin, Inc., 1963), p. 125.
[21]Howard Y. Weatherbee, "Personnel Data Systems and the Computer," *Personnel*, July-August 1968, p. 58.
[22]See Charles E. J. Cassidy, "Electronic Data Processing and the Personnel Function: The Present and the Future," *Personnel Journal*, June 1966, pp. 352-356.

Figure 8.1

BAND SAW OPERATOR[23]
JOB DESCRIPTION

1. COMPANY NAME: __X. Y. Z. Co.__   2. PAGE NO. __1A__   LINE NO. __5__
(Part I of Manning Table)

3. PLANT NAME: _____   4. DEPARTMENT: __Production Lathe__

5. JOB TITLE: __BAND-SAW OPERATOR__
(List first most common title used in plant and any additional titles - separate by semi-colons)

6. MINIMUM TIME NOW REQUIRED TO TRAIN A REPLACEMENT: __200 hours__

7. SPECIAL PHYSICAL REQUIREMENTS: __NONE__
(State unusual requirements of job - eyesight, strength or other, and what portion of the job requires this trait.)

8. SUPERVISION: __Receives work assignments from Foreman, completing them according to prescribed standards.__
(Indicate type of supervision received or given)

9. DESCRIPTION OF WORK PERFORMED:
SUMMARY *(Give overall picture of job in one or two sentences.)* Cuts sheet metal blanks to specified dimensions using a power-driven band saw.

Steps performed in the job	Percent of Time	Exactly How Performed (Include special skills, machinery, tools, judgments, decisions)
*a. Marks sheet for entry, according to specifications	13%	Lays out lines to be cut using T square, compass, triangle and chalk or scriber.
b. Clamps marked sheet to work table	5%	Uses clamps to fasten workpiece to table.
c. Directs lubricating fluid against cutting edge	2%	
d. Cuts blank from sheet **	80%	Starts saw and turns handwheel or engages power-driven feed to move stock against blade of saw.

10. COMMENTS: (Use this space to enter additional information explaining items on this form; to give additional facts about this job; to indicate where job fits into industrial process; to explain difference between this and similar jobs; to define any special terms peculiar to the job; or any other pertinent information.)

Worker must exercise care to avoid amputating fingers.

Indicate most essential skill with *.
Indicate next most essential skill with **.

Figures 8.1 and 8.2[24] give examples of job analysis reports. While the form of each varies, both cover the basic elements listed above—with the

[23]Jucius, *Personnel Management*, pp. 104-105.
[24]Buffa, *Modern Production Management*, pp. 656-657.

Figure 8.2

JOB ANALYSIS WORK SHEET 24.

Machine and Manufacturing Co.

Job title BROWN & SHARPE MACH. OPERATOR, CAM LAYOUT   Code 12:104
Other titles AND CUTTING
Suggested title
Dept. CHUCKER   Dept. No. 12   Supr. P. Wurtz
No. on job   Lead Man
Persons interviewed Joe Hall
Analyst E.B.S.   Date

Job Summary (key phrases that cover job):
Makes cams for, sets up, and operates Brown & Sharpe machine.
Procures materials, tends machine, sharpens tools.

Work Performed: What-How-Why (Use additional sheet if req'd)
1. Makes cams for Brown & Sharpe machine setups. Works from blueprints and M.O.T. to calculate travel lengths and rises on cams required to advance tools, set depth of cuts and timing of tools. Scribes pattern on cam and cuts out on doall saw, finishing by hand. Designs tooling for machine.
2. Sets up machine. Works from blueprints and M.O.T. to set up cams and gears for required sequence of operations. Times machine; checks parts to be sure of proper set up.
3. Operates machine. Checks parts periodically as machine automatically produces parts. Sharpens and replaces tools as they wear. Oils machine periodically (3 times/day). Gets stock and cams in preparation for next job.

Equipment, machines used:
Brown & Sharpe #2   Doall Saw
Precision tools for checking work   Hand tools.

Requirements of Job (Minimum)
(Think of the job—not the man)

SKILL
1. Education Requirements - Must be able to read blueprints, use precision gauges and know how to sharpen tools to required angles for materials used. Uses shop math. to calculate required travel and rises on cam.
2. Experience Requirements   Five years plus one year on cam making.
3. Initiative—Ingenuity - Machine set up, cam making. Alert to new ideas and techniques.

EFFORT
4. Physical Demand - Runs last 1 - 3 days. Maximum lift of 35 lbs. only periodically to get and feed stock to machine (2 - 3 times/day).
5. Mental-Visual Demand - Calculations and layout of cams. Read precision gauges, grind tools.

RESPONSIBILITY
6. Equipment or Process - Bad collet may cause excessive wear or breakage up to $25. If machine out of time, possible damage up to $400.
7. Material or Product - Proper cams essential to make good parts. Works from raw bar stock.
8. Safety of Others - Whipping bar stock.
9. Work of Others - None.

JOB CONDITIONS
10. Working Conditions - Noise, dirt (oil).
11. Unavoidable Hazards - Minor hand cuts from chips.

Employee Joseph E. Hall (signed)   Supervisor P. Wurtz (signed) exception of hours of work, wage levels, and number of employees and supervisors. These records enable control over many aspects of personnel operations. First, cumulatively they give an inventory of the precise manpower needs within a company. Second, they provide guidelines for operating managers and so to some degree control his handling of personnel and insure integration and coordination of individual personnel requirements in each operating area.

In conjunction with classifying jobs and defining their specifications, jobs must also be assigned wage and salary levels, if personnel costs are to be controlled. In order to assign wage and salary levels to jobs, each job or job category must be evaluated, in relation to other jobs within the company, and to pay scales in the community and industry in general. Job evaluation techniques may involve simply ranking or grading the jobs within a company relative to each other and then assigning a salary or wage to each rank or grade. Or, they may involve analyzing the components of each job, assigning points (or weight) to each component, and fixing pay levels on the basis of the total points per job or job category.[25]

By defining the requirements for each job (job specification) and assigning a wage and salary level to each job, control standards are established for personnel costs and assignments. These standards enable control both the number of employees and their wages and salaries—basic elements affecting personnel costs. These standards, when used in conjunction with personnel and recruiting records, enable control over the assignment of personnel and the filling of these positions—either from the company's labor pool or through hiring.

Job specifications also facilitate appraisal of worker performance, and in turn control of promotions and raises when they are supplemented by appraisal standards. Worker appraisal standards are needed to insure that worker performance will be evaluated objectively and consistently throughout a company. Appraisal forms are used to communicate these standards and to maintain control of the way employees are judged by their supervisors. Figure 8.3 gives an appraisal report form used by one company.

Some companies go further and establish even more specific criteria for appraising job performance, especially at the clerical level. For example, Figure 8.4 shows one company's appraisal standards for a stenographer-typist and file clerk's job. Since the standards are spelled out in such detail, the task of evaluating worker performance is considerably simplified.

Judgment of performance can be very subjective, and personal chemistry can lead supervisors to favor one worker over another. There is no way to eliminate personal likes and dislikes. But with appraisal standards

---

[25]See, for example, Paul Pigors and Charles A. Meyers, *Personnel Administration* (5th ed.; New York: McGraw-Hill Book Company, 1964), Chapter 21.

Figure 8.3

ABC COMPANY
ENGINEER APPRAISAL FORM

ABC COMPANY

NAME _____ CLOCK NO. _____ POSITION _____ DATE _____
APPRAISED BY _____ DATE INTERVIEWED _____

	UNSATISFACTORY	FAIR (Somewhat below average)	GOOD	EXCELLENT (Somewhat above average)	OUTSTANDING (Well above average)
	1 2 3	4 5	6 7 8	9 10 11	12 13 14 15

1. INITIATIVE
Enterprise; drive; capacity for independent action; degree to which he assumes responsibility when orders are lacking; degree to which he follows through on a job despite obstacles.

2. COOPERATIVENESS
The trait of working wholeheartedly both with and for others in an open-minded objective fashion; possession of the qualities of tact, courtesy, friendliness and tolerance.

3. EXPRESSION
Facility in expressing ideas both orally and in writing. This implies the ability to communicate ideas in a logical, coherent fashion and the ability to summarize.

4. QUANTITY OF WORK
Amount of useful output in the light of the opportunities afforded by the job. The output may be written or otherwise.

5. QUALITY OF WORK
The general excellence of all kinds of output, including written material, with consideration given to the difficulty of the job. Accuracy, thoroughness and dependability of output should be considered, but not quantity. In the case of supervisors, this trait includes skill in directing and guiding others.

6. CREATIVENESS
Originality, including imagination and inventiveness.

7. ENGINEERING OR TECHNICAL JUDGEMENT
Skill in analyzing situations and arriving at sound conclusions from available facts even though the available data may be incomplete or seemingly contradictory.

8. VERSATILITY & ADAPTABILITY
Willing and capable of doing successfully several lines of work, as need arises.

9. GENERAL COMPANY INFORMATION
The degree of understanding of procedures of major and minor company policies and conformance to them. (See Inst. 3 B)

10. BUDGET AND/OR SCHEDULES
Ability to perform within budget limitations and/or according to schedules and commitments.

11. PROFESSIONAL INTEGRITY
Degree of willingness to face facts and follow course of action indicated.

166

Figure 8.4

PERFORMANCE STANDARDS[26]
STENOGRAPHER-TYPIST AND FILE CLERK

		Hours	Minutes	%
1.	Total Hours Paid For: (Daily)	8	480	100
	Total Hours Allowance: (Daily)	1	60	12.5
	Total Net Productive Hours: (Daily)	7	420	87.5

LINES
2. 30 Lines Per Letter: Dictated and Transcribed
    30 Lines Per Letter: Straight Copy

LETTERS
3. Production (Net Production Time) — in Seven (7) Hours, or 420 Minutes:
    Dictated and Transcribed Letters (30 lines each) $= 10\text{-}\frac{1}{2}$ letters, or Straight Copy
    Work (30 lines each) $= 21$ letters

TIME STUDY ANALYSIS
4. Fifteen (15) Minutes Average Dictation Time for 30-Line Letter
    Twenty-Five (25) Minutes Average Transcription Time for 30-Line Letter
    Twenty (20) Minutes Average Copy Time for 30-Line Letter

AVERAGE DAILY TIME
5. Net Production Time: Seven (7) Hours, or 420 Minutes:
    Minutes Per Dictated Letter (40) $= 10\text{-}\frac{1}{2} - 30$-Line Letters in Seven (7) Hours
    Minutes Per Copied Letter (20) $= 21 - 30$-Line Letters in Seven (7) Hours

Note: Typing time to transcribe a full page or equivalent from voicewriting machine cylinders or records is figured at 20 minutes per letter. The average cylinder contains approximately 120 lines of typing. The number of cylinders completed per day should total 7 or more. In general, stenographers spend 65% of productive time on dictation and transcription and 35% on typing from copy or manuscript, resulting in a combined total production of 13 full pages per day.

FILING
6. (a)   Fifty (50) Units of Mail Per Hour using a numerical file system is the average and includes General File upkeep.
    (b)   One hundred fifty (150) Units of Mail Per Hour, filing alphabetically, is the average and includes General File upkeep.

These production standards are based on the results of numerous surveys of stenographic work and represent actual production of stenographers having average ability.

CODE ARRANGEMENT:
    Have steno or typist place initials on copy.
    Use "T" for transcribing from longhand material or typed copy.
    Use "D" for dictated letters.
    Use "V" for voicewriting machine.
    Make notation on working paper describing material typed if not practical to make copy such as contracts, complicated statements, and legal documents.
    Show typing time on each letter or typed material.

[26]"Setting Standards for Clerical Performance," *Management Review,* October 1953, p. 590.

and report forms a company can move closer to having a network of more objective performance standards upon which promotions can be based. These standards communicate to workers what the company considers good and bad performance and so also function to direct their efforts into desired channels.

Personnel controls are also developed to monitor employee turnover and injuries, both critical aspects of the efficient use of personnel within a company. Most companies have periodic reports on the level of activity in each of these areas. Control reports are also needed on the effectiveness of recruiting efforts in meeting manpower planning goals, another critical area of personnel management.

Of the three operating and staff areas discussed in this chapter, personnel makes the greatest use of non-financial controls. As in other areas, personnel controls are closely linked with overall company plans and financial controls. Personnel functions not only to insure that manpower resources are as adequate as financial and facility resources to meet planned needs, but also to control the total costs of manpower. These costs are controlled by monitoring both the efficiency of personnel usage and the wage and salary levels within a company. Aside from the control reports within the wage and salary administration area, however, the actual tools are outside the financial accounting area.

For this reason, the personnel area provides the best example of how the network of operating and staff controls in a company extend far beyond the financial accounting controls discussed in Chapter 7. It is also a good example of the close relationship between planning and control tools. Once plans, objectives and policies are quantified, these quantified plans, objectives and policies become control standards both to guide action and to subsequently compare performance against plan.

As in the marketing and manufacturing areas, personnel has available a wide range of tools to facilitate control. The areas covered by these control tools are generally the same in all companies. But the final form of the reports and their standards will vary with the situation. The discussion in this section, as in the earlier sections, is designed only to give a feeling for the nature of control tools and systems used in personnel and some examples of the form in which these controls and their standards appear.

OVERALL CORPORATE CONTROL AND OPERATING AND STAFF CONTROL

Overall corporate control, like lower level operating and staff control, requires use of non-financial (in addition to financial) controls, if top corporate managers are to monitor effectively the activities within a company which affect financial results. The non-financial controls used in overall corporate control cover all operating and staff areas of a company and are similar to those described in this chapter, though usually they are not as detailed.

In an effort to define and categorize top management controls, Paul Stokes has divided them into eight key performance areas:[27] finance; operations; productivity; market position; service relations; public, customer, and government relations; employee relations and development; and ownership and member relations. As can be seen from the list, financial controls are only one aspect of the overall controls used within a company—a fact that often comes as a surprise to executives who are used to thinking of controls exclusively as accounting and finance oriented. Stokes' list includes areas covered earlier in this chapter, as well as additional areas important in overall corporate control. The following paragraphs discuss each of these categories and give selected examples of the non-financial controls used by top management.

Financial controls concern the flow of money through a business and give a picture of a company's financial condition at any one time. Examples of these controls are given in Chapter 7.

Operating controls, according to Stokes, are those controls which deal directly with the day-to-day functioning of an organization. Like controls in other areas, these controls will differ from company to company and operation to operation, and in some instances they will overlap with financial or productivity controls. As an example of operation controls, he lists the following key indicators on which operating control reports would be needed by top management in a freight transport company.

1. Number of cars per train compared to standard.
2. Tons carried per car or truck.
3. Ratio of long hauls to short hauls.
4. Cost per ton-mile.
5. Ratio of less-than-carload lots (LCL) or less-than-truckload lots (LTL) to carload or truckload lots.
6. Frequency and value of damage per shipment.
7. Frequency and value of lost freight per shipment.
8. Customer complaints compared with standard.
9. Demurrage charges collected or paid per month.
10. Maintenance cost per unit.
11. Labor cost per ton-mile.
12. Cost of maintenance of buildings, grounds, or trackage per ton-mile.

Productivity controls monitor the results in the form of goods or services. The areas covered by these controls are labor, materials, capital

[27]Paul M. Stokes, *A Total Systems Approach to Management Control* (New York: American Management Association, 1968).

and equipment. The following list enumerates the variety of ways in which units of production per man-hour can be reported on for control in the labor area:

1.   Boxes packed per hour (warehousing or production).
2.   Number of welds per hour (production).
3.   Number of bottles filled per minute (packaging).
4.   Number of words typed per minute (office-clerical).
5.   Number of pages proofread per hour (office-clerical).
6.   Number of forms processed per hour (office-clerical).
7.   Number of transactions posted per hour (accounting-clerical).
8.   Number of customers handled per hour (sales-clerical).
9.   Number of orders processed per hour (billing).
10. Number of bushels picked per hour (production).

The controls needed by top management in the marketing area identified by Stokes are those that measure results against plans (for example, actual versus budgeted sales), share of market (company sales versus industry sales and total potential sales), cost of sales and selling ratios, percentage of complements and complaints, and customer opinion surveys. In addition, top management would also want to review those control reports covered in the marketing section of this chapter which are relevant to their operation.

Services controls are developed for those categories (basic, desirable, or deluxe) which the company has decided to offer. The key indicators most often reported on for control in the services area are, according to Stokes:

1.   Number of services offered versus number offered by competitors.
2.   Cost of services as a percentage added to base operating costs.
3.   Cost of services per sales dollar.
4.   Level and types of complaints this year versus last year.
5.   Frequency of service versus competitor's service.
6.   Do most customers feel that you give them "a little more"?
7.   Number of free services versus service for which there is a charge.

Stokes next considers controls over the company dealings with outside parties: public, customer, and government relations. Indicators, similar to those listed above, are given for each party. For example, the following factors might be covered in control reports on customer relations:

1.   Dollar value of goods returned as a percentage of sales.
2.   Average length of time required to adjust customer complaints versus standard.
3.   Time required to perform warranty service versus standard.
4.   Number of employees trained and encouraged to greet customers cordially.
5.   Average dollar value per sale.
6.   Percentage of repeat orders.
7.   Percentage of customers who have established charge accounts.

8. Dollar value of special or custom orders versus total sales.
9. Average cost per unit of maintaining warranties.
10. Time required to process service calls versus standard.
11. Average length of time from order to delivery versus standard.
12. Percentage of orders shipped on time.
13. Percentage of orders requesting special handling, wrapping, and so on.
14. Average dollar sales per regular customer versus overall average.

The controls developed by Stokes in employee relations and development cover labor costs, salary levels, college recruiting, employee selection, communications, morale and accident prevention. Both formal and informal controls are discussed by Stokes in his study of the last performance area, ownership and member relations.

The basic thrust of Stoke's study is to isolate those operating and staff areas which must be covered in any effective overall corporate control system. His study extends the discussion earlier in this chapter, by exploring all the operating and staff areas which are important in management control.

In covering all control areas in his study, Stokes is not able to discuss in complete detail each area. And many managers will disagree on his choice of specific controls and the way in which he categorizes these controls. However, his general approach is valid—first, examine those key areas which are most important to total company success, and second, develop controls (both financial and non-financial) in these critical areas.

CONCLUSION

It is impossible to discuss management control without some consideration of the specific operating and staff controls developed and used throughout a company. Developing operating and staff controls follows the basic management control process. First, responsibility for control development is fixed with the operating or staff manager, and the amount of assistance needed from the accounting and finance department and the systems department is determined. Next, the overall planning and control structure is studied, the individual needs of the operating or staff department are defined, and the general purpose and nature of the controls and their standards are determined. Third, the specific control forms and reporting systems are developed.

A wide range of control standards and control reports have been discussed in this chapter and ample illustrations have been given. Because these controls were developed for individual operations, they cannot be used in their presented form in a wide variety of control situations.

The purpose of this chapter was not, however, to give forms which the reader can use. Rather, it was to show the process by which these controls are developed. Each manager will have to study the specific requirements of his situation and in turn develop controls unique to his situation.

The process he follows will be the same and the pattern of controls will be the same: some of the controls will be integrated very closely with overall company financial control systems, while others will be quite distinct from them. His control reports will be comparative ones, measuring the deviation of actual results from standards, as in all control areas. But the exact standards used and comparisons made, their timing, the report format, and the like, will most likely be different from those shown in this chapter.

In addition to the control systems discussed in this chapter, there are a number of additional mathematical, graphic, and computer tools which can be used in control. These tools are discussed in the next two chapters.

The discussion in this chapter is continued in Chapters 13 and 14, where two integrated control studies are discussed. Chapter 13 concerns an overall financial control system at a large electrical equipment company. The discussion covers mainly the structure of the corporate control system and the overall financial control reports in each major operating and staff area, though some consideration is given to the overall non-financial operating controls developed to supplement the financial controls. Chapter 14 concerns the controls developed for the circulation marketing department at a national publication. This discussion shows how an integrated network of operating controls was developed from a study of individual operating needs, and how only after operating controls were developed in this way was the operating system integrated with the overall company financial control system.

DISCUSSION QUESTIONS

1. Describe the different ways in which the first three steps in the management control process are applied in each of the three business areas covered in this chapter.

2. In what ways does the purpose (or purposes) a control tools is designed to serve affect the final form of a control report (and its standards) on a manufacturing department's expenses?

3. In what ways does the control situation affect the kind of tools used in the personnel area?

4. Why are manufacturing controls tied more closely to overall company financial controls than are personnel controls?

5. Outline the network of controls used in the marketing area. In how many different ways are the standards and the deviations from standard expressed? Give an example of how the nature of the operation being controlled dictated the form of the standards.

6. All control tools and systems involve some comparison of actual results with standards. Describe three different kinds of comparisons that are made through the manufacturing controls described in this chapter. What different control purposes does each serve?

7. Describe how you might develop and evaluate alternative control tools to meet the requirements of an advertising manager of a replacement parts manufacturer in the automobile industry, or the requirements of a specific marketing or manufacturing operation with which you are familiar.

8. Discuss the ways in which the controls used in the personnel area can differ from the overall company financial controls described in the last chapter. In what ways are they closely related?

9. Describe and discuss some of the major differences between the controls used in an operating area and those used in a staff area.

10. List some of the characteristics common to all types of controls described in this chapter.

11. List the major differences and similarities between the operating and staff controls discussed in this chapter and the accounting and finance controls discussed in Chapter 7.

12. List and discuss the major differences and similarities between overall company controls and individual operating and staff controls. Point out the areas in which these two levels of controls are identical.

13. In what ways is the concept of overall company control developed in this book different from the more traditional, accounting-oriented approach to overall control.

STEP THREE: SOME GRAPHIC AND MATHEMATICAL TOOLS USED IN MANAGEMENT CONTROL

The purpose of Chapter 9 is to classify and discuss some more widely used graphic and mathematical techniques useful in performing more effective management control. These tools are most often used in operating control and in the computer systems area, although they also have application in accounting and finance control. The discussion is not written for the technician, nor does it concentrate on technical considerations. Rather, it is designed for the business executive or potential business executive with little training in mathematics or other fields of science who wants to learn how these techniques can be used to manage better.

The first part of the chapter describes the basic approach underlying the use of these techniques, model building and simulation. In the following sections, a number of graphic and quantitative techniques are described, and examples given of how they are applied to specific business problems.

Like the budget, these techniques are first of all planning tools, in that they help quantify and visualize a plan. Like the budget, which provides a quantitative test of a plan, these graphic and mathematical tools enable the planner to refine and improve his plan. Once settled in final form, like the budget, these graphic and mathematical representations in turn serve as control tools, since they become standards against which actual progress can be measured and controlled.

THE BASIC APPROACH: MODEL BUILDING AND SIMULATION

The techniques described in the following sections make use of the basic model building and simulation approach. In using each technique a graphic or mathematical model of the situation under study is first developed. Many of the models are then manipulated in some way to simulate the situation variables, in order to give the planner outcome information upon which to base his decision. The following are brief definitions of model building and simulation.

Model Building.

A model is a representation or abstraction of an actual object or situation, which attempts to explain the behavior of some aspect of that object or situation.[1] While a model is only a representation of reality and so is less complex than reality, it must be sufficiently complete to approximate those aspects of reality being investigated.

The three most common types of models are:[2]

Physical. A three-dimensional scale reproduction of the system. A toy plane would be an example of a physical model. This type of model is used when studying the geometric or physical relationships of a system.

Diagrammatic. A schematic representation of activities. Examples of diagrammatic models are the flow charts shown below in the discussion of PERT/CPM.

Mathematical. Equations or formulas which describe the operations symbolically. Examples of mathematical models are given in the discussion of linear programming and decision theory below.

The basic steps in model building are:

1. Observe the situation, and define the problem and the objective.
2. Investigate controllable input factors.
3. Study the network of interconnections and observe changing inputs and outputs until an hypothesis (a model or statement of how changing inputs are expected to affect outputs) is reached.
4. Evaluate uncontrollable factors.
5. Test the model for validity.
6. Repeat steps 2-5 until a model is found that predicts as reliably as is necessary to solve the management problem.[3]

Simulation.

Simulation is a method of approaching a problem first by constructing a model which abstracts elements of the real situation that are pertinent to the problem, and second by manipulating this model in such a way as to

[1]David W. Miller and Martin K. Starr, *Executive Decisions and Operations Research* (2nd Ed.; Englewood Cliffs, N.J.: Prentice-Hall, Inc., 1969), p. 145.

[2]American Institute of Industrial Engineers, *Journal of Industrial Engineering*, August 1967, back cover.

[3]Billy E. Goetz, *Quantitative Methods: A Survey and Guide for Managers* (New York: McGraw-Hill Book Company, 1965), pp. 84-90.

draw some conclusions about the real situation.[4] Business managers use simulation to visualize the components of the situation, in order to determine an effective solution to the problem.

Simulation takes many forms (for example, flying a plane in a wind tunnel, manipulating mathematical formulas in order to solve linear programming and queuing problems, and playing computerized executive business games)[5] and very often involves the use of a computer.

Several examples of the use of model building and simulation are given in the following sections of this chapter and in Chapter 10.

GRAPHIC CONTROL TOOLS

A graphic control tool is a diagrammatic model of an operation or plan. The graphic tools discussed in this section generally fall into two categories, dynamic and static. Dynamic graphic controls (such as the Gantt chart shown in Figure 9.3) are used for on-going projects, for they are posted and checked periodically and decisions are made based on these posting. Dynamic graphic controls basically feed back information to the decision maker in a form that makes it easier for him to check for deviations and introduce any changes needed to keep activities on target. A static control chart (such as a company's organization chart) is developed at the outset of a process or operation, and usually originates as part of the planning process. Once the plan and planning standards are established and charted, the chart is used as a guideline to alert the manager to deviations from the original plan.

The discussion in this section concentrates on some of the major dynamic control charts: Program Evaluation and Review Technique (PERT) and Critical Path Method (CPM); Gantt Charts; and line charts. The section concludes with a review of the better known static graphic control tools.

PERT and CPM.

PERT (Program Evaluation and Review Technique) and CPM (Critical Path Method) are two dynamic graphic control techniques that

---

[4]John Dearden and F. Warren McFarlan, *Management Information Systems: Text and Cases* (Homewood, Illinois: Richard D. Irwin, Inc., 1966), p. 92.

[5]For an explanation of the various types of simulation see Joel M. Kibbee, "Management Control Simulation," in *Management Control Systems*, eds., Donald G. Malcolm and Alan J. Rowe (New York: John Wiley and Sons, 1960), pp. 300-320. See also Thomas R. Prince, *Information Systems for Management Planning and Control* (Rev. ed.; Homewood, Illinois: Richard D. Irwin, Inc., 1970), Chapter 17; Jay W. Forrester, *Industrial Dynamics* (Cambridge, Mass.: The M.I.T. Press, 1961); Charles P. Bonini, *Simulation of Information and Decision Systems in the Firm* (Englewood Cliffs, N.J.: Prentice-Hall, Inc., 1963); and Paul S. Greenlaw, Lowell W. Herron, and Richard H. Rawdon, *Business Simulation in Industrial and University Education* (Englewood Cliffs, N.J.: Prentice-Hall, Inc., 1962).

can aid in the planning and scheduling of projects. PERT and CPM both use graphic network techniques to develop the maximum utilization of manpower, machines, and time in the accomplishment of a project.[6] Through PERT and CPM techniques, a project is divided into its components in order to determine the sequence of activities needed to complete the project. Normally the entire project is then presented in flow chart form.

Through the use of the flow chart, PERT and CPM help the manager to visualize the interrelationships of all aspects of a project. Both methods can be used to decide whether to undertake a project, to develop a reasonable plan for carrying out a project, and to control the progress of the project. These techniques are widely used in solving such business problems as construction and new product planning and control, as well as in military missile programs.

PERT and CPM differ in some respects. PERT is mainly used to plan and schedule complicated jobs where previous experience is lacking. For this reason PERT uses three time estimates, the most optimistic, the most pessimistic, and the average or most likely. CPM, on the other hand, is used where there has been enough experience to determine with reasonable accuracy how much time is required to complete each activity in the project. CPM thus uses only one estimate of time for each job.[7]

When first used, PERT (sometimes called PERT/Time) was concerned only with the time needed to complete each component of a project and the total time for the project. Subsequently, PERT/Cost was developed. The technique, which is still in the developmental stage, is concerned with both the time and the cost of completing each component and the total project.[8]

The following is an example of the use of PERT scheduling in introducing a new product line.[9] The first phase is to outline the steps involved in completing the project, the relationships of each step to the others, and the expected time required to complete each step. In this case the expected time is arrived at by making three time estimates, optimistic (To), most likely (Tm) and pessimistic (Tp), and using the following equation:

$$\frac{To + 4tm + Tp}{6} = \text{Expected time}$$

Based on this initial analysis, a flow chart is drawn up, as shown in Figure 9.1. In the figure the numbers in parentheses are the expected times

[6]Dearden and McFarlan, *Management Information Systems*, p. 63.

[7]Prince, *Information Systems*, p. 104.

[8]Richard I. Levin and Charles A. Kirkpatrick, *Planning and Control with PERT/CPM* (New York: McGraw-Hill Book Company, 1966), p. 153.

[9]Dearden and McFarlan, *Management Information Systems*, pp. 80-83.

Figure 9.1

PERT SYSTEM

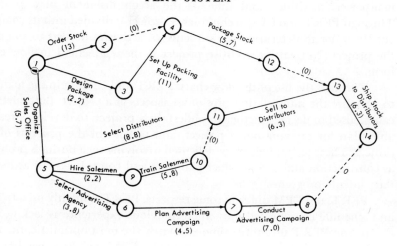

in weeks for each step, the lines the steps to be taken, and the circles the start and finish of each step.

The next phase is to study the interrelationships of all the steps and calculate the earliest expected time and latest allowable time for each series

Figure 9.2

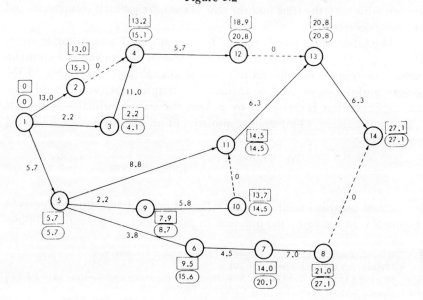

of steps. The earliest expected time is calculated by adding up the expected times for each step. These figures are written in boxes on the chart shown in Figure 9.2.

The latest allowable time is calculated by starting from the end of the project (circle 14) and working backwards, subtracting the expected time of each preceding activity. For example, it is anticipated that it takes only 18.9 weeks to design the package (circles 1 to 3) and package the stock (circles 4-12), so this expected time figure was written in the box next to circle 12. However, it will take 27.1 weeks to complete organizing the sales force, selecting distributors, and selling and shipping stock to distributors (circles 1, 5, 11, 13 and 14). Thus there is more time available or allowable for the packaging phase. This allowable time of 20.8 weeks (27.1 weeks minus 6.3 weeks) for the packaging steps is written in the oval next to step 12.

The final phase is to translate the network chart into a tabular format and to give actual dates for the expected and allowable times. Such a tabular summary is given in Table 9.1.

Table 9.1

PERT SYSTEM

Event	Nomenclature	Expected Date	Latest Allowable Date	Slack Time (in weeks)
1	Start ordering stock & package design	5/ 7/63	5/ 7/63	0
2	Finish ordering stock	8/ 6/63	8/20/63	2.1
3	Start packaging facility	5/22/63	6/ 5/63	1.9
4	Start package stock	8/ 7/63	8/20/63	1.9
5	Start dist. sales, hire sales, select ad. agency	6/14/63	6/14/63	0
6	Start plans ad. campaign	7/11/63	8/22/63	6.1
7	Start conducting ad. campaign	8/13/63	9/24/63	6.1
8	Finish conducting ad. campaign	10/ 1/63	11/12/63	6.1
9	Start salesmen tng.	6/29/63	7/ 5/63	.8
10	Finish tng. salesmen	8/ 9/63	8/15/63	.8
11	Finish selec. distrib.	8/15/63	8/15/63	0
12	Finish pkg. stock	9/14/63	9/28/63	1.9
13	Finish selling to distributors	9/28/63	9/28/63	0
14	Finish shipping stock to distrib.	11/12/63	11/12/63	0

PERT/CPM can be applied to almost any type of project planning problem in business.

Gantt Charts.

Gantt charts are among the better known and most widely used dynamic graphic control tools. A Gantt chart consists of a series of horizontal lines or bars, each of which represents a given amount of planned performance over a specified period. Below each bar is a second contrasting bar representing actual accomplishment, as of a certain date. Thus, a glance will reveal whether a product is ahead of schedule, behind schedule, or on schedule.

A Gantt chart for a polishing department is shown in Figure 9.3.[10] This chart shows work scheduled and completed as of the end of work on Wednesday. The letters represent explanations for the condition shown on the chart according to the following key:

R—down for repairs
A—operator absent
I—idle capacity
M—lack of materials
P—power failure
T—lack of tools

Figure 9.3

GANTT CONTROL CHART

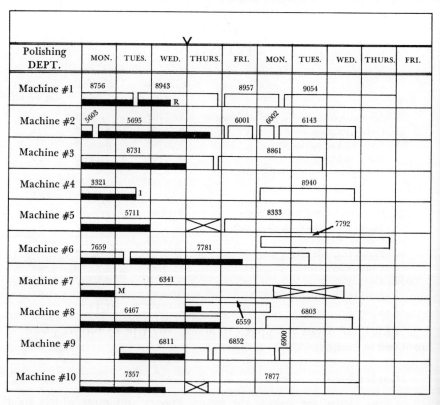

The amount of work scheduled for each machine is shown by a light line, and the amount completed by the black bars. The numbers above the light lines refer to the factory order being processed. As of Wednesday evening machine No. 4 has no work scheduled and work which has been delayed has been rescheduled on machines Nos. 5, 7 and 10 (shown by the "X" marks). Machine No. 1 is down for repairs and no attempt has yet been made to reschedule the work alloted to it. Machines Nos. 6 and 8 have been scheduled for new order based on the work done ahead of schedule.

While useful, Gantt charts have their limitations. They must be posted regularly, like any other schedule chart, to be of value. There are physical limitations, as was discovered by one manufacturer who attempted unsuccessfully to maintain 400 Gantt charts at one time. Their use must, therefore, be limited to operations that are small enough and simple enough to be monitored by manual control tools.

Line Charts.

Simple line charts are another commonly used dynamic graphic control tool. An example of such a chart is given in Figure 9.4. It is taken from *The National Observer* study described in Chapter 14.

In the chart, budgeted circulation is first drawn in. Periodically, actual results are drawn in, so that actual results can be compared easily to the standard or the plan. Such a chart can be used to visualize many types of control comparisons.

Figure 9.4

THE NATIONAL OBSERVER

Circulation Budget and Results 1963-64[11]

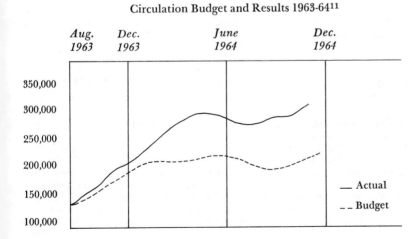

11Robert J. Mockler, *Circulation Planning and Development for The National Observer* (Atlanta, Georgia: Georgia State College, 1967), p. 28.

Static Control Charts.

Static control charts are mainly pictorial representations of standards. They include such charts as break-even charts, organization charts, wage classification charts, and histograms.[12] Examples of many of these are found throughout this study.

MATHEMATICAL TOOLS

Mathematical tools can also be useful in management control. Five major ones are discussed in this section: linear programming, dynamic programming, probability and decision theory, queuing or waiting line theory, and game theory. Like the graphic techniques discussed above, these are mainly planning techniques, useful in quantifying planning and control standards.

Linear Programming.

Linear programming is a mathematical technique employed in business for finding the best uses of the firm's limited resources, including money, raw materials, machines, space, transportation equipment, time and personnel, to accomplish specific goals.[13] The adjective "linear" is used to describe a directly proportional relationship between or among two or more variables. For example, if a 10 per cent increase in productive hours causes a 10 per cent rise in output, the relationship between productive hours and output is linear. "Programming" refers to the use of mathematical techniques to determine the best solution.[14]

The basic requirements for the use of linear programming are:[15]

1.   There must be a specified objective. For example, a furniture company uses one facility to produce both tables and chairs and wants to find the most profitable product mix.

2.   There must be alternative courses of action, one of which will achieve the objective. For example, should the furniture company allocate manufacturing capacity to tables and chairs in the ratio of 50:50? 25:75? 70:30? Some other ratio?

[12]Earl P. Strong and Robert D. Smith, *Management Control Models* (New York: Holt, Rinehart and Winston, 1968), pp. 101-115.

[13]Richard I. Levin and C. A. Kirkpatrick, *Quantitative Approaches to Management* (New York: McGraw-Hill Book Company, 1965), p. 198.

[14]Linear programming has sometimes been called mathematical programming, but this is incorrect. Linear programming is only one type of mathematical programming. There are also non-linear types of mathematical programming, such as dynamic programming, which is discussed below. See Alexander Henderson and Robert Schlaifer, "Mathematical Programming: Better Information for Better Decisions," in *Scientific Decision Making for Business: Readings in Operations Research for Non-Mathematicians* ed. Abe Shuckman (New York: Holt, Rinehart and Winston, Inc., 1963), pp. 149-223, for a complete discussion of mathematical programming.

[15]Levin and Kirkpatrick, *Quantitative Approaches to Management*, p. 199.

3. Resources are in limited supply. A limited number of machine hours are available; consequently, the more hourse scheduled for tables, the fewer chairs can be made.
4. The variables must be interrelated. For example, if profit is $8 per table and $6 per chair, the total profit will reflect the ratio of tables to chairs.
5. The company's objective and operational limitations must be expressible as (or approximated by) linear mathematical equations or in inequalities. For example, the furniture company's objective, dollar profit objective, can be expressed in this simple equation:

> p (profit) = $8A_1 (number of tables) + $6A_2 (number of chairs).

The following is an example of how linear programming can be used to control a company's production mix. A company has two products in its line—Autoscopes and Flexibars.[16] Each Autoscope produces $40 profit and each Flexibar yields $50 profit.

The company wants the answers to the following questions:

1. What combination of products uses plant facilities best and still maximizes profits?
2. Do we have enough testing capacity?
3. Can we change product mix and still maximize profits?

The three main operations in the plant are machining, assembling, and testing. Table 9.2 shows available production time and time used in each department by each product.

Table 9.2

PRODUCTION TIME

	Machinery	Assembling	Testing
each Autoscope requires	1 hour	5 hours	3 hours
each Flexibar requires	2 hours	4 hours	1 hour
Total Production time available	720 hours	1800 hours	900 hours

As in the case of the furniture company described above, we can express the total profit from the operation in an equation: profit = $40 times the number of Autoscopes + $50 times the number of Flexibars. If we substitute X for the number of Autoscopes and Y for the number of Flexibars, the equation can be simplified to: p = 40X + 50Y.

---

[16]General Electric, *G-E Linear Programming* (Phoenix, Arizona: Information Services Division, General Electric Company, 1966), pp. 3-8.

First, the *machining* time available for each product is calculated. If only Autoscopes were made, 720 could be produced (1 hour divided into 720 available hours). If only Flexibars were made, 360 could be produced (2 hours divided into 720 available hours).

Next, the *assembling* time available for each product is calculated. If only Autoscopes were made, 360 could be produced (5 hours divided into 1800 available hours). If only Flexibars were made, 450 could be produced (4 hours divided into 1800 available hours).

Last, the *testing* time available for each product is calculated. If only Autoscopes were made, 300 could be produced (3 hours divided into 900 available hours). If only Flexibars were made, 900 could be produced (1 hour divided into 900 available hours).

These calculations give the maximum and minimum ranges for the solution. By plotting these ranges on a single chart, the entire range of possible solutions can be visualized (Figure Five). The shaded area represents the range of feasible solutions.

Figure 9.5

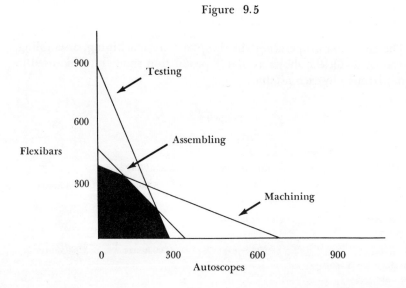

Once these limits have been established, profit calculations can be made. The formula given above is p = 40X + 50Y. We arbitrarily pick a profit which by inspection is close to what could be expected in the situation, $25,000. The formula then reads $25,000 = 40X + 50Y. If only Autoscopes were made, 625 would have to be made to produce this profit ($25,000 divided by 40). If only Flexibars were made, 500 would have to be made to produce this profit ($25,000 divided by 50). This hypothetical line is now plotted on the chart (Figure 9.6).

The same calculations are then made at a $15,000 profit level and plotted on the chart in Figure Five, since $25,000 profit does not intersect the feasible solution area. This line does intersect the feasible solution area, but does not give maximum use of facilities.

Figure 9. 6

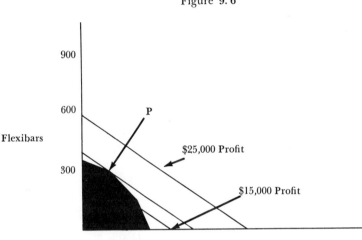

Since the lines will be parallel regardless of the hypothetical profit figures selected, we arbitrarily draw a line that intersects the shaded area where the dollar value is highest—point P. The X and Y values at the point of intersection show that producing 120 Autoscopes and 300 Flexibars will give maximum profits and maximum use of facilities.

The reader should keep in mind that while the problem was solved graphically here, such an approach can be used only when there are a limited number of variables. Where there are more than three variables, mathematical techniques must be used.

In addition to solving production, scheduling or facilities allocation problems, linear programming can be used to solve a variety of business problems, such as:

1. Finding the best way to transport and warehouse products, taking into account customer demands at various locations around the country and varying costs of transportation.

2. Finding the best method of allocating raw materials to several manufacturing plants.

3. Determining optimum inventory levels.

4. Scheduling assignment of personnel, such as airline stewardesses and pilots, in situations where there are complex routing and work assignment restrictions.

5. Reducing trim losses in cutting rolls of paper, textiles, and other such materials.

6. Allocating limited amounts of electronic service equipment in manufacturing and testing operations.

7. Determining an optimum diet and subsistence levels.

8. Assigning personnel to engineering project planning groups in accordance with project priority.

9. Finding the most economical blend of grain and wheat products and of oil and chemical products, taking current supplies and demands into consideration.

This list is by no means complete, but it gives some idea of the variety of business problems that linear programming can help solve.

Dynamic Programming.

When the relationship between variables is not linear but continuously changing, linear programming cannot be used in solving resource allocation problems. In the furniture company example mentioned previously, suppose that the profit realized was not constant but varied between $0 and $8 per table and $0 and $6 per chair, depending upon such things as the timing of the run, market conditions, consumer acceptance, and economic fluctuations. In this instance the company's resources must be allocated by a technique that incorporates decisions made over a period of time.

Dynamic programming is one of the best known techniques for solving business problems in which resources are allocated in a sequence of interdependent decisions over a period of time and the objective is to obtain the maximum return on the entire sequence of decisions.[17] In such instances, dynamic programming can show management how some gain from one decision can be sacrificed to make possible a greater gain from another decision.

Dynamic programming can be used for solving a variety of business problems, from marketing and production to financial planning. For example, a particular market has three advertising media: A, B, and C. The cost per advertisement in A is $2,500, in B, $5,000, and in C, $10,000. The advertising director of a manufacturing company with a total advertising budget of $20,000 can use dynamic programming to calculate the total cost involved under various combinations of advertising frequencies in media A, B, and C, and to predict probable sales from each of the combinations.[18]

Assuming that historical figures were available which showed the range of unit sales (optimistic to pessimistic) that might be produced from each ad, then Table 9.3 could be constructed.[19]

According to the table, the best course of action under either optimistic or pessimistic assumptions would be two appearances in A, one in B and one in C.

Other business problems that can be solved through dynamic programming include allocating salesmen to marketing areas, allocating funds for

Table 9.3

TOTAL COSTS AND TOTAL EXPECTED SALES FOR SEVEN KEY
COMBINATIONS UNDER BOTH PESSIMISTIC AND
OPTIMISTIC ASSUMPTIONS

# of Ad Inserts (A, B, C)	Pessimistic Assumptions		Optimistic Assumptions	
	Total Cost	Total Expected Sales	Total Cost	Total Expected Sales
(0, 4, 0)	$20,000	350	$20,000	360
(2, 3, 0)	20,000	510	20,000	550
(1, 2, 0)	20,000	540	20,000	580
(0, 2, 1)	20,000	510	20,000	590
(2, 1, 1)	20,000	580	20,000	690
		—		—
(4, 0, 1)	20,000	530	20,000	640
(0, 0, 2)	20,000	300	20,000	350

dividends, planning capital requirements over a period of years, and determining shipping and warehouse arrangements.

Decision Theory.

Decision theory is a method used to select from several alternatives the best course of action to achieve a desired objective in a given situation under conditions of uncertainty.[20] It enables the decision maker to analyze a set of complex situations with many alternatives and many different possible consequences. Decision theory is sometimes referred to as decision making under uncertainty or statistical decision theory.

[18]Richard B. Maffei, "Planning Advertising Expenditures by Dynamic Programming Methods," in *Scientific Decision Making in Business*, ed. Shuchman, pp. 209-216.

[19]Adapted from Maffei, "Planning Advertising Expenditures," p. 212.

[20]Harold Bierman, Jr., *et al.*, *Quantitative Analysis for Business Decisions* (Rev. ed., Homewood, Illinois: Richard D. Irwin, Inc., 1965), p. 55.

Decision theory makes use of probability theory. Probability theory is a technique used for drawing inferences from statistical data. It deals with events of a special kind: random events, whose outcome is determined by chance.[21] The probability of an outcome can be most simply understood as the percentage of times a particular outcome will occur if an event is repeated a great many times. For example, in tossing a coin the probability that heads will come up is 50 per cent, because an infinite number of tosses has to produce about half heads and half tails.

Through the use of probability theory the decision maker can judge which events are more probable than others, when faced with a decision under uncertainty. Combining this probability estimate with the expected consequences (potential profit or loss) of each possible event, he can weigh the potential profit against the probability of each alternative outcome, determine the risk, and decide which course of action is most *likely* to yield the greatest gain.

Decision theory has been used effectively in a wide range of business situations, such as capital budgeting and product pricing as well as determining where to drill oil wells, how much inventory to carry, whether or not to buy a new machine or introduce a new product, and whether to make or buy an item.

The systematic approach to making a decision under uncertainty is given by Robert Schlaifer:[22]

1.   Attach a definite numerical *value* to the consequence of every possible act given every possible event.
2.   Attach a definite numerical *probability weight* to every possible event.
3.   For each act separately, use these weights to compute a *weighted average* of all the values attached to the act.
4.   Select the act whose weighted average value is highest.

The following problem and solution illustrates how these steps are carried out in practice.[23] Suppose we have a product to market at a price of $50 per unit. We have to invest $5000 in fixed costs and are uncertain whether sales will be 100 units, 250 units or 1000 units. The profit (or loss) at each level of sales has been calculated: $3000 loss at 100 units, $0 at 250 units, $15,000 profit at 1000 units. These figures are written in the first and third columns of our decision chart in Table 9.4.

Next, the chances or probability of an event occurring (100 units, 250 units, and 1,000 units sale) are estimated by the decision maker, and written in the second column of the chart in Table 9.4.

Step three is to multiply the profit anticipated (outcome) by the probability of it occurring (probability weight) to arrive at a weighted average.

[21]Miller and Starr, *Executive Decisions and Operations Research*, p. 73.
[22]Robert Schlaifer, *Probability and Statistics for Business Decisions* (New York. McGraw-Hill Book Company, 1959), p. 5.
[23]Bierman, *et al.*, *Quantitative Analysis*, pp. 6-8.

Table 9.4

COMPUTATION OF EXPECTED PROFIT FROM NEW PRODUCT

Sales (Units)	Probability (Weight)	Profit	Weight X Profit
100	0.40	— $ 3,000	— $1,200
250	0.40	0	0
1,000	0.20	15,000	3,000
	1.00		$1,800

The last step is to make the decision. The expected profit or expected monetary value for marketing the product is $1800, compared with zero for rejecting the project. Hence, using decision theory, we proceed to market the product (this conclusion assumes that the consequences measured in dollars also measure utility).

This is admittedly an oversimplified example of how decision theory works, but it illustrates the basic technique—quantifying judgmental factors and unknown outcomes—which underlies decision theory.

Queuing or Waiting Line Theory.

Bottlenecks, backlogs, and idle capacity are common problems in business. Each of these arises from a variable rate of arrival of some kind of unit requiring some kind of service, and by a variable rate of completing the service required.[24] Queuing, or waiting line, theory is a mathematical technique used in scheduling and handling the arrival and service of these units, for through it the manager can determine the most economical balance between the cost of waiting for service and the cost of providing additional facilities.

A study conducted by Boeing Aircraft to determine the number of clerks that should man a factory tool crib counter illustrates how waiting line theory can be used to solve a business problem.[25] At the Boeing factory, the tools used by assembly line and shop mechanics are stored in special rooms or "tool cribs." Clerks hand out the tools when mechanics arrive at the crib counter and request tools. The mechanics return the tools to the clerks when no longer needed. In this situation, management wants the lowest possible overhead, or fewest clerks; the factory foremen want their mechanics to spend a minimum of time waiting in line and so argue for a greater number of clerks.

Study of the operation showed that the average time between arrivals of mechanics was 50 seconds and the average time required by a clerk to

[24]Goetz, *Quantitative Methods*, p. 426; Bierman, *et al.*, *Quantitative Analysis*, p. 328.

[25]Georges Brigham, "On a Congestion Problem in an Aircraft Factory," *Operations Research*, November 1955, pp. 412-428.

fill a mechanic's request was 60 seconds. If arrivals were evenly spaced, therefore, two clerks would be more than enough to man the tool crib. However, since service times varied and arrivals occurred at random, at certain times a long line of mechanics would build up, while at other times clerks would be idle. Queuing theory was, therefore, employed to predict the *average* length of time an arriving mechanic would have to wait before being served. Using the appropriate mathematical model or formula,[26] the average waiting time was calculated to be 33.8 seconds with two clerks, 4.7 seconds with three clerks, and 0.8 with four clerks. Since there was an average of 540 requests during a $7\frac{1}{2}$ hour working day, increasing the number of clerks from two to three would reduce the mechanics' waiting time by approximately $4\frac{1}{2}$ hours. However, the amount of time clerks were idle would be increased by $7\frac{1}{2}$ hours a day for each additional clerk. If the cost of idle time was $7 per hour for mechanics and $3 per hour for clerks, the average daily cost of idle time could be calculated as follows:[27] with two clerks, $53.50; with three clerks, $45.40; with four clerks, $63.80. Based on the study, three clerks should be assigned to this tool crib.

Queuing as waiting line theory can be applied to a variety of business situations, where questions are raised concerning numbers of services or service facilities or the method in which the service is offered. These include: checkout stands at grocery stores, loading and unloading docks, secretarial typing pools, toll booths at bridges and tunnels, airline maintenance shops, retail store service counters, repair facilities for factory machine maintenance, telephone order taking or answering operations, job shops or departments producing custom orders, hospital emergency rooms, and electronic computer centers.

Game Theory.

Game theory is a mathematical technique helpful in making decisions in situations of conflict, where the success of one party tends to be at the expense of others and where the individual decision maker is not in complete control of the factors influencing the outcome.[28] For example, a general whose forces face the enemy, an industrialist whose products compete with others, a player in a poker game, and a politician fighting other candidates for an office are all involved in struggles that may be classified as game situations.

The simplest example of game theory is the two person zero-sum game: in a two person coin flipping match, when one person loses a coin

[26]Frederick S. Hillier and Gerald J. Lieberman, *Introduction to Operations Research* (San Francisco: Holden-Day, Inc., 1967), pp. 307-310.

[27]Hillier and Lieberman, *Introduction to Operations Research*, p. 347.

[28]Bierman, *et al.*, Quantitative Analysis for Business Decisions, p. 226; Martin Shubik, "The Uses of Game Theory in Management Science," in *Scientific Decision Making in Business*, ed. Shuckman, p. 332.

the other person wins a coin, so that the sum of one person's losses and the other person's gain is zero (that is, losses equal gains). Decision making in such a game situation is more difficult than in the situations discussed in the programming sections above, for when one party wins, the other loses. The individual has to work out how to achieve as much as possible, taking into account the fact that there are others whose goals are different and whose actions have an effect on all his decisions.[29]

The following is a simple illustration (two person zero-sum game) of how game theory can help in developing marketing strategy.[30] Two competing companies, Jones and Smith, each prepare a display featuring one of its products in a supermarket at the beginning of each week. Once the display has been set up it cannot be changed for the remainder of the week.

The Jones Company has three products, A, B and C, which it may display in competition with the Smith Company's products, D, E and F. The Jones Company marketing manager constructs the chart shown in Table 9.5 and estimates the chances of success of each of his products against each of Smith's products.

Table 9.5

		Smith Company Displays		
		D	E	F
Jones Company Displays	A	good	fair	fair
	B	fair	good	poor
	C	poor	fair	good

He then gives numerical values to each of his value judgments—1 for poor, 2 for fair, and 3 for good—and inserts them in his chart (Table 9.6).

Table 9.6

		Smith Company Displays		
		D	E	F
Jones Company Displays	A	3	2	2
	B	2	3	1
	C	1	2	3

Using game theory[31] it is possible to calculate the best strategy for the Jones Company: feature product A one half of the time, product B one sixth of the time, and product C one third of the time.

---

[29]Shubik. "The Uses of Game Theory," p. 333.
[30]Levin and Kirpatrick, *Quantitative Approaches to Management*, pp. 304-305. Used with permission of McGraw-Hill Book Company.
[31]Levin and Kirkpatrick, *Quantitative Approaches to Management*, pp. 268-304.

The theory of games provides a conceptual framework within which most competitive problems can be formulated.[32] It is especially useful in solving such problems as developing strategy for introducing new products or for meeting other forms of market competition.

CONCLUSION

The graphic and mathematical tools discussed in this chapter are among the many the manager may draw upon in developing controls and control standards. Some of the tools discussed in this chapter are no more than simple diagrammatic techniques, such as Gantt charts, which have very limited application. Others involve the use of advanced mathematical techniques, usually classified as management science or operations research techniques, which can be applied in a variety of control situations.

Some of the control situations in which these tools are applicable have been identified in this chapter. Additional situations are described in the next chapter, where computer applications using some of these mathematical techniques are discussed.

Generally these graphic and mathematical tools are used in visualizing and quantifying plans or in evaluating alternative plans. As such, they are principally planning tools. However, like other selected planning areas which are included in this study, such as budgeting, these tools are also used in management control. For example, a PERT chart is a graphic representation of a plan, which is used as a control mechanism to monitor progress towards the planned goal. Corrective action can be taken at any of the intermediate phases of the project, if schedules are not met. Linear programming, dynamic programming, and other operations research techniques are used in making such decisions as what of the optimum blend or mix of products, or product components or inventories. These blends or mixes can then be used as control standards, as in an automated oil plant where whenever the sensing device detects the standard mix is not being maintained action is taken automatically to correct the porportions of the mix. In other words, wherever the graphic and mathematical tools discussed in this chapter are used to produce quantified plans that in turn serve as control yardsticks, these tools can also be considered management control tools—in the same way that budgets and sales forecasts are.

The preceding discussion has attempted to outline briefly some of the graphic and mathematical tools more commonly used in management control, to define them, and to show how they may be used for control. The discussion was not intended to convey technical knowledge, but only to expand the reader's understanding of the tools available and how they can be used in management control. In an actual business situation, the

---

[32]Russell L. Ackoff and Patrick Rivett, *A Manager's Guide to Operations Research* (New York: John Wiley and Sons, Inc., 1963) p. 51.

manager would have to work with trained technicians in using most of these tools.

Since many of these tools are used in conjunction with computer systems, and serve as a mathematical basis for systems and computer simulation, they also provide an important introduction to the discussion of information systems for control in the next chapter.

DISCUSSION QUESTIONS

1. Discuss the relationship of the process used for building a model and the problem-solving/decision-making process outlined in Chapter 1.
2. Define the difference between static and dynamic graphic controls and give examples of each.
3. PERT/CPM are techniques that help in controlling projects. This chapter describes how a PERT system was developed in planning and controlling the introduction of a new product. Describe how you would go about applying PERT/CPM to control in another area of business with which you are familiar.
4. How is a Gantt chart used for management control in an operating situation? Can you describe any ways in which it can be used outside the manufacturing area? What are the major limitations on its use in any situation?
5. Comparative line charts are also useful in a limited number of control situations. Discuss examples with which you are familiar of where line charts could and could not be used effectively for control.
6. In what ways can linear programming be used to schedule and control distribution and warehousing, and in what ways can dynamic programming be used to control advertising expenditures?
7. How valid do you think the Jones Company's decision based on game theory was? In your opinion, did the application of game theory to the situation improve the allocation of display space?
8. Discuss the ways in which decision theory is helpful in control of such areas as inventory management.
9. Discuss the ways in which the tools described in this chapter serve to coordinate the planning and control functions.
10. Describe other situations (both operational and corporate) not mentioned in this chapter in which the techniques discussed in this chapter can be used for management control.

CHAPTER 10

STEP THREE: INFORMATION PROCESSING SYSTEMS USED FOR MANAGEMENT CONTROL

Chapters 7, 8 and 9 have described the control tools, systems and requirements found in three major business areas: accounting and finance controls; operating and staff controls; and graphic and mathematical controls. The control tools and systems in these areas must be maintained—data must be recorded and stored and information on performance results fed back to the manager. Such a system to process and store data and to provide feedback information on performance results is needed to make comparisons of results to standards, to uncover deviations and to take corrective action.

A company's data processing system provides the information flow needed in these control areas. This chapter concerns developing data processing systems for management control. The areas covered in the discussion are: data processing systems and management control; major kinds of business information processing systems; ways in which electronic data processing (EDP) systems can be used for management control; the systems approach and business organization for control decision making; and guidelines for developing information processing systems for control.

DATA PROCESSING SYSTEMS AND MANAGEMENT CONTROL

The simplified diagram of the management control process given in Chapter 2 is shown again in Figure 10.1 below. In carrying out the "performance" and "measurement" phases information on performance results must be collected and communicated through some mechanism which enables

194

comparison of those results to a standard. Effective management control thus requires systematically organized and developed information processing and reporting systems.

Figure 10.1

THE CONTROL PROCESS

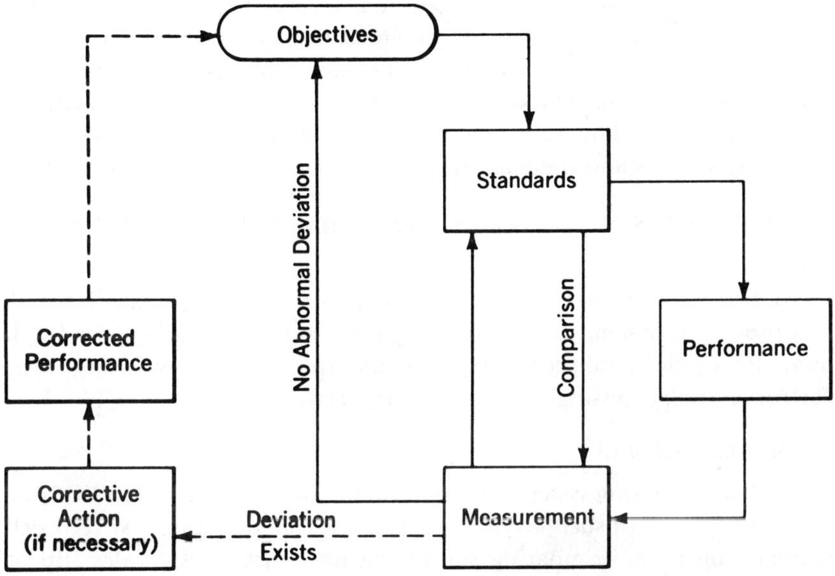

The reporting of performance results can take many forms. The reports comparing actual and budgeted balance sheet and cash flow figures shown in Chapter 7 are examples from the accounting and finance areas. The various reports shown in Chapter 8 in marketing, manufacturing, and personnel are examples from the operating and staff areas. The Gantt and line charts shown in Chapter 9 are examples from the graphic control area.

A great number of control reports are based on information stored and processed by a company's data processing system. In many instances that system will actually produce the reports. The data processing system required to produce control reports can be very simple. For example, the information on the number of coupon replies received from a circulation advertisement is obtained from a clerk in the mail-opening section who counts the coupons and enters the daily total on a cumulative record, which also has written on it the number of replies needed to justify the cost of the ad. In most cases, however, the job of information collecting and reporting is not so simple, especially in larger companies employing *computerized* data processing systems. Because of their complexity and widespread use in business today, the discussion in this chapter concentrates on EDP systems, although the principles underlying them are applicable to all types of business data processing systems.

A distinction is often made between data processing systems and management information systems. Data processing systems refer to the mechanical processes by which data is collected, recorded and communicated. When data processing systems are designed to meet the needs of specific management information systems, for example, to support an operating control system in the marketing area, they are called management information systems. The following discussion covers both the nature of data processing systems and their use in meeting management control needs.

DATA PROCESSING SYSTEMS: SOME BASIC DEFINITIONS

The orderly collection, storage, and dissemination of information needed for control decision making is one of the major functions of a company's data processing system. Data processing may be performed in three ways: manually; by electrical accounting machines (punched card systems); or by electronic data processing machines (computers).

Manual Systems.[1]

A data processing system for a very small business would most likely be a manual system. In such a system, a business transaction is first recorded manually on some originating source document (such as a sales slip or shipping receipt). The transaction is then transferred to a journal (a chronological record of transactions) and then to the ledger, where the transactions are grouped together in accounts (for example, accounts receivable). Many action documents (such as monthly invoices, production and purchase orders, or shipping instructions) are issued on the basis of these records, as are many reports used for control and planning (such as comparative sales and production reports, profit and loss statements, and balance sheets).

Manual systems are normally no more than basic accounting systems and are usually sufficient to provide with minor modifications most of the control information needed by managers of small companies.

Electrical (or Electromechanical) Data Processing.[2]

Electrical data processing systems offer significant advantages over manual systems, and many small and medium-sized companies find these

---

[1]Frederick P. Brooks, Jr., and Kenneth E. Iverson, *Automatic Data Processing* (New York: John Wiley & Sons, Inc., 1963), Chapter 2.

[2]E. Jerome McCarthy, J. A. McCarthy, and Durward Hermes, *Integrated Data Processing Systems* (New York: John Wiley & Sons, Inc., 1966), pp. 52-65.

systems useful and economical. Even though more firms will probably switch to computers as their cost continues to decline, a basic understanding of electrical accounting systems is important to understanding the concept of electronic (computer-based) data processing systems.

Both electrical and electronic data processing systems make use of the unit record principle. In a system using this principle, a transaction is recorded on one document—punched card, paper tape, or magnetic tape, for example. This single record (or source document) is then used over and over again to produce such documents as the inventory, sales, and accounts receivable records.

Electrical data processing involves the use of punched cards on which the data is recorded, and machines for interpreting, reproducing, sorting, selecting merging, matching, tabulating, and reporting these cards and the data on them. For this reason, electrical systems and machines are usually called punched card systems and machines. Since the different versions of these machines are neither strictly electrical or strictly mechanical, the systems using them are sometimes called electromechanical systems.

The functions performed by a data processing system employing electrical machines are:

1. *Card Punching.* The first step is to punch the required data onto a card. A sample of a punched card is given in Figure 10.2. The punching is usually done by a human operator using a card (or key) punch machine, although in some instances the punching is done automatically.

2. *Card Verifying.* A second operator—usually an experienced one—checks the accuracy of the original punching. The operator takes the source document and the newly punched card and repeats the original punching operation on a similar card punch machine. This machine, the card verifier, does not punch new holes but compares the keys pressed by the verifier operator with the holes already punched in the card and stops everytime there is an error.

3. *Card Reading.* The cards are then processed and the punched holes are converted into electrical impulses as the cards pass under tiny wire brushes and contact with an electrical source is made through the hole. The machine processes these timed electrical impulses in accordance with the way it has been "programmed" or wired to act.

4. *Card Interpreting.* If desired, electrical processing equipment can print the information punched on the card across the top of the card.

5. *Card Reproducing.* If required, electrical processing equipment can reproduce some or all of the information punched on one set of cards on another set of cards.

6. *Card Sorting, Selecting, Merging, and Matching.* Depending on the need, electrical processing equipment can perform any of these functions. If management desires a report on sales made by each salesman, a sorter can be used to *resort* the sales cards and group them by salesman. If the management of a

Figure 10.2

AN IBM PUNCHED CARD

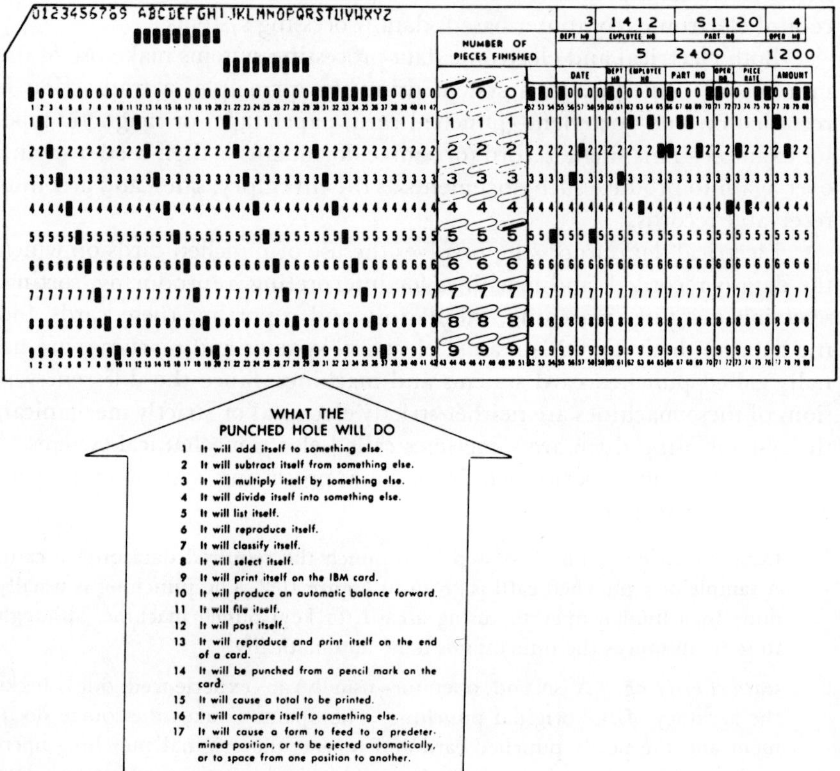
0123456789 ABCDEFGHIJKLMNOPQRSTUVWXYZ
NUMBER OF PIECES FINISHED
3 1412 S1120 4
DEPT NO
EMPLOYEE NO
PART NO
OPER NO
5 2400 1200
DATE
PIECE RATE
AMOUNT
WHAT THE PUNCHED HOLE WILL DO
1 It will add itself to something else.
2 It will subtract itself from something else.
3 It will multiply itself by something else.
4 It will divide itself into something else.
5 It will list itself.
6 It will reproduce itself.
7 It will classify itself.
8 It will select itself.
9 It will print itself on the IBM card.
10 It will produce an automatic balance forward.
11 It will file itself.
12 It will post itself.
13 It will reproduce and print itself on the end of a card.
14 It will be punched from a pencil mark on the card.
15 It will cause a total to be printed.
16 It will compare itself to something else.
17 It will cause a form to feed to a predetermined position, or to be ejected automatically, or to space from one position to another.

magazine wants to enter a new subscriber's name in its proper place in the subscriber mailing file, a collator can be used to *select* the right spot. The collator can also be used to *merge* two sets (decks) of cards or to *match* two sets of cards—for example, to match current orders against a file of past customer purchase records in order to create an invoice.

7. *Printing.* Once cards have been put into the desired sequence, a deck of cards can be run through the machine and both the alphabetic and numerical information desired can be printed on a report form. The machine can add and subtract numerical information as the decks run through, accumulate the totals, and print them at desired places in the report. These machines can print invoices and shipping documents. They can generate all forms of management control reports—for example, sales, accounts receivable, production, inventory, payroll or commission reports.

While a data processing system built on electrical accounting machines has limitations and can never provide a fully integrated information system, it is an economical tool for smaller companies and specific operations. Such systems are relatively easy to understand and use, and present few of the technical complexities found in electronic data processing systems.

Electronic Data Processing Systems.

In business today the word computer has come to mean an electronic data processing machine. Strictly speaking, a computer is any calculating device, and the term could be correctly applied to an abacus or an adding machine, as well as to a modern computing machine. In recent years, however, the term has come to apply to a special type of modern calculating machine.

There are a number of ways to classify computers.[3]

1. *Method of Operation: Analog or Digital.*   The analog computer does not compute directly with numbers but manipulates some physical quantity, such as voltage or length or shaft rotation.[4] Analog computers operate on the principle of a parallel or analogue between numbers and physical quantities, and in the analog computer the various quantities in the problem to be solved are represented by corresponding physical quantities in the machine. For example, the simplest type of analog computer is a slide rule, where lengths represent numbers and are manipulated to solve a problem.[5] Modern electronic analog computers use electronic circuitry to represent physical properties and processes.

   The digital computer records, computes, and reports in terms of absolute digits, that is, it counts things, such as electrical impulses, to obtain results. A simple type of digital computer is the adding machine.

2. *Purpose: General or Special.*   Computers which can be used for any type of data processing are called general-purpose computers, and those designed for a particular industry or application are called special-purpose computers.

3. *Relationship of Equipment: On-Line or Off-Line.*   When the input and output devices are wired directly to the main computer unit, it is an on-line computer system. Airline reservation systems are on-line systems. Since most input and output devices are not connected in this way, most computer systems are off-line.

The discussion in the remaining parts of this chapter is concerned mainly with digital computers, the type of computer in most common use in business today. Several characteristics typically found in digital computers differentiate them from electrical accounting machines. These char-

[3]Richard N. Schmidt and William E. Meyers, *Introduction to Computer Science and Data Processing* (New York: Holt, Rinehart and Winston, Inc., 1966), pp. 2-3.

[4]E. W. Martin, Jr., *Electronic Data Processing: An Introduction* (Rev. ed.; Homewood, Illinois: Richard D. Irwin, Inc., 1965), p. 102.

[5]John Dearden, *Computers in Business Management* (Homewood, Illinois. Dow Jones-Irwin, Inc., 1966), p. 13.

acteristics are speed, internal memory, and stored programs. The electronic circuitry is what gives the electronic computer its great speed. While electromechanical devices, such as the electrical accounting machine, are characterized by speeds of hundreds of operations per second, electronic devices, such as the electronic computer, can perform millions of operations per second.[6] Electronic computers can also hold data and instructions in an electronic representation in an internal memory unit, enabling use of a stored program and adding to processing speed.

The major types of equipment used in the electronic data processing (or computer) center and their functions are:[7]

Type of Equipment	*Function*
1) Central processing unit, containing:	
—an integral memory	—program and data storage
—arithmetic unit	—computation
—control circuits	—direct operation and control of system
—operator console	—operating unit
2) Magnetic tape units: random access strip, disc, or drum files	—mass data storage
3) Card reader; paper tape reader; console typewriter; data collection units; magnetic ink reader: optical character reader	—input of information
4) Printer; card punch; console typewriter; graph plotter; display device	—output of information

A simplified outline of the interaction of these units is given in Figure 10.3:

Figure 10.3

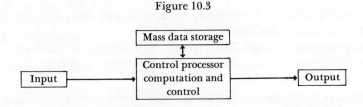

[6]Irving I. Solomon and Laurence O. Weingart, *Management Uses of the Computer* (New York: Harper and Row, Publishers, 1966), p. 202.
[7]Gordon B. Davis, *An Introduction to Electronic Computers* (New York. McGraw-Hill Book Company, 1965), p. 13.

The functions performed in an EDP system are similar to those performed in an electromechanical system: information is prepared, fed into the system through punched card readers, magnetic or paper tap readers, and optical scanners, or directly through keyboard-type machines; it is either processed or stored for processing at a later date; information is generated for use through a printer, typewriter, cathode (TV-like) tube, graphic display, sound machine, etc.

A company cannot, however, simply buy a computer and set it to work. Instructions for each job it is to do must be "programmed" for it in computer language. This translation process is a demanding one, for the "programmer" must have considerable knowledge and skill in the use of the computer in order to provide effective programs or instructions to complete the assigned task. Programming also can be a very time consuming task, depending upon the complexity of the system and the experience level of the programmer. However, once a program has been developed for a particular operation it can be recorded in the computer's memory or storage and used at will when the proper input is fed in.

Degree of Mastery Needed.

The executive interested in performing management control more effectively in today's business environment cannot avoid learning something about electrical and electronic data processing. While he does not necessarily need to learn how to program or how to operate a console, he does need to be familiar with how information systems are developed, the kinds and timing of reports they can produce, the calculations and other functions they can perform, and the costs of these information services, so that when participating in the designing of information systems for control in his operation he will not ask for the impossible or for information services whose costs exceed the benefits derived from their use. And he must know enough about EDP systems to be able to use available information systems effectively.

ELECTRONIC DATA PROCESSING SYSTEMS APPLICATIONS IN MANAGEMENT CONTROL

One of the best ways to understand how EDP information systems can be used for management control is to review some of their principal uses in business today.

Information Storage and Record Keeping.

Although the earliest computers were not developed for the record-keeping function, their potential in this area was soon recognized, and today the record-keeping application takes up considerably more computer time than any other application. The computer is particularly useful for processing a large number of items where only a small amount of processing is required for each item. In general electronic computers can be used effectively wherever the following conditions are met:

1.   A considerable amount of simple calculation is involved.
2.   The logic of the problem contains many special cases and exceptions.
3.   Answers must be precise.
4.   There is cyclical processing, that is, the particular job is processed every day, week, etc.
5.   There is repeated use of input data, that is, the same data can be used to produce a variety of output reports.

The keeping of employee payroll records is the most common use of computers today. Besides calculating the employees' pay, after making all deductions, writing the check, and making the journal entry for accounting purposes, the computer system can produce considerably more management control information. It can among other things calculate employee costs by profit center, or by operation, maintain other employee tax records, provide analysis of types and grades of personnel, and process data for promotion and movement of personnel.

At Lockheed Missiles and Space Company, the payroll is prepared by an electronic data processing system.[8] This system provides for the preparation of paychecks promptly and accurately and the development and maintenance of proper records of employee earnings. It also provides for the preparation of required control reports on taxes and on statistics required by governmental agencies and management. The computer system calculates time card and labor data, computes statutory payroll taxes, collects internal deductions, and accumulates employee earnings. It is, as a result, a valuable tool for accumulating important management control information.

A computerized data processing system can also be used for processing and maintaining customer account records. Department stores, banks and many manufacturers, and such government agencies as the Internal Revenue Service, also have massive problems to overcome in maintaining an accurate record of all transactions affecting the status of a customer's account. For example, large magazines, where a subscriber list can run as high as 14,000,000 names in the case of such publications as *Readers Digest*, must have a way of processing orders cheaply, since each subscriber pays only a few dollars for his subscription. They must also have accurately recorded subscriber address information, since the publication is delivered by mail and the customer is resold by mail. Computers are, therefore, ideally suited to handling subscriber record keeping. The kinds of management control information such computerized systems can record and produce is described in detail in Chapter 14, in the description of *The National Observer* study. Like large magazine publishers, all companies with complex customer account servicing problems now make use of computerized data processing systems.

Other management control applications of computerized systems are found in inventory accounting and in production planning and scheduling.[9] For example, Thomas and Betts Company has cut the length of its control reporting cycle from one month to ten days by means of a one-pass computerized system for handling all inventory control. All orders go directly to the computer, which maintains the inventory records for six warehouses across the country. The computer produces all the control documents, invoices, and shipping papers. The AC Spark Plug Division of General Motors Corporation also employs computer control of its inventory system. As a result, inventory control has been improved a number of ways: inactive stock items have been slashed from 20% to 0.05%; parts shortages have been cut in half; direct labor savings have increased; and contract delivery performance has improved 90%.

Compton and Knowles Company has developed a computerized system which combines inventory control with production scheduling. When an inventory item is out of stock, the computer generates a production order, including: department, work center, operation to be performed, job code and obtainment code, setup hours, standard hours required, description of the requirement, and scheduled due date.[10]

Advanced EDP Systems.

The more exciting applications of electronic data processing are outside the area of routine record-keeping.

While there is some disagreement as to whether a company can ever have a "total information system"[11] that is, a completely integrated data processing system—considerable progress is being made towards greater integration of information systems.

[9]L. James Sasanecki, "Introduction to EDP—Controlled Inventory Control," *Management Services* (November-December 1967), p. 35. For a description of how other companies have used the computer for inventory control see: William A. Price and Edward J. Neppl, "Automated Inventory Control," *N.A.A.-Management Accounting* (October 1966), pp. 52-58; C. E. Viscione, "3 Automatic Warehouses . . . Luxurious? . . . 'No, They Are Practical and Economical' ", *Factory* (October 1964), pp. 100-102; Anthony A. Vallario, "An Inventory Control System with Profitable By-Products," *Management Services* (January-February 1967), pp. 31-36; and William N. Smith and G. F. Reichenbach, "Maintenance Material Inventory Control," *N.A.A.-Management Accounting* (August 1967), p. 51.

[10]William J. McLaughlin, "EDP Contribution to a Manufacturing Operation," *Financial Executive* (April 1966), pp. 14-26.

[11]John Dearden, "Can Management Information Be Automated," *Harvard Business Review* (March-April 1964), pp. 128-135.

Within an integrated system for a mail-order sales operation, for example, a single entry would be made for a sale. This entry would then be input into the computer which would perform the following functions:

1. Check whether present customer account is in arrears, and whether customer's credit status justifies charging present purchase.
2. Record sales in sales record.
3. Produce customer invoice.
4. Enter transaction in Accounts Receivable file.
5. Check availability of item of inventory.
6. Withdraw item from inventory, update inventory balance, and schedule interview replacement.
7. Issue shipping instructions.
8. Report sales by media for advertising planning and control.

The possibilities of integration in mail-order operations are virtually unlimited, since a mail-order operation is handled almost entirely internally, and customer contact is limited to automated correspondence. Even here, however, the so-called "total systems" with which this author has worked have never achieved the ideal of serving all the information needs of the decision makers with a single EDP information processing system.

Rollaway Bearing Company provides an example of an advanced computer system used for control in the production area.[12] Rollaway used the computer to convert engineering designs automatically into precise manufacturing instructions, including: directions as to the operations that must be performed; the sequence in which they must be performed; the work methods that must be employed; the raw material form that must be used; the exact tools and fixtures that will be required, in-process dimensions and temperatures, if applicable; time standards; and detailed cost estimates.

Many advanced computer systems are real-time systems—that is, a system in which data is processed at such speed that output may be fed back to control current operations. In a real-time system information is updated frequently enough to be considered correct at all times, and the information can be retrieved as quickly as needed.[13] An airline reservation system is one of the most familiar real-time EDP systems. Each reservation office ticket counter has an input-output electric typewriter wired directly to a large, centralized computer system. This machine is used to determine whether seats are available and to reduce the "inventory" of seats available for that particular flight, if the customer reserves a seat. American Airlines' SABRE system is one of the many such systems used by airlines companies.[14]

---

[12]"Automated Manufacturing Planning: Computer Solves a Big Production Problem," *Business Management* (January 1966), pp. 41-43.
[13]Dearden, *Computers in Business Management*, p. 275.
[14]Martin, *Electronic Data Processing*, pp. 12-13.

Real-time systems are also used for the control of hotel and motel reservation operations. For example, the more than 700 Holiday Inns throughout the world are linked together by a computer-controlled reservation-communication network.[15] Each Holiday Inn has a system terminal connected to the main computer center. The clerk at any Inn pulls a call card for the inn where the reservation is to be made and places it in the system terminal on an adjoining keyboard. The clerk keys into the terminal the code number of the inn at which the reservation is to be made, the type of room accommodation desired, the number of nights and the dates, and types out the guest's name.

This information is transmitted instantly to the control center in Memphis, Tennessee. There the computer determines whether the reservation can be made. If it can, the computer notifies the inquiring clerk and sends a confirming message both to the inn originating the request and to the inn at which the reservation has been made. If the reservation cannot be made, the computer notifies the inquiring clerk and suggests other accommodations available at the requested inn and at other Holiday Inns in the same geographical area.

Retailers use real-time computer systems to control credit clearing operations. For example, the Carson, Pirie, Scott department store in Chicago uses an in-store system that enables its personnel to check a customer's credit in a matter of seconds by dialing the customer's account number on a telephone.[16] The computer returns a spoken answer, either authorizing the sale or giving other instructions.

Repetitive Computations and Comparisons.

The computer is an extremely useful tool in performing complex mathematical computations, such as those needed for operations research and PERT/CPM. Examples of situations where the computer could be used to support operations research were given in the linear and dynamic programming sections in the preceding chapter.

Systems Simulation.

Once a control system has been designed, the essence of it can be simulated in a way that permits the system developer to test and refine the system using a computer. Because of the computer's ability to do extensive complex computations quickly, it is possible to develop more sophisticated computer systems models.

A business system is simulated by making a quantitative description of it. This description is called a model. The model is then programmed for

15William B. Walton, "Holiday Saves $128 Million in First Year," *Journal of Data Management* (May 1967), p. 34.
16Philip Kotler, "A Design for the Firm's Marketing Nerve Center," *Business Horizons* (Fall 1966), pp. 65-66.

a computer, which can compress real time and permit the effect of years of operations to be studied in a few minutes.

Industrial dynamics is a good example of the use of systems simulation in business. Jay W. Forrester was a pioneer in developing the industrial dynamics approach to the study of the business organization and decision making.[17] Using this approach the business organization is viewed as interrelated flows of many variables—materials, money, information, manpower, and capital equipment. Through the use of simulation, management can study the effects of the interrelationships of these variables on organizational performance, allowing management to determine how a change in one variable will effect the other variables. For example, an optimum inventory system may cause serious difficulties in the production department, so that the inventory system is best understood in the context of a simulation model which includes production, inventory, sales, and so on.

Information Retrieval.

One of the major problems of our technological civilization is the staggering volume of information the individual is expected to use. Approximately 60,000 books, 100,000 research treatises, and 1,300,000 articles are published each year throughout the world.[18] As a result, people are finding it increasingly difficult to keep up with the literature on subjects of interest to them, and there is much needless duplication of research.

The computer can provide assistance in solving this information retrieval problem. One system being developed uses key words to identify subject matter.[19] An article or a subject, such as the Van Allen belt, is identified by metals, radiation, Van Allen belt and space. These key word identifiers and a brief abstract are stored on magnetic tape for reference for use by researchers.

Various governmental agencies and scientific organizations have established information retrieval systems. Each document is read and abstracted, and a list of key words that indicate the documents information content is prepared. For example, Chemical Abstracts Service (CAS), a government agency, periodically offers magnetic tapes containing references to printed reports of scientific and technical research.[20]

Guidance and Control.

Guidance and control systems also make use of computers. The computer receives information, makes the necessary calculations instan-

---

[17]Jay W. Forrester, *Industrial Dynamics* (New York: John Wiley & Sons, Inc., 1961).
[18]Martin, *Electronic Data Processing*, pp. 15-16.
[19]Davis, *Electronic Computers*, p. 35.
[20]Speeding Up the Search," *Chemical Week* (February 18, 1967), p. 49.

taneously and continuously, and then adjusts the process being regulated. Missile and ship guidance, and manufacturing process control are some of the uses of the computer in this area.

NIKE missiles are controlled by computer. The guidance computer tracks the enemy plane by radar and transmits instructions to the missile to adjust the missile's speed and flight path to intercept the plane as it changes course.

Guidance and control of ships is another use of the computer. For example, a computer has been placed aboard the Scripps Institution of Oceanography research vessel *Thomas Washington*.[21] The computer has four main jobs to do:

1. Performing the regular routine logging of the marine environment, including measuring water depth, checking sea-surface temperature and salinity, calculating wind speed and direction, and air temperature and humidity.
2. Collecting data for specific scientific experiments.
3. Working towards a more accurate knowledge of the ship's position, and providing better knowledge of the origin of the data it is receiving.
4. Providing the scientist with general purpose computational capacity with which to analyze previously unanticipated relationships from reduced data, so that the scientist will be able to write completely new analysis programs or modify old ones while at sea.

In process industries, such as oil refining and chemical production, computers often form an integral part of the control network that operates the process. In these situations the computer is applied to a continuously changing situation to control and maintain optimum performance of the system.[22] For example, using automated control equipment a computer can adjust mixes and blends in a continuing chemical process when they deviate from prescribed standards. At the Western Division of Chevron Oil Company, management uses its computer facilities for product blending and refinery operation planning.[23] Among the questions answered by the computer are: how much more a Product A can be made without reducing the production of other products, how much would it cost to increase by a certain amount the output of Product A, and what is the best method of getting rid of production bottlenecks?

Other Computer Applications.

The computer performs many other functions not directly related to management control.

American Telephone and Telegraph Company has installed about 400,000 digital circuits in its Bell System and plans to convert all of its

21"Seagoing Computer Will Aid Marine Research by Giving Instantaneous Solution to Problems," *Management Services* (September-October 1967), p. 12.

22Solomon and Weingart, *Management Uses of the Computer*, p. 205.

23"Hands on Computers," *Chemical Week* (November 18, 1967), p. 156.

circuit lines to digital circuits eventually.[24] When telephone calls go between exchanges a digital computer transmission system chops the electrical signals into samples 8,000 times a second. The system measures the samples and transmits the resulting numerical value in a computer-age Morse code between telephone offices. At the receiving office, electronic equipment sorts the signals, decodes them, and reconverts them into the varying, continuous electrical current that carries the voice to the telephone at the end of the line.

The computer has become a valuable tool in today's colleges and schools. At the Massachusetts Institute of Technology, for example, successful experiments with *programmed instruction* using the computer have been conducted in the area of managerial accounting.[25] Computers are now used to help teach mathematics, reading and spelling to 6,000 elementary school students in the New York City School System.[26] Computers are also being used for language translation.[27]

Computer decision simulation or management gaming is another use of the computer for education.[28] For example, several times each year groups of Proctor and Gamble employees, including new sales personnel and management trainees, are asked to spend six hours playing Venture, a computerized management decision-making game.[29] And an International Business Machines Corporation game carries computer involvement a step further than most business games: rather than relying on the computer as merely an umpire, players use the machine to analyze problems and alternatives before they decide what to do.[30]

These and other applications, such as "heuristic" programming,[31] while not directly related to control, give some idea of the extensive use of computerized systems in other areas of management decision making.

THE SYSTEMS APPROACH AND BUSINESS ORGANIZATION FOR CONTROL DECISION MAKING

The growing use of the computer is having a revolutionary impact on business today. In larger companies, many operating executives have

---

[24]"Why Ma Bell Chops Up the Signals," *Business Week* (January 13, 1968), pp. 82-84.

[25]Zenon S. Zannetos, "Programmed Instruction and Computer Technology," *Accounting Review* (July 1967), pp. 566-571.

[26]Judson Hand, "Tireless Teacher Makes Debut," *New York Daily News* (June 14, 1968), p. 5.

[27]Martin, *Electronic Data Processing*, p. 16.

[28]John R. Carson, "Business Games: A Technique for Teaching Decision-Making," N.A.A.—Management Accounting (October 1967), p. 32.

[29]Elliot Carlson, "The Versatile Business Game: Its Growing Use in Industry," *Management Review* (September 1966), p. 46.

[30]*Ibid.*

[31]Charles L. Hinkle and Alfred A. Kuehn, "Heuristic Models: Mapping the Maze for Management," *California Management Review* (Fall 1967), pp. 61-62.

found the revolution chaotic, for it has come in the form of the intrusion of the computer and computer personnel into their operations. They have felt their authority and control slowly stripped away by a movement they little understand, and because of this they have resisted it.

The computer is not, however, the villain. What normally happens is that the introduction of the computer sets in motion a systematic reevaluation of what the business is and how it can operate most efficiently. This reevaluation exposes the real problem—the gradual fragmentation of decision-making systems within a company over the years, the exposure of the problem in turn leads to an effort to reestablish smoothly working, fully coordinated decision-making systems within the business. Systems theory provides a conceptual basis, as well as principles and guidelines, for establishing a more efficient system within a business for control decision making.

A system may be defined as an orderly grouping of separate but interdependent components for the purpose of attaining some predetermined objective.[32] Three important aspects of systems are implied by this definition. First, the arrangement of components must be orderly and hierarchical, no matter how complex it may be. Second, since the components of the system are interdependent, there must be communication among them. Third, since a system is oriented towards an objective, any interaction among the components must be designed to achieve that objective.

Systems theory, and the various aspects of it explored by scientists,[33]

---

[32]A number of variations on this definition exist. For example, Warren Brown, "Systems, Boundaries, and Information Flow," *Academy of Management Journal*, Vol. 9, No. 4 (December 1966), p. 318, defines a system as "a group or complex of parts (such as people, machines, etc.) interrelated in their actions towards some goal," and Richard A. Johnson, Fremont E. Kast and James E. Rosenzweig, *The Theory and Management of Systems* (2nd ed.; New York: McGraw-Hill Book Company, Inc., 1967), p. 4, state that "a system is "an organized or complex whole; an assemblage or combination of things or parts forming a complex or unitary whole."

[33]A number of authorities working in diverse fields of specialization, such as biology, communications theory and business management, have contributed to the development of systems theory. Four of the better known of these authorities are Ludwig von Bertalanffy, Kenneth Boulding, Norbert Weiner and Herbert Simon. Johnson, Kast and Rosenzweig, *ibid.*, p. 6, n. 1, assert that von Bertalanffy was the first to use the term "Systems Theory." For further information on von Bertalanffy's *Systems Theory see his Problems of Life: An Evaluation of Modern Biological and Scientific Thought* (London: C. A. Watts and Company, Ltd., 1952) and a series of papers by von Bertalanffy, Carl G. Hempel, Robert E. Bass, and Hans Jonas, published under the overall title "General Systems Theory: A New Approach to Unity of Science," in *Human Biology*, Vol. 23, No. 4 (December 1951), pp. 302-361. For the works of the others, see Kenneth E. Boulding, "General Systems Theory—The Skeleton of Science," *Management Science*, Vol. 2, No. 3 (April 1956), pp. 197-208; Norbert Wiener, *The Human Use of Human Beings: Cybernetics and Society* (Boston: Houghton Mifflin Company, 1950); Herbert A. Simon, *The New Science of Management Decision* (New York: Harper and Row, Publishers, 1960).

are important to business and business managers for a number of reasons.[34] First, since the systems approach is objective-oriented, systems organization automatically centers attention upon the objectives for which the firm has been established and helps to generate concerted and coordinated activity towards attainment of these objectives. Second, systems theory stresses the interdependence of elements, so that a manager is continually forced to view the components of a business in relation to each other. Third, systems theory provides a systematic approach to developing information processing systems for management control.

The systems approach underlies the development of all effective information processing systems used in management control. It is important, therefore, to understand the impact of the systems approach to information systems development on a company's organization structure and decision-making processes.

The systems approach forces the manager to look upon his business organization as an information network, with the flow of information providing the decision makers at varying management levels with the information needed to make decisions of all types. These information-communication systems necessarily link together the components needed to operate a business successfully, i.e., the people, plants and machines assembled for the purpose of achieving both the general corporate objective of making money and the individual corporate objective of making money by engaging in a specific type of profit-making business enterprise.

Traditional business organization theory emphasises the relationships between people by focusing on the tasks to be performed, the job positions and responsibility for each job position. In *Management Systems* McDonough and Garrett give some of the principles of organization that show the traditional, personnel-oriented approach to organization. [35]

1. Be sure that adequate provision is made for all activities.
2. Group (departmentalize) activities on some logical basis.

[34]Within the last few years a number of authors have studied the application of systems theory to business operations:

Robert N. Anthony, John Dearden and Richard F. Vancil, *Management Control Systems: Cases and Readings* (Homewood, Illinois. Richard D. Irwin, Inc., 1965).

John Dearden and F. Warren McFarlan, *Management Information Systems: Text and Cases* (Homewood, Illinois. Richard D. Irwin, Inc., 1966).

Daniel O. Dommasch and Charles W. Laudeman, *Principles Underlying Systems Engineering* (New York: Pitman Publishing Corp., 1962).

Donald G. Malcolm and Alan J. Rowe, *Management Control Systems* (New York: John Wiley and Sons, Inc., 1960).

Adrian M. McDonough and Leonard J. Garrett, *Management Systems: Working Concepts and Practices* (Homewood, Illinois: Richard D. Irwin, Inc., 1965).

Henry M. Paynter, *Analysis and Design of Engineering Systems* (Cambridge, Massachusetts: The M.I.T. Press, 1961).

Thomas R. Prince, *Information Systems for Management Planning and Control* Rev. ed.; (Homewood, Illinois: Richard D. Irwin, Inc., 1970).

[35]McDonough and Garrett, *Management Systems*, p. 9.

3. Limit the number of subordinates reporting to each executive.
4. Define the responsibilities of each department, division and subdivision.
5. Delegate authority to subordinates wherever practicable.
6. Make authority and responsibility equal.
7. Provide for controls over those to whom authority is delegated.
8. Avoid dual subordination.
9. Distinguish clearly among line authority, functional authority, and staff relationships.
10. Develop methods of coordination.

These principles clearly focus on the person-to-person relationships within an organization and on the physical and functional departmentalization of the business unit. The commonplace block-diagram organization chart reflects this concept. Such relationships are, of course, important in thinking about organizations, but overemphasis of these relationships can obscure the information and communication links so vital to effective control within the corporation.

When changes are introduced within the traditional organization structure, normally new departments or units are added or new responsibilities are given to existing departments. Sometimes these additions or changes are made to meet new business needs, sometimes to take maximum advantage of an individual executive's particular combination of talents, and sometimes merely to adjust to the personalities of individual executives. Such a fragmented development process almost invariably leads to some decrease in the effectiveness of the decision-making processes within an organization.

The systems approach to organization attempts to avoid this problem by focusing on the dynamic interaction and intercommunication among components of the system. Systems theory subordinates the separate units or departments of a business to decision-making information and communication networks. Understanding this difference is fundamental to understanding how systems theory has affected business organization and decision making.

The initial chart picturing a business organization restructured around the information flows, instead of around the authority and responsibility units, does not look substantially different from more traditional organization charts, for during the first phases of the changeover only a few departments have been added and some job responsibilities shifted. The change in basic organization philosophy has a profound effect, however, for it creates major changes in the way an organization functions—changes that affect the lives of all the individuals operating within the business system·and changes that after a period of time produce major adjustments in the structure of the business organization. Both in theory and in practice, therefore, the systems approach is revolutionary for an established business.

The revolution has in fact occurred in most larger companies, because the introduction of electronic data processing, with its enormous capacity for storing and processing information and its enormous expense, is forcing business to use a systems approach to organization development. The computer has in a sense been the catalyst for reevaluation and change. For some companies the transition has been smooth, for others it has been chaotic.

When introducing a computer, many companies tend to approach the changeover in the traditional way—piecemeal, department by department. Such an approach only reinforces the fragmentation and disruption of information and decision-making systems.

Instead, as most companies sooner or later discover, before major decisions concerning computerization or company-wide information systems are made, management must reevaluate the entire flow of business, not merely the individual operations being computerized, in order to isolate the major decision-making areas, their interrelations, and the information needed to make these decisions most effectively. In other words, the systems approach has proved in practice to be the best one.

For example, in a large merchandise mail-order business which had decided to change to computerized order processing and information handling, the first inclination was to write programs in steps, first for marketing, then for order processing, billing, inventory control, and so on, for each of the components or departments currently operating in the company.

It soon became apparent that this was not the best approach. At this time management directed the systems group to study overall planning factors: the nature of the business in which the company was then engaged, the business in which the company hoped to be engaged within the next five years, and the environment in which the company would operate in the future.

The group next constructed a chart of the flow of the business operation, starting with the coupon advertisement offering the product and asking for the order, and following the customer's order through processing and billing until the product is shipped, the merchandise restocked, and the bill paid. For each phase in the flow chart a supplemental list was made of the significant planning, control and operational decisions necessary to perform that phase well. The information that was needed was then determined.

Only after the above studies were completed was a decision made as to which aspects of the business process could most economically be computerized, which could best be done clerically, and which were of sufficiently minor importance to the overall functioning of the business that they would be done in a less than ideal way or not be done at all. As a final step, the actual organization of the operation was restructured around the picture of the business which had been developed in the systems studies.

The diagram of the restructured organization may have looked to the casual observer like the traditional organization chart of the former organization, for there were departments for marketing, order processing, billing and credit, product procurement and inventory control, and liaison among all these operations. But the changes made to bring the organization into line with the known decision-making needs of the business were enormous.

On closer examination it was clear that the new organization had little relation to the old organization. Pockets of personal strength had been wiped out and antiquated reporting relationships had been changed drastically. Major adjustments had been made in the daily interworkings between departments and in the groupings of functions within each department. For example, advertising was now a marketing department, order processing included customer service, and product procurement and warehousing were combined. In other words, what is commonly called an "authority" organization structure had given way to a "systems" organization structure.

The reevaluation showed that the old organization had not grown dramatically with the business but was a conglomeration of old operating procedures, compromises made to accommodate personality differences, and the like. Although the changeover was painful, it revitalized the operation.

The advantages of following the systems approach may seem obvious to the reader. Yet it is still an approach rarely followed in practice. In an existing business concern the tendency is to look at the business as a series of departments, with department heads who perform various functions, the totality of which is the "business." What this business is, how it flows, and how its parts interrelate is likely to be known only by those who grew up with the business and now head it. And even they may not have a clear understanding of some of the newer aspects of the business.

The mail-order company cited in the example above was fortunate. In spite of the problems caused by the introduction of systems thinking into the organization, the company finally adjusted to and profited from the systems approach. Many companies faced with computerization have taken the easy way out. Instead of starting with a thorough reevaluation of their businesses from a systems viewpoint, they have computerized their operations piecemeal. Letting presently established organizational structures control the systems study and development creates a number of problems: first, it leaves the antiquated organization structure intact and hinders the development of an effective mechanism for improved decision making; and second, it leads to inefficient use of the new, automated, computerized processing equipment.

The systems approach is revolutionizing business decision making, for it can provide more comprehensive information, faster, at the point and in the form it is needed to make better business decisions. Adapting the organization to the information systems needed for effective planning, control and operational decision making enables a company to take advantage of new facilities for storing and processing information, which can in turn lead to competitive advantages and greater profits.

Drastic organizational changes do not necessarily have to occur at the time a study of the business system is made, since a company may have grown and developed in tune with its growing business. But this is the exception. Some changes will always occur, and over the long run they are usually major.

The executive familiar with the fundamental changes in business philosophy forced upon business by the introduction of electronic data processing and the development of systems theory will be better prepared to meet the challenges they present. He will not be confused by the continuing change brought about by the systems approach to organization and decision making, nor will he consider electronic data processing a threat to this position. Instead, he will be able to control and guide that change in the most profitable directions, and at the same time expand his capacity for more effective management performance.

DEVELOPING A NEW INFORMATION SYSTEM FOR CONTROL: GUIDELINES FOR OVERCOMING SOME TYPICAL PROBLEMS

During the past few years the author has worked with a number of companies in developing information systems for planning, control and operating decision making. All of the companies were of moderate size, over $50,000,000 in annual sales. In each case a large portion of the business was done through direct-response selling—that is, selling a product or service through an advertisement or mailing piece which asks the customer to write directly to the company to order the item advertised. The products these companies sold through direct-response advertising ranged from magazine subscriptions and book club memberships to phonographs and television sets.

As they grew, each of these companies saw the need to convert to a computer data processing system. For all of them the conversion was a difficult task. Because there were many similarities in the problems encountered in developing the systems and in the ways these problems were overcome at each of these companies, it seemed that others might benefit from a review of the lessons learned about identifying and overcoming these problems.

The Decision to Develop a New System.

In each company the development of the new system began the same way: management decided to install a new computer to process orders, to maintain the file of customer names for billing and repromotion, and to generate planning and control reports. In all instances the customer names were currently being maintained on punch cards, but the lists were growing so fast that the punched card systems were becoming inefficient and uneconomical.

In no case was there a formal feasibility or cost study which compared the old card electromechanical and new tape electronic systems and which determined how much time and expense would be involved in developing the new system. At first this may seem puzzling, since many people with experience in the field recommend such studies.[36] Most companies, however, are slow to adopt management theory to practice, and the situation encountered at the mail-order companies studied is probably more the rule than the exception.

Formal feasibility studies were not conducted because each company already seemed to have made an instinctive commitment to a new computerized system. As a result, the mission of the systems manager was to develop the new system and perform the conversion as economically as possible, not to determine whether or not the new system should be installed or what would be involved in the development and conversion phases.

The first problem common to all these companies, therefore, was the lack of a preparatory or feasibility study. Fortunately, in all instances the economy and efficiency of an updated, high-speed, computerized processing system proved beneficial to company operations.

Preparing for the Systems Study.

The actual systems development work was begun in the traditional way. A group from the systems analysis section was appointed to develop a systems proposal and prepare programs for the new computer. Then all the operating managers affected by the new information system were notified that the study was to be undertaken.

Corporate management gave verbal support to the project, but did not appoint a corporate officer to head the study group and, in fact, attended few of the group's meetings during the year or so spent developing the new information system.

The second problem, therefore, was the lack of top management guidance, support and, most important, participation in the systems development study.

The Changing Scope of the Initial Study.

Because no feasibility study was done, the exact scope of the systems development study and the time and effort needed to develop a new information and control system were not clearly spelled out from the beginning.

---

[36]See, for example, James Greenwood, *EDP: The Feasibility Study—Analysis and Improvement of Data Processing* ("Systems Education Monograph, No. 4;" Washington, D.C.: Systems and Procedures Association, 1962), and Thomas Hindelang, "EDP Feasibility Study—An Indispensible Prerequisite for EDP Success," *Computer Applications Service*, V, 1965, pp. 36-41.

In retrospect it seemed that management thought of the project as writing a program for a new computer. Only as the systems development group delved deeper into their study did the scope of the undertaking expand into a true information systems study, which was what management finally determined they really needed and wanted.

Through the study group's efforts management came to realize that no judgment about where a computer can be used effectively and economically is possible until the decision-making processes within the company and the flow of information needed for decision making are studied and defined. A computer system can be a great aid in decision making, but only if it is structured to meet the specific decision-making needs of the company using it.

Because no one had expected the project to be so complex, it had to be modified as it progressed. The confusion, resistance and waste of time and money this caused could have been avoided by defining the mission broadly rather than narrowly at the beginning. Then management could have either provided the time, manpower and money needed to do a complete project, or lowered their sights and settled for a system of more limited scope.

The third problem, therefore, was not understanding that a total information system was needed, not realizing what such a study entailed, and not providing the people, organization, time, and money needed to complete the study.

The Initial Phase of the Study.

Because at the outset the project was narrowly defined as a computer program writing project, the systems study group first examined each of the individual operations being computerized. As the work progressed, however, the group found they needed to do more background work before they could understand these operations and they began exploring in more depth such areas as:

1. The general nature of the business and the markets within which the company operated.
2. The company's entire business process, from order receipt to customer payment.
3. The kind of information needed for decision making at the various critical points in the business process.
4. The timing and format of the information needs.[37]

The businesses being studied were mail-order selling operations. Sales or inquiries were solicited by mailings, by magazine or newspaper coupon ads, or by radio and television commercials asking for customer orders.

[37]These are the steps recommended by Prince, *Information Systems*, pp. 23-24.

The products sold ranged from $500 television sets to $2 gift merchandise and magazine subscriptions. Sales were solicited from former customers, from the general consumer market, and from customers served by other divisions of the company. Most sales were on credit, but lower-priced merchandise was frequently sold on a cash-with-order basis. The companies were, therefore, retailers, and all of the functions normally handled in the retail store would have to be handled by the new system.

Once the general nature of the business was defined, the systems group looked at the internal flow of business. Orders and payments were received in the mail room. Payments were sent to the collection section, which deposited the money and credited the payment to the customer's account. Orders were sent to the application section. If the order was from a customer in good standing, it was processed; if not, it was sent to the credit department for clearance or rejection. Once the cleared orders were processed, the products were shipped and customer billing begun. In all, five operating sections were involved:

1. Production or product procurement, including warehousing.
2. Marketing.
3. Accounting and financial analysis.
4. Fulfillment: order processing and file maintenance, including billing.
5. Credit.

As the systems group extended their study, they found how little they knew about the areas other than order processing, and how much they would need to know to develop a sophisticated information system to meet information requirements in all these sections.

The systems study group encountered some problems when they began the necessary detailed study of each of the five areas. Although they had been told to call upon all sections involved in the operation, no one person in each operating section was designated to help the study group and no executives from the operating departments were appointed members of the study group.[38] Since the systems group was part of the fulfillment (order processing and file maintenance section and since they could obtain little assistance from the other four operating sections, they naturally tended to create a system designed principally for the fulfillment area, a system that would only secondarily serve the information needs of the other sections.

At each company it was necessary for a corporate executive to intervene to resolve the problem. At one of the companies, for example, the marketing manager met with the system group, saw the inadequacies of the new system, discussed the problem with them, and recommended expanding the study group to include a representative from each operating

[38]The importance of involving operating executives directly in the systems study is emphasized by such authorities as Dearden and McFarlan, *Management Information Systems*, p. 49.

section. Four operating managers were then appointed to the group, although most of the work was still done by the original study group of systems analysts. A timetable for completion was developed at the same time.

Only at this point, therefore, was the true breadth of the new system officially recognized. What had originally been basically an order processing and file maintenance system now became a total information system, and the group was given the manpower needed to complete the project successfully.

Prior to this step, the scope of the project had been limited, not because management wanted it to be limited, but because they had not provided the mechanism or organization to implement a broader study. The fourth problem, therefore, was that representatives of each operating section were not made part of the original study group and so did not participate in the work of the systems development.

Defining Information Needs.

The next step in developing the information system was to have each operating section define its functions, the kinds of decisions it made, the information needed to make these decisions, and the form in which that information was needed.

This was not a simple task. First, the operating managers were reluctant to spend the time required to do this. Each felt that he knew his job and that describing it in a report would be a waste of time. In addition, he felt that he would be reporting to the systems analysts, although he had been told that the system would be serving his needs and thought that the analysts would be reporting to him. Second, a systems analyst needs considerable skill at interviewing in order to draw out information about future or ideal operating needs, for the operating manager tends to speak of the information he now gets, instead of what is required to make good decisions.

Again the corporate officer closest to the study was forced to intervene. He explained that a periodic review of job objectives and functions was good business and normal, that the systems group really was working for the operational managers, and that the new system was a wonderful opportunity to relieve operational managers of a considerable amount of detail work and to give them better reports, in a more readable form. However, the price to be paid over the short run was that each operational manager would be required to devote time and attention to the project. If the operational managers did not give such time, they could not justifiably complain later of lacking the information needed to make decisions or of not having it in the form needed to make decisions quickly.

The fifth problem, therefore, was getting a clear definition of the information needs of each of the decision makers within the system.

Balancing the Information Needs of Each Operating Section.

Because of the lack of direction from management and support from the operational managers, and because of the systems analysts' training in machine applications, it was difficult for the systems group to maintain a "total information system" perspective and to be objective in balancing the needs of each operational group in the new system.

This point often escapes the systems theorist. Prince, for example, overlooks it when he describes the job of the systems analyst:

The system analyst, like the financial accountant, the financial manager, the sales manager, and the production manager, is concerned with designing observations of certain manifestations of a business organization. But unlike the other cited trained observers, the systems analyst does not respond to any traditional set of theories associated with a functional area of the business. . . .

The systems analyst is concerned with the information dimension of decision-making activities throughout the business organization. . . .

The systems analyst desires to establish the ideal set of information systems that is compatible with the major decision-making requirements in the existing unique environment of a particular business organization.[39]

While ideally the systems analyst is supposed to have the perspective to view an entire business system objectively and to pull together all aspects of an operation, there is no guarantee that he will. The systems analyst is often a trained programmer. Because of his background and training he tends to be machine-oriented and to think in terms of the efficiency of machine applications instead of operational decision-making needs. Like the sales manager, production manager and financial manager, then, the systems analyst also has a functional bias.

The ability to view an operation objectively and in its entirety is not an exclusive characteristic of any particular functional area in a corporation. It is a characteristic of effective management. Any good manager, in any functional area, should be able to maintain a broad, comprehensive, objective viewpoint.

In the companies studied the problem of maintaining a balanced viewpoint was further compounded by the fact that the systems group in a mail-order operation is part of the fulfillment operation. Where compromises had to be made, therefore, the group tended to accomodate either machine efficiency or the efficiency of the processing system for the fulfillment area.

As a result, operational managers came to believe that the information needs of their areas—whether product procurement or marketing—were considered secondary to the needs of the fulfillment area. However, these managers were not willing to devote the time needed to help shape the new system to their own needs. The systems group wanted to be objective,

39Prince, *Information Systems*, pp. 16-17.

but in the absence of sufficient guidance from top management and from the operating managers, they naturally concentrated on satisfying the needs of the areas they knew best: fulfillment and computer applications.

The situation at this point was chaotic. For example, the marketing section wanted daily manual tabulations of customer orders received by media and a report on them daily. This would enable the marketing section to make quicker decisions on the profitability of promotions. The systems group immediately reacted negatively, for the request would require adjustments and delays in their order processing system. In other words, the systems group revealed an unconscious bias towards creating the most efficient fulfillment system possible, even at the expense of efficiency in other operating sections.

The same kind of problem arose when the credit manager asked that certain credit checks be built into the system, when the marketing manager asked that the billing envelopes be enlarged so that he could enclose promotional material in them, when the product procurement manager asked for an on-line perpetual inventory sub-system, when the financial analysis group asked for a returned merchandise count by promotion, and so on.

The situation fortunately did not get out of hand, for in all these cases objectivity was supplied by the informal intervention of a corporate executive, who knew systems, understood all the operations affected by the system, and was well-liked by the persons working on the development of the system. It was this executive who prevented the systems group from fashioning the parts of the system to suit machine efficiency exclusively and arbitrated the compromises necessary to create a system that served the needs of all operational areas. It was he who filled the gap left when top management failed to become directly involved in the project.

The sixth problem, therefore, was maintaining objectivity and balance in the new system.

The Final Determination of the Costs and Performance Characteristics of the New System.

Not only did management under-estimate the costs and complications of developing the system, they also underestimated the costs and performance characteristics of the final system. Fortunately, even though the costs of the final system were higher than anticipated, the savings under the new system were sufficient to justify its installation.

But modifications in the design and size of the new system occasioned sizeable delays. In all cases the computer ordered turned out to be too small. The order was changed, delays resulted, and management had to adjust to increased costs. The machine hardware configuration (that is, number of drives, printers and computer specifications) also changed and its final form differed radically from that originally proposed to the manufacturer. Management also had to adjust to some basic changes in the system performance. It was found, for example, that the new system could not substantially decrease order processing time, and that it could provide only a modified on-line inventory control.

While some changes are inevitable, a more complete feasibility study would have reduced the number and size of these changes. The seventh problem, therefore, was making a commitment for the new computer before completing a detailed study of costs and the computer configuration needed for the new system.

The Organizational Impact of the New System.

The systems development program at the companies studied led to major changes in the organization structures of the companies. As a result of the project, attention was shifted from what each department had done in the past—that is, which department had handled what functions—to the operations and functions that were needed to run this type of business successfully.

Some personnel with narrow viewpoints saw the study as a threat to their positions. And they were right. For the study made it obvious that certain changes in the organization were needed. Other personnel, however, realized that a business is dynamic, and that internal changes are constantly needed to meet changing market conditions and improve operating efficiency. To these persons the new system represented an opportunity, not a threat.

While the adjustments came easily for some, for others who were not prepared for the changes and resisted them the adjustments were painful. Some pockets of bureaucratic resistance were wiped out, for a number of departments were eliminated and their remaining functions were put under existing departments. For the most part this was healthy, but in the process some good people were unfortunately lost. With proper forethought and planning, these people could have been retained.

The eighth problem, therefore, was not anticipating the changes in organization structure and the dislocations in personnel that would be occasioned by the new system, and not developing plans and educating personnel to meet these changes.

Other Benefits Derived From the New System.

A number of other benefits resulted from the new systems in these companies. In addition to a thorough reevaluation of corporate goals, and the interaction of the various functional operations needed to achieve these goals, a considerable amount of coordination and education occurred.

A spirit of cooperation gradually developed as operating personnel found that their ideas were needed and used. In turn, the interchange helped to educate operating personnel in the problems of other operating departments, and in management objectives and policies, both for the coming year and for the longer term.

Such coordination and education benefits did not happen by chance. They came about because in administering the later stages of the system's development management took the time to listen to ideas and follow up on them, and to communicate the nuances of corporate policies and the rationale behind them.

Where deviations from plans or operational deficiencies were found, they were not made a cause for reprimand. Rather, the problems were explored to find their causes, and means were developed to prevent their recurrence.

As a result, a well-knit operating group emerged from the systems development program. Operating personnel had a common purpose. They knew what was expected of them and what the major problems of the business were. They knew that they had the freedom to innovate and make mistakes, and that their suggestions would be considered. Most important, they knew why they were doing what they were doing and how it fit into the rest of the company's operations.

All of these side benefits of the systems development project could have been lost if time and attention had not been devoted to cultivating them.

Summary of Guidelines.

Managers cannot expect everything to go smoothly in developing a new system, but they should not use this as a rationale for tolerating unnecessary inefficiency. Systems development is a new area, in which most managers lack experience. Clearly, performance in this area can be improved, and this discussion has attempted to establish some guidelines for improving systems development programs on the basis of the experience of the companies studied.

These guidelines may be summarized as follows:

1. Systems development should begin with a feasibility study.
2. A corporate executive (or other responsible company manager) should be appointed to head the systems development group (where the system being developed affects a major segment of a company's business) and he should participate actively in the work. Control points should be developed, where top corporate management can participate in and demonstrate their support of the project.
3. The scope of the project should be defined early, so that management will have realistic expectations for what the systems development program will accomplish and will know how much work will have to be done to fulfill these

expectations. Adequate time, money and manpower must be allocated for the project.

4. The study group should include someone from each operating section affected by the new system, to insure the direct involvement of these areas in the project. Deadlines for each stage of the project should be set, to insure the continuing involvement of all parties.

5. Time should be taken to develop an adequate definition of the major decision-making areas within the business system and of the information needed for effective decision making in each of these areas.

6. Balance and an overall company perspective should be maintained in the new system. Extreme care should be taken to see that no one functional area dominates the structure and development of the system.

7. The final commitment for machinery should be withheld until a very precise idea of what is needed has been formed.

8. Major changes in organization structure and major dislocations in personnel will occur, and plans and programs should be developed for making these changes and dislocations as painless as possible. This includes educating everyone concerned in what is happening.

9. Time and effort should be taken to realize the education and coordination side benefits possible from a systems development program.

10. The study should result in the preparation of a formal report listing all the findings, conclusions and recommendations

The companies examined in this study had alert, bright, and realistic management. Although there were problems, once they were recognized, management took the necessary steps to resolve them.

These steps could, however, have been taken earlier in the systems development programs, thus avoiding many of the problems. Instead of false starts, which made the normal activities required to develop a system seem like problems, each step could have been conceived of positively, as a necessary activity in the normal development of a new information processing system for management control. In this way, there would have been less negative feeling about the project and fewer hours and dollars would have been lost in carrying out the project.

CONCLUSION

Three types of data processing systems used in management control have been discussed in this chapter: manual, electrical, and computerized. The discussion focused on computerized systems.

Data processing systems are needed in all control areas. Accounting and finance must have mechanisms for the collection and reporting of information needed to fulfill accounting and financial control objectives. In large and medium-sized companies, a company-wide computerized or punched card system is the mechanism used, leaving the accounting and finance personnel free to concentrate on more important analytical and management jobs. In smaller companies, the accounting department or manager often maintain the data processing system used in accounting and other types of control.

The operating and staff areas also require data processing systems to meet their control needs. On one level, the control systems and tools in these areas are closely tied to those in the accounting and finance areas, since financial controls are an important aspect of every operating and staff area control system. On another level, the control needs in the operating and staff areas are distinct from financial control, so that operating and staff controls extend beyond accounting and finance controls. In larger companies, operating and staff control needs are largely fulfilled by company-wide computerized or punched-card data processing systems, except in those specific instances where it is more economical for an individual department to prepare its own reports and maintain its own records. For example, in a mail-order advertising operation the marketing department clerks often can more economically prepare reports on specific seasonal campaigns (based on overall figures maintained by the computer systems department) than can the computer department, where expensive and valuable programmer time would be used.

Many graphic and mathematical control tools are used in accounting and finance control, as well as in operating and staff control. Many of these tools also require the use of data processing systems. For example, data processing systems often supply the information used in comparative control charts and perform mathematical computations used in operations research work.

This chapter has attempted to describe the major components of computerized data processing systems and their principal uses in management control. Their potential for further contribution is vast and exciting. The reality of a checkless society is not far off, for example, and within this generation it is likely that we will see a considerably expanded network of credit transfers of funds. For example, payments at retail stores may be charged directly to a customer's bank account, thus greatly reducing the need for currency and artificial money transfer media such as checks. Because of these limitless horizons for computer applications for business decision making, the executive must understand and learn how to use these tools, if he is to perform management control in tomorrow's corporations.

This chapter has also outlined specific guidelines for developing information processing systems used for management control. As was seen in the discussion of actual systems development projects, the development of a data processing system is closely linked with the development of the control system it supports. For example, in the mail-order marketing study the operating manager first identified the control requirements in his operating area and the general outline of the control tools and system he needed. The operating manager and systems development manager then worked together in designing the specifics of the control system and its supporting processing system. The primary job of the systems manager in this study was to design and create the processing system needed to support the operating control tools and systems; his secondary job was to assist the operating manager in specifying the operating control needs.

While the guidelines given for developing a data processing system were drawn from the study of only one type of control situation, they are in modified form universally applicable. No matter what the level or kind of management, one must still define the scope of the system and the control needs of those using it, study the feasibility of the system before becoming involved in it, maintain the overall management planning viewpoint in designing the system, and anticipate the organization changes resulting from the new system. These principles are thus applicable to all types of management control—whether it be overall corporate accounting and budgetary control systems or specialized operating and staff control systems.

The systems approach guides the development of an effective information processing system for control. Systems theory focuses on the interaction of systems components in achieving objectives, and is fundamental to an understanding of how systems development works. It is only within the total perspective of the business flow from department to department and from decision maker to decision maker that a truly effective information processing system can be developed.

DISCUSSION QUESTIONS

1. Discuss the relationship between a company's data processing system and its accounting and finance controls, operating and staff controls, and graphic and mathematical controls.
2. A data processing system is the system designed to record, store and communicate data. At what point does a data processing system become a management information system for control?
3. Discuss the distinction between the role of the operating manager in designing and using a control system and the role of the systems manager in developing the data processing needed to put the operating control system to work.
4. Why is it so important to define decision-making needs before developing data processing systems?
5. Why do you think that the computer, instead of the information system, receives so much attention? Why is it a major mistake to focus on the computer, instead of the information system?
6. It has been said that when converting to computers the major economies come from the systems study and not from the introduction of the computer. Discuss.

7. Discuss the ways in which computers have become indispensable to efficient information systems for control in large companies.
8. Name and discuss other uses to which computers can be put for management control.
9. What are the dangers of letting computer technology control development of information systems for control?
10. Why is it so important to have an economical computer system for storing and retrieving information?
11. List the mistakes made by the mail-order companies discussed in this chapter in introducing a new computer-based information system. Why was it natural to make each of these mistakes?
12. Since it was natural to make these mistakes, do you think it is necessary and helpful to have a more scientific approach to systems development? In what ways does systems theory provide such an approach?
13. The idea of a system is not new, for we see natural systems at work all around us every day. What then is new about systems theory and its application to business decision making?
14. How much of an effect do you feel the growth in business's use of computers has had on business's development and acceptance of the systems approach?
15. List and discuss the ways in which the systems approach has affected business organization structure.
16. What other applications of the computer to business control operations not discussed in this chapter can you think of? How "limitless" do you think the applications of the computers to business operations are? What areas do you feel will always be beyond computer applications?

CHAPTER 11

STEP FOUR IN THE MANAGEMENT CONTROL PROCESS: EXERCISING CONTROL

Once control tools and systems have been developed, the manager must be prepared to use these tools and systems to exercise control. This chapter concerns the exercise of control, the fourth step in the management control process.

This chapter first outlines the basic principles and concepts guiding the exercise of control. A number of actual situations are then examined: introducing and using a corporate budgetary control system; using control tools in making planning decisions; making operating control decisions and taking corrective action at the operating level. The final section of the chapter discusses the importance of the behavioral sciences to the exercise of control.

THE BASIC CONCEPT AND PROCESS

The preceding five chapters discussed different aspects of step three in the management control process, developing control tools and systems. In step four in the process, the manager develops effective ways to use the control tools and systems he has selected for controlling and making control decisions. In many instances control is exercised automatically— performance is checked and adjustments are made by automated equipment. The thermostat of a home heating system is an example of this type of automated control,[1] as are many modern chemical plant operations.[2]

---

[1] Arnold Tustin, "Feedback," *Automatic Control* ("A Scientific American Book;" New York: Simon and Schuster, Inc., 1955), pp. 10-23.

[2] Eugene Ayres, "An Automatic Chemical Plant," *Automatic Control* ("A Scientific American Book;" New York: Simon and Schuster, Inc., 1955), pp. 41-52.

The type of control being discussed here is not, however, automatic control that is built into the control system's mechanism, but the type of control that involves executive judgment and executive action in using control tools and systems.

In theory, the exercise of control involves three steps:

1. Comparing actual results with standards.
2. Determining the significance and cause of any deviations.
3. Initiating whatever corrective action appears needed.

In practice, however, there is a preliminary step which in many situations has a major impact on the exercise of control—setting an atmosphere conducive to control action while developing and implementing control tools and systems. Where the manager whose operation is to be controlled participates in defining the standards and developing the kind and form of the control system, the standards are more likely to reflect actual operations, the form in which results are reported is more likely to meet the manager's specific decision-making needs, and the manager is more likely to be responsive to taking immediate corrective action when deviations occur. This was seen in the valve manufacturer study in Chapter 3, where the participative approach was used to involve the production supervisor and marketing manager in the development of the cost control system, in order to overcome their resistance to any new system. The first step in the exercise of control, therefore, is to create a positive atmosphere for taking action when developing and implementing new controls.

The second step in exercising control involves comparing actual performance to established criteria. Frequently, this is done as part of the control reporting system. As was seen in the earlier discussion of accounting control reports, for example, income statements are often designed to show comparisons between actual results and standards. These reports also attempt to show the relative importance of deviations, through giving the amount or percent of the deviation.

Not all control comparisons are done as part of the reporting system, however. Frequently, the executive must work only with result reports or observed results. In these situations, he must develop his own comparisons of these results with standards with which he is familiar or which are contained in other documents.

Next, the significance of any deviations is determined. This step is sometimes called evaluating performance, and cannot be performed effectively if the earlier stages of the management control process have not been well executed. For example, in a recent system development study conducted for a mail-order company, each manager determined the critical control points in his operation, the standards required to measure performance at these points, and the kind of information he needed to control his particular operation. In this way management was certain that the standards used and the performance information fed back would provide more effective measurement and control of performance. If the information feedback had not been tailored to the decision-making needs of the manager, if the critical control points or aspects of an operation had not been accurately identified, or if the standards did not accurately reflect the actual situation, then reliable comparisons could not have been made.

The process of investigating the causes of deviations may lead in many directions. On the one hand, the standard may have been wrong, the information may have been inaccurate, or some other misunderstanding may have occurred. On the other hand, the problem may actually be an operational one, which requires executive action. Where only one operation is involved, for example circulation marketing, the investigation consists of examining the operation and/or consulting with the operating manager or supervisor. The investigatory process becomes more difficult where the deviation could have been caused by more than one company operation. In such cases, one may have to examine both the individual operations involved, as well as the interaction between them.

The true causes of deviations, therefore, may require considerable probing. For example, when profits began dropping at a mail-order company studied, the initial information seemed to show that the problems were increased costs in acquiring new customers and servicing their accounts, a greater number of persons defaulting on their accounts, increasing product costs, and the like. However, this was not enough information to enable management to solve the problems, for as it turned out, these problems were only symptoms of more basic problems.

As a result, more information was sought, and many questions were asked. Had there been a change in the kind of customer serviced by the company, which in turn required a change in product strategy? Since company customers were younger, did credit screening policies also need changing? Was the computerized system, which had been ahead of its time five years ago, now out of date and uneconomical? Had warehousing procedures failed to keep up with the changing product mix? What was the exact cost of handling complaint letters? What was the effect of complaint correspondence on sales?

All areas—advertising, warehousing, account servicing, and product procurement—had to be examined in depth before the real problems were identified and corrective action could be initiated. Only when the basic planning and strategy problems—market direction, equipment modernization, and process streamlining—had been identified accurately could an effective solution be formulated and action taken.

In probing for the meaning of each deviation from standard, both favorable and unfavorable variances should be investigated. While it is important to track down problems which may be signalled by a negative deviation from standard, a positive deviation may present an opportunity for improvement and so deserves equal attention.

Taking action is the last step in exercising control. There are many ways in which control can be exercised and many levels at which corrective action can be taken. At the corporate level in large companies the exercise of control is usually handled by a specific corporate department or executive. Since a major part of the corporate control job is to coordinate the various financial control systems at the lower operating levels of the corporation, usually through budgetary controls, the exercise of control is very often only *initiated* by the control department. The corrective action itself is carried out by the lower level managers in charge of the operating departments, with the control department following up to see that corrective has been taken.

At lower levels in the organization, the manager may both determine the causes of deviations and the action to be taken, and administer the carrying out of corrective action. In these instances, the distinction between management functions blurs, and it makes little sense to draw a fine line between what is considered part of the control function and what is part of the administrative function. For example, in *The National Observer* study described in Chapter 14 the circulation manager observed results, studied the causes of deviations and took whatever action was needed to adjust advertising schedules.

In a resource allocation situation, on the other hand, the control function would be limited to developing investment and income comparisons. Here only a *recommended* course of action based on financial considerations would be presented, and other departments would weigh these recommendations with other factors in determining a final course of action.

Control action can thus be indirect, direct, or advisory; varying as it does from from initiating and monitoring corrective action, to administering corrective action, to providing supporting control analyses. As in many other steps in the control process, the execution of this step depends on the requirements of the control situation.

No matter what the control situation, however, the process followed in exercising control is basically the same. When exercising control, the manager must set the atmosphere for control during the development and implementation stage. He must have standards and information appropriate to the kinds of control decisions he faces. He must develop creative solutions to the problems, and work to maintain a constructive atmosphere when initiating and carrying out corrective action.

UNDERLYING PRINCIPLES

In exercising control the manager can limit himself to insisting upon compliance—protecting assets, policing, checking accuracy, reprimanding, and the like. However, this is too restrictive a viewpoint.

Management control dictates that the manager also strive to attain more positive goals in exercising control. The primary aim of management control is to stimulate better use of assets, to create new ways of doing business, to coordinate better the efforts of individual operating departments, and to educate operating personnel so that their efforts are more closely geared to accomplishing specific corporate objectives—in short, to create an enabling atmosphere, whose vistas are broadened, not narrowed, by the controls.

Above all, management control requires that a balance be maintained between compliance and stimulation in exercising control. For example, when variances from budget caused by operating deficiences are noted, the control executive must decide what balance can be struck between criticizing operating personnel for non-compliance and taking constructive steps for educating them in corporate goals. He must also determine how much use can be made of the discussions of the variances to better coordinate funtional operations, such as production and marketing, without at the same time destroying the control system's value in maintaining compliance.

Achieving the balance between the compliance and creative use of controls is not an easy task. Jerome points out the difficulty of finding this balance:

> I want to refer again to the basic dilemma faced by any management in its attempt to achieve a controlled operation. This is the dilemma of attempting to achieve a workable balance between creativity and conformity. Or, expressed somewhat differently, this is the problem of encouraging initiative on the part of subordinates by keeping operations flexible, and minimizing the chances of error by keeping operations standardized.[3]

This capacity of executive control for motivating constructive action, developing initiative and generating progress is, according to Jerome, "by all odds its most important characteristic."[4]

Considerable tact and judgment and a high degree of regard for the individual are required to exercise management control effectively. The approach discussed in this section can at times seem inefficient over the short run, since it often involves lengthy discussions with individuals in exploring the causes of problems and developing a true understanding by the individual of the management implications of the problems. In the long run, however, following such an approach can lead to more efficient use of corporate resources and better management control.

[3]William Travers Jerome III, *Executive Control—The Catalyst* (New York: John Wiley and Sons, Inc., 1961), p. 75.
[4]Jerome, *Executive Control*, p. 34.

EFFECTIVELY INTRODUCING AND USING A NEW CORPORATE CONTROL SYSTEM

A study of the introduction of a new budgetary cost control system at H. J. Heinz, Inc. in the mid-1950's illustrates how the underlying principles of management control can be effectively put to work in implementing a new control system at the corporate level.[5]

The H. J. Heinz company was established in 1869. The company and its subsidiaries are principally engaged in processing, packing and selling an extensive line of quality food products. At the time of the study, the company had twelve factories and numerous related production facilities, and over seventy sales branch warehouses, located throughout the country. Overall company objectives and basic policies were clearly defined and distributed to all employees through a brochure entitled *Statement of Policies and Objectives of H. J. Heinz Company*. Planning and control was performed within the framework of these objectives and policies.

The company's overall organization is shown in Figure 11.1.[6] The comptroller's division was responsible for all profit planning and control. The policies guiding the comptroller's operation emphasized its positive role in the organization and defined clearly the department's staff function. The department thus considered it "a very challenging problem to get competent staff and special study groups to make effective analyses and give sound advice without assuming (or giving the impression of assuming) any part of line authority and without attempting to take personal credit for successful programs carried through by the line organization."[7]

In an effort to improve financial control of corporate operations, the company decided to introduce a new standard cost and variance reporting system. Manufacturing costs accounted for 65% of the sales dollar and so were considered a major area to focus on in improving controls. As part of the new system, decentralized individual factory cost accounting departments were formed to administer the new cost control system.

The new system was developed by the corporate Cost Accounting Department and was introduced in stages, starting with the home-office plant in Pittsburgh. Once the Pittsburgh plant had been converted to the new system, it was used for training personnel to introduce the new system at the company's other plants.

In introducing the new system, time and money were allocated for educating and training all those involved in the new system. Home-office teams spent from three to six months at each factory location to introduce

[5]Controllers Institute Research Foundation, Inc., *Management Planning and Control: The H. J. Heinz Approach* (New York: Controllers Institute Research Foundation, 1961).

[6]Controllers Institute, *The H. J. Heinz Approach*, p. 8.

[7]Controllers Institute, *The H. J. Heinz Approach*, pp. 30-31.

Figure 11.1

ORGANIZATION CHART

H. J. Heinz Company

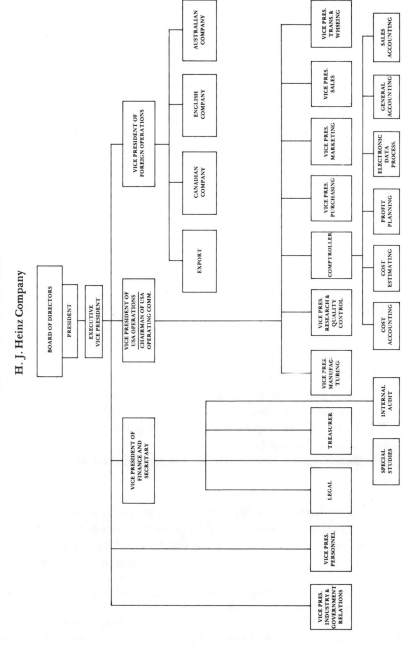

the system and indoctrinate those who would be using it. Personnel were given the opportunity to take courses in cost accounting at company expense, and when certain home-office accounting functions were phased out, surplus personnel were given the option of transferring to factory cost accounting departments. The education and training program was not terminated once the new system was introduced. A continuous learning program was maintained, including periodic seminars for factory personnel working with the system.

Both initially and as the program continued, those responsible for performance originated the standards used within the new control system. The company's philosophy was that the personnel at each factory were in the best position to establish standards and budgets for their operation. This approach not only brought more realism into the standards, but also evoked livelier interest in the new system among factory personnel. All standards and budgets were, however, still subject to review and approval by the home office.

The process followed in developing standards at Heinz thus involved factory operating personnel and staff units. Conferences were held to encourage an interchange of ideas, cross fertilization of thinking, and diverse scrutiny of proposals. This group participation not only helped develop better standards, it also provided the manpower needed to perform the vast amount of work necessary to develop detailed standards, and at a later date to foster more widespread knowledge of standards and conformance to them at lower operating levels.

While standards were generally fixed at the time of annual review, allowance was made for changing these standards where circumstances, such as wage or material price increases, warranted it.

Variances were reported on and reviewed at many levels. Daily meetings were held at the factory level to review daily variance reports, diaries were maintained by foremen, reports were issued on significant and recurring variances, and regular periodic review meetings were held among factory and home-office accounting personnel.

In analyzing operating variances from standards, the main emphasis was on finding and correcting the causes of variances *in order to improve future performance*. The creative emphasis led to the analysis of favorable as well as unfavorable variances. As explained by the company,

The line of thinking, of course, is that something caused the favorable variance—either unexpected effectiveness of factors of production or some reduction in standard cost which needs re-examination. If the causes of improvement are positive and can be identified, their possible permanence can be appraised; and if the development, whatever it is, can be passed on to other factories or departments, it will improve the overall company profit picture. There are frequent improvements in the company's products, recipes, processes, and costs, and some of these are directly traceable to properly-investigated variances from standards and budgets.[8]

The profit planning department at Heinz operated under a similar participative philosophy. The primary purpose of the profit planning department was to coordinate and consolidate the various division budget plans. At Heinz the budget plans themselves were not as important as the planning and budgetary processes which helped coordinate the operating divisions. Profit planning was "not a course in 'forward accounting' but a system whereby business plans are screened, evaluated, and reduced to realistic, attainable objectives in a well-coordinated program of action—and the responsibility of their attainments is then specifically delegated to those most logically responsible for results—and, it should be emphasized—*to those who have had an opportunity to participate in the planning and development of these activities.*"[9]

Thus Heinz strove in both cost accounting and profit planning to emphasize the creative, educational, and coordination benefits of their control systems, rather than the compliance aspects. In this way Heinz was able to use the systems for *management* control instead of limiting it to *accounting* control.

In management control the educational and cordination benefits of an operating control system are as important as meeting any specified budgets. Controls can highlight problems for management and lead them to more creative solutions to these problems. When, as was done at Heinz, operating personnel are brought into control development and participate actively in the control process, especially in setting standards and reviewing performance, they are educated in overall corporate directions and self-checks and balances are thus built into individual operations.

The discussion of the Heinz study has deliberately only touched on the highlights of the exercise of control at the corporate level, in order to focus on guidelines for good practice. A more extensive discussion of overall corporate control systems, and the way control is exercised within them, is given in Chapter 13.

PROVIDING COMPARATIVE FINANCIAL ANALYSES FOR PLANNING DECISIONS

A control section is often called upon to provide quantitative analyses to be used in comparing proposed courses of action. The transportation company study discussed earlier in this book provides an example of this kind of control situation. In that study, the control section was asked to provide a financial analysis of two competing types of equipment systems,

[8]Controllers Institute, *The H. J. Heinz Approach*, p. 55.
[9]Controllers Institute, *The H. J. Heinz Approach*, pp. 73-74.

an all gas bus system and a combination electric trackless trolley and gas bus system. The bases used for comparison were total investment, annual operating costs, and return on investment over a thirty-year period.

First, the total "cost" of each investment alternative was calculated. In making the calculation, a ten-year life-span was used for gas buses and fifteen-years for electric trackless trolley buses. Purchases of other types of equipment over that period, such as a new power plant in five years, were also included in the calculations at their present value. A discount rate of 6% was used, the rate the company could earn on its excess capital. The calculations showed that the all bus system would cost about 5% more than the combined system, or about $200,000 more.

Second, the yearly operating costs were calculated. These showed a slight saving with the combined system, which was roughly equivalent to the increased investment in this alternative. As a check against these two calculations, a calculation was made of all annual charges to income for both alternatives over a thirty-year period. This last calculation showed the two alternatives roughly equal.

Next, an estimated forecast of revenue was made for each alternative. An analysis of the area served by the company showed that a considerable amount of new construction could be anticipated over the next thirty years. Since the all bus operation would provide greater flexibility in serving this shifting market and also generate more income from excursion business, the all bus system could be expected to produce higher revenues and earnings. The all bus system also showed a reasonably higher return-on-investment than the alternative combined system. (Both alternatives yielded an ROI above the minimum required by the company).

The control function technically ended at this point, with a recommendation based on the quantitative analysis to adopt the all bus system. This quantitative analysis was, however, supplemented by an examination of other factors affecting the decision, such as customer service factors (speed, comfort, capacity) and public service factors (safety, air pollution, traffic congestion, appearance). For example, the trolley buses were faster and had a larger passenger capacity than the gas buses, but required ugly overhead lines which made them much less flexible in traffic. This analysis, like the quantitative analysis, showed the all bus system to be the best.

While these other non-quantitative considerations were not part of the control analysis, they were none the less important to the decision and had to be given recognition by the control analyst. The final decision was clearly a planning decision to be made by top management, and the analyst made it clear in his report that he was just providing supporting analysis to help the planner make a better decision.

The exercise of control in these types of control situations is fairly limited, since the control function is confined to testing alternatives quantitatively and making financial projections. It normally involves making only a qualified recommendation, based on financial considerations. In these situations the final action would be taken by company managers responsible for planning decision making.

DETERMINING THE CAUSES OF DEVIATIONS AT THE OPERATING LEVEL

Deviations from standards should trigger action. When a circulation marketing manager sees from comparative result statements that his subscription ad in the *New York Times* is not bringing in an economical number of orders, he acts to develop a stronger ad, change the day or page on which it is run, or run the ad in another publication.

Not all control situations are so simple and straightforward, however. The following is a description of a production quality control problem in the production area, which illustrates some of the difficulties that may be encountered in making control decisions and exercising control.

The situation involves a plant that manufacturers quarter panels[10], the panels which cover the four quarters of a car, including the wheels, and are the successors of the fender. The panels are made on four separate production lines, each line headed by a huge hydraulic press that stamps the panels out of sheet-steel blanks. When the flat steel arrives at the plant by rail from various suppliers, it is unloaded and carried to a machine which cuts identical size blanks for all four hydraulic presses. Blanks go to the presses by fork lift trucks in pallet stacks of 40 each, and the schedule is so arranged that there is always a supply of blanks on hand when the presses are started up on the morning shift.

The men involved in the situation were:

1. Oscar Burger, Plant Manager—a tough manager in his late fifties; known for his willingness to listen to others; considered antiunion by the employees.
2. Robert Polk, Production Chief—a hard-nosed driver, very able technically, but quick-tongued and inclined to favor certain subordinates; also considered antiunion by the employees.
3. Ben Peters, Quality Control Manager—reserved, quiet, and cautious when dealing with others; extremely confident in his figures.
4. Ralph Coggin, Industrial Relations Manager—a fairly typical personnel manager; sympathetic to employees; relies on human relations techniques in dealing with the union.
5. Andy Patella, Shop Steward—antagonistic to management and eager to prove his power; has developed rapport with Industrial Relations Manager Coggin.
6. George Adams, Supervisor on Line #1—steady, solid, and well respected by his men.

[10]Perrin Stryker, "Can You Analyze This Problem," *Harvard Business Review*, May-June, 1965, pp. 73-78; and "How to Analyze That Problem," *ibid.*, July-August, 1965, pp. 99-110.

7. James Farrell, Supervisor on Line #2—irrascible, ambitious, and somewhat puritanical; very antiunion.
8. Henry Dawson, Supervisor on Line #3—patient, warmhearted, and genuinely liked by his men.
9. Otto Henschel, Supervisor on Line #4—aloof, cool, and a bit ponderous; neither liked nor disliked by his men.
10. Tom Luane, Scheduling Supervisor—persistent, analytical, and systematic; has some training in problem analysis procedure, but lacks experience.

The problem arose on a Wednesday morning when the reject rate rose severely on Lines #1, #2 and #4 because of burrs on the quarter panels. At a morning meeting it was learned that production pressures were great because of high sales, so a solution was needed quickly. The metal blanks had been checked immediately by quality control and were said not to have caused the problem. Engineering checked the presses and found them not to be the cause of the problem.

The previous day a worker (Joe Valenti) had been suspended by supervisor Farrell on suspicion of drinking at work, and many of the men were angry and threatening to take a strike vote. Many of the managers at the meeting immediately jumped to the conclusion that the burring was the result of sabotage by the workers.

During the day Polk rechecked the blanks and presses, and Peters checked the quality control records to see when the reject rate had last hit its current level. Coggin talked to Patella to see if sabotage might really be the problem and what might be done about it. The four supervisors were visited by Polk; Henschel and Farrell believed sabotage to be the cause of the problem, while Adams and Dawson felt that the cause might be elsewhere.

At a meeting that afternoon, Burger reviewed with his managers the information they had gathered in checking out the initial "hunches" on what was the cause of the problem. Patella had confirmed to Coggin that the workers were angry and ready to strike, so that Coggin was convinced that worker sabotage was the cause. Polk found that the presses and blanks were okay and concluded that Valenti must be reinstated immediately, if the problem was to be solved. The fact that no rejects were found on Line #3 was attributed to the loyalty of the men there to their supervisor, Dawson, who was considered easier to work with. Burger, the plant manager, came to the conclusion that Polk was right, and that he would either have to reinstate Valenti and undercut Farrell, or risk continued sabotage and perhaps a strike.

Luane, the scheduling supervisor, suggested that before taking any rash action, a more systematic analysis of the problem be made. The problem was first defined as the rapid increase of burrs on Lines #1, #2 and #4—to over 10%—a major deviation from the prescribed standard of 2%.

Extensive questioning revealed that while all lines used the same flat sheet steel, Line #3 was making a different type of panel than the other lines, a panel which had a shallower "draw." Further investigation showed that a new manufacturer had started supplying blanks on Wednesday morning, that these panels contained a new alloy, which tended to burr more in deep "draw" processes. The situation was remedied by having the supplier change the alloy used in making the blanks.

All the facts were known to the managers, but it took an objective, systematic analyzer to make the other managers forget an emotional incident—the Valenti suspension and worker reaction—and look for other causes of the problem. Only after complete specifications for each aspect of the problem—what, where, when, and to what extent—were spelled out did the managers abandon their emotional biases and direct their efforts along productive lines.

This incident illustrates a number of points about the search for the causes of deviations in exercising control:

1. The true cause of a deviation is not always immediately apparent.
2. One should guard against jumping to conclusions based on hunches or emotions, for these emotional biases often get in the way of objective analysis.
3. A systematic, objective approach to finding true causes of deviations is needed.

Investigating the true causes of operational deviations can extend beyond the operation to questioning the validity of control standards and the accuracy of result information. Every time a budget comparison is made a manager should always ask, "Is the budget a good yardstick?" The budget is a plan, which is sometimes based on wishful thinking and used by some managers to prod people on to more productivity. In all instances, therefore, the accuracy of the standard against which performance is measured should be rechecked first.

The result figures should also be questioned. In a mail-order operation, where a large volume of orders are coded by low-paid clerks, key punched by typists and processed by a computer, the chance of reporting error is high. Thus when the manager interpreting results finds a major deviation, he should always recheck the reporting process. Only after checking the accuracy of the standards and result information would he investigate other variable factors in the situation which may have caused the deviation, and examine each of these variations.

The above example is taken from the production area and involves a very limited control problem. A more comprehensive and detailed discussion of operating control tools and systems, and the way in which control is exercised in the marketing area, is given in Chapter 14.

TAKING CONTROL ACTION

Three types of control action can be observed in the three company studies reviewed above: indirect, supporting or advisory, and direct.

In the Heinz Company study, the corporate control department administered setting up a new accounting control system which was to be used to monitor operating results. As for exercising control, the cost accounting departments worked with the operating personnel in a staff capacity, encouraging and guiding the operating managers who actually took whatever corrective action was needed. In this study, while the control department initiated corrective action, it did not directly administer the carrying out of that action. This type of control action, therefore, is called indirect.

In the transportation company study, the objective of the control effort was mainly to provide comparative analyses to be used in making a planning decision. The control tools were thus designed to support that decision area. The analyst considered factors other than financial ones, weighed them in his analysis, and presented recommendations based on both a quantitative and qualitative analysis. He was, however, only recommending or advising the planning manager, not making the decision.

In the operational situation at the stamping plant, the burr problem was both analyzed and corrected by operating managers who had direct responsibility for the operation. In this situation, the control action was thus administered directly by those who did the control analysis, and so is called direct control action.

These studies thus serve two functions. First, they illustrate the different phases involved in the exercise of control—development and implementation of a new control system, comparative analysis, deviation analysis, and taking corrective action. Second, they illustrate three different ways in which corrective action, the fourth phase of the exercise of control, can be taken.

Like so many of the illustrative studies in this book, these examples are not necessarily typical of situations the reader may encounter in his work. For example, comparative analysis very often involves comparing actual results with standards, as is done in the comparative reports shown in the accounting and operational control chapters, not the kind of comparative analysis shown in the transportation study discussed in this chapter. For many readers, the introduction of new computerized information systems for control, such as the one discussed in the last chapter, is a much more familiar implementation situation than the cost accounting one discussed in this chapter. And for readers not working in the manufacturing area, an example of analyzing deviations in a situation in his area would be much more relevant.

It would be impossible to cover all types of control action in one chapter or even in one book. First, the situations are too numerous and varied. Second, rarely can one capture the intricacies of a dynamic day-to-day working situation on paper. An effort is made, therefore, in this chapter and in the preceding ones only to give the reader a sense of the various kinds of situations and solutions which might be encountered in the exercise of control. In Chapters 13 and 14, two familiar types of control situations are studied in greater depth—corporate financial control and marketing operational control. These studies are integrating studies, showing how the whole control process is used. Because of this, they give the reader a more comprehensive view and deeper insight into the intricacies of exercising control in typical business situations.

As can be seen from the in-depth studies, as well as from the illustrative studies already discussed, the exercise of control is rarely simple. Not only are the situations themselves often complex, but in most instances it is necessary to work with and through people in introducing new systems, and in uncovering the causes of deviations and taking action to correct deviations. Because of this, behavioral science tools are important in exercising control, and a knowledge of them can be of great help to the manager in performing this fourth step in the management control process.

THE BEHAVIORAL SCIENCES AND MANAGEMENT CONTROL

All too often the exercise of control is reduced to a mechanical process which ignores human needs and the factors important in motivating human beings to take action. The operations researcher presents "ideal" quantitative solutions; the systems approach reduces the decision-making process to a logical sequence of cause and effect, which can be programmed in a master brain, the computer; and finance and accounting provide the all-too-familiar view of the operation as the impersonal movement of money to produce a profit for the stockholder.

Behavioral science until recently has not been given adequate consideration in the science of management control. Yet human behavior affects major aspects of management control.[11] As has been pointed in a recent study by Robert Dawson and Dorothy Carew, the effectiveness of many control systems depends more on human attitudes and social environment than on the system itself.[12]

Management control is exercised through the business organization and the people working within it, so that without their cooperation control cannot be exercised effectively. Exercising control thus requires knowing and effectively using behavioral science tools, if the manager is to

[11]Arnold S. Tannenbaum, ed., *Control in Organizations* (New York: McGraw-Hill Book Company, Inc., 1968), *passim*.

[12]Robert J. Dawson and Dorothy P. Carew, "Why Do Control Systems Fall Apart?," *Personnel*, May-June, 1969, pp. 8-16.

motivate others positively and gain the maximum benefits from his control system.

Behavioral science, which is the study of human behavior, whether in groups or as individuals, has been defined as:

> A combined endeavor of many fields investigating all aspects of behavior, leading to understanding of human beings as individuals and in social relations. Behavioral science therefore includes many studies in the fields of anthropology, bio-chemistry, ecology, economics, genetics, geography, history, linguistics, mathematics, neurology, pharmacology, physiology, political science, psychiatry, psychology, sociology, statistics and zoology.[13]

The major behavioral sciences are psychology, sociology, and anthropology. Behavioral science includes those aspects of these and the other fields cited above which concern human behavior. Many authorities use the term "human relations" as equivalent to "behavioral science," although the two are not necessarily the same.[14]

Behavioral science is an important management science because it helps managers understand and direct people better. It provides tools for effectively introducing innovations and changes, resolving organization conflicts, stimulating creativity, and developing strong leaders.[15] The behavioral sciences thus touch on many aspects of human behavior important in management control. Three of these are discussed in the following sections:

1. What motivates people in their work environment?
2. How to direct people more effectively.
3. How to discipline people.

What Motivates People in Their Work Environment?

Each individual's behavior can be viewed as an action designed to satisfy his own needs. Every person has needs that are never fully satisfied, and the presence of unsatisfied needs motivates an individual to act. If the action arising from a need is directed to some goal or objective that results in the elimination of the need, then there can be said to be a motive for the action.[16]

A person is motivated to work in order to satisfy some need. In its simplest form, a worker's need, motivation, or goal setting occurs as fol-

13Harold M. F. Rush, "What Is Behavioral Science?," *The Conference Board Record* (September, 1965), p. 38.

14Allen I. Kraut, "Behavioral Science in Modern Industry," *Personnel Administration* (May-June, 1967), pp. 32-37.

15Maneck S. Wadia, *Management and the Behavioral Sciences: Text and Readings* (Boston: Allyn and Bacon, Inc., 1968), p. 22.

16John F. Hall, *Psychology of Motivation* (Chicago: J. B. Lippincott Company, 1961), p. 30.

lows: first, a need, such as hunger or self-fulfillment arises in a person; second, the person recognizes that he must satisfy this need and so is motivated to action; third, he takes action to satisfy that need, by getting a new job or deciding to keep working at his present job.

Douglas McGregor, drawing on the work of Abraham Maslow, has arranged needs into a five-level hierarchy:[17]

1. *Physiological needs.* Man's most basic needs are his physiological needs, that is, those needs he must satisfy to function as a normal human being, such as the needs for food and shelter.

2. *Safety needs.* Man has an instinctive need to protect himself and his family and to make himself as safe as he can from danger, threat and deprivation.

3. *Social needs.* Man is basically a social animal, who does not want to be alone, and so has a great need for belonging, for association, for acceptance, and for giving and receiving friendship and love.

4. *Ego needs.* Ego needs can be divided into two classes: those that relate to one's self esteem, such as self-confidence, independence, achievement, competence and knowledge, and those that relate to one's reputation, such as status, recognition, appreciation, and respect.

5. *Self-fulfillment needs.* Most men feel that they must fulfill a role in life. Self-fulfillment needs include the realization of one's own potentialities, continued self-development, and continued creativity.

Man's basic physiological needs are usually satisfied when he obtains employment or goes on relief, for with the money he receives he is able to buy food and obtain shelter. Safety needs are partially satisfied by job security, so long as arbitrary management actions do not create uncertainty about continued employment or reflect favoritism or discrimination. In the business environment, the worker satisfies his social needs by belonging to work groups. The typical worker in mass-production industries has little opportunity to satisfy his ego and self-fulfillment needs through his job. As a result, these needs are a major stimulant in motivating men to seek supervisory management jobs, since these jobs have decision-making responsibility and do allow a man to satisfy ego and self-fulfillment needs.

Both Douglas McGregor and Abraham Maslow discuss these five needs in terms of a hierarchy of importance, with higher needs (social, ego and self-fulfillment) being acted upon only after lower needs (physiological and safety) are satisfied. While it is possible to speak theoretically of needs in a five-level hierarchy, in practice this is not the case. Man tries to satisfy a diversity of needs at the same time. Higher needs emerge and are acted

[17]Douglas McGregor, "The Human Side of Enterprise," *Management of Human Resources*, Paul Pigors, Charles A. Meyers and F. T. Malm, eds. (New York: McGraw-Hill Book Company, Inc., 1964), pp. 57-58; Abraham H. Maslow, *Motivation and Personality* (New York: Harper and Row, Publishers, 1954).

upon before lower needs have been completely satisfied. Thus a worker, in performing his job, is trying to satisfy many needs at the same time.

The study of needs provides only a partial explanation of human behavior, for the same needs may lead to different responses or satisfiers (for example, two hungry people may choose different foods to satisfy their hunger) and the same action may be motivated by different needs (for example, one person may work to earn money and another to gain prestige or power). Need, therefore, is only one of the many factors which influence how a person will react to a specific situation. Other factors affecting an individual's response to his environment are previous experience, expectancy, level of aspiration, group relationships, ethical values and religious beliefs, cultural influences, an individual's emotional make-up, health, and the like.[18]

A person's past success or failure can influence the way he responds to all of his work environment. For example, if a person believes, based on experience, that he can reach a goal, he will be more inclined to try to reach a goal and satisfy a need. The expectation of rewards can also increase the attractiveness of a task, and if a worker is certain that he will receive a raise or a promotion or some other kind of satisfaction from performing a different job, he may be more inclined to accept the job and perform it well.

Aspirations may be divided into two basic categories: the desire to achieve success and the desire to avoid failure. The individual who has an overwhelming desire to achieve success will set high, challenging goals for himself. He is the worker who will accept a difficult job. The person who desires to avoid failure will choose only those goals he is confident that he can achieve. He is the worker who is content to do the same job day after day, because he is sure he can handle the job.

Group membership, the characteristics of the group, and the individual's place in the group, all influence the way in which a person responds to his needs. When a group accepts and attempts to enforce certain standards, the individual has group discipline as well as personal discipline compelling him to conform to these standards. The stronger the group bonds, the more deeply the individual's attitudes are interwoven with the group norms. Thus, the worker who is a union member will be affected by the union's action, beliefs, and desires.

Ethical and religious beliefs may also affect the manner in which a person responds to his needs, for religious training can provide a person with norms or standards, and conditions his attitudes towards his environment. For example, as a result of this moral training, a person may not perform an action or a job he believes unethical, even though another

[18]Timothy W. Costello and Sheldon S. Zalkind, eds., *Psychology in Administration* (Englewood Cliffs, N.J.: Prentice-Hall, Inc., 1963), pp. 64-66.

worker might. Every person is also influenced by the customs, habits, and the traditions in his society. Generally speaking, the chief influence on a person's development of these customs and habits is his family, and in many cases a person takes the same beliefs, traditions and customs as his parents.

Each person has a different emotional make-up and a different personality. There are those who are by nature nervous, tense, and anxious; and those who are by nature calm and relaxed. Each one will respond differently to a work assignment, a challenge, or tense working conditions. And the healthy person will be more likely to respond to his needs than the sick person, although they both may have the same needs.

All of the factors discussed in this section condition the way an individual reacts to business situations. Understanding the reasons why people behave the way they do in organizations is an important first step towards controlling behavior, for once behavior is understood, it is a much easier task to predict and control it.[19]

Leadership.

In order to institute controls and exercise control successfully, the manager must be able to lead and direct people effectively. Effective administration depends upon the manager's ability to motivate his workers and discipline them when necessary. One person may want power; another may want money. Whatever the object or desire, behind every purposeful human act there is some need, either conscious or unconscious, that prompts a person to act.[20] This driving force which impels a person to take some action is motivation, and the manager must identify motives if he is to stimulate individuals to effective action.

As can be seen from the discussion in the last section, motives are often individual and personal, and so are often obscure not only to the manager trying to motivate, but also to the worker being motivated. Effective motivation depends upon being able to discover the often obscure basis for an individual's (or group of individuals') action in any given situation. The manager should never assume that other people's motives are the same as his own. Rather, he should probe to uncover the basic motivators operating in the situation at hand. Garret Bergen and William Haney have developed a helpful checklist to guide the executive in this process:[21]

[19]Chris Argyris, *Personality and Organization* (New York: Harper and Row, Publishers, 1957), p. 5.

[20]Herbert G. Hicks, *The Management of Organizations* (New York: McGraw-Hill Book Company, Inc., 1967), p. 235.

[21]Garret L. Bergen and William V. Haney, *Organizational Relations and Management Action: Cases and Issues* (New York. McGraw-Hill Book Company, Inc., 1966), pp. 16-21.

1. *Frames of reference.* People frequently see the same situations in different ways. Am I treating this as a black and white problem? Am I aware that my own frame of reference is only one man's view? What is my interpretation of the perceptions of other individuals and groups concerned with the problem?

2. *Self-interest.* Most people are self-centered, and their primary goals are their own needs and desires. Am I making it easy for the people concerned to satisfy their own interests in this situation, as well as to do what I expect of them in order to meet our organization goals?

3. *Economic, material incentives.* Money talks, but it may say different things to different people. Am I assuming too much that people are motivated by the basic needs that money can buy? Have I looked to see whether money is just a means to another end for the people concerned?

4. *Emotional security.* People need to feel reasonably safe and secure. Do the people with whom I am dealing know where they stand in the organization? What has been done lately to help them understand what is expected of them and what support then can one expect from others, including me?

5. *Self-esteem.* The preservation of self-respect is a dominant need of men and women at work. Is what I am doing or planning to do likely to maintain the self-respect and human dignity of the people involved in this situation?

6. *Feelings and sentiments.* Nonlogical emotional behavior is natural, for people feel as well as think. Am I taking feelings into account in this emotion-laden situation? Or am I looking for a "logical" approach to a non-rational situation?

7. *Group behavior.* Group factors are inevitable in organizational relations and influence strongly the behavior of individuals. What reference groups are involved here? How do group codes, norms, or customs affect the situation?

8. *Conflict.* Ambivalence should be expected. Have I identified the horns of the dilemma? Am I ready to deal contructively with the areas of conflict?

9. *Multiple plus.* The human equation is not likely to balance unless all components gain a "plus." Will I "plus" myself with a "minus?" How can I work things out so that all receive at least a partial "plus?"

10. *Individual differences.* Individuals differ in many important respects. Am I doing everything I can to make full use of the diversity and range of human talent in our organization? Am I resisting the tendency to stereotype?

This simple set of guidelines covers the key areas that the manager should probe in uncovering motivation: the individual's needs or balance of needs, the individual's emotional and psychological make-up (the kind of person he is), and the group or social relationships affecting the situation. The answers to these questions provide a basis for stimulating people to a desired action.

Involving an individual in setting his own goals or standards has proved to be an effective way to stimulate him to better achievement, because it gives him a sense of participation, a sense of belonging in a meaningful way, and even a degree of independence in that his achievements are measured against his own standards. Involving the individual also provides better control, since the greater a worker's understanding of a standard, the more likely he is to maintain it.

Worker involvement is particularly important when organizational changes are made.[22] For example, as was seen earlier in this chapter when the Heinz Company introduced their new control system, those affected were involved from the beginning and were allowed to suggest ways to improve the system. This participative approach was a key factor in the success of the new system.

According to Tannenbaum, Weschler and Massarik, the participative approach in introducing changes is one that gives the worker an opportunity to suggest ways in which changes might be made.[23] Worker participation in changes is an important way to spark employee enthusiasm. For example, in one situation an office supervisor, on discovering that a form used for years was out-dated, commented to one of his subordinates that there must be a way that he (the subordinate) could improve it. The next day the employee came in with a newly designed form that took only half as long to fill out.[24]

Resistance to change will in almost every instance be less intense when those affected participate in the actual planning of the change.[25] If workers participate in the planning of changes in weekly scheduling of jobs, for example, they will be more inclined to go along with the new schedule than if they had not participated in the planning of the changes. Not involving those affected by an organizational change may intensify resistance to change and create unnecessary problems.

In the same way that a worker should know his goals and standards, he should also know the results of his work—that is, to what degree he met the standards or achieved the goals. A session in which the manager communicates his judgments to the subordinate about his performance, discusses the reasons for the judgments, and advises the subordinate on ways in which he might improve is fundamental to the business organization.[26] At the same time, the manager should also communicate with

[22]Thomas A. Wicker, "Employee Commitment: Key to Smooth Change," *Supervisory Management* (July 1967), pp. 31-33; A S. Hatch, "Explaining Changes: If You Don't, the Grapevine Will," *ibid.* (April 1967), p. 40.

[23]Robert Tannenbaum, Irving R. Weschler, and Fred Massarik, *Leadership and Organization: A Behavioral Science Approach* (New York: McGraw-Hill Book Company, Inc., 1961), p. 86.

[24]Paul J. Meyer, "8 Ways to Spark Employee Enthusiasm," *Supervisory Management* (February 1966), p. 41.

[25]Gordon L. Lippitt, "Management Change: 6 Ways to Turn Resistance into Acceptance," *Supervisory Management* (August 1966), pp. 21-24.

[26]Douglas McGregor, *The Human Side of the Enterprise* (New York: McGraw-Hill Book Company, Inc., 1960), p. 78.

his workers informally from time to time, in order to inform them of the results of their work.

Along with understanding objectives and standards, the worker should have a clear picture of his relationship with others in the organization and how his job fits into the overall operation. It is hard for anyone to identify with an operation if he does not have a clear picture of how it is set up.[27] This step is becoming increasingly important, as traditional organization boundaries are broken down by the development of complex computer-based information systems. In the systems study described in Chapter 10, for example, an understanding of interdepartment relationships (as well as objectives and standards) was important to the success of the new system and was achieved by letting each department participate in the development study.

These guidelines were followed in *The National Observer* study discussed in Chapter 14, through distributing result reports more widely, through increased informal personal contacts, and through face-to-face reviews of performance with the worker involved. *The Observer* study also showed how effective a motivator delegation could be, for through delegation of certain tasks, the subordinate's job was made larger and more meaningful, his participation in the department increased, and his performance improved.

Incentives, therefore, are not always in the form of increased pay. They can be rewards which fulfill other needs of the individual, such as more responsibility, increased participation in management decision making, appreciation, and a greater feeling of job security. In addition to these positive motivators, there are negative motivators, such as threats of punishment or deprivation of present benefits. The manager's job is to develop the incentives appropriate to the situation and then deliver the promised rewards.

Leadership, however, involves more than understanding individual and group motivation, defining jobs and their objectives, keeping workers informed, appraising performance periodically and giving adequate rewards for performance. Leadership also involves the ability to inspire workers to improve performance and the ability to make right decisions. Timing is also important, as are the ways in which communications are made, personality differences and crises are handled, and general daily interpersonal relationships are conducted.

Leadership may be defined as interpersonal influence, expressed in situations and directed, through the communication process, toward the attainment of a specified goal or goals.[28] Leadership always involves at-

27Burt K. Scanlan, "Motivation: Are You Touching All the Bases?," *Supervisory Management* (January 1967), p. 30.
28Tannenbaum, Weschler and Massarik, *Leadership and Organization*, p. 24.

tempts on the part of a leader (influencer) to affect (influence) the behavior of a follower (influencee) or followers. It is the ability to persuade others to seek defined objectives enthusiastically. It is the ultimate act which brings success to all of the potential that is in an organization and its people.[29] Without leadership an organization cannot function.

Leadership ultimately depends on the personal characteristics of the leader himself. There is no doubt that while managers can be trained to improve their leadership qualities, some people are born better leaders than others. As Albert Dorne, late president of Famous Artists Schools, pointed out, it is the same with a writer or artist: you can develop talent to its limit, but some people are born better writers, artists, and leaders than others. This does not mean that a person should not study art or writing or leadership. It simply means that one should recognize the importance of native genius and the limitations of training.

Discipline.

Since management control often involves correcting the actions of subordinates, the handling of discipline is an area of behavioral science of particular significance to this study. The two major areas of organizational discipline are the development of a system of rules and the administration of that system. The general function of a system of rules is to insure efficient organizational effort by reducing random, undirected individual effort. Sooner or later, some of these rules will be broken.

It will then be necessary for the manager to take appropriate action. The following checklist provides some helpful guidelines in carrying out the disciplinary function:[30]

1. Do I have the necessary facts?
    a. Did the employee have an opportunity to tell his side of the story fully?
    b. Did I check with the employee's immediate supervisor?
    c. Did I investigate all other sources of information?
    d. Did I hold my interviews privately to avoid embarrassing the employee?
    e. Did I exert every possible effort to verify the information?
    f. Have I shown any discrimination toward an individual or group?
    g. Have I let personalities affect my decision?

2. Have I administered the corrective measure in the proper manner?
    a. Did I consider whether it should be done individually or collectively?
    b. Am I prepared to explain to the employee why the action is necessary?

[29]Keith Davis, *Human Relations at Work* (New York: McGraw-Hill Book Company, Inc., 1967), p. 96.

[30]Walter E. Baer, "Discipline: When an Employee Breaks the Rules," *Supervisory Management* (February 1966), p. 23.

For instance:

—Because of the effect of the violation on the employer, fellow employees and himself.

—To help him improve his efficiency and that of the department.

c. Am I prepared to tell him how he can prevent a similar offense in the future?

d. Am I prepared to deal with any resentment he might show?

e. Have I filled out a memo for his personnel folder or a letter describing the incident, to be signed by the employee? A copy of this memo or letter should be given to the employee, and he should be told that he may respond in writing—for the record.

f. In determining the specific penalty, have I considered the seriousness of the employee's conduct in relation to his particular job and his employment record?

g. Have I decided on the disciplinary action as a corrective measure—not a reprisal for an offense?

3. Have I done the necessary follow-up?

a. Has the measure had the desired effect on the employee?

b. Have I done everything possible to overcome any resentment?

c. Have I complimented him on his good work?

d. Has the action had the desired effect on other employees in the department?

JUDGMENT, CREATIVITY, AND MANAGEMENT CONTROL

Another important aspect of exercising management control is the executive judgment needed in evaluating the factors affecting a decision, as well as the creativity required in developing new directions. For example, in an equipment acquisition decision the calculations of return on investment can be made so that the executive has available certain quantitative tools to work with. But the executive must create the alternatives, that is, he must develop the possible courses of action which the financial group analyzes. And once the quantitative analysis is complete, the executive's decision does not hinge solely on these quantitative factors. It is affected by other factors, such as what weight he gives to possible obsolescence, competitive market position, possible political developments, and the like, before making his decision.

Statisticians such as Robert Schlaifer have made some effort to quantify judgmental factors through decision theory, but no complete substitute has yet been found for the executive's decision-making experience and the intuitive insights he develops from that experience. And it is unlikely that any complete substitute for them will ever be found. The success of all management control decision-making will always ultimately depend in some degree on the maturity of the decision maker's experience, judgment, and creative instincts.

CONCLUSION

The exercise of control is considered by many to be the essence of management control, for it is the step which brings action into line with plans and so fulfills the ultimate purpose of control.

The steps in the exercise of control are:

1. Develop an atmosphere for effective control action when creating controls and control standards, and when introducing new controls.
2. Compare actual results with standards.
3. Determine the significance and cause of any deviation.
4. Initiate and take whatever corrective action appears necessary.

A number of company studies were discussed, which illustrated various aspects of the exercise of control. The Heinz study showed how a new corporate control system and standards were developed and implemented in close cooperation with those who would use the system and how this approach helped the system succeed. The transportation company study briefly illustrated how a comparative analysis, differing somewhat from comparative analyses discussed in earlier chapters, can be developed to support planning decisions. The quarter panel study illustrated some of the difficulties involved in determining the causes of deviations.

Each of these studies involved a different kind of control action: indirect, supporting or advisory, and direct. Because the corporate control department focuses on financial control, it usually controls operations indirectly. For example, if the corporate financial budgets indicate that costs are out of line, the operating management will most often investigate the precise causes of the deviations and specify the action to be taken, whereas the control department will monitor the situation to see that costs are in fact brought into line by operating management. Financial and statistical analysts, and in many instance operations researchers, focus on providing analyses designed to support planning decision making, for they are the scientific technicians who can provide a more rational, quantitative evaluation of alternative courses of action. Where operating management is responsible for both the control analysis and the operation being controlled, the control action is direct, since the exercise of control is handled entirely by operating management.

Additional examples of situations involving the exercise of control are found throughout the study. The accounting and operating control chapters, for instance, are filled with examples of comparative reports analyzing results in relation to predetermined control standards for such as company assets, income, total sales and salesmen, advertising, manufacturing expenses, operator output, inventory, and stenographer performance. Each of these reports presents control analyses of deviations and would trigger action similar to that described in the quarter panel study—the cause of the deviation would be analyzed and control action taken.

In exercising control the manager should strive to strike a balance between maintaining compliance and stimulating the creative use of assets. When a deviation from a prescribed standard occurs, the control executive must correct the deviation, often through a subordinate or a line manager. He can insist harshly on compliance with standards and so produce a variety of defensive, negative reactions by the subordinate or line manager. Or, by studying human behavior and the control needs of the situation, the manager may be able to institute the corrective action in a way that stimulates a positive reaction from the subordinate.

Knowledge of behavioral science is equally helpful in developing new controls, for this is the time at which the general tone and orientation of the control system is established in the worker's mind. In the Heinz study, for example, the new system was introduced and installed with full participation of those who would subsequently be controlled by the system. Installing the system in this way created an atmosphere of constructive participation of all concerned, thus making it easier subsequently to exercise positive control within the new system.

As can be seen from the discussion in this chapter, the exercise of control involves much more than just comparing actual performance to standards and initiating action. It requires making sure that when developing and implementing controls a positive atmosphere for the exercise of control is developed, usually by involving those who will be using the system in the development of the system and its standards. It requires questioning the bases for control comparisons, to be sure the standards and the result information provide a reliable basis for making a decision. It requires considerable time and ingenuity in uncovering the causes of deviations, and a certain amount of creative imagination in developing ways to improve operations. When taking corrective action, the exercise of control requires taking care to look first at ways to improve operations and only second for ways to correct errors. It requires paying attention to the possible education and coordination benefits, both when developing and instituting controls and when taking corrective action. And it requires an awareness of human factors and a knowledge of how to motivate human beings.

This chapter has attempted to outline an approach to exercising control, by defining the kinds of control action which can be taken, the way in which action is taken in various situations, and the limits of control action. Since the discussion has deliberately been limited to the control area, little attention has been paid to describing the actual administrative action taken in the various situations in adjusting operations. For example, if at a control review meeting, the corporate budget department has pointed out that advertising costs per order are too high and the operating manager has presented a corrective plan for using lower-cost media, the control problem is ended—except to monitor the situation to see that the corrective action has been effective. How the operating manager directs his subordinates or adjusts his marketing plan in taking corrective action, while important, are not part of the control function—and so not included in this study.

The exercise of control is related to all the other steps in the control process. Factors affecting the exercise of control are identified in the first and second steps of the management control process, and a definition formed of the kind of control to be exercised. During the third step in the control process, the design and structure of control tools and systems is affected by the kind of control decisions to be made using them. And in some control systems, such as chemical control processes, the exercise of control is built into the mechanics of the control system. Control reports, which are discussed in the following chapter, are also vital to the exercise of control, since they often signal when control action is needed.

Because of the dynamic nature of the control process and the close and continuing interrelationships among the steps in the process, the exercise of control is ultimately understood only within the perspective of the total process. Chapters 13 and 14 present integrated studies of the management control process at work, and so provide an opportunity to study in depth the relation of the exercise of control to the other steps in the process.

DISCUSSION QUESTIONS

1. What are the different steps followed in exercising control, and how do they relate to the other steps in the management control process?
2. Why do you think it is so difficult to maintain a balance between compliance and creative stimulation in exercising control?
3. In what ways can the exercise of control be used to educate and coordinate the efforts of others?
4. List five of the techniques employed in the Heinz study to use the new control system in a positive way to improve operations through education and stimulation of operating personnel.
5. Describe some of the difficulties which may be encountered in determining the true causes of deviations from standards.
6. Discuss the limitations of the exercise of control in situations where quantitative analysis are provided to aid in making planning decisions.
7. List and discuss the different kinds of control action which can be taken, and the circumstances under which each might be taken.
8. Describe and discuss some of the ways in which behavioral science tools can be used in the exercise of control.
9. Studies of motivation tend to emphasize the selfish interest of the individual. Nowhere do the behavioral sciences seem to discuss the interests of the owners or investors of capital. Shouldn't a better balance be struck between the two points of view?

10. Frequently, one gets the feeling that the behavioral scientists cater to too much to the individual. Is this true? Or are they in reality saying that to study and understand the individual gives the manager greater power to manipulate subordinates more effectively and so limit their freedom even more? Discuss.

11. Each of us knows that on occasion a good "chewing out" is the best and only way to deal effectively with a situation. Discuss situations in which the emotional and psychological atmosphere justifies using such an approach to assert one's authority or to achieve a business goal.

CHAPTER 12

STEP FIVE:
CONTROL REPORTING

While control reporting is called the last step in the management control process, in practice it may be performed at many points in the process. As part of step three, a manager may write a report describing the design of a new control system or have prepared a comparative financial control report. Control reports may also be written as part of the exercise of control, the fourth step in the process, where the report outlines a manager's analysis of a control problem and his recommendation for the corrective action to be taken. A control report may even be written on the background factors affecting the development of a control system, and so be an outgrowth of step two in the control process. Control reporting thus relates to many steps in the control process. It is placed fifth and last in the process not because it necessarily follows all the other four steps, but because it is usually one of the last steps a manager performs in a control situation before administrative action is taken.

This chapter attempts to provide focus to the different aspects of control reporting that have been discussed throughout this study and to give a comprehensive overview of the subject. The discussion covers five areas: the nature of control reports, an approach to writing control reports, the factors which affect control reporting within a corporation, ways in which control reporting can be performed more effectively, and the manager's basic viewpoint in using control reports.

THE VARIOUS KINDS OF CONTROL REPORTS

Control reports, which usually contain some numerical data, range from basic data reports to analytical and action reports.

Basic data reports for control may be no more than simple daily chronological lists of checks received or sales made. Or, the data may be reshaped to suit some specific control purpose, such as a statement of expenses and profits by profit center or of sales by product line. Another kind of basic information report would be one informing personnel about what standards have been established. Most control reports, however, are usually more than just basic information reports.

Many control reports involve comparisons of actual results to some standard. Comparative control reports can cover every operating area and, as was seen in Chapter 7, are used widely in the financial control area.

Control reports are not limited to reporting only quantitative information. The report writer may analyze why deviations occurred. Or, he may go even further and present a recommended course of action for improving performance. In some instances, a control report will contain no figures, for example, when presenting the outline of a new information system for control or communicating non-quantitative performance expectations to department personnel.

Control reports, in short, encompass any kind of reports which affect management control decision-making—from computer print-outs of quantitative data to management analysis and action reports. Because control reporting is such a broad subject, the following discussion does not, and could not, cover every specific kind of control report made in a company. Rather, it focuses on the major types of reports, the major areas in which control reporting is important, and the major problems encountered in control reporting within a corporation.

PREPARING CONTROL REPORTS

A business report is a factual presentation of data or information directed to a particular reader or audience for a specific business purpose.[1] A control report is one type of business report.

Management control, as defined in Chapter 1, is:

A systematic effort to set performance standards consistent with planning objectives, to design information feedback systems, to compare actual performance with these predetermined standards, to determine whether there are any deviations and to measure their significance, and to take any action required to assure that all corporate resources are being used in the most effective and efficient way possible in achieving corporate objectives.

Management control reports are defined as any business reports which directly affect any aspect of the performance of management control —from designing the system and setting the standards, to instituting corrective action.

In order to perform control, the manager must first create the control system needed, or evaluate the existing system to determine if it meets his

---

[1]Leland Brown, *Effective Business Report Writing* (2nd ed.; Englewood Cliffs, New Jersey: Prentice-Hall, Inc., 1963), p. 3.

needs. A report may be written on the results of this systems study—for the manager's subordinate, his superiors, or merely for his own reference files.

The report might be structured around a modified outline of the management control process. The first part would give a summary of the purpose of the report, its method, and the major findings and recommendation. The remainder of the report would cover the key factors affecting the situation, the alternative courses of action, and the control action recommended. The section headings in the report could be drawn directly from the outline of the process, or could be modified to suit the individual situation.

In the case of the valve manufacturer described in Chapter 3 for example, the report might take the following format:

Introduction. This section would describe: the problem faced by the manufacturer, developing a new cost control system for one of its valve production divisions; the purpose of this report, to examine the present control system (or a modified version of it), recommend whether or not to change, and, if change is introduced, how to handle it; the methodology of the report, basically the management control process; and a recommendation, probably to adopt a modified version of the new system.

Key Factors Affecting the Situation. This section would describe those characteristics of the company, industry and market which affected the solution: the company was small and competed on the basis of price, so that it needed tight cost control; its largest selling valve (Valve A) seemed underpriced. This section would also describe the nature of the control situation (the five sections of the valve production department, only two of which Valve A passed through; overhead costs varied considerably by section), the nature and purpose of the controls and control standard (cost accounting controls and sectional standards), and any factors affecting the exercise of control (both production and marketing management resisted any change).

Available Alternative Controls. This section would describe both the present and the alternative proposed cost control systems, and the various alternative ways a new system might be introduced and control exercised, if a new system was adopted.

Evaluating Alternatives and Reasons for Recommending a Solution. This section would list the advantages and disadvantages of each system: Valve A passed through only two of five production sections, yet the present cost system used a single overhead standard for all five sections, instead of separate cost standards for each section; this led to inaccurate pricing, since overhead costs were different for each section; while the new system gave more accurate cost information, it required more work to collect needed information; the old system was simple, but did not give accurate enough information to make good pricing decisions. Weight would then be given to each advantage and disadvantage: accurate cost information was essential for the company to compete successfully on the basis of price, a factor which far outweighed the nominal increase in information collecting costs. The new system should, therefore, be adopted.

This section would also give the details of the new system, such as the forms to be used and the procedures for collecting information.

Implementing the New Control System.   This section would explore ways of introducing the new system. It was decided to use the participative approach, because there was considerable resistance to change. Responsibilities for carrying out the action plan and for exercising control under the system would also be spelled out in this section.

Another example of a control report on systems development was found in the systems development study for a mail-order company described in Chapter 10. In this situation, each operating manager who would use the new system prepared reports on his operating area, which in general followed the above format. These reports defined the decision-making and operational needs of each area, and presented and evaluated various information systems which might serve these needs. These individual reports were used in developing a single, coordinated information system for the whole division and in writing the summary report describing the entire system.

Not all control reports are as involved as those described above. Some control reports are limited to merely quantifying plans or defining performance standards. The most common control report of this type is a budget plan. A budget plan report can take many forms. There are proforma income statements and balance sheets, either for an entire company or for any division of a company's operation. There are sales budgets, production costs budgets, return on investment and share of market budgets, unit production budgets, warehousing and inventory budgets, and manpower budgets. There are reports that merely list the standard overhead charge per man-hour in a flexible budget. All of these reports, examples of which are found in earlier chapters, are basically figure reports, although they may be supplemented by explanations of how certain standards were arrived at and were to be used.

Once a system has been designed and standards set, management control depends on having actual result information and then comparing it to standards. A result report may be no more than an information report, giving only the actual result data. For example, a manager may need to have an aging of accounts receivable that he can then compare to anticipated results, which have been reported to him earlier and which he has on file. While it may be necessary to make a simple result report at times, it is not the most effective kind of management control result report.

Wherever possible a result report should give both the anticipated or budgeted results and the actual results, visualized in a way to make comparison easy. Table 12.1 shows such a comparative report. This report gives the manager basic information he needs to identify certain areas which may need corrective action at the factory level.

Table 12.1

ANNUAL INCOME STATEMENT[2]

	Budget		Actual		Difference†		Remarks
	Amount	%	Amount	%	Amount	%	
Net Sales............	$800,000.00	100.0	$900,000.00	100.0	$100,000.00	12.5	
Cost of Sales.........	560,000.00*	70.0	650,000.00	72.2	90,000.00	16.0	
Gross Profit on Sales..	$240,000.00	30.0	$250,000.00	27.8	$ 10,000.00	4.16	
Selling Expenses.....	$112,500.00	14.06	$135,000.00	15.0	$ 22,500.00	20.0	
Administrative Expenses..........	67,500.00	8.44	63,000.00	7.0	4,500.00†	6.6†	
Total Expenses......	$180,000.00	22.50	$198,000.00	22.0	$ 18,000.00	10.0	
Operating Income....	$ 60,000.00	7.5	$ 52,000.00	5.8	$ 8,000.00†	13.3†	
Financial Expenses...	4,000.00	.5	4,500.00	.5	500.00	12.5	
Estimated Net Income (7% of Sales)......	$ 56,000.00	7.0	$ 47,500.00	5.27	$ 7,500.00†	13.4†	

*Inventory of Finished Goods, $4,000.00.
†Indicates decrease.

As the report in Table 12.1 shows, a comparative control report generally goes beyond merely giving two lists of numbers. It also calculates the amount or percentage or trend of any deviations, and the relative importance of each element. Table 12.1 contains both horizontal (difference of actual from budget) and vertical (% of total actual and budget sales represented by each element) analysis. Where possible comparative reports should go even further and highlight the deviations and exceptions, in order to save the manager time and avoid giving him information he does not need or will not use. In this way he can control and manage by exception. For example, where the report is a long one, it should be selective and show only major deviations, such as those which exceed 5% or $1,000. An example of such a report is given in Table 12.2.[3]

Comparative control reports may also contain analysis or be supplemented by analysis reports. For example, in the control report on factory

[2]Adapted from John J. W. Neuner, *Cost Accounting: Principles and Practice* (6th ed.; Homewood, Illinois: Richard D. Irwin, Inc., 1962), p. 530.
[3]Adapted from J. Brooks Heckert and James D. Willson, *Business Budgeting and Control* (3rd ed.; New York. The Ronald Press Company, 1967), p. 211.

Table 12.2

ABC COMPANY[4]

Sales Analysis Report

Salesman Under Budget 5 Per Cent or More Year to Date

District Pittsburgh

Current Month and Year to Date

Description	Salesman No.	Current Month			Year to Date		
		Actual Sales	Under or Over Budget* Amount	%	Actual Sales	Under or Over Budget* Amount	%
PERFORMANCE SATISFACTORY		$ 827,432	$112,610 *	15.8 *	$4,623,096	$497,830 *	12.1 *
UNDER BUDGET PERFORMANCE:							
Abernathy	2609	32,016	1,760	5.2	102,600	6,300	5.8
Bristol	2671	17,433	1,390	7.4	61,080	4,270	6.5
Caldwell	2685	19,811	1,320	6.2	70,100	4,600	6.2
Fischer	2716	24,033	1,470	5.8	84,390	5,090	5.7
Gordon	2804	8,995	480	5.1	31,600	1,810	5.4
Inch	2827	27,666	1,820	6.2	97,010	5,930	5.8
Long	2982	4,277	600	12.3	15,020	900	5.7
Mather	3007	39,474	3,800	8.8	138,400	8,540	5.8
Owens	5066	43,189	4,400	9.6	151,800	9,080	5.6
Subtotal		216,894	17,040	7.3	752,000	46,520	5.8
District Total		$1,044,326	$ 95,570 *	10.1 *	$5,375,096	$451,310 *	9.2 *

* Figures marked with an asterisk are over budget; all others are under budget.

overhead given in Table 12.1, there is no explanation of why the deviation in selling expenses occurred nor of how the deviation might be corrected. In this instance, the manager was probably able to check the deviation out verbally or knew from experience exactly what it meant, so that he did not need an explanation of the deviation in the report. In other instances, however, it may be necessary to include deviation analysis in comparative control reports or have someone investigate the situation and write a supplemental report on why the deviation occurred. On occasion, control reports will present plans for corrective action. For example, a report analyzing accounts receivable may recommend ways to reduce receivables by limiting sales to certain customers. Or, a report analyzing plant capacity may recommend ways to improve efficiency. Rarely, however, is a control report only an action plan. Rather, where action is recommended, the action plan will usually be the last part of an entire control study.

FACTORS AFFECTING CONTROL REPORTING

Ideally, every manager should be given any report he feels he needs to operate effectively. In practice, however, this cannot always be done, for there are many factors which limit the kinds and number of reports that can be furnished to a manager. Control reporting is limited by the information and reporting systems, the equipment, and the people involved in the reporting process. Each of these factors affects the cost of reporting and sets limits on the timing and number of reports. Each must be considered in weighing a report's value against its cost, in order to determine whether or not to institute it.

The Information Reporting System.

While modern information systems and advanced computerized equipment, such as those described in Chapter 10, provide enormous capabilities, they also have many limitations. These limitations affect control reporting.

The limitations upon the kind and number of control reports that can be prepared are evident during the early stages of systems development. In developing an information system for control, the information needs of each operating area have to be balanced with the information needs of other operating groups in a company. Many compromises have to be made to strike this balance. Compromises also have to be made in most information systems[4] because certain information requested cannot be delivered in the time or form needed at a reasonable cost. For example, in the mail-order company study described in Chapter 10 the marketing department could get certain reports only every other week, instead of weekly, and

---

[4]Rudolph E. Hirsch, "The Value of Information," *Journal of Accounting*, June 1968, pp. 41.

certain reports requested by order servicing were eliminated, because their cost did not seem to be justified by their value.

Further limitations are introduced once a reporting system is in operation. Rigid schedules are set and computer time is carefully allocated, because the cost of buying or renting computers is high. As a result, changes in schedules are not easy to make, for they usually require dislocating some other reports, which affects other managers' needs. Once a system is developed, programmers are assigned to other duties and personnel are trained to produce and use the scheduled reports. As a result, the addition of new reports requires reassigning programmers and additional programming expense—a major problem in today's larger information systems.

When a new report or change in report format is requested immediately after the new system has been introduced, the manager is under pressure to explain why he waited until then to request the report and did not build it into the original system. The obvious answer, of course, is that he didn't think of it. Managers cannot be expected to know, down to the last detail, what they want in a control report and the exact form in which they want it, before a system is in operation. Nor can they really be expected to know everything about how a complex, computerized information system works and what reports it can or cannot prepare.[5] And in many instances, business conditions simply change quickly, leading to new report needs.

Most companies now recognize the need for constant changes in information systems. Many companies perform a periodic systems audit, especially after a new system has been introduced.[6] During this audit, a manager may discover that certain information he needs is not being generated. For example, a manager may not have realized when a system was being developed that external market information and trade data could be made available on computer.[7] Changes occur continually in systems, as managers become more educated in system capabilities, as past errors in systems design are corrected, as managers articulate their needs better, as business conditions change, and as new systems become available. It is in fact not unusual to see system changes occur only a week or a month after a new system is introduced.[8] In spite of this increased awareness of the need for change, there is resistance to change in an estab-

[5]Russell Ackoff, "Management Misinformation Systems," *Management Science*, December 1967, p. 152.

[6]Benjamin Conway, "The Information System Audit: A Control Technique for Managers," *Management Review*, March 1968, pp. 37-48.

[7]J. Daniel Couger, "Seven Inhibitors to a Successful Management Information System," *Systems and Procedures Journal*, January-February, 1968, p. 18.

For further discussion of information needs, see Robert Beyer, "A Positive Look at Management Information Systems," *Financial Executive*, June 1968, pp. 50-52, 54, 56-57; and Malcolm Macdougall, "Disseminating Information within a Company," *Systems and Procedures Journal*, May-June 1968, pp. 28-32.

[8]Alan J. Rowe, "Coming to Terms with Computer Management Systems," *Financial Executive*, April 1968, p. 71.

lished information system, so that any changes will always create aggravations and cannot always be done easily.

Despite the limitations of modern information systems, they are vast improvements over manual systems, and can in many instances generate better control reports faster than can older manual or electro-mechanical systems. In order to use computerized information systems effectively, however, a manager must become involved in their development and learn how to use them.

The Equipment.

The capacities of information processing and reporting equipment have a major impact on control reporting, especially in the areas of information storage, information processing, report output, and programming.

A company cannot possibly store all the information that would be needed for every kind of control report, for it would be extremely expensive and could never be justified by its benefits. Thus the company must limit the amount of information retained to that which it considers essential. This applies to computer as well as non-computer storage.

When information is stored on punched cards or in files, storage is limited by the amount and cost of floor space and cabinets, the cost of punching cards or filing material, the time involved in searching these files to retrieve the information needed, and the like. It is much easier to store *everything*, and the average individual will do so until he runs out of space or until he experiences extreme difficuties in finding information he wants quickly. Such indiscriminate storage of information is uneconomical and inefficient, and each individual manager must take a disciplined approach to selecting what to file and what to throw away.

A computer also has limited information storage capacity. While the amount of information stored in a computer system will vary with the size of the system, there is always some limit to a system's storage capacity. Basically, storage is of two types, internal and external. Internal or main storage is done within the central processing unit of the computer itself. The size of this storage is usually relatively small, from 4,000 to 1,000,000 characters of information. In most cases a company will have to use external or auxiliary storage, such as magnetic tapes, disks, drums, or punched cards.[9]

Information kept in storage must be retrieved in order to be used in report preparation.[10] A processing unit for reading or retrieving information from auxiliary storage media may represent as much as 10% of the

[9]Frederick G. Withington, *The Use of Computers in Business Organizations* (Reading, Massachusetts. Addison-Wesley Publishing Company, 1966), p. 233.
[10]Richard S. Nauer, "Reference It; Retrieve It; Reproduce It," *Systems and Procedures Journal*, March-April 1968, pp. 32-36.

cost of the computer itself.[11] As a consequence, a company may have to limit the number of auxiliary units to be used and so limit the use of external information storage in control reporting.[12]

The time necessary to retrieve information also affects the preparation of control reports. If information is kept in internal or main storage, the access time, which is in effect the time interval between the instant the data is called from storage and the instant at which delivery is completed, is relatively short. For example, in reporting by closed circuit television, as in brokerage houses, the access time is only a few seconds. However, if the data is in an external or auxiliary storage unit, the access time can be quite long. For example, if information is on magnetic tape, the tape must be found, mounted on a tape drive, and the entire tape run through in order to retrieve the exact information wanted.

The running time in many instances can be fairly long, even though the information required is not extensive. For example, a tape file may list all of a magazine's subscribers (filed in alphabetic order by state or mailing zone) and carry complete information on the subscribers and all their transactions with the company. The information wanted may be only the names on those subscriptions which expire during the current week, but the entire list will have to be run through to get his information. This approach is called sequential access retrieval. The necessity to run the entire tape in sequential access retrieval severely limits the use which can be made of stored information for control reporting.

Information retrieval time can be considerably shortened with random access systems. Under a random access system, every piece of information in a file does not have to be passed through a retrieval unit. Instead, the information is stored on magnetic drums and the information is retrieved directly from where it is stored.[13] Random access systems are still expensive, however, and it may be some time before economical random access systems are ready for widespread commercial use.

While sophisticated computers can perform calculations at spectacular speeds, they are limited in the operations they can perform. A computer can perform such arithmetic operations as addition, subtraction, multiplication, and division. It can also perform logic or comparison operations, such as comparing two figures to determine which is greater or lesser.[14]

---

[11] John A. Postley, *Computers and People* (New York: McGraw-Hill Book Company, 1960), p. 31.

[12] For a discussion of information storage, see Milton J. Cooke, "The Data Base Revolution," *Systems and Procedures Journal*, March-April 1968, pp. 20-22; and Charles H. Nicholson, Jr., "Building Data Banks for Multiple Uses," *Systems and Procedures Journal*, May-June 1968, pp. 18-22.

[13] John S. Murphy, *Basics of Digital Computer Programming* (New York: John F. Rider, Publisher, Inc., 1964), p. 117.

[14] John Scott and McCready Young, "Challenge to Electronic Data Processing," *Financial Executive*, February 1964, p. 29.

However, normally a computer cannot determine the reasons why one figure is greater or lesser than the other.

A computer system makes use of various output devices to transmit information, such as magnetic tape, punched cards, cathode picture tubes (TV-like tubes), and printed output. High speed printers have been developed which print entire lines from 120 to 160 characters long[15] at one time, at speeds ranging from about 150 to 1,000 lines per minute or more. But even with this great speed, there are limits upon the amount of printing that can be done at a particular time, which affects the effectiveness of computer usage for control reporting. For example, the author recently had an interest rate schedule calculated by a computer for a pricing chart; the actual calculations took two seconds, but over a minute was needed to print the chart. Control reporting is also limited by the fact that only one report can be printed out at a time on any printing device.

For a computer to perform any operation, it must be programmed. This is probably the most limiting aspect of computers today. A program is a sequence of instructions and routines for performing a desired operation.[16] A computer can do only what it is programmed to do.[17] For every type of report that the computer generates, a program must be prepared telling the computer how to do it.

When the same control reports are prepared regularly, the same computer programs can be used. However, in many instances, a manager will ask for a report that has not been prepared before. For example, the marketing manager may want a report giving sales information by customer, rather than by the type of product sold. The data for this report may exist, but the computer program necessary to generate the report must be prepared, if such a report has not been requested and run before.

Considerable time is needed to translate written instructions into one of the computer languages. And programmers, who do this work, are in short supply and are highly paid. For example, the new system whose development was described in Chapter 10 required thousands of hours of programming—six programmers working four months—before the system was computerized. Because programming takes time, the interval between initial request and delivery of the report may be many days or even weeks. Because programmers are expensive, the cost of preparing the report may be too high to justify running the report, unless it is needed on a regular basis. Programming thus affects what control reports can be prepared

[15]Withington, *The Use of Computers in Business Organizations*, p. 27.

[16]C. Orville Elliott and Robert S. Wasley, *Business Information Processing Systems* (Homewood, Illinois: Richard D. Irwin, Inc., 1965), p. 544. See also R. F. Garland, "Computer Programs: Control and Security," *N.A.A. Management Accounting*, December 1966, pp. 43-45.

[17]George Glaser, "Plain Talk About Computers," *Business Horizons*, Fall 1967, p. 33.

and when they can be given to management.[18] Work is being done on automated programming devices, but until they are commercially available, programming severely limits a manager's ability to request new kinds of reports within a computerized system.

Both a company's information system and the computer equipment it uses affect management control reporting. The information system, and its related computer equipment, establish a framework for the amount, types, and timing of report generation. While such systems offer enormous capabilities for improved control reporting, their limitations must be understood in depth, if an effective and efficient management control system is to be developed.

Human Factors.

A successful management control reporting system depends as much on people as it does on machines. All reporting systems are affected to some degree by the capacities and limitations of the human beings working within the system—from the programmer and key punch operator working in a computerized system, to the analyst preparing interpretive reports, to the manager interpreting and using the report.

Reporting by machine is only as accurate and as reliable as the data fed into the machines and the programs directing machine operations. People make the programs and develop the input data. People thus have a major impact on the success of computerized reporting systems.

Human factors also affect other areas of control reporting. For example, a manager or his assistant may be asked to analyze and report on deviations in a particular operation. The success of this report depends on two factors: the subordinate's ability to analyze and evaluate data, and his ability to digest the material and write a report on it in clear, forceful language. If his judgment is weak and the true importance of each factor is not seen, if the conclusions are not synthesized into a realistic solution, or if the report is vague and disorganized, then the control report will be of little value.

Human factors also affect the interpretation of reports. While a machine may tell the manager where a control problem exists, interpreting the cause of the problem usually depends on the manager's insight and the way the manager "sees" the problem. Rarely will any reporting system anticipate all the needs of each decision maker: his temperament, his reading habits, his knowledge gaps, his work routine, his personal preferences, and the like. All of these factors affect the way he reads, interprets, and uses control reports.

[18]See B. Rothery, "Assessing Programming Progress," *Data Processing Magazine*, August 1967, pp. 40-41, "Estimating the Programming Load" *Data Processing Magazine*, July 1967, pp. 36-37, and "Problems of Computer Programs Change," *Data Processing Magazine*, March 1968, pp. 68-69.

Human factors thus affect all phases of the reporting cycle: information collection, processing, analysis, communication, and interpretation. And they must be taken into account both when developing information systems and when searching for the reasons behind deviations from standards.

SOME GENERAL GUIDELINES

No matter what the situation, there is one basic rule in control reporting: the control report must meet the needs of the situation and of the decision maker, as regards both form and content. This is not always an easy task. Before undertaking any control report, therefore, one should probe deeply the use to which the report will be put, by asking such questions as:

Who will be reading the report? Is it intended for more than one person? At what management level are they?

Precisely what kinds of decisions will be made based on the report? Exactly what information will be needed to make the report?

How significant will the decisions be that are made based on the report?

How important will the report be in helping make the decision?

Is the report to supply all the information needed to make the decision, or does it deal with only one aspect of the situation?

How much time will the reader generally have available for reviewing the report?

Should just the highlights of a study be given, or should the writer try to include all pertinent background analysis material in detail?

Is the report to be a decision document, in which case recommendations should go at the beginning? Or is it to be a review report which merely presents facts?

What is the best form to present the figures? What is the best way to show comparisons clearly? Should the size of deviations be shown in percentages or in absolute amounts?

These questions help focus the writer's attention on why the report is being written, who will be using it, and the purpose for which it is being written, and so serve as guidelines for approaching control reporting. They also help the writer determine what aspect of the management control process the report concerns.

Other factors which should be considered when preparing a control report are timeliness, accuracy, clarity and conciseness, and the report's precision in highlighting deviations, fixing responsibility and generating corrective action.

Any control report must, of course, be timely. The sooner the manager knows that a situation is out of control, the sooner he can correct it. And nothing is more frustrating than to receive result information too late to correct the situation.

If intelligent corrective action is to be taken, the information in a control report must be accurate. However, accuracy sometimes depends on checking and double-checking, which can be time-consuming. A balance must, therefore, be struck between timeliness and accuracy. If a report is needed within a very short time, a degree of exactness may have to be sacrificed. It should be remembered that many times a timely estimate is a lot more valuable than a late report accurate to the penny.[19]

A control report must be clear, brief and to the point. It should be as short as possible, yet contain all essential information. All unimportant facts must be eliminated from a report.

Consistency of terms and values is important to report clarity. Meanings and terms should not change in mid-report.[20] For example, inventory valued at lower of cost or market should be valued this way all through the report, not changed to some other method of valuation in the middle of the report.

Table 12.3

DEPARTMENTAL COST REPORT[21]
INCLUDING COST-CONTROL DISTINCTIONS
DEPARTMENT A

	Budget	Actual	Variance
Direct materials	$10,500	$10,200	$(300)
Direct labor	18,400	18,800	400
Factory overhead—foreman's responsibility			
Indirect labor	2,800	2,900	100
Idle time	500	550	50
Supplies	340	325	(15)
Stationery	110	106	(4)
Salaries—staff	800	750	(50)
Depreciation—equipment	4,800	4,800	
Total foreman's responsibility	$38,250	$38,431	$ 181
Factory overhead—other's responsibilities			
Salaries—department head	1,200	1,200	
Depreciation—building	2,200	2,200	
Payroll taxes	810	870	60
Insurance	220	220	
Total departmental costs	$42,680	$41,921	$ 241

[19]"Management Reports: Technique and Usage," *Financial Executive*, October 1964, p. 45.

[20]Michael J. Recter, "Reports That Communicate," *Management Services*, January-February 1967, p. 30.

[21]I. Wayne Keller and William L. Ferrara, *Management Accounting for Profit Control* (2nd ed.; New York: McGraw-Hill Book Company, 1965), p. 252.

Wherever possible, control reports should be comparative in nature. Actual performance data alone may be of little significance unless compared with a target or yardstick, such as budgets, standards, or past performance. It is one thing to report that direct labor costs for the month were $25,000; it is quite another thing to report that direct labor costs for the month were $10,000 over budgeted costs.

Control reports should emphasize responsibility for any deviations discovered. In comparing actual costs with standard costs, it is important to distinguish between those costs which are not controllable. Doing this makes it easier for management to determine problem areas and evaluate operating performance. Table 12.3 illustrates a cost control report distinguishing costs by area of responsibility.

The control report must communicate in the most effective way possible specific information useful in performing management control. It is useful at this point, therefore, to review some of the basic guidelines for good communication given by authorities in the field. The following are ten guidelines for written communications:[22]

1. Write on the level of your reader's understanding.
2. Watch your pace.
3. Keep your sentences short.
4. Put your qualifying ideas in separate sentences.
5. Use paragraphs to break your text into readable units.
6. Avoid too much use of the passive voice.
7. Use verbs
8. Be direct.
9. Keep your tone appropriate.
10. Be specific.

And the following are ten guidelines for verbal communications:[23]

1. Stop talking!
2. Put the talker at ease.
3. Show him that you want to listen.
4. Remove distractions.
5. Empathize with him.
6. Be patient.
7. Hold your temper.
8. Go easy on argument and criticism.
9. Ask questions.
10. Nature gave man two ears but only one tongue, which is a gentle hint that he should listen more than he talks.

By following these guidelines, control reporting—either verbal or written—can be made more effective.

THE MANAGEMENT CONTROL VIEWPOINT

The instinctive reaction of many managers is to assume that a control report is correct, and to spend their time studying the kinds of action that could be taken based on the information in the report. It is puzzling why so many middle managers fail to question the bases and accuracy of control reports, and why a figure report so often seems to take on an aura of sacred truth—no matter how inaccurate the figures or how unusable the form in which they are presented.

A manager should always start by questioning the basis of his decision. In a situation involving a comparative control report, the manager's first step should be to question the mechanism used to prepare the report, the source documents used, the purpose for which the report was prepared, and the like. Next, the standards should be scrutinized. For example, if higher management set the sales goals, they may be a little higher and the costs a little lower than might honestly be anticipated, if the objective is to provide lower-level management with incentive goals; if the manager of the operation being controlled set the standards, they may be a little conservative, if he is looking to make his job a little easier. Only after a manager has raised such questions and obtained satisfactory answers to them should he procede to take action.

Strong management control administration is also needed to eliminate control reports no longer needed. Especially in large organizations reports will often continue to be generated and circulated long after their usefulness has ended. Again only the manager receiving the report can effectively maintain control over control reporting, for he is in the best position to judge their usefulness and initiate requests for elimination of reports no longer needed. A strong administrator will, therefore, question not only the content and form of a control report, but also its very existence.

This study is intended to give a manager broader perspective from which to approach performance of the control function. In the control situations described in this chapter, as in the others described elsewhere in this study, the manager is forced to examine all phases of the control process when dealing with a specific problem. For example, the user of a control report will instinctively study how the report was put together, and the one who prepares the report will instinctively study in depth the uses to which the report will be put—if he works within the perspective of the management control process.

Simply because another department, such as information systems or corporate financial control, may be responsible for generating control reports, a manager should not side-step his basic management responsibilities. When using control reports his responsibility remains to understand their place in the total management control process and to be certain they fulfill basic control purposes effectively—no matter who is responsible for preparing them.

CONCLUSION

Many aspects of control reporting have been covered in the first eleven chapters of this study. This chapter has attempted to give focus to these earlier discussions and present a systematically organized approach to control reporting.

The discussion in this chapter covered the various kinds of control reports, the approach used in preparing each kind, the major factors affecting control reporting, some guidelines for report preparation, and the manager's basic viewpoint in using control reports. The discussion was not meant to be a substitute for a book on good report writing and presentation. Rather, it was designed only to touch briefly on those points of most relevance to reporting in the *control* area.

The control report is an indispensable tool of management control. It is the feedback link in the control cycle. Without the effective feedback of result information and without the effective communication of the method to be followed in correcting deviations, there can be no management control.

DISCUSSION QUESTIONS

1. What are the major factors that distinguish management control reports from other types of business reports?
2. List and describe the various types of control reports.
3. Discuss the differences in approach when preparing a comparative report on performance results and one recommending corrective action.
4. Discuss the differences in approach when preparing a comparative report on performance results and one recommending a new information system.
5. Describe the basic outline followed in preparing management control reports, and describe how it relates to the problem-solving/decision-making process described in Chapter 2.
6. Why is it so important that a control report be comparative? How does this requirement relate to the essence of management control?
7. How should deviations be reported? Why is vertical and horizontal analysis so important in control reporting?
8. What are the major systems and equipment limitations a sales manager might face when requesting a change in calculating commissions for his salesmen?
9. Even when a fairly good control information and reporting system has been developed, people do not always use it or use it well. Discuss why this is so.

CHAPTER 13

A CORPORATE FINANCIAL CONTROL SYSTEM

The five steps in the management control process have been discussed in detail in Chapters 3 through 12. In an effort to give perspective to those discussions, these last two chapters present integrated studies of the control process at work on two levels: an overall corporate control system and an operating control system.

This chapter discusses a typical corporate financial control system. The discussion is based on Robert Deming's study of Frost Electric Company, and covers the planning base of the system, the budgetary standards, the data gathering and reporting mechanisms, and the use of the system by corporate executives in exercising control. The chapter concludes with an evaluation of the system by several corporate controllers.[1]

THE PLANNING BASE

The study of the overall company financial control system at Frost began with an examination of Frost's organization and planning process.

The Frost Company was founded in 1890, and a younger brother of the founder was Chairman of the Board in 1963. The company manufactured three types of electrical equipment: power tools, including welders, bench saws, planers, drill presses, lathes, and other stationary equipment; builders' supplies, including residential and commercial lighting fixtures, electric heaters, heat controls, ventilating systems, heat hoods, and intercom systems; and electric motors used for a wide variety of commercial and industrial purposes, including manufacture of conveyors, fans and blowers, machine tools, pumps, home appliances, furnaces, and many other applications.

[1]Robert H. Deming, *Characteristics of an Effective Management Control System in an Industrial Organization* (Boston: Division of Research, Graduate School of Business Administration, Harvard University, 1968).

Figure 13.1

FROST COMPANY

Condensed Organization Chart
Domestic Operations, September 1962

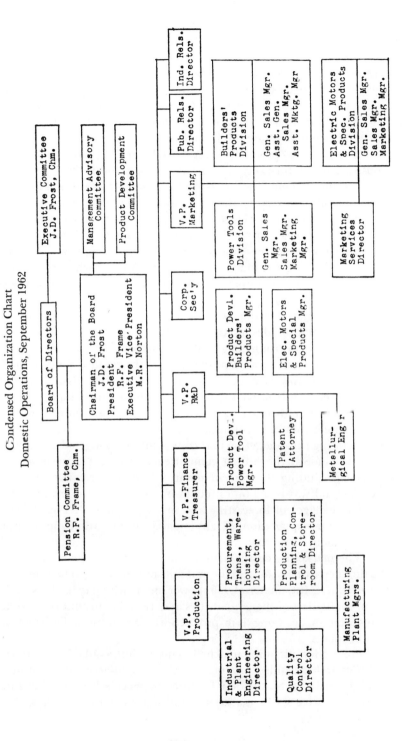

From 1947 to 1962 consolidated annual sales had risen from $36,000,000 to $192,000,000 and net earnings from $2,800,000 to $13,100,000. The company had both domestic and foreign manufacturing facilities, and had become the leading manufacturer in the industry, holding approximately 10% to 15% of the total composite domestic market.

The company's organization, which was described briefly in Chapter 5, is given in summary form in Figure 13.1.

The planning process at Frost started with long-range planning, which consisted of establishing overall objectives, defining new product plans, and developing long-range (five-year) economic forecasts and five-year forecasts of dollar and unit sales by product line. The long-range, strategic planning was done by the Management Advisory and Product Development Committee, assisted by the market research manager. In their planning, major emphasis was given to forecasting, and very little time was spent on defining nonfinancial objectives. In fact, when questioned, the three chief officers expressed differing view on many facets of the overall company objectives.

Operational planning was basically profit planning, and began with an eighteen-month sales forecast. This forecast was done by the forecasting and inventory control manager. While this forecast was based on the five-year sales forecast, it was adjusted to meet the requirements of marketing promotion plans, seasonal patterns, and new product plans. The eighteen-month forecast was broken down by month for the coming year, and by quarter for an additional six months. It covered all major product lines. This eighteen-month sales forecast was reduced by 5% to 10% in preparing the operating cost budget, so that costs would be budgeted conservatively.

Each month the billing committee prepared a three-month billing forecast (including the current month). This forecast was for each sales division, and was based on estimates by the marketing product managers and the manager of forecasting and inventory control. Top management required an explanation of any significant deviations in it from the eighteen-month forecast.

The marketing department submitted requests quarterly to the production department for specific amounts of product. Production converted these requests into material, manpower and machine quantities, and based on an evaluation of these quantities and available inventories, production plans were made. Long-term production plans were made based on new product plans.

Production planning matched plans against available inventories and facilities and scheduled production, while manufacturing plant managers administered the production facilities to meet schedules. Inventory requirements were set by marketing, and were taken into account in short-term scheduling.

Annual expense budgets were prepared as part of the planning phase and used as standards for expense control. It was through the sales forecasts and the expense budgets, therefore, that planning and control were closely integrated at Frost.

DEVELOPING BUDGETS AND STANDARDS

The finance department handled the coordination of expense budgets. Prior to 1963, each year the finance department asked all department managers to submit budget estimates. Each manager in turn requested budget estimates from his subordinates, wherever possible.

Starting in 1963, the financial analysts prepared budgets for each department and the department or section manager was responsible for questioning it and justifying changes. The new budgetary procedure, which was still in the development stage, was as follows:

1. Develop past history.
2. Issue questionnaire.
3. Prepare annual budget and recommend ways through cost reduction that the department might meet the budget.
4. Review budget with responsible manager and through negotiation or fiat decide upon a budget that will then be reviewed with the manager of the cost control and budget department.
5. Review the approved budget with the respective functional vice presidents.
6. Submit the official budget, approved by the manager of the cost control and budget department and the functional vice president, to the Management Advisory Committee for final approval and arbitration of any unresolved differences.

Marketing Department.

In general, all expense budgets in the marketing department were prepared on the basis of previous year's budgets, with adjustments being made for such things as increased sales forecasts. Most marketing costs were fixed, and not variable with sales. The finance department matched combined marketing expense budgets with other expense budgets and matched them against sales in order to come up with profit estimates. Where profit estimates were below the standards set for each product, finance, the marketing manager and other managers involved met together to develop a final budget within profit standards.

The sales promotion and advertising budget was prepared separately by the advertising managers by product line, working with the market service manager. Generally, this budget was limited to around 5% of sales. This was usually the first budget cut, if profits and profit forecasts were below standard.

Detailed budgets and a projected operating statement for the company were then prepared and submitted to the Management Advisory Committee (MAC) by the finance department. Once reviewed and approved by the MAC, these budgets became official company goals for the coming year.

Standard Cost System.

The standard cost system used in the production area was built on cost centers and estimated plant capacity.

A cost center was defined as a group of like machines (with respect to the cost of owning and operating), no matter where they were located. There were 70 cost centers spread over a variety of factory operating departments in various manufacturing facilities. Overhead costs were accumulated by cost center and a fixed and variable rate per unit of time was determined for each one. Each job was charged with the rate(s) of the cost center(s) through which is passed. Any one factory operating department usually contained many cost centers, and each cost center spanned several factory operating departments.

Total plant capacity was calculated at 90,000 hours per week and adjusted annually. Based on this total, the capacity of each cost center was determined. All standard cost center overhead rates were based on capacity operation within a cost center.

Standard cost rates were established for labor, material, and overhead. Standard labor times were calculated for each job in the tool engineering department from the standard or formula data established by the time study section, and included set-up time. The standard or allowed labor time was priced at the labor rate assigned to the cost center performing the operation. The procurement section established standard material costs based on actual costs, and each job ticket carried standard material costs.

Overhead was charged to the product on the basis of standard fixed and variable cost center rates. The process used to calculate such rates was to compute the direct costs associated with each center and add to this the various distributed, non-direct costs (e.g., staff departments, general plant overhead) and divide by capacity hours.

Production Department.

Both staff and factory operating budgets were based on the direct labor hours.

Each staff department was allocated a fixed budgeted expense, plus a variable amount determined by the number of direct labor hours produced by the shop each month. The rate at which the variable expense budget was to be calculated was contained in the budget. Each month the department manager was given the number of planned production hours and he calculated his own total budgeted expenses for the coming month. A budget performance statement was prepared at the end of each month for each department, showing actual and budgeted performance.

A department foreman's operating expense budget was made up of two items: 1) supervisory salaries and wages and indirect labor and 2) an additional amount, which was determined by the jobs he processed through the various cost centers.

As for supervisory salaries and wages, each factory department had a rate sheet that showed the fixed and variable budgeted dollars for supervisory and indirect labor. The fixed portion of supervisory salaries was composed of the foreman's annual salary and the assistant foreman's annual wages, whereas the variable portion was composed of the proportionate share of the lead man's wages based on a ratio of one hour of supervision for each 20 hours of planned direct labor. The fixed and variable amounts for indirect labor were based on historical levels, adjusted periodically for the addition or deletion of certain services. The department foreman was not charged with, and so did not have a budget for, the cost of direct labor.

The department foreman's budget for other operating accounts was based on hours spent in each cost center in his department during the month, weighted by cost center rates for each expense account. This was determined by the jobs assigned to him by production planning and by the cost centers through which these jobs were scheduled. The total budget for each department expense account was the accumulation of identical accounts from all the cost centers utilized by a manufacturing department during a particular month.

A manufacturing department foreman did not receive a pre-set budget monthly, but did receive a monthly estimate of the total hours planned for his department by production planning, and he could apply his departmental budget rates to calculate his allowed supervisory and indirect labor budgets. He also had available a composite rate factor for each major account. This rate factor was a weighted average standard based on a typical cost center mix that he could apply to the planned hours to arrive at an estimate of the budget allowance he would receive for each expense account. At the end of each month he received a performance report, showing actual expenditures, collected on a cost center basis and summarized in a data processing report.

Research and Development.

The R and D budget was prepared on the basis of past experience, adjusted for anticipated new programs and services. Generally, R and D expenses were limited to 3% of estimated domestic sales, but were adjusted to accommodate new projects by the MAC. The major expense in this department was for people, the engineering staff.

Product Pricing.

The standard for pricing was to hold manufacturing costs to 52% or less of gross sales value for builders' products, 45% for electric motors, and 65% for power tools. Any variances were reviewed by the MAC. In addition to the cost/price ratios mentioned above, other factors which were taken into account in pricing were: competitive prices and conditions, share of market, end use of item, payback period, utility of product, relationship with other products in line, and what the market would bear. Each year prices were reviewed in relation to costs when preparing the next year's unit cost book.

Monthly Forecast of Operating Results.

Each month the financial department prepared an estimate of operating profits, sales, and costs for the next three months. This was based in part on the billing committee's billing forecast, but mainly on the most recent spending and cost trends. These forecasts were not related to the annual budget or sales forecast. The forecast was designed to enable managers to take steps to bring the forecast back into line with the annual budget during the coming quarter. This forecast was in essence a red flag, through which the financial manager could alert the MAC to the fact that results for the coming quarter might not be in line with the budget.

THE CONTROL SYSTEM: OVERALL COMPARATIVE FINANCIAL RESULT REPORTS

The Blue Book.

A series of financial result reports (referred to as "The Blue Book") was prepared monthly. The Blue Book contained an 11-page parent company section, as well as a breakdown of results for each foreign and domestic subsidiary. The parent company section contained:

1. An overall statement of income and surplus.
2. An operating statement for each product division.
3. A breakdown of cost of goods sold.
4. A balance sheet.
5. A detailed inventory breakdown by tools, parts, and accessories, according to their state of completion by location.
6. A statement of property accounts.
7. An analysis of variances.
8. A detailed breakdown of factory expenses.
9. Income and expense details.

Representative examples of these statements are given in Figures 13.2 through 13.6. In addition to the reports in the parent company section,

Figure 13.2

INCOME AND SURPLUS

Parent Company

Note: All Figures Stated In Thousands

INCOME	Month of February						Year to Date 5 Months thru Feb.					
			ACTUAL						ACTUAL			
	BUDGET	%	This Year	%	Last Year	%	BUDGET	%	This Year	%	Last Year	%
GROSS SALES												
Less: Cash Discount												
Service Allowances												
Transportation												
Merchandising Allow.												
NET SALES												
Cost of Sales												
MANUFACTURING MARGIN												
Less: Salesmen's Comp.												
Salesmen's Expenses												
Promotion												
Service Operations												
Other Selling Expenses												
Total Selling Expenses												
Administrative & General												
Development Eng.												
Parent Service Fee												
Total Expenses												
OPERATING INCOME												
Add: Other Income												
Inter-company Profit												
Non Recurring Income												
Service Fees-Subsid.												
INCOME BEFORE TAXES												
Less Taxes on Income												
NET INCOME												
Provision for Depreciation												
EARNED SURPLUS												
Net Income												
Dividends from Subsidiaries												
TOTAL INCOME TO SURPLUS												
Less: Cash Dividends												
Net Surplus of Period												
Add: Balance at Beginning												
Other Credits												
Less: Stock Dividends												
Other Charges												
EARNED SURPLUS AT END												

there was also an income and surplus statement for each domestic subsidiary, each of the eight foreign subsidiaries, and the consolidated company.

Figure 13.3

BUDGET FISCAL YEAR
OPERATING STATEMENT

Parent Company

	Total All Sales	Total Power Tools	Total Building Products	Total Electric Motors & Special Products
Total Gross Sales	$	$	$	$
Less: Cash Discount				
Service Allowances				
Transportation				
Net Sales				
Cost of Sales				
Standard				
Variance				
Other Costs				
Total Cost of Sales				
Manufacturing Margin				
Less: Salesmen's Compensation				
Salesmen's Expenses				
Promotion				
Service Operations				
Export Operations				
Other Selling Expenses				
International Planning				
Total Selling Expenses				
Administrative & General				
Development Engineering				
Total Expenses				
Operating Income				

Figure 13.4

COST OF GOODS SOLD

Parent Company

Month of: February,	Direct Material	Direct Labor	Overhead	Total
Standard Cost of Goods Shipped				
Add: Volume Variance				
Rate Variances				
Use Variances				
Total Manufacturing Cost				
Add: Other Cost of Goods Sold				
Other Costs and Expenses				
Total Cost of Goods Shipped				
Less:Cost of Goods Sold to Other Subsid.				
Less:Transfers to Promotion				
Cost of Goods Sold—Customer				
Manufacturing Cost Rates				
* on Standard Hours				
on Actual Hours				
* Includes Sub. Std. Hrs.				
5 Months To: February 25,	Direct Material	Direct Labor	Overhead	Total
Standard Cost of Goods Shipped				
Add: Volume Variance				
Rate Variances				
Use Variances				
Total Manufacturing Cost				
Add: Other Cost of Goods Sold				
Other Costs and Expenses				
Total Cost of Goods Shipped				
Less:Cost of Goods Sold to Other Subsid.				
Less:Transfers to Promotion				
Cost of Goods Sold—Customer				
Manufacturing Cost Rates				
* on Standard Hours				
on Actual Hours				
* Includes Sub. Std. Hrs.				
FACTORY BUDGET	Direct Material	Direct Labor	Overhead	Total
Current Month — Budget				
Variance				
Year to Date — Budget				
Variance				

Figure 13.5

DETAILS OF FACTORY OVERHEAD EXPENSES

Parent Company

	Month of February			Year to Date 5 Months thru February			
	Budget		Actual		Budget		Actual
	Official	Flexible	This Year	Last Year	Official	Flexible	This Year	Last Year
Overhead Departments								
Production Planning								
Production Control								
Receiving and Stores								
General Planning & Supervision								
Industrial Engineering								
Inspection								
Industrial Relations								
Training								
General Engineering								
Process								
Tool Design								
New Mfg. Methods								
Tool Room								
General Factory								
Maintenance-Plant								
Mech. & Equip.								
Mechanical and Electrical								
Special Appr.								
Tool Crib								
Plant Protection								
Plant Utilities								
Gen. Factory Fixed and Unallocated								
Overhead Adjustment								
Freight & Express - Inbound								
Cafeteria								
Provision for Year End Payroll								
Contingent Compensation								
Holiday and Vacation Pay								
Unutilized Plant Capacity								
Total								
Less: Direct Overhead Transfer								
Total Factory Ledger								
Count Variance (Closed Orders)								
Total Overhead								
Std. Rates Chgd. to Inv.								
Add:Rate Var. Chgd. To Cost of Goods Sold								
Use Variance								
Volume Variance								
Total Overhead								
Std. Rates Chgd. To Cost of Goods Sold								
Plus: All Production Variance								
Total Mfg. O.H. In Cost of Goods Sold								

282

Figure 13.6

INCOME AND EXPENSE DETAILS
Parent Company

Column headers (both panels):

	Month of February			Year to Date 5 Months thru Feb.		
	Budget	Actual		Budget	Actual	
		This Year	Last Year		This Year	Last Year

Left panel row labels:

Salesmen's Salaries & Expenses:
Domestic: Salaries
 Contingent Comp.
 Expenses
 Export
 Total

Promotion:
Promotion
Contingent Compensation
 Total

Service Operations:
Marketing Service
Product Service
Service Branches
Unallocated Overhead
Contingent Compensation
 Total

Other Selling Expenses:
Training – Sales
Product Distribution
Special Sales
Forecasting & Inventory Cont.
Regional Managers Office
District Sales Office Exp.
Customer Service
Unallocated Overhead
Auto Transportation
Order
Duplicating
Dwellings – Staff
Market Research
Santa Barbara Warehouse
Boston Warehouse
Finished Stock & Shipping
Traffic
Export
International Planning
Marketing Mgrs.
Marketing
Contingent Compensation
 Total

Right panel row labels:

Administrative:
Controller's Office
Cashier's Office
Secretary's Office
Public Relations
Purchasing
Credit & Collections
Audit
Payroll & Cost
Budget
Treasurer's Office
General Accounting
Data Processing
General Administrative
Unallocated Overhead
General Office Bldgs. & Grds.
Dwellings – Rented
Contingent Compensation
 Total

Development Engineering:
Unallocated
Power Tool Div.
Records & Packaging
Experimental Machine Shop
General
Electrical & Tests
Building Products
Elec. Motors & Spec. Prod.
Contingent Compensation
 Total

Other Income:
Interest
Rental Income
Profit on Sale of Assets
Sundry
 Total

Operating Graphs.

These monthly reports gave in graphic form gross sales, cost of sales, total selling expenses, total expenses, net income, annual rate of earnings per share, total inventories, and net working capital. In the graph the current year's results were compared with the prior years'. A sample operating graph is shown in Figure 13.7.

Figure 13.7

SUMMARY OF OPERATING RESULTS—CONSOLIDATED
(6 MONTHS—FISCAL)

("000" omitted except in percentages and per share earnings)

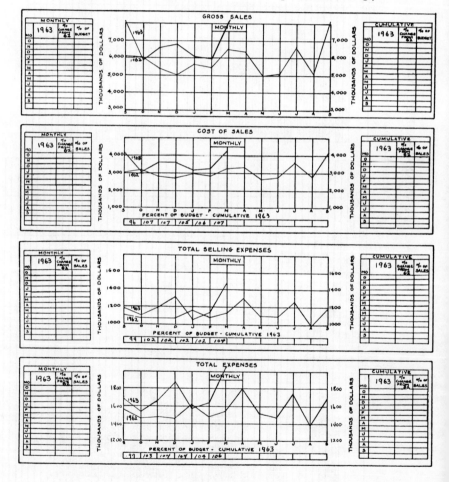

Figure 13.8

ORDEROMETER

Based on Gross Sales
Value of Customers'
Orders and Billing

COMMENTS

Note: The Orderometer Report for fiscal 1963 will not include the same period as the Company's Financial Reports (10-2-62 - 9-30-63). Therefore, the year-to-date totals will not co-incide with Sales Statistical Reports by $682,533 of billing.

Report No. 16

For This Week   FROM: 1-15-63   TO: 1-21-63

| Description | Billing | | | Orders Received | |
Domestic	Actual	Quota	%	This Week	Last Year
Power Tools					
Builders' Products					
Electric Motors					
Special Products					
Service					
TOTAL					
EXPORT					
GOVERNMENT					
OTHER					
GRAND TOTAL					

For The Fiscal Year To Date   FROM: 10-2-62   TO: 1-21-63   16   WEEKS

| Description | BILLING | | | ORDERS RECEIVED | | UNFILLED ORDERS | |
Domestic	ACTUAL	QUOTA	%	LAST YEAR	THIS YEAR	LAST YEAR	THIS YEAR	LAST YEAR
Power Tools								
Builders'Prod.								
Elec. Motors								
Spec. Products								
Service								
TOTAL								
EXPORT								
GOVERNMENT								
OTHER								
GRAND TOTAL								

ISSUED BY DATA PROCESSING DEPT. 1/26/63

285

Daily Cash Report.

This was a daily one-page report of cash balances, deposits and withdrawals in domestic banks, and a summary of outstanding credits and collections.

THE CONTROL SYSTEM: OPERATING CONTROLS RELATED TO THE OVERALL FINANCIAL CONTROL SYSTEM

A variety of comparative control reports on performance were used at all supervisory levels to appraise performance for which supervisors were responsible.

Marketing Department.

Sales Performance. Gross sales were monitored by an Orderometer and Daily Flash report. The Orderometer, which was a weekly tabulation of billings and orders received, compared actual weekly billings with the official sales goal set at the first of the year, compared orders received that week with orders received in the same week of the previous year and showed these same figures on a fiscal-year-to-date basis. An example is given in Figure 13.8. Every management person, from the chairman to plant managers, was sent a copy of this report, and all levels of management indicated that the Orderometer was one of the most important action documents they received.

Top corporate and marketing managers also received the Daily Flasher (see Figure 13.9), a slip of paper showing sales billing for the day and for the month.

Figure 13.9

DAILY FLASHER

Gross Sales Forecast and Performance
for the Month of March

Budget		$12,089,700
Forecast for March		$12,369,000
Forecast to March 30		12,369,000
Actual to March 29	$12,090,116	
Actual for March 30	1,408,216	
Actual through March 30		13,498,332
Accumulated EXCESS		$ 1,129,332
Shipping Days Remaining 0		

Divisional Performance. Each month all division sales managers and the marketing vice president received an operating performance report by division for the past month, comparing actual performance with budget. A sample of this report is given in Figure 13.10. This was used to pinpoint

Figure 13.10

BUILDERS' PRODUCTS DIVISION
INCOME BUDGET & PERFORMANCE REPORT FOR THE MONTH OF MARCH 1963

INCOME	Month of March, 1963					Year to Date 6 Months thru March, 1963					
	BUDGET	%	Actual				BUDGET	%	Actual		
			This Year	%	Last Year	%			This Year	%	Last Year	%
GROSS SALES											
Less: Cash Discount											
Service Allowances											
Transportation											
Other											
NET SALES											
COST OF SALES											
MANUFACTURING MARGIN											
Less: Salesmen's Compensation											
Salesmen's Expenses											
Promotion											
Service Operations											
Export											
International Planning											
Other Selling Expenses											
Total Selling Expenses											
Administrative & General											
Development Engineering											
Total Expenses											
OPERATING INCOME											
Add: Other Income											
Inter-company Profit											
INCOME BEFORE TAXES											
Less Taxes on Income											
NET INCOME											
Provision for Depreciation											

Note: All Figures Stated in Thousands

287

significant variances and take action. For example, if cost of sales was rising in general, individual product costs were examined and consideration was given to raising the prices of those which had risen. Or, if selling or other expenses were out of line, the individual subdepartment budget comparisons (described below) were examined to determine the exact cause. The vice president generally checked all major variances with his divisional sales managers. The MAC also reviewed these reports and asked the market vice president to explain major deviations and the action he took based on them.

Subdepartment Group Performance. Each month a budget comparison report was prepared and sent to each responsible manager within the marketing department. An example is given in Figure 13.11. In general,

Figure 13.11

DEPARTMENTAL BUDGET AND PERFORMANCE REPORT

Date: ___March___
Dept: ___Promotion___

THIS MONTH 5 WEEKS				YEAR TO DATE 6 MONTHS			
Budget	Total Actual	VARIANCE Favorable (Unfavorable)		Budget	Total Actual	VARIANCE Favorable (Unfavorable)	Actual Last Year
			178 Salaries				
			221 Displays				
			222 Merch. Fixtures				
			225 Electros, Cuts, Etc.				
			260 Printing — No Tax				
			265 Merch. of Advertising				
			266 Direct Mail				
			270 Production Printing				
			275 Repairs — Equipment				
			283 Office Supplies				
			285 Supplies — Misc.				
			297 Films & Visual Aids				
			302 Art Work				
			304 Service Fees				
			306 Prep. of Adv.—Other Med.				
			310 Transp. & Post.				
			380 Advertising Time				
			382 Advertising Space				
			390 Telephone				
			391 Telegraph				
			393 Travel				
			551 Use, Sales, Excise Tax				
			601 Prom.—Give Away				
			602 Special Discount or Allow.				
			603 Co-op Advertising				
			604 Sales Promotion Allow.				
			605 Co-op Adv. Whslers.				
			901 Memb. & Subs.				
			913 Sales Campaign Expense				
			971 Preconditioning Expense				
			981 Shows & Exhibits				
			982 District Promotion				
			983 Consumer Adv. Fund				
			108 Overtime				
			227 Demonstration Mat'ls				
			997 Profit on Inter-Co Exp.				
			999 Departmental Income				
			Sub-Total				
			998 Adv. & Sales Prom. Var.				
			Total				

marketing managers worried very little about monthly variations, but only about balancing the total budget by the end of the year, since the monthly figures did not always accurately reflect operations.

An example of this was the control of budgeted advertising funds. While the finance department prepared and issued reports on budget, actual commitments, actual expenditures, and remaining available funds, these reports came too late for the fast-moving advertising business. Thus, each advertising manager kept his own records and submitted his own report on uncommitted funds, which were reviewed by the market services manager and the marketing vice president. Internal controls in this instance were more effective than overall financial controls. The manager of forecasting and inventory control also developed his own individual control tools to keep overall inventory levels within budget, since the financial controls were not adequate.

Production Department.

Overall Control. The vice president of production had three control reports which he said gave him complete control over operations: a summary budget report on staff operations; a summary report on shop operations; a summary report on shop operations; and the overhead variance report. Monthly meetings were held, in which the production vice president asked managers reporting to him for explanations of budget variances.

Staff Budgets. Since staff department budgets were based on budget rate schedules, containing both a fixed amount by month and a rate based on direct labor hours, staff managers did not receive a budget each month. Rather, they were given an estimate of production hours for the coming month and from this calculated their total budget for the month. At the end of each month they received a report of actual expenses and reported on the reasons for any major variances to the vice president. Emphasis was on controlling total expenses for each individual account within the section.

Operating Budgets. Monthly each department foreman also received an estimate of production hours from the finance department. At that time, he calculated an estimated budget, based on the fixed dollars budgeted and the variable rate for supervisory salaries and wages for indirect labor accounts and on cost center rates for other accounts. He then forecast what he thought his actual expenses might be and calculated a forecast variance, which he reported and explained to the general foreman. A summary of these forecast reports were used by the vice president. At the end of each month he received a report comparing actual and budgeted expenses, as shown in Figure 13.12. This report was backed up by reports breaking down actual costs and budgets by cost center within each account number. Direct labor accounts were excluded from all these expense reports. These reports were also reviewed by the vice president.

Figure 13.12

FACTORY EXPENSE CONTROL REPORT

Dept.	Account		Std. Hrs.	Budget	Actual	Var.	To Date Hrs	Budget	Actual	Var.	4 Week Var.	Mo.	Yr.
17	34108				39186	39186 CR			39186	39186 CR	39186 CR	10	1
*17	34141	9	1116900	222598	183630	38968	1116900	222598	183630	38968	38968	10	1
17	34154	1	1116900	398166	474196	76030 CR	1116900	398166	474196	76030 CR	76030 CR	10	1
*17	34179	9	1116900	550694	551259	565 CR	1116900	550694	551259	565 CR	565 CR	10	1
17	34248	9	1116900	3825	2306	1519	1116900	3825	2306	1519	1519	10	1
17	34250	9	1116900	590	77	513	1116900	590	77	513	513	10	1
17	34251	9	1116900	12013	7600	4413	1116900	12013	7600	4413	4413	10	1
17	34275	9	1116900	180341	229517	49176 CR	1116900	180341	229517	49176 CR	49176 CR	10	1
17	34285	9	1116900	164396	166173	1777 CR	1116900	164396	166173	1777 CR	1777 CR	10	1
17	34324	53	281425	117131	109606	7525	281425	117131	109606	7525	7525	10	1
17	34331	53	281425	92696	95468	2772 CR	281425	92696	95468	2772 CR	2772 CR	10	1
17	34919	9	1116900	34685	15979	18706	1116900	34685	15979	18706	18706	10	1
17	37141	9	1116900	2785	924	1861	1116900	2785	924	1861	1861	10	1
17	37154	9	1116900	31897	10238	21659	1116900	31897	10238	21659	21659	10	1
*17	37178	9	1116900	71287	39366	31921	1116900	71287	39366	31921	31921	10	1
*17	37275	9	1116900	44868	48651	3783 CR	1116900	44868	48651	3783 CR	3783 CR	10	1
17	37285	9	1116900	23322	447	22875	1116900	23322	447	22875	22875	10	1
			16199450	1951294	1974623	23329 CR	16199450	1951294	1974623	23329 CR	23329 CR		

*Contain a fixed element

Three levels of control review were used: first, the general foreman with his department foreman; second, the plant managers with the general foreman and the financial department; third, the plant staff managers with the production vice president.

The general foreman met with individual department foremen monthly to review department budget performance. After reviewing total department results, he reviewed individual accounts in which deviations had occurred. Within each account an attempt was made to isolate the cost center which caused the variance. Corrective action was then discussed. *Only unfavorable variances were reviewed.*

The plant managers met with budget and control representatives of the finance department to discuss possible adjustments in standard rates. The plant managers met with the general foremen monthly to review general problems, but individual department deviations were not discussed at these meetings.

Overhead Variance Analysis. An overall report on overhead variances was issued each month, as shown in Figure 13.13. This report was rearranged by the industrial engineering manager to give the following: material rate variance, material use variance, labor rate variance, labor use variance, overhead volume variance, and overhead budget rate variance. These reports were only of interest to the product managers, although they were distributed to all company managers.

Research and Development Department.

While reports comparing expenses to budget were prepared, they were used by the R and D vice president only to keep people cost conscious. His main interest was in getting value for each dollar spent. His control centered on the quality of the item produced and how well individual project schedules were being met. His control was thus more a project control system than a budgetary control system. The important standard for this operation was the percentage of the current year's sales which were accounted for by new and improved products and accessories. The standard or goal was 20%.

Finance Department.

The finance department, like other staff departments, had an expense budget. Both the controller and vice president of finance were interested mainly in total performance figures, and not in individual accounts, except where total expenses exceeded budget.

THE CONTROL SYSTEM: OTHER OPERATING CONTROLS

As is often the case, the financially oriented control reports were of greatest interest to higher management and were a means of orienting operational

Figure 13.13

ANALYSIS OF PRODUCTION OVERHEAD VARIANCES
PARENT COMPANY

CREDIT HOURS

- Programmed Credit Hours
- Performed Standard Credit Hours
- Sub-Standard Credit Hours

PRODUCTION VARIANCES

VOLUME:
- Programmed Volume Variance
- Deviation from Program*
- Total Volume Variance

RATE AND SPENDING:
- Budget Changes, Allocated Budgets**
- Budget Changes, Unallocated Budgets**
- Expenditures over Allocated Budgets
- Expenditures over Unallocated Budgets
- Sub-Standard, Variable
- Count, Set-Ups, Etc.
- Total Variance

* EXPLANATION OF DEVIATION FROM PROGRAM:
- Hrs. in Excess of Program $2.05/Prog. Rate
- Sub-Standard Cr. Hrs.152% $2.02 Absorp Rate
- Volume Under Absorption
- Deviation from Program

1. Actual Monthly Absorption Rate
2. Programmed Absorption Rate
3. Standard Absorption Rate
   CURRENT VARIANCE IN ABSORPTION RATE
   3 Minus 1 =

ANALYSIS OF PRODUCTION OVERHEAD VARIANCES
PARENT COMPANY

CREDIT HOURS

- Programmed Credit Hours
- Performed Standard Credit Hours
- Sub-Standard Credit Hours

PRODUCTION VARIANCES

VOLUME:
- Programmed Volume Variance
- Deviation from Program*
- Total Volume Variance

RATE AND SPENDING:
- Budget Changes, Allocated Budgets
- Budget Changes, Unallocated Budgets
- Expenditures over Allocated Budgets
- Expenditures over Unallocated Budgets
- Sub-Standard, Variable
- Count, Set-Ups, Etc.
- Total Variance

* EXPLANATION OF DEVIATION FROM PROGRAM:
- Hrs. in Excess of Program $2.05 Prog. Rate
- Sub-Standard Cr. Hrs.126% $2.00 Absorp Rate
- (Over) or Under Absorption
- Deviation from Program

1. Actual Monthly Absorption Rate
2. Programmed Absorption Rate
3. Standard Absorption Rate
   CURRENT VARIANCE IN ABSORPTION RATE
   3 Minus 1 =

managers towards company profit goals. While breakdowns of individual accounts were interesting, most operating managers (except production) did not pay much attention to variations in individual accounts but only to bottom line figures.

Current operating control was maintained by a series of operating control tools developed within each area, to meet specific operating requirements. The following discussion covers some of these specific operating controls at Frost.

Marketing Department.

Field sales control was maintained in two monthly reports:

1. *Summary of salesmen's activity.* Each district sales manager prepared a report by salesman, showing the number of calls to distributors, the number of distributors' salesmen's calls to users, as well as the number of stock checks made. Quarterly and semi-annual summaries were made and compared with divisional and district averages. Top management did not review these reports, only marketing management.

2. *Summary reports of sales and expenses by salesman.* These reports were made on a year-to-date basis by division, district and salesman, and were broken down into individual expense categories. These reports were translated into percentages of sales and compared to historical averages. Top management did not review these reports. They were used by marketing management to spot unfavorable deviations and correct them.

Other special reports used for marketing were:

1. *Summary of territory sales.* This monthly report showed dollar sales, sales quotas and percent of quota by district and salesman. This report was distributed to top management and marketing management, and was used to evaluate salesman performance, spot sales trends and pinpoint weak areas.

2. *Analysis of orders received.* This weekly report was a breakdown of the Orderometer report, and enabled management to spot weak areas several weeks faster than did the territory sales report. Results were compared to average year-to-date volume and the average weekly quota. Current week, year-to-data and past-13-week figures were shown. Marketing management and the executive vice president used this report.

3. *Product performance report.* This report, issued monthly only to marketing managers, showed sales by product, by division, by district, and by salesman. In this report performance was measured against quota.

4. *Customer volume report.* This report, issued monthly to marketing managers and salesmen, showed dollar sales by customer and was broken down by division, by district, and by salesman. It was used in a number of ways: to focus on customers not giving Frost a sufficient percentage of their business; to spot declining accounts; to assign salesmen and set quotas; to judge the relative importance of an account when providing promotional and other services to an account.

5. *Customer classification reports.* This report, issued quarterly for the power tool division only, summarized dollar sales by type of account. This report was used by marketing management to evaluate the changing importance of the various types of distribution (e.g., retailers, wholesalers, specialty hardware).

6. *Market share reports.* These quarterly reports compared Frost sales by product division with competitor sales, and were used by all management levels to spot adverse product trends, to discover areas where new products were needed, to learn which products gave Frost a commanding share of the market and where prices might be increased, and to ascertain the size of the total market in planning for the future.

7. *Market penetration report: Competitive geographical position.* This report was prepared annually by the market research department for all divisions. It was based on figures reported by most of the firms in the industry. The report for each product division contained a summary statement comparing Frost sales with those of manufacturers of similar products; a summary of Frost's market share percentages for the major geographical regions; a summary showing Frost's market share by district for the last three years, compared with the national average; and a trading area breakdown for each district. The information contained in this report was used as a reference point from which trends could be measured, as an indicator of weak districts and trading areas within districts, as a basis for questioning performance, and as an indicator of high potential volume areas where Frost had not yet obtained its share.

8. *Unit cost book and the CPR.* Marketing management used the unit cost book and its related cost-to-price ratios to indicate where action might be required. These tools were used to make pricing decisions (increase or decrease) and decisions on dropping or redesigning products, as well as to spot increased product costs.

9. *Advertising Controls.* Product advertising managers kept their own records of commited funds.

In addition to these reports, marketing management also used company control reports discussed earlier, such as the short-range billing forecast, the orderometer and daily flashes, for control.

Production Department.

In addition to the overall financial control reports described above—the report on shop operations (including production department expense budget reports), staff budget reports, and the overhead variation analysis—the production department made use of the following control procedures.

Quality control was primarily the responsibility of the department foremen. But quality control inspectors were used to check on quality, and any rejected products were charged to the scrap account of the department responsible. A weekly and monthly report on units inspected, tested, and passed was issued by the vice president of production to foremen. Any unit which failed to have at least 95% passed was checked. The director of quality control was responsible for instituting corrective action, but the foreman generally took action immediately in his department when he saw rejects rising. A report on scrap was issued weekly, which compared budgeted with actual scrap.

Control of production output was accomplished in three ways: by the monthly production report, which showed the rate of production to the sales rate and was designed to avoid excessive inventory buildup; by the weekly overall report on shop operations, which was used to control labor efficiency; and by a monthly report comparing the hours planned and scheduled by production planning with the actual hours delivered by the factories.

Control of costs through comparative budgetary financial reports was supplemented by two groups of reports, one on the reduction of labor-cost standards and one on reduction of material standard costs. The goal in each area was 4% reduction per year.

Research and Development Department

The main control in this department was project control. Each month a report was issued by R and D, showing the actual versus estimated cost and time schedule for each project by division. The report showed by project the following information: the three-year sales estimate, estimated tooling and development costs compared with expenditures to date, estimated factory costs versus the most recent cost estimate, original and current planned list price and cost-price-ratio, and the original and current engineering release date. This report was reviewed by the Product Development Committee.

Control of the movement of a product from engineering to production was handled by the Production Engineering Committee, composed of representatives from marketing, R and D, and the purchasing and tool engineering production sections. The committee used Gantt charts for control.

Project costs were accumulated by the finance department, which recorded all costs related to a project and issued a monthly statement on them. Product development managers used these reports to keep tabs on spending on each project, and to supplement the analysis done using the operating budget comparisons.

THE CONTROL SYSTEM: PERSONNEL CONTROLS

Control was exercised in personnel in four areas: evaluation of production supervisors, appraisal of other manager performance, sales personnel compensation control, and overall analysis of payroll and personnel.

As for factory supervisors, the first level of evaluation was their performance in relation to budgeted costs, scrap value, and quantity of output. The next level considered such characteristics as ingenuity, resourcefulness, ability to handle people, etc.

As for management personnel appraisal, the executive vice president had recently developed a management appraisal plan, which included a management inventory. The appraisal was done by the manager's superior and by joint superior committee reports.

As for sales personnel compensation control, field sales personnel received a base salary and contingent compensation or bonus based on an individual sales quota. The amount of such compensation was determined by his individual performance over 80% of quota and by his district's performance. The percentages were so calculated as to give him 80% of his contingency based on his own performance and 20% on overall performance of his product division. The contingent compensation was calculated and paid at the end of each six months, at which time a new quota was established. The district managers' compensation plan was very similar to that for the salesmen.

As for personnel and payroll analysis reports, a series of graphs were prepared for the executive vice president, showing the number of people in direct labor, service operations, factory overhead, field sales force, and other overhead. Hirings and separations were also shown, as were total payroll costs. The executive vice president used these reports to control overhead, personnel, employee turnover, and total payroll expenses in relation to total sales.

THE CONTROL SYSTEM: CAPITAL BUDGETING

The capital budgeting process was basically different for the manufacturing and non-manufacturing departments. In manufacturing areas it was built around a project analysis report, while in non-manufacturing areas it was based on need.

In non-manufacturing areas, functional vice presidents were responsible for the preparation of a capital budget request for their departments. Each vice president would ask his section heads and they in turn would ask their supervisors for a statement of capital needs and the reasons supporting each request. The vice president would then summarize the amounts for his department, compare the total with that for the previous year, adjust the budget if necessary, and submit it to the industrial and plant engineering section of the production department for inclusion in the company's capital budget. These reports were consolidated without review, and presented to the Management Advisory Committee and the Board of Directors. Once the capital budget had been approved, the responsible head could spend up to the approved amount on items listed in the budget proposal and could substitute any other item that he believed could better fulfill the need.

The capital budget in the manufacturing department consisted of three sections: replacement equipment, new equipment, and improvement and addition to buildings. Each section was supported by a detailed list of the machines or projects that were recommended for acquisition, including type, date and cost of machine. All items costing over $500 were included in this budget.

Annually, foremen and section heads submitted requests for new or replacement equipment for the coming year to their department heads. In general, Frost strove to replace all machines over 12 years old. A machine load report was also prepared to see what additional machines would be needed to meet sales forecasts. New machinery generally had to have a three-year or less payback. The tool engineering manager and plant managers then met and prepared a total list of machines wanted. This list was reviewed by the vice president of production, and added to based on his knowledge of long-range plans and new product programs. An overall dollar limit on total capital spending was determined from a plot of the 10-year relationship between the expenditures for capital equipment and the sales value added in processing.

The capital budget was then presented to the Management Advisory Committee and the Board of Directors. Each functional vice president presented his own budget to the Board and explained the reasons for the proposed level of spending. The Board mainly used last year's figures for evaluating the overall level of spending. In general they tried to keep new spending roughly equal to depreciation.

In controlling actual expenditures, the Board and the Management Advisory Committee were mainly interested in whether total actual spending (which was reported to them) was under budget. The production vice president, however, had the tools engineering department make a detailed project evaluation of each proposed machine purchase prior to authorizing its actual purchase. This evaluation was reviewed by all concerned foremen and department heads. Only after this detailed review was the equipment actually purchased. After a machine was purchased, the tool engineering section followed performance for one year to see that technical specifications were met.

TOP MANAGEMENT USE OF THE CONTROL SYSTEM

Mr. Frost, the Chairman, used mainly the Blue Book, the Orderometer and the Daily Cash Report. His major control standards were historical figures. The figures he watched most closely in the Blue Book were earnings per share, operating profit, total expenses and cash-to-inventory ratio. Any variances in these key control areas prompted him to investigate the causes for the deviation. He used the Orderometer to compare current orders with last year's orders, and current billings with quota. If current billings were under quota for several weeks, production schedules and inventory levels would be checked, as would the current unfilled order position (back orders were kept to under ten days). Mr. Frost used the Daily Cash Report to watch 1) the balances maintained in various banks compared with a preset, desired ratio, 2) the overall cash balance compared with commitments coming due, 3) the investment of idle cash and 4) the level of payroll. In reviewing the annual budget, he worried most about earnings per share. In exercising control Mr. Frost generally depended more on his contact with people than on reports—an attitude typical of men who started their own businesses and continued to manage them as they grew into large industrial enterprises.

Mr. Frame, the President, used the Blue Book (especially the consolidated and parent company income statements and balance sheets), the Orderometer and the Monthly Financial Forecast of Operating Results. The figures most important to him in the income statement were 1) earnings per share, 2) return on investment and sales, 3) comparison of actual sales and profits to budgeted sales and profits, 4) the cost of sales and any indicated trend, 5) sales expense, development expense, and administrative and general expense, and 6) profit ratios for the product divisions. The balance sheet items of most concern to him were 1) cash, to determine the reasons for any changes, 2) accounts receivable, to see that they were not increasing relative to sales volume, and 3) inventory. Mr. Frame used the Orderometer in the same way as did Mr. Frost. He used the Forecast of Operating Results primarily to examine the forecasted profit and, if it was below budget, to determine what, if any, corrective action could be taken to attain budgeted profit.

Mr. Frame also reviewed other control reports. Through the report of shop operations he monitored major expense areas of plant operations and checked to see that ratios were what he thought they should be. The Report of Units Inspected, Tested, and Passed gave Mr. Frame a general feel for the units with which the factory was having trouble. Mr. Frame also analyzed the market share reports, and based on this analysis he might 1) initiate development of a new product to fill a gap, 2) hold a conference with marketing to determine why a downward trend developed, 3) instruct the sales force to give broad attention to the line and not jump overboard on a new item, and 4) plan corrective action to reverse a negative trend. He also reviewed in detail the Annual Unit Cost Control Book.

While no reports were made on R & D activities, Mr. Frame closely watched projects in that area using four critical control factors: 1) anticipated or projected cost of project compared with actual, 2) actual project progress compared with scheduled completion dates, 3) percentage of annual sales accounted for by new products and 4) the number, novelty and success of project developments, especially in relation to competing companies. In deciding on new project proposals, he considered the following factors: 1) estimated sales volume, 2) estimated profitability of the item relative to tool and development costs, 3) profit history of related or similar projects, 4) marketing strategy considerations, i.e. whether it was needed to fill a gap in the line and prevent competitive inroads, and 5) plant capacity.

Mr. Norton, the executive vice president, used mainly the Blue Book, the Orderometer, and the Personnel and Payroll Analysis Report. The first two he used in much the same way as did Mr. Frost and Mr. Frame. He used the last report to watch the turnover, as well as the number, of employees in overhead areas. Like Mr. Frame, he also watched closely allocation of R & D funds and market share reports.

EVALUATION OF THE CONTROL SYSTEM

The Frost Company's control system was evaluated by a committee of four control executives from major U.S. corporations. The evaluation was broken down into five parts: overall evaluation; company objectives; sales forecasting and budget planning; the control system; capital spending.

Overall Evaluation.

The Frost Company had grown and prospered in a highly competitive industry. The company had been managed successfully by two top men on the basis of personal feel and rules of thumb developed over time, with a minimum amount of detailed controls. The functional executives were capable and employees generally appeared cost conscious. Top management was, however, attempting to guide and control today's corporation with control devices similar to those they used when sales volume was one-fifth of its current rate. This has led to major weaknesses in the control system, which will become evident as management is transferred to new hands.

Company Objectives.

In the area of company objectives, the evaluation committee saw two problems. First, overall product and marketing objectives and strategies were not clearly spelled out, so that there was no clear guideline for allocating R & D funds. Second, the company did not have a definite return-on-investment goal, sufficient emphasis was not given to return-on-investment in the control system, and lower level managers were not impressed with the importance of return-on-investment.

Sales Forecasting and Budget Planning.

The committee made several suggestions for improving sales forecasting and budget planning at Frost. In the five-year sales forecast, alternative forecasts should be made. The first and most realistic forecast would be one which allowed for no increase in share of market, included a mortality curve for older products, and recognized technological changes. Alternative long-term forecasts would then be developed for varying market conditions.

The eighteen-month sales forecast should give consideration to field managers' estimates of sales and budgets, and these estimates should be considered in developing the profit plan. At present sales quotas are imposed on the field. Alternative eighteen-month forecasts would then be developed, based both on field information and on management objectives. Various alternative annual profit plans would then be developed from the forecast, and the impact of each profit plan on return-on-investment calculated. Initially, the preliminary profit plan and its expense categories would be communicated to operating and staff managers, with the expense figures used as targets. Subsequent adjustments would then be made in advertising, R & D budgets, manufacturing and marketing budgets, and pricing, in developing a final profit plan. The components of this profit plan would be the yardsticks for control. Under the present system, department budgets are built from the ground up without reference to an initial profit plan, and so are not well integrated within an overall company plan.

The committee felt that R & D budget planning needed better control. At present, there is no priority list of projects, ranked by their potential return-on-investment and by their contribution to achieving overall company goals. The 3% guideline, like so many other control standards at Frost, is based on history rather than on planned need. A strategic planning basis is lacking, both for allocating total available corporate funds among R & D, advertising, capital equipment and other discretionary items, and for determining what the total R & D budget should be.

The practice of lowering the sales estimate by 5% to 10% was criticized. The committee felt a better practice would be first to create a realistic profit plan, and then to raise the sales goal by 5% to 10%. The committee also criticized the new cost budgeting plan, which has recently been developed and which would generally let the finance department dictate the budget. In general, the committee agreed with the principle that those using a budget should participate in its creation.

The committee had a number of comments on the expense budgets in general. They felt that fixed and variable costs were not adequately segregated; that captions, arrangement, classifications and content were not self-explanatory, so that the immediate impact of the reports was diminished;

and that cost-volume relationships in general were not highlighted in the budgets. For example, with regard to a sales item it was not possible to analyze whether a variance was due to a price or a volume variance, because the budget format did not identify these elements.

As for pricing, the rigid cost-price ratio standards, combined with the emphasis in marketing on unit sales, often led to underpricing some products—that is, even where a higher price could be charged, marketing would use the cost-price ratio to set a price, simply to get a greater unit volume. These problems could arise because not enough emphasis was given return-on-investment and cost-price relationships throughout the control system.

The Control System.

The major criticism of the total control system was that it swamped the reader in a mass of detail and lacked cohesiveness. The committee found that there was a gap between the reports top management used and those used at the operating level—that is, variances in the summary reports could not be traced to the detailed reports for responsible areas without time-consuming work—and that the system could be improved in many ways, to promote economic thinking, to report on an exception basis, and to provide maximum psychological impact on those using them.

As an example, the committee reviewed in detail the department manager's monthly budget performance report (Figure 13.12). An examination of the report shows that it does not break expenses down by subclassifications or give subtotals by areas of cost controllability, it does not segregate fixed and variable costs, it is not well integrated or tied into summary control reports or the profit plan, and it uses a cost accounting system that is so complicated and involves so much detailed work that it discourages use by department managers.

In this report, as in all Frost's control reports, no effect is made to highlight significant variances, either by marking them with an asterisk or by having a clerk do a summary of major variances. Probably the strongest criticism was that the report is based on financial controls and does not represent an accurate picture of the operations, so that it is not in practice used by operating managers. For example, the advertising manager maintains his own expense control report and ignores the monthly budget comparisons. The monthly budget comparison report thus merely gives the accounting department a very general idea of what has happened with advertising expenses, but it is not a control tool which can be used to control performance in this area of operations.

In reviewing control reports, managers throughout the company focused on unfavorable variances. Instead, both favorable and unfavorable variances should be analyzed. Review practices should also be strengthened to probe individual variances with the manager responsible. The system was partially at fault in this regard, because it encouraged control of total costs and discouraged analysis of variances by individual items.

A major example of the lack of cohesiveness in the present system was the Monthly Forecast of Operating Results. In preparing it no explanations were given for variances between the annual budget and sales forecast and the current estimate. On the surface it would appear that the annual budget was not adequate for monthly control, and as a result a separate control tool was developed. However, in creating the new control tool, care was not taken to integrate it within the total control system.

Capital Spending.

The company's return-on-investment between 1947 and 1962 declined from 15% to 10%, and part of this decline can be traced to an inadequate capital budgeting system. In this area, Frost's management again relied on historical standards. An analysis showed that 80% to 90% of Frost's capital spending was merely to stay in business, which on the surface indicates that they are underspending. This was to be expected, since management was limiting capital spending to current depreciation. A better procedure would have been to prepare a list of capital projects many times larger than the one presently used at Frost, and to calculate a return-on-investment for each item. In this way, management would be more likely to take advantage of technological improvements. Analysis of project justification reports also made it clear that control criteria, such as a three-year payback period, were not being followed in practice.

CONCLUSION

The Frost Company's overall control system is in many ways typical of control systems in small and medium-size companies. First, it is heavily accounting and finance oriented, and so has limited usefulness in many operational control areas. Second, because of the accounting orientation of the overall control system, a whole network of other controls has been developed over the years, which were only loosely linked with the overall control system. Third, because the owners and founders still manage the company, control was exercised largely through personal contact, so that there was little incentive to develop a truly self-sustaining control system. Fourth, standards were based largely on historical experience, instead of on planned goals.

There is no doubt that overall control is exercised within the Frost Company. The personal involvement of the owner-management personnel insures careful scrutiny of operations. The control system is probably not, however, as effective as it could be.

As the company moved more heavily into computer data processing, the problems with the system would become more visible to management, and steps would be taken to solve them. The control decision-making needs of all managers would probably be given more equal weight with those of the production manager. Cost accounting requirements would be segregated from the expense control requirements in other areas, and different standards and different data accumulation and reporting systems would be developed to meet the needs in each area. Steps to improve the control system could, of course, have been taken without converting to computers, by following the management control process as outlined in this book. But in most business situations some kind of catalyst is needed to generate change, and in the control area such a catalyst is often the introduction or expansion of computer systems.

The Frost study also illustrated various ways in which a control system can be used by executives, depending on their different control needs and different personal characteristics. Mr. Frost, the Chairman, felt his major responsibility was to stockholders, so he concentrated on earnings per share and the control tools which kept that figure in line. Because he was so familiar with the operation, he bypassed the regular control system and relied heavily on personal contacts in exercising control. Mr. Frame, the President, made the most complete use of the control reports in reviewing operations. Mr. Norton, the Executive Vice President, favored graphic presentation of control comparisons and was responsible for introducing the operating graphs shown in Figure 13.8. He also introduced controls over personnel levels, as a means of controlling costs and cost efficiency in that area—another example of how the deficiencies in Frost's control system were filled somewhat haphazardly as the need arose.

The Frost study was designed to illustrate both good and bad control practices. Frost's control system was obviously a working control system. It was, however, basically an accounting financial control system. The system was most effective in controlling costs in the manufacturing area, probably because an accounting system lends itself most easily to accounting cost controls, and in providing overall financial control for the company. Since it focused on overall financial controls, it enabled control of total costs but encouraged burying of individual variances in all areas. It was not an effective control tool for uncovering operational problems, so that a whole network of supplementary operational controls developed in a somewhat haphazard way outside the manufacturing area. Frost's system was thus not an integrated control system.

The following chapter studies a control system in one operating area, marketing. In that study, the control process was more rigidly adhered to, first by basing the system's development on the needs of the operation and its manager, and second by integrating these operational controls with overall financial controls. By relying on the fundamental approach underlying the management control process, a better integrated and operationally more useful control system was developed.

DISCUSSION QUESTIONS

1. Describe the characteristics of an overall financial control system.
2. Why is it so difficult to adapt such a system for operational control?
3. Why do you think a company's overall control system is of often basically just a financial control system?
4. In what ways does a systems department (and the introduction of the computer) provide a means of developing a truly integrated overall control system, serving both operational and overall accounting control areas?
5. Why can it be said that the statement shown in Figure 13.10 only shows the accounting department whether costs have been controlled on a periodic basis, but does not enable control of costs in the advertising department? Why was the advertising manager forced to develop his own controls to control costs and performance on a current basis?
6. The review committee felt that Frost's control system was not self-sustaining and would be ineffective if the principal executives left the company. Explain the reasoning behind this statement.
7. In what ways do you think that having the control system developed and administered entirely by the finance and accounting departments at Frost hindered the development of a broad-based control system?
8. In what ways does reliance on control through personal contact hinder development of an effective overall control system?
9. What steps would you take to improve the control systems at Frost?

CHAPTER 14

PUTTING THE CONTROL PROCESS TO WORK IN AN OPERATING SITUATION

This chapter presents an in-depth study of how the management control process can be adapted and applied in an operational control situation.

On one level, operating controls are closely linked with overall company financial controls. As was seen in the previous chapter and in Chapter 8, many of the control reports operating managers use are finance and accounting oriented. On another level, however, the operating manager needs a network of controls outside the accounting area, in order to control costs and performance in his area. While this network of controls is designed to ultimately produce maximum profits (like overall corporate controls), they are not necessarily accounting-type controls nor structured like accounting and financial controls.

Not only is his control system different from that of the corporate controller, but the individual operating manager also exercises control in a much different way than does a corporate control department. Normally, the individual operating manager is more likely to do the detailed analysis of deviations, and often both recommends the action to be taken and administers the corrective action taken. The dimension of his problem is also considerably smaller than those of the corporate controller.

In spite of these differences, the control process followed on both the operating and corporate control level is the same, as can be seen from the Frost Company study in Chapter 13 and *The National Observer* study in this chapter. The application of the process may not always be simple, nor is it always easy to see initially, so that considerable ingenuity is usually needed to adapt the process to the situation at hand. This is the art of management control. The management control process, however, still provides the scientific framework for dealing with the situation, for it gives a systematic approach for developing controls and effectively exercising control.

The discussion in this chapter is structured around the first four steps in the control process, with one addition—a section on integrating operating and corporate controls. The parts of the discussion are: defining the control situation and developing an approach to it; identifying key factors; developing an operating control system; integrating internal operating controls with overall corporate controls; and the exercise of control. Control reports are discussed at the points in the study where they were developed and used.

DEFINING THE CONTROL SITUATION AND DEVELOPING AN APPROACH TO IT

The National Observer, which was introduced on February 4, 1962, by Dow Jones and Company, was designed to be the first national family weekly newspaper in this country.[1] After one year of publication the circulation of the new paper had dropped from 240,000 to around 130,000 copies a week. At this point, Dow Jones realized that something had to be done, and quickly, if the new publication was to be successful. The company decided to seek outside help with experience in market planning and control for publications of general consumer interest.

A preliminary study showed that the major factor which had led to *The Observer*'s circulation marketing problems was the new publication's over-reliance on past corporate experience. Because of the operating savings involved, all the paper's marketing operations had been placed under existing Dow Jones departments. As a result of this, the marketing methods that had been so successful for *The Wall Street Journal* (Dow Jones' daily financial-business newspaper) were used in marketing the new publication (a general news weekly), and *The Observer*'s staff did not have the freedom to develop marketing plans and controls tailored to its own needs. In addition, under *The Observer*'s existing fragmented organization structure, the exercise of control was difficult.

On the basis of this preliminary analysis, the scope of the problem was narrowed to the circulation marketing area. The control effort was to be subsequent to, and built upon, a new planning program. The controls were to be designed to help the circulation manager meet planned objectives, and were to be developed by the circulation manager with the assistance of outside consultants. While the controls were to be mainly

---

[1]Robert J. Mockler, *Circulation Planning and Development for The National Observer: A Research Study on Business Applications of Management Planning and Control Principles* ("Research Paper No. 39"; Altanta, Georgia: Bureau of Business and Economic Research, School of Business Administration, Georgia State College, October 1967), and, "How Systematic Management Planning Helped a New Product Succeed," *University of Washington Business Review* (October 1966), pp. 65-72.

internal operational controls, these internal controls were to be integrated with overall corporate financial controls.

Once the paper's basic problems, the objective of the control effort, and the responsibility for developing controls were defined, an approach to dealing with the situation was developed. First, a new marketing plan was to be created for *The Observer*, including new marketing objectives, policies and programs. Then a new system for control was to be developed to check performance against plans. Last, new administrative procedures and organization policies would be developed to facilitate the exercise of control.

IDENTIFYING KEY FACTORS

Overall Circulation Planning Factors.

The initial phases of the study involved developing a new marketing plan for *The Observer*. First, the paper's market had to be redefined. On the basis of their brief, initial analysis of the industry, Dow Jones had concluded that a large segment of the nation's readers were not reached by major local weekly newspapers and news magazines, or was dissatisfied with what they found in them. In filling that market gap Dow Jones had concentrated on the newspaper market, because of their past marketing experience in this area and because they owned newspaper printing presses. Actually, their market was the national weekly news magazine market. A new marketing objective was thus developed: to compete aggressively against the weekly news magazines, and to exploit local newspaper markets only where economical.

New policy guidelines were then developed. Under the new marketing program, subscription, instead of newsstand, sales were emphasized, credit and discount offers were made for the first time, a mail-order marketing staff was recruited, and servicing and fulfillment operations were strengthened to handle a greater volume of subscription sales.

A new marketing strategy with a heavy emphasis on selling discount introductory subscriptions was developed, as was a new pricing structure. New selling programs were introduced. They included:

1. Concentration of subscription selling in the more productive seasons—winter, late summer and fall.
2. Use of advertising headlines emphasizing female and family appeals, and incorporating strong emotional appeals which related *The Observer* to basic human needs and aspirations.
3. Introduction of proven mail-order advertising techniques, such as the use of insert cards, photographs, larger coupons and color, and the placing of ads near the front of a publication.
4. Concentration of advertising in mass circulation publications, and more

selective advertising in small circulation magazines and less use of direct-mail solicitations.

5. Variation in the size of ads to suit the type of publications.
6. Exploitation of new outlets for selling subscriptions.

Through the new marketing plans and programs the cost of obtaining new orders was cut in half, a saving in excess of $1,000,000.

The Nature of the Operation Being Controlled.

Once the planning base for the new control system had been established, the nature of the operation being controlled was defined. The job of the circulation management is a complex one, and varies a good deal from publication to publication. At a newspaper, for example, the circulation manager is responsible for delivering papers locally to readers' homes and to newsstands each day before the morning and evening rush hours. At a national publication, on the other hand, the circulation manager's job requires administering a large advertising program and considerable market planning.

At *The Observer*, the concept of the circulation manager's job had vacillated between these two extremes. With the shift in emphasis to subscription sales, therefore, the job of circulation management for the paper needed redefinition, to insure the continuing success of the new circulation program.

In general, a circulation manager's primary responsibility is to maintain a stable and continuing circulation growth, while keeping expenses at a minimum. In order to do this successfully for *The Observer*, his job would include:

A. Analyzing markets and determining marketing strategy.
B. Developing a price structure and a plan for managing circulation.
C. Creating and implementing subscription, renewal and single-copy sales programs.
D. Establishing budgetary and other circulation controls.
E. Organizing and staffing the operation.
F. Managing and supervising the overall operations of the circulation department.
G. Coordinating circulation activities with those of other departments, especially the fulfillment and distribution departments.
H. Assuming responsibility for short-term circulation performance and for long-range circulating planning.

Circulation management for *The Observer* was, therefore, a many faceted job, of which control was only one aspect. Control was a necessary link, however, in performing the circulation manager's many planning and administrative duties.

The flow of business in *The Observer*'s circulation operation was relatively simple to outline broadly. Subscriptions were sold to the public, through such media as magazine and newspaper advertising, direct mail, radio and TV advertising, telephone selling, and door-to-door salesmen, usually for a trial period of six months. At the end of this trial period, solicitations were sent to subscribers in an effort to get them to renew their subscriptions for one year or more. Each year thereafter solicitations were sent to regular subscribers to obtain their renewal again. Additional new subscriptions were sold to replace those subscribers who did not renew and to increase the total circulation of the publication. Copies of the paper were also sold each week through newsstands.

The functional areas which the circulation manager thus had to supervise and manage in carrying out his job were many:

A.	Advertising Planning	G.	Renewal and Billing Planning
B.	Direct Mail	H.	Liaison with Subscriber Service
C.	Field and Phone Selling		and Accounting
D.	Educational Sales	I.	Art and Production
E.	Newsstand and Home Delivery	J.	Office Services and Internal
F.	Miscellaneous Sales Operations		Record-keeping

Controls were especially important in the selling functions (A through E) and in Renewal and Billing (G). And the information system required for circulation marketing control was closely linked with those used by the Subscriber Service and Accounting departments.

As a last step in defining the control situation, several additional characteristics of a circulation operation were isolated.

1. The large number of low-priced sales.
2. The requirements of servicing and reselling customers over a long period of time.
3. The remoteness of the customer.
4. The need for a high degree of automation to manage circulation economically.
5. The importance of having as much personalized service as possible in order to strengthen reader loyalty.

The Nature and Purpose of the Control System and its Standards.

The new control system had to take all these factors into account. It had to provide information on both new subscription sales from a variety of sources and on renewals, as well as on newsstand sales, and it had to provide the circulation manager with this information quickly and economically. To meet these needs, an automated data processing and reporting system was needed, based on the report format outlined in the next section of this chapter.

The overall unit-sales and expense budget standards used in circulation were initially based on past performance: Dow Jones management wanted to do better—that is, lose less money and have a larger circulation—than they had the year before. Subsequently, standards for circulation performance were developed from an overall profitability analysis. Circulation management and overall company management first determined just how much circulation was needed and how much had to be spent to obtain that circulation. The job of the circulation manager was then to deliver the mutually agreed on circulation within the mutually agreed on spending budget. Since circulation income was directly proportional to circulation levels, no separate budget standards were established for circulation income. Overall financial planning and overall circulation planning were thus closely integrated and formed the basis from which control standards were developed.

Specific performance standards were next developed for the critical control areas of the circulation operation in line with these overall budget standards. These areas included: total annual selling expenses by advertising media; the cost per new order (credit and cash) for each media; the percentage of payments received on these orders; the percentage of these orders which were renewed; total subscription orders needed per week; total expected weekly cancellations; weekly newsstand sales needed; and weekly circulation goals. The control standards within the system were thus developed to meet the specific decision-making needs of the circulation manager, and were closely linked with overall company budgetary standards and plans.

Factors Affecting the Exercise of Control.

Several management and organization problems which would affect the implementation of a new system and the exercise of control were also identified, as part of the analysis of key factors affecting the control situation. These included outlining the present organization structure and isolating the attitudes of key executives towards change. In general, top management resisted change and tended to favor following traditional procedures and patterns of action. And as can be seen from the discussion of the organization structure of the circulation operation later in this chapter, the present structure did not facilitate effective planning and control of the circulation operation.

DEVELOPING AN OPERATING CONTROL SYSTEM

An information system for control was next developed, covering both the internal operating controls needed by the circulation manager to direct his operation and those controls needed by Dow Jones management to control overall corporate operations. Various alternative types of data processing systems were studied. Since it was anticipated that *The Observer*'s circulation would grow to over 300,000 in the next few years, it was decided that a computerized information system would be the most efficient one for control data processing and reporting.

The new system was developed by a systems study team composed of equipment representatives and Dow Jones personnel. The system was basically a subscription record-keeping and billing system, which maintained subscriber records, recorded sales and payments, printed labels for weekly shipment of the publication, produced subscriber bills and renewal notices, and the like. Because the system maintained all subscription records, reporting for circulation marketing planning and control was part of the new system. The system was developed along the lines outlined in Chapter 10, with the circulation manager specifying his reporting system requirements. The major difference was that the reporting system was first developed and introduced into the existing punched card system, and only after it was tested and assimilated by operating personnel was it converted to computer.

The information needed for *internal control purposes* was dictated by the requirements of planning and managing circulation, and of selling subscriptions and single copies. The information on which control reports were needed included:

1. Current and cumulative sales results and weekly paid circulation estimates.
2. A periodic actual count, or inventory, of paid circulation.
3. Renewals and payments.
4. Selling costs.
5. Circulation income.
6. Test results.

Reports on Sales Results and Weekly Paid Circulation.

In early 1963 there were two weekly control reports which gave information on *The Observer*'s circulation, and on its subscription and single-copy sales. The first gave the number of new subscriptions received that week from each sales effort.[2] Through it the circulation manager was able to judge the effectiveness of current sales promotions on a weekly basis and to plan future promotions. This report did not need to be revised.

The second report, a weekly summary of circulation and sales results, did need revision, however, because it was not accurate or complete enough for circulation management needs, and in mid-1963 this report was expanded to include the following information for the current week:

[2]Within each general sales source (e.g., direct mail) each promotional effort (e.g., a mailing to *Changing Times* subscribers) is given an individual key number designation, so that information from this particular sales effort can be easily identified and evaluated in relation to the success of the overall sales program.

1. Total subscription sales by sales source,[3] term of subscription and type of payment—i.e., cash or credit.
2. Subscription terminations in three categories:
   a. Non-renewals, by expiration date.
   b. Credit subscriptions stopped for non-payment, by order-entry date.
   c. Terminations requested by the subscriber, by either expiration or order-entry date.
3. Subscription renewals by expiration date and subscription payments by order-entry date.
4. A count of delivered circulation and an estimate of paid subscription circulation. Figures on single-copy sales were incorporated into this part of the report to arrive at a fairly accurate estimate of total paid circulation for that week.

This new control report gave the circulation manager current information on the three key input and outflow factors affecting circulation performance: new subscription sales; payments; expirations and renewals. Any variation affecting circulation results would be exposed immediately through this report, so that circulation management could quickly take corrective steps to control overall performance.

One additional sales report, a daily report on the results of current sales tests, was instituted. This report enabled the earliest possible use of test results to improve overall sales performance.

Inventory Report.

A quarterly subscription inventory report was introduced in mid-1963. This report listed all currently active subscriptions by month of expiration, term and type of subscription,[4] and sales source.

The report gave the pattern of expirations over the coming year, as well as the circulation strength—i.e., the numbers of long-term versus short-term subscriptions. This report told the circulation manager not only when, but also how many, subscriptions would expire and need to be replaced over the coming years. As such, this report was a key control element in circulation planning and, as circulation grew, it would eventually be needed monthly.

---

[3]Subscription sales sources were classified as follows: direct mail; radio, newspaper and magazine advertising; house ads; development; community and telephone; independent subscription agents; education and clergy; gift; over-the-counter, employee and institutional; solicitations of home-delivery expires. The term "sales source" is also loosely applied to individual sales promotions within these categories, though such individual sales promotions are more correctly called "sales efforts." For example, a sales effort would be an ad in the March 21, 1964, issue of *The Saturday Evening Post*, whereas the general sales source would be magazine advertising.

[4]The types of subscription included: regular subscriptions, introductory subscriptions, gift subscriptions, education and clergy subscriptions. The terms were broken down as follows: 20 weeks, 27 weeks, 38 weeks, one year, two years, three years, five years.

Table 14.1

THE NATIONAL OBSERVER—CIRCULATION DEPARTMENT

Subscription Selling Costs of 1964 Promotions—March 1964[1]

I. DIRECT MAIL

Date	Pcs. Mailed	Returns	Actual % Return	Budgeted % Return	Actual Cost/Sub[2]
12/30	998,246	19,772	1.980	1.60	$3.44
1/6	595,593	16,586	2.784	1.60	2.44
1/13	592,598	12,806	2.160	1.60	3.15
1/20	693,575	13,884	2.002	1.60	3.40
1/27	530,714	10,012	1.886	1.60	3.60
January	3,410,726	73,060	2.147	1.60	$3.18
2/3	551,095	10,974	1.992	1.30	$3.42
2/10	1,133,976	26,310	2.320	1.30	2.93
2/17	532,825	8,806	1.652	1.30	4.12
2/24	771,917	16,484	2.139	1.30	3.19
February	2,989,813	62,584	2.094	1.30	$3.25

II. PRINT AND BROADCAST ADVERTISING

	Date	Cost	Returns	Actual Cost/Sub	Budgeted Cost/Sub
Magazines[3]	Jan.	$28,967	7,796	$3.72	
	Feb.	26,042	7,952	3.28	
Total		$55,009	15,748	$3.50	
Newspapers	Jan.	$25,506	6,400	$3.98	
	Feb.	18,091	4,750	4.23	
Total		$43,597	11,150	$3.90	
Radio and TV:					
A. Godfrey	Jan-Mar	$67,000	13,800	$ 4.90	
CBS Radio News	3/14-15	10,500	842	12.47	
Other Radio	Jan-Mar	6,159	1,456	4.23	
Today TV Show	3/26	6,964	1,050	6.63	
Total		$91,223	17,148	$ 5.34	
Production		$ 5,000			
Total Advertising		$194,829	44,046	$4.43	$4.50

III. OTHER SOURCES

	Date	Cost	Returns	Cost/Sub
House Ads	Jan-Feb	$ 800	2,222	$ .36
Gift	Jan-Mar	$1,000	1,266	$ .79
Community & Agency	Jan-Mar	Commission Only	778	$1.00
Educational	Jan-Mar	$6,064	5,262	$1.15
Telephone	Jan-Feb	Salary & Promotion	1,476	$2.75
Dept. Store Env.	January	$5,863	1,244	$4.72
Adserts	February	$5,760	1,180	$4.88

(1) All figures have been disguised. However, the general relationships among the various components of the report have been maintained to indicate the economics of circulation.

(2) Further information on evaluating sales sources is given in Figure One B.

(3) More detailed information on these results is given in Figure One C.

Renewal and Billing Reports.

The existing monthly renewal and payment reports gave final renewal and payment results, after all promotions were completed. These reports were expanded in mid-1963 to show renewals and payments by sales source and by subscription type and term. The circulation manager used these reports both to study the effectiveness of his renewal and billing promotions and to estimate how many of the present subscribers shown in the inventory report could be expected to renew over the coming year.

Reports on Selling Costs.

Since no regular report on subscription sales costs was being made prior to mid-1963, a new monthly report on these costs was instituted (see Tables 14.1, 14.2, and 14.3, below). This report gave subscription order costs for each sales source, and for the larger sales efforts. Information on administrative costs and on renewals and payments was included (see

Table 14.2

THE NATIONAL OBSERVER—CIRCULATION DEPARTMENT

Evaluating Subscription Sales Sources—March 1964[1]

As the following examples show, a number of factors in addition to the basic cost per order must be taken into consideration in determining the value of each promotion.

	Cost/Sub	Payment Percent	Other Cost Factors	First Renewals	Second Renewals
Direct Mail (Jan-Feb)	$3.20	84%[2]	None	29%[2]	64%[2]
Magazine Ads (Jan-Feb)	$3.50	76%[2]	Production Costs	31%[2]	66%[2]
Telephone (Jan-Feb)	$2.75	56%[2]	Administrative Costs	N.A.	N.A.
Dept. Store Env. (Jan)	$4.72	97%[2]	No Subscriber Billing	N.A.	N.A.

Even though the cost per new subscription from advertising is higher than that from direct mail, these two subscription sales sources appear to have about equal value after conversions and renewals. While department store envelopes have a high cost per new order, there are no subscriber billing costs and practically no bad pay. The cost per new subscription from telephone sales is the best of the four sources listed, yet when the bad pay and additional administrative costs are added in, telephone sales would seem at this time to be one of the more expensive sources of new subscription business.

(1) All figures have been disguised. However, the general relationships among the various components of the report have been maintained to indicate the economics of circulation.

(2) Estimates.

Table 14.3

THE NATIONAL OBSERVER—CIRCULATION DEPARTMENT

Magazine Return Breakdown—March 1964[1]

JANUARY	Cost	Returns	Actual Cost/Sub
Commentary	$ 76	34	$ 2.29
Tablet	325	120	2.71
Saturday Review	725	228	3.18
New Yorker	1,189	362	3.29
Our Sunday Visitor and Register Unit	812	234	3.47
Newsweek	3,340	946	3.53
Life	14,642	4,066	3.60
Reporter	340	88	3.87
U.S. News	6,555	1,656	3.96
Scholastic Teacher	276	30	9.20
AMA News	686	32	21.43
Total	$28,967	7,796	$ 3.72

FEBRUARY	Cost	Returns	Actual Cost/Sub
Saturday Evening Post	$18,859	6,578	$ 2.87
Harpers	493	122	4.04
Family Weekly	3,767	796	2.73
Tablet	77	14	5.50
Christianity Today	275	50	5.50
St. Anthony Messenger & Christian Herald	900	160	5.63
Atlantic	1,356	198	6.85
Grade Teacher	315	34	9.27
Total	$26,042	7,952	$ 3.28

(1) All figures have been disguised. However, the general relationships among the various components of the report have been maintained to indicate the economics of circulation.

Table 14.2), when that information affected the evaluation of individual sales efforts.

This report simplified evaluation of sales promotions and enabled faster decisions on which promotions should be terminated and which continued and increased to maximize circulation profits. For example, in late February 1964 a regional test ad in *The Saturday Evening Post* brought in subscriptions at less cost than direct-mail promotions (see Tables 14.1 and 14.3). As a result, some direct-mail promotions were replaced by a full-page ad in *The Post* in April. When certain radio advertising did not do as well as department store envelope promotions (see Tables 14.1 and 14.2), planned radio advertising was replaced by advertising on department store remittance envelopes.

Income and Expense Reports.

Since the inception of *The Observer*, the accounting department had prepared monthly circulation revenue reports and monthly reports on total circulation department expenses. No changes were needed in this area.

Test Result Reports.

Since accurate test result information was needed to evaluate new selling methods, a reliable test control system was needed. This system covered testing procedures, record keeping and reporting.

Before a test was undertaken, it was necessary to determine the size of what was being tested (for example, an American Express Credit Card holder list of 1,000,000 names), or the significance of the element being tested (for example, a new price offer of 29 weeks for $2.87 versus the established offer of 27 weeks for $2.67). This was necessary in order to establish the optimum form, size and cost of the projected test. In the case of the American Express mailing list, a random sampling of 1% to 2% (10,000 to 20,000 names) would give an accurate indication of the value of the list in selling *The Observer*. As for the new price offer, if it were tested in direct-mail solicitations, a sampling of over 30,000 names from at least three different lists would be necessary to get an accurate reading,[5] since the difference in price was small.

The estimated cost of the test was then weighed against the potential usefulness of the information to be learned from the test. For example, if the test of the American Express list was successful solicitations could be mailed to over 900,000 additional names; if the test of the new price was successful, the new price could be used in all direct-mail selling—a potential of 18,000,000 mailing pieces per year. However, if the total American Express list had been only 50,000 names, it probably would not have been worth running the test. A test was run, therefore, only if the information learned from it could subsequently be used to improve subscription returns or lower selling costs in promotional efforts large enough to amortize the cost of the test.

[5]While there are some general rules of thumb for interpreting test results, a good deal of experienced judgment is needed to read results accurately. For example, when the difference between the returns from two equal parts of a test is greater than twice the square root of total returns, the result can be assumed to be 95% correct. If there were 225 orders from the $2.87 offer and 300 orders from the $2.67 offer, the difference between the returns from the two parts of the test would be 75. This figure is greater than 50, which is twice the square root of the total returns ($225 + 300 = 525$; $\sqrt{525} = 25$; $2 \times 25 = 50$). Therefore, it is almost certain that the $2.67 offer will always do better than the $2.87 offer. Further tests would be needed to say definitely how much better the $2.67 offer will do, though it should always do at least 10% better.

More complete and accurate records of test results, and closer liaison with *The Observer*'s subscriber-service department when conducting tests, were also needed under the new control system:

A. When information on payments was required for evaluation of a new sales effort, as in radio and telephone sales, results had to be segregated and recorded outside the regular reporting system.

B. When test results were needed on the day the orders were received, the information had to be collected and tabulated separately by hand.

C. In new-subscription sales tests and in renewal and billing tests, a representative random sample of subscriber records had to be obtained in a way that would not disrupt automatic billing systems. New forms also had to be prepared for reporting test results.

D. When new advertising media, such as newspapers, were being tested, the head of the subscriber-service department had to alert his order-recording personnel to any difficulties in identifying orders to insure accurate reporting.

The closer liaison between the circulation and subscriber-service departments provided control over the many activities involved in testing and helped insure maximum efficiency in processing test orders and recording test results.

As the new circulation program developed, advance information on all subscription sales plans, not just testing, was sent to the subscriber-service department for evaluation. This was done in order to be certain that the capacities of the subscriber-service department were taken into consideration before going ahead with any promotions.

INTEGRATING INTERNAL OPERATING CONTROLS WITH CORPORATE CONTROLS

Once the *internal control system* for the circulation department had been developed, an *overall corporate control system* was developed. Because *The Observer* was so new and changes were occurring rapidly, corporate management wanted and needed very close control of the paper's operations. New monthly and yearly reports to corporate management were, therefore, introduced. These reports gave both the circulation manager and Dow Jones management a comprehensive review of *The Observer*'s overall circulation performance. Standards were established through the semi-annual budget reports. Results were reported through monthly result reports.

Semi-Annual Budget Reports.

Under the new control system, circulation and sales budgets, as well as expense budgets, for the following year were prepared in the fall, and

Table 14.4

THE NATIONAL OBSERVER—Circulation Department

Estimated Subscription Sales and Circulation—1964*

	Jan.	Feb.	March	First Quarter	April	May	June	Second Quarter	July	August	Sept.	Third Quarter	Oct.	Nov.	Dec.	Fourth Quarter	Year
Subscription Circulation (Paid) Beginning of Period:	100,000	100,000	109,600	100,000	127,600	150,200	118,800	127,600	116,400	114,000	86,400	116,400	95,600	115,000	131,600	95,600	100,000
I. Additions:																	
Subscription Sales:																	
Direct Mail	26,200	35,600	39,000	100,800	12,800	2,000	2,000	16,800	4,000	14,000	32,400	50,400	25,200	18,000	12,400	55,600	223,600
Advertising	10,000	17,000	15,000	42,000	8,400	1,200	1,200	10,800	2,000	4,000	12,800	18,800	6,000	2,000	400	8,400	80,000
House Ads in DJ Publications	800	800	800	2,400	600	600	600	1,800	600	600	600	1,800	600	400	200	1,200	7,200
Development and Testing	1,200	3,600	2,200	7,000	200	200	200	600	200	1,600	3,600	5,400	3,600	1,200	200	5,000	18,000
Community and Phone	1,000	1,200	1,200	3,400	2,000	2,000	2,000	6,000	2,000	2,000	2,000	6,000	2,000	2,000	2,000	6,000	21,400
Subscription Agency	200	200	200	600	200	200	200	600	200	200	200	600	200	200	200	600	2,400
Education and Clergy	1,600	1,200	600	3,400	—	—	—	—	—	—	1,000	1,000	6,000	3,000	1,000	10,000	14,400
Regular and Christmas Gift	200	200	200	600	200	200	200	600	200	200	200	600	200	200	5,800	6,200	8,000
Over the Counter, Employee and Institutional	1,800	1,800	1,800	5,400	1,200	1,200	1,200	3,600	1,400	1,400	1,400	4,200	1,400	400	1,000	2,800	16,000
Solicitation of Home Delivery Expires	2,000	—	—	2,000	—	—	—	—	—	—	—	—	—	—	—	—	2,000
Total Subscription Sales	45,000	61,600	61,000	167,600	25,600	7,600	7,600	40,800	10,600	24,000	54,200	88,800	45,000	28,200	22,500	95,700	393,000
Renewals: Long-term	8,000	10,000	4,000	22,000	4,000	10,000	14,000	28,000	8,000	6,000	6,000	20,000	8,000	6,000	6,000	20,000	90,000
Short-term	14,000	14,000	12,000	40,000	—	—	—	—	16,000	20,000	16,000	52,000	6,000	2,000	2,000	10,000	102,000
Total Additions	67,000	85,600	77,000	229,600	29,600	17,600	21,600	68,800	34,600	50,000	76,200	160,800	59,000	36,200	30,500	125,700	585,000
II. Losses: Long-term Expires	15,000	24,000	9,000	48,000	5,000	17,000	20,000	42,000	8,000	8,000	8,000	24,000	8,000	8,000	8,000	24,000	138,000
Short-term Expires	44,000	42,000	40,000	126,000	—	—	—	—	51,000	63,600	51,000	165,600	23,600	5,600	5,500	34,700	326,400
Education and Gift Expires	2,000	—	—	2,000	2,000	2,000	2,000	6,000	—	—	—	—	—	—	—	—	8,000
Credit Stops	6,000	10,000	10,000	26,000	—	—	2,000	2,000	8,000	6,000	8,000	22,000	8,000	6,000	8,000	22,000	72,000
Total Losses	67,000	76,000	59,000	202,000	7,000	19,000	24,000	50,000	67,000	77,600	67,000	211,600	39,600	19,600	21,500	80,700	544,400
Net Subscription Gain (or Loss) for Period	—	9,600	18,000	27,600	22,600	(1,400)	(2,400)	18,800	(32,400)	(27,600)	9,200	(50,800)	19,400	16,600	9,000	45,000	40,600
Subscription Circulation (Paid) End of Period	100,000	109,600	127,600	127,600	150,200	148,800	116,400	116,400	114,400	86,400	95,600	95,600	115,000	131,600	140,600	140,600	140,600
Unpaid Copies Delivered	12,000	10,000	6,000	6,000	6,000	6,000	6,000	6,000	6,000	6,000	6,000	6,000	6,000	6,000	6,000	6,000	6,000
Total ABC Subscription Circulation End of Period	112,000	119,600	133,600	133,600	156,200	154,800	122,400	122,400	120,400	92,400	101,600	101,600	121,000	137,600	146,600	146,600	146,600
Other ABC Circulation End of Period:																	
Newsstand and Home Delivery	16,000	16,000	16,000	16,000	16,000	16,000	16,000	16,000	16,000	17,000	17,000	17,000	17,000	18,000	18,000	18,000	18,000
Young Salesmen Program	3,600	3,800	4,000	4,000	4,200	4,400	4,600	4,600	4,800	5,000	5,200	5,200	5,600	5,800	6,000	6,000	6,000
Total ABC Circulation End of Period	131,600	139,400	153,600	153,600	176,400	175,200	143,000	143,000	141,200	114,400	123,800	123,800	143,600	161,400	170,600	170,600	170,600

*All figures have been disguised. However, the general relationships among the various components of the flow plan have been maintained to indicate the economics of circulation.

revised at mid-year. The mid-1963 budget report, the first coordinated *Observer* circulation budget ever submitted to corporate management by the circulation department, gave a complete breakdown of sales and expenses for the whole *Observer* circulation operation.

The final circulation and sales budget for 1964, as submitted to management in November of 1963, was basically the circulation plan (see Table 14.4). A similar budget was prepared which gave detailed expense projections for each of the departments working on *The Observer's* circulation activities. A prose summary of the sales plan for the coming year was attached.

Monthly Result Reports on Circulation, Sales, and Expenses.

A new monthly result report was instituted to give corporate management all the information it needed on a regular basis to follow *The Observer's* progress. This report compared actual results with budgeted goals for both the current month and the year to date. A copy of the March 1964 report is given in Table 14.5. Comparisons with the previous year's performance were not possible because adequate information on results for 1962 and early 1963 was not available.

Attached to this report was the circulation manager's report on the cost-per-order of subscriptions by all general sales sources and by major individual sales efforts and tests. Samples of these attachments are given in Tables 14.1, 14.2 and 14.3.

Each quarter a cover memo outlining plans for the coming period and explaining overall circulation performance for the past period was added to the monthly result report to management. Semi-annually, actual and budgeted expense comparisons by sales source were also included in the report. Monthly expense reports were issued to corporate management by the business department.

Since the monthly result reports were an extension of the circulation manager's internal control reports and the annual budget report, they were relatively easy to prepare. Since they were consistent with other records kept in the new control system, anytime corporate management wished more complete information on circulation and sales results, it was readily available to them from a single source.

Copies of the monthly summary report were also sent to all department heads who worked on *The Observer's* circulation activities, as well as to the managers of *The Observer's* subscriber-service, editorial, advertising sales, production, and business departments. This reporting system not only enabled all company managers to follow *The Observer's* circulation progress more closely than they had in the past, it also helped draw together the paper's circulation operation by encouraging information communications among *Observer* department heads.

Table 14.5

THE NATIONAL OBSERVER—CIRCULATION DEPARTMENT

Circulation and Subscription Sales Report—March 1964[1]

	First Quarter Jan - Mar 1964		March 1964	
	Budget	Actual	Budget	Actual
Subscription Circulation (Paid) Beginning of Period:	100,000	100,000	109,600	142,800
I. Additions:				
Subscription Sales:				
Direct Mail: Regular	100,800	164,818	39,000	87,400
Testing				
Advertising: Regular	31,800	34,532	11,000	12,586
Reader's Digest (Oct. '63)[2]	2,000	2,240	600	618
Radio	8,200	8,418	3,400	5,178
House Ads in DJ Publications	2,400	3,250	800	1,512
Development: Dept. Store Envelopes	2,200	3,668	200	2,248
Adserts	1,400	1,456	200	842
Testing	3,400	-	1,800	-
Community and Phone	3,400	2,588	1,200	1,050
Subscription Agency	600	684	200	164
Education & Clergy: Individual	600	1,388	400	514
Bulk - Classroom	2,800	3,974	200	486
Gift	600	1,266	200	18
Over the Counter, Employee & Inst.	5,400	7,038	1,800	2,366
Solicitation of Home Delivery Expires[3]	2,000	3,480	-	46
Total Subscription Sales	167,600	238,800	61,000	115,028
Renewals: Long-term[4]	22,000	27,010	4,000	4,800
Short-term[4]	40,000	35,618	12,000	14,000
Total Additions[4]	229,600	301,428	77,000	133,828
II. Losses: Long-term Expires[4]	48,000	41,800	9,000	10,000
Short-term Expires[4]	126,000	118,000	40,000	48,000
Education and Gift Expires[4]	2,000	1,000	-	-
Credit Stops[4]	26,000	48,000	10,000	26,000
Total Losses[4]	202,000	208,800	59,000	84,000
Net Subscription Gain (or Loss) for Period[4]	27,600	92,628	18,000	49,828
Subscription Circulation (Paid) End of Period[4]	127,600	192,628	127,600	192,628
ABC Grace Carried[4]	6,000	14,000	6,000	14,000
Total ABC Subscription Circulation End of Period[4]	133,600	206,628	133,600	206,628
Other ABC Circulation End of Period:[4]				
Newsstand and Home Delivery	16,000	14,500	16,000	14,500
Young Salesmen Program	4,000	5,200	4,000	5,200
Total ABC Circulation End of Period[4]	153,600	226,328	153,600	226,328

(1) All figures have been disguised. However, the general relationships among the various components of the report have been maintained to indicate the economics of circulation.

(2) These returns are in addition to the 21,804 returns received in 1963.

(3) Net figure after deducting credit losses.

(4) Estimates.

THE EXERCISE OF CONTROL

Implementing the new control system was done in three phases. First, the reporting system was developed to meet the circulation manager needs. Second, changes in reports and reporting systems were introduced piecemeal into the existing punched card system—some reports were added, some old reports revised, and some reports were prepared manually by clerks in the circulation department. Third, once the desired reporting system was in operation and tested, the systems group proceeded to convert the new system to computer.

This three-phase implementation of the new system worked very well in this situation, for it prevented the build-up of resistance to change, enabled testing of new report forms, and made the transfer to computer seem more controlled and rational. Because the new system was introduced piecemeal, operating personnel saw it as an adjusting of the old system, and as a result, the natural resistance to all new changes which sometimes arises in these situations did not develop. There was some minor resistance to the larger new reports, but because they were introduced slowly there was time to explain the reports and give people a chance to get used to using them. Since people were given an opportunity to use reports and express their views on them, many improvements in them were made during this phase. Since the individual changes were part of a systematically developed total system, they did not appear to be haphazard or whimsical. And because of the preparatory work done, when it came time to convert the system to computer the change appeared to be more a conversion of the existing system than the introduction of a totally new (and so possibly confusing and disruptive) system, thus making it easier for the operating personnel to adapt to and use the new system.

Control systems and tools are, however, only one part of management control. Equally important is the process of exercising control—the ability to make use of these basic tools in controlling the day-to-day operations. In addition to having adequate control tools and control systems, two conditions must be fulfilled, if the exercise of control is to be effective. First, the manager must possess the required administrative abilities. Second, the company must provide the manager with the organization and the corporate management policies which permit the exercise of control.

The Observer's new circulation program, therefore, also included recommendations for changes in organization and administrative practices, where such changes affected the continuing effectiveness of the new control program. The circulation activities of all Dow Jones publications were centralized under a corporate circulation sales director (see Figure 14.1). Excluding the field staffs of the telephone, educational, and newsstand sections, about thirty-five people were needed to handle these activities.

The functions listed in the boxes on the left were the responsibility of section heads who handled all three Dow Jones publications and who reported directly to the sales director. Those functions listed in the right-hand boxes (connected by dotted lines) were the responsibility of each circulation manager, although the sales director had direct authority over these operations.

Figure 14.1

DOW JONES CIRCULATION DEPARTMENT
ORGANIZATION STRUCTURE

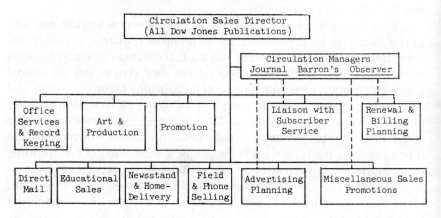

Within this organization structure, *The Observer*'s circulation manager was a staff man, without line authority, whose responsibilities were limited to planning and creating promotions. The new paper's circulation operations were for the most part handled by functional departments which had formerly handled only *The Journal* and *Barron*'s. As a result, *The Observer*'s problems were not always given adequate attention, and there was a tendency to do things in *The Journal*'s way, rather than in a way suited to the new paper's marketing needs.

When the new program was introduced in 1963, *The Observer*'s circulation manager was informally given greater authority over his operations. This informal authority enabled him to exercise personal leadership, and so develop enough coordination and control of circulation activities to put the new program into operation, without disruptive changes in the present organization structure.

The circulation manager exercised informal control in several ways. He spent considerable time helping resolve problems which arose within the individual sections. For example, on one occassion he offered his help in designing new reporting forms for the record-keeping section when new promotions were undertaken. On other occasions he helped develop a salesmen's compensation plan for the telephone sales section and helped work out special local newsstand distribution arrangements.

The circulation manager kept each section that worked on *The Observer*'s circulation operation informed on all *Observer* circulation activities. He also consulted with them about any planned promotions they might be working on. These discussions helped a great deal:

1. Section heads came to realize that *The Observer* needed considerable attention.

2. Because they were brought in on the development of plans, section heads became more receptive to the new *Observer* circulation program.

3. Personnel in these sections gained a better understanding of the relation of their work to the whole *Observer* program.

In order to deepen their involvement with *The Observer*, wherever possible the new paper's circulation manager would delegate responsibility for new promotions to the sections concerned. For example, the production manager was given considerable freedom in designing and carrying out many development projects, not only because he had an aptitude for this work, but also because it enabled him to participate more fully in the new program.

Through this personal leadership, exercised informally, *The Observer's* circulation manager was able to realize the full potential of the new circulation program, and by mid-1964 the paper's circulation had been doubled. Such an informal arrangement could not, however, be considered a permanent solution to the organizational problems within the circulation department. As *The Observer's* circulation increased, the demands of the new paper would put further strain on Dow Jones' present circulation organization. Moreover, personal relationships within a corporation change frequently, and such changes would eventually restrict the exercise of informal authority. Without centralized authority for coordination and control of *The Observer's* circulation operations, the many benefits of the new program might soon be dissipated.

To insure the success of the new circulation program over the long-term, therefore, a new organizational plan was proposed (see Figure 14.2):

In addition to the above plan, an outline was made of the duties performed in each functional area.

The new plan was a hybrid one, which gave the circulation managers ample control over their operations, without disrupting the present departmental operations. The newsstand, telephone and educational sales departments would remain functional departments, handling all three publications under the advisement of each circulation manager. This would be done because it allowed more economical use of field personnel around the country. The art, production, promotion, and record-keeping departments also would continue to service the three publications, because these operations required special skills which made functional specialization more efficient. However, all the other circulation operations would be centralized under the circulation manager of each publication, so that he would have direct authority over the major subscription selling operations. Since the new organization plan would have required only minor shifts in responsibilities and reporting relationships and the addi-

Figure 14.2

DOW JONES CIRCULATION DEPARTMENT

Proposed Organization Structure

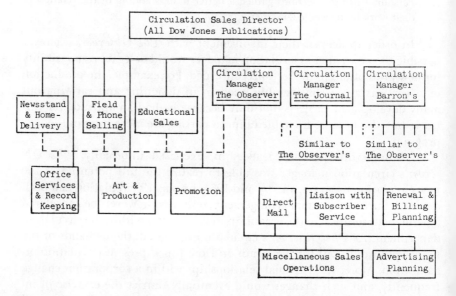

tion of only three clerks, the change could have been made without major personnel readjustments or undue expense.

It was recommended that the proposed organization structure for Dow Jones' circulation department be adopted sometime in 1966, when *The Observer*'s circulation would approach a level where it could support its own organization.

CONCLUSION

The National Observer study illustrates the complexities of putting the management control process to work. In *The Observer* study, the basic management control process was followed both in developing a new control system and in exercising management control. In an attempt to increase circulation, the fundamental problem was first defined, a new marketing objective and new marketing policies were developed, and new marketing programs were instituted. Only then was the control problem dealt with. The next step at this point was to identify the needs of the operation being controlled, the purpose and standards for the system, and the organization and administrative problems affecting the exercise of control.

Once these key factors had been identified and step two in the process was completed, a new control system was developed and introduced.

Admittedly, the description of *The Observer* study does not cover all the steps followed in developing the mechanics of the new control information and reporting system. But sufficient information is given to show how the control system was designed and how step three in the control process was carried out at *The Observer*.

In exercising control within the system, much of the action for improving operations was taken directly by the circulation manager. After comparing results with performance standards, he might replace direct mail with magazine advertising, expand test programs into full campaign promotions, or cancel promotion programs. Because of the existing organization structure, however, control could not always be exercised directly, and in many instances informal channels had to be used. Because of the problems caused by the organization structure, overall organization changes designed to make control easier were also recommended as part of the study.

In exercising control the circulation manager followed the fundamental guidelines given in the discussion of the fourth step in the control process in Chapter 11. He participated in developing overall standards for planning and controlling his operation. He specified the critical control points, quantified standards for each of these points, defined the information he needed to make decisions, and helped construct the form in which the information would be reported. He exercised control through comparing results with standards and initiating corrective action. While in some instances he took the corrective action directly, in many instances he worked through other departments and motivated them to take the action. Throughout the study, he worked to maintain a constructive atmosphere and used the system for educating all operating personnel and stimulating them to greater productivity.

The National Observer study also illustrates how various control tools and systems interact at the operational level. First, following the guidelines given in Chapter 8, a network of operating controls were developed based on the needs of the situation and of the decision maker. Second, financial controls were developed for the circulation area. These financial controls were integrated both with the network of operating controls and with overall corporate accounting and finance controls similar to those described in Chapter 7.

While the sophisticated scientific tools described in Chapter 9 were not used within *The Observer*'s circulation control system, selected mathematical tools were used in controlling testing. These tools helped reduce the cost of testing and enabled better and faster use of test result information in full-scale promotions.

A coordinated data processing and reporting system was developed to administer the control system. The data system was initially a punched card system, but was later converted to a computerized system. Because the systems approach described in Chapter 10 was used in developing the control system, the transition from punched card to computer system was orderly.

The National Observer study thus not only shows the management control process at work, but also shows the interaction of many control areas in an actual operating situation. Because it shows how the various aspects of the control process interact in an actual business situation, *The National Observer* study was presented as the final chapter in this book. However well one may have mastered the various steps in the control process and however familiar he may be with the various control tools and systems, it is only through understanding how they all come together to enable a manager to control better that one understands the essence of management control.

DISCUSSION QUESTIONS

1. Describe the steps in the process followed in developing controls and exercis- control at *The National Observer*.
2. Discuss the ways in which the management control process was adapted to this control situation.
3. Planning is an important base upon which all control is built. Discuss the ways in which planning factors affected the development and use of controls at *The Observer*.
4. Name the critical control points and the specific standards used in *The Observer*'s control system. In what way were they developed from the nature of the operation being controlled and the needs of the decision maker when exercising control within the system?
5. The control system at *The Observer* was an integrated reporting system with two parts, internal and corporate. What was the distinction between these areas of control? In what ways were they related?
6. Describe each report within *The Observer*'s control system. In what ways is or is not each report related to the peculiar requirements of a circulation marketing operation. Be specific. Should any additional reports have been included? Should any of the reports have been eliminated?
7. Describe the way in which the circulation manager used each report to monitor his operations.
8. In what ways did organizational problems affect the exercise of control for The Observer's circulation operation?
9. In what ways were human relations and administrative skills important in exercising control at *The Observer*?
10. In what ways was the systems approach used in developing the control re- porting system for *The Observer*'s circulation operation? How did it differ from the applications described in Chapter Ten?
11. What mathematical tools were used in *The Observer*'s circulation marketing control system?
12. Summarize the guidelines you have developed for adapting the control process to different levels and kinds of control problems.

CHAPTER 15

CONCLUSION

This chapter gives a summary of the concepts discussed in this study, some methods for controlling the controller, a brief history of the study of management control, and some concluding notes on building a unified science of management control.

THE MANAGEMENT CONTROL PROCESS: A SUMMARY OF THE STUDY

This study presented an integrated view of management control by focusing on the *process of management control*—rather than on individual control tools, or on the different control jobs within a company, or on the different kinds of control problems faced by the manager.

Management control situations are diverse in nature. They may involve designing a new control system or developing control standards, analyzing and measuring deviations of actual performance from standards, developing a quantitative basis for determining where to invest limited capital resources, taking corrective action, or simply examining a situation to determine exactly what the control problem is. The level of the problems may also vary, from the operational control problems faced by middle managers, to the overall corporate control problems faced by a company's controller or the problems faced by the systems and management sciences departments. The tools a manager can use in performing control include economic planning and forecasting techniques, accounting and finance controls, individual operating controls, graphic and mathematical tools, data processing systems, and behavioral science tools.

Despite the diversity of control tools and situations, the basic approach in using these tools and dealing with each control situation is the same, the management control process:

1. Diagnose the situation in order to define the control problem and the method for dealing with it.

2. Examine the control problem and review the facts in order to find the key factors affecting the problem and its solution.

3. Develop, test, and evaluate alternative control tools and systems, and ways to implement them.

4. Exercise control.

5. Prepare a written report if necessary.

Because of the complexity of the management control process and its application and because of the variety of management control problems arising at all management levels, putting the process to work is not a simple job. The process is most easily applied in lower-level operational control situations, for the scope of these situations is narrower. Corporate control situations and resource allocation problems are more complex, so that applying the process in these situations requires greater perception, judgment and creativity. In spite of these difficulties, however, in all these situations the control process provides a reliable basis for control problem solving and decision making.

This study has examined in detail how the steps in this process are carried out at different management levels within the corporation and applied in different kinds of control situations. It has also explored the ways in which various management tools in the economics, accounting, operating, mathematical and graphic, systems, and behavioral sciences areas are used for control.

Economic planning and forecasting are important to the foundations of management control. Company planning starts with the study of the economic environment, and based on this study of its environment and a study of internal company factors, sales forecasts are developed, which in turn became the control standards by which the performance of the production, marketing and other areas is judged and controlled.

A company's accounting and finance areas are also important to control. Basically, accounting provides overall control of company assets, costs and profits, generates accounting statements, keeps company books, and handles payroll and collections. Finance provides the control tools needed to measure how efficiently management is putting assets to work. The control functions in these areas are carried out mainly through the budgetary process and financial analysis.

Operating controls are closely tied into the overall company control system, but are distinct from these overall controls in many ways. Each operating and staff area, each business segment, and each manager needs a network of controls specifically tailored to meet the needs of his operation. Some of these controls will be overall finance and accounting controls. Most of them, however, may be quite distinct from accounting-type controls, even though they will all be designed to achieve maximum company profitability.

Management control also makes use of mathematical, graphic and other model building tools. The tools discussed in this study, such as PERT/CPM, decision theory, and linear programming, are not easy to master, but they are essential to modern management control decision making.

The systems approach provides guidelines for developing data processing systems for control. Computers are essential to the operation of larger information systems, and they give these systems expanded capabilities and versatility, while at the same time setting limits on them. Computers are also useful in many other areas of control decision making, such as information retrieval, mathematical and statistical decision making, network development, systems simulation, accounting and finance, and reporting.

The exercise of management control was given special emphasis throughout this study, both because of its difficulty and because of its importance to successful control. Almost every control situation requires some control action—checking to see if the standards or the system are adequate, measuring and comparing actual results against standards to see if there is any deviation, and taking whatever corrective action may be needed. The requirements of each situation and the manager's individual characteristics dictate the kind of control exercised, as was seen in the discussions of the Heinz Company, the production burr problem, the transportation company equipment decision, and the Frost Company and *National Observer* studies. In all cases, the successful exercise of control depended on maintaining the proper balance between compliance and creativity and developing a healthy atmosphere for exercising control.

The behavioral sciences provide advanced techniques useful in improving the exercise of control. Behavioral science can help managers gain a better understanding of human motivation, and enables them to more effectively set standards, institute changes in control and control systems, and take action to correct deviations from performance standards. The behavioral sciences have not received the attention they deserve within the science of management control, even though they provide tools without which effective control cannot be maintained.

The last control area covered in this study was reporting. Where control reporting depends on automated equipment, foresight and planning are needed to develop reporting systems flexible enough to handle all major decision-making needs that may arise within a company. Where reports are prepared and written by company personnel, attention must be paid to the communication techniques used and the human factors affecting the reporting. While there are general guidelines for effective reporting, each business area has its own peculiar reporting requirements, which must be studied and taken into account in individual reporting situations.

The science of management control will continue to grow as new tools and techniques are developed, and as new studies refine the concepts and principles of management control. None the less, a science of management control does exist now to guide the manager in his daily work. This book has attempted to introduce the reader to that science. Hopefully, this study will help the manager carry out his job better and provide the business researcher with a useful framework upon which to build a more complete science of management control.

CONTROLLING THE CORPORATE CONTROLLER

The emphasis in this study has been on control as exercised by any manager at any level in a company. In practice, most companies view control more narrowly, as a job performed by a finance or accounting executive, using mainly financial and accounting controls, supplemented by a few non-financial controls as needed. The Frost Company study is an example of such a control situation.

The problem of monitoring control activities in these situations where control is narrowly defined is two-fold: first, how do you control the financial and accounting control operation; and second, how do you control the wide variety of other control activities within the company?

The degree of control a top company manager will have over the control operation can depend both on his organization of control activities and on the degree of his participation in developing the company's overall control system, his understanding of other control systems within his company, the amount of information feedback he gets from individual operating and staff areas, and the use he makes of his company's control systems.

In most companies, annual reviews are made by outside accounting firms, and these reviews are one form of control. They are, however, usually done annually and so provide no interim, continuing check on control activities. Nor do they necessarily provide any check on the non-financial controls within a company.

In a small company, a company president can monitor control activities almost entirely by personal observation. In these situations separate organization units for control may not be needed to monitor control activities. As the size of the company grows, a company manager's ability to monitor control activities personally diminishes.

Some large companies have found that designating a control executive whose job is separate from the accounting and finance executives' jobs provides an adequate crosscheck on financial and accounting control and enables the expansion and coordination of other control activities within the company. Another check on control activities in large companies can be provided by the information systems group, if this group does not report directly to the control or accounting executive, for the systems group is responsible for evaluating the adequacy of control systems (including financial and accounting controls) in meeting the various control needs within a company.

Control reporting systems themselves often have crosschecks built into them. For example, at a mail-order company studied recently, short-term "flash" reports were issued on the projected profit results of current promotions as part of the marketing reporting system. These reports used estimates for bad debts and returned merchandise which were based on the accrual percentages used in the financial reports. Some months later, reports on financial results for the entire marketing area were issued as part of the financial control system used by the accounting department. A review of the individual marketing reports on all promotions during one period showed considerably better cumulative profit results than the financial report on total marketing area profits for the same period.

An investigation revealed many errors in the financial reporting systems. Accruals of projected bad debt expenses had been inadequate, and actual bad debts were running 30% ahead of accruals (customers were normally given two years to pay). Accruals for returned merchandise were also below actual figures. In addition, the allocation of customer service charges was inaccurate, which led to many missed profit opportunities. For instance, on one occasion a major promotion effort was cancelled because the projected profit was inadequate. Subsequent analysis showed that if correct estimates of customer service expenses had been used the proposed promotion would have shown an adequate profit and so have been undertaken. These errors were uncovered because the financial control system was supplemented by a marketing control system, and the company president periodically compared the reports generated by the two systems.

The lesson learned from this experience was that ultimately only by having a system of crosschecks, by understanding how the control tools and systems within the company work, and by taking time to use them can a corporate president (or the control executive designated by him) maintain control over the company's control activities.

THE HISTORY OF THE STUDY OF MANAGEMENT CONTROL

While the science of management control is still developing, it is not new. Many authorities have attempted to define aspects of control and outline the science. These earlier works, which are reviewed in this section, form a base upon which this study is built.

The beginning of the study of management control can be found in the works of the general management theorists. In 1916, for example, in one of the earliest efforts to develop a science of management, Henri Fayol, gave the following definition of management control: "Control consists of varifying whether everything occurs in conformity with the plan adopted, the instructions issued, and principles established. It has for object to point out weaknesses and errors in order to rectify and prevent recurrence."[1] Fayol was thinking mainly in terms of compliance control within a manufacturing-oriented company. This viewpoint prevails in his definition of control and in his discussion of the various processes and tools needed for controlling a business operation effectively and efficiently.

A review of the studies of general management theory and practice that followed Fayol reveals both a continuing interest in the subject and an ever-increasing awareness of the importance of control to successful business management.[2] In their definitions of the control process, the authors of these studies continue to stress setting standards, checking conformity of actual performance to standards, and correcting deviations. And like Fayol, in their discussions of control tools and techniques, these authors for the most part concentrate on the mechanics of the overall corporate control process, and stress the use of control in maintaining compliance.

Although useful, these studies of management control leave much to be desired. First, because they are brief, they do not cover the wide range of situations faced in making management control decisions—by both individual managers and corporate control departments. Second, because these studies concentrate on control tools and techniques, they fail to present an integrated concept of management control and the management control process. Third, because the authors each develop management control theory and principles within the framework of their own overall concepts of the discipline of management, they do not provide a broad

[1]Henri Fayol, *General and Industrial Management* (New York: Pitman Publishing Corporation, 1949), pp. 107ff.

[2]The following are some of the better-known studies to appear (or reappear) during the last five years:

William H. Newman, *Administrative Action: The Techniques of Organization and Management* (2nd ed.; Englewood Cliffs, New Jersey: Prentice-Hall, Inc., 1963), Chapters 24-26.

George R. Terry, *Principles of Management* (4th ed.; Homewood, Illinois: Richard D. Irwin, Inc., 1964), Chapters 26-30.

Justin G. Longnecker, *Principles of Management and Organization Behavior* (Columbus, Ohio): Charles E. Merrill Books, Inc., 1964), Chapters 24-26.

Koontz and O'Donnell, *Principles of Management*, Chapters 28-31.

Ernest Dale, *Management: Theory and Practice* (New York: McGraw-Hill Book Company, 1965), Chapter 26.

Max D. Richards and Paul S. Greenlaw, *Management Decision Making* (Homewood, Illinois: Richard D. Irwin, Inc., 1966), Chapter 12.

William H. Newman, Charles E. Summer and E. Kirby Warren, *The Process of Management: Concepts, Behavior, and Practice* (2nd ed.; Englewood Cliffs, New Jersey: Prentice-Hall, Inc., 1967), Chapters 27-30.

conceptual basis for developing a unified science of management control. Fourth, because these studies concentrate on the compliance aspects of control, they neglect exploring other positive aspects of management control. As a result, no consistent or complete body of management control theory and principles has evolved or can be developed from the works of the general management theorists.

Prior to 1960 very little effort was made to study management control as a separate discipline—a distinct decision-making/problem-solving process that could be used by any manager in any functional area. In *Top Management Organization and Control* (1941 and 1951) Holden, Fish and Smith concentrated on explaining the control techniques used in their day in such areas as organization, costs, salaries and wages, product lines, and the quality of key personnel.[3] Outside of a few pages on the process of control, however, the book contains no discussion of the fundamental theory and principles of management control. Nor does it make any attempt to build a conceptual basis for further scientific study of the field.

Rose and Farr attempted much more in *Higher Management Control* (1957).[4] After defining control, the authors describe their experiences in setting up control systems for manufacturing operations. However, the emphasis of this book is still on the techniques used in the early 1950's by a controller or control department in a corporation, not on control as a broader management function practiced by all managers.

In 1957 the Financial Executive Institute sponsored a study of the installation of a new system for budgetary control at the H. J. Heinz Company.[5] Although the study primarily concerns the internal control problems faced by the corporate controller, it contains a significant departure from the viewpoint that prevails in compliance-oriented, internal control studies. In the Heinz study the authors emphasize how the control process can be used to stimulate creativity, innovation, education and coordination —all of which tend to be de-emphasized in studies of internal corporate control, where compliance to standards is emphasized. Another Institute study on General Electric Company also broke new ground in control by studying the relation of planning and control at the corporate level.[6] In

---

[3]Paul E. Holden, Lounsbury S. Fish and Hubert L. Smith, *Top-Management Organization and Control: A Research Study of the Management Policies and Practices of Thirty-One Leading Industrial Corporations* (New York: McGraw-Hill Book Company, 1951).

[4]T. G. Rose and Donald E. Farr, *Higher Management Control* (New York: McGraw-Hill Book Company, 1957).

[5]*Management Planning and Control: The H. J. Heinz Approach: A Case Study in Management Planning and Control Objectives, Organization and Methods with Particular Emphasis on the Part Played by the Comptroller's Division in This Work* (New York: Controllers Institute Research Foundation, Inc., March 1961).

[6]*Planning, Managing and Measuring the Business: A Case Study of Management Planning and Control at General Electric Company* (New York: Controllers Institute Research Foundation, Inc., March 1961).

addition, the Financial Executives Institute has sponsored a number of other studies in the control field, but these deal almost exclusively with techniques and tools of control from the controller's or financial officer's viewpoints.[7]

There are a number of studies which deal with control tools in the accounting field, whose authors attempt in various ways to relate their fields to management control. These include: Anthony, *Management Accounting Principles* (1965); Keller and Ferrar, *Management Accounting for Profit and Control* (1966); Heckert and Willson, *Business Budgeting and Control* (1967); Korn and Boyd, *Accounting for Management Planning and Decision Making* (1969); Flink and Grunewald, *Managerial Finance* (1969); and Edward F. Norbeck *et al., Operational Auditing for Management Control* (1969).[8] *Management Controls* (1964)[9] edited by Bonini, Jaedicke and Wagner, presents a series of papers on current management control techniques in such areas as simulation, accounting, economics and the behavioral sciences. All of these studies, however, again concentrate on control tools.

Management control also makes use of operations research and statistical tools. The use of operations research and statistics in business decision making is explained in detail in: Schlaifer, *Probability and Statistics for Business Decisions* (1959); Bierman *et al., Quantitative Analysis for Busi-*

[7]Michael Schiff and Martin Mellman, *Financial Management of the Marketing Function* (New York: Financial Executives Research Foundation, 1962).

Raymond Villers, *Research and Development: Planning and Control* (New York: Financial Executives Research Foundation, 1964).

David Solomons, *Divisional Performance: Measurement and Control* (New York: Financial Executives Research Foundation, 1965).

Glenn A. Welsch and Burnard H. Sord, *Management Planning and Control* (New York: Financial Executives Research Foundation, 1968).

Peter O. Dietz, *Measurement of Return on Investment in Pension Funds* (New York: Financial Executives Research Foundation, 1968).

Robert K. Mautz, *Financial Reporting by Conglomerate and Concentric Companies* (New York: Financial Executives Research Foundation, 1968).

Frederick A. Lovejoy, *Measuring the Productivity of Organizations* (New York: Financial Executives Research Foundation, 1968).

[8]Robert N. Anthony, *Management Accounting Principles* (Homewood, Illinois: Richard D. Irwin, Inc., 1965).

I. Wayne Keller and William L. Ferrara, *Management Accounting for Profit Control* (2nd ed.; New York: McGraw-Hill Book Company, 1966).

J. Brooks Heckert and James D. Willson, *Business Budgeting and Control* (New York: The Ronald Press Company, 1967).

Solomon J. Flink and Donald Grunewald, *Managerial Finance* (New York: John Wiley and Sons, Inc., 1969).

W. Winston Korn and Thomas Boyd, *Accounting for Management Planning and Decision Making* (New York: John Wiley and Sons, Inc., 1969).

Edward F. Norbeck *et al., Operational Auditing for Management Control* (New York: American Management Association, 1969).

[9]Charles P. Bonini, Robert K. Jaedicke and Harvey M. Wagner, eds., *Management Controls: New Directions in Basic Research* (New York: McGraw-Hill Book Company, 1964).

ness Decisions (1965); Hillier and Lieberman, *Introduction to Operations Research* (1967); Brabb, *Introduction to Quantitative Management* (1968); Miller and Starr, *Executive Decisions and Operations Research* (1969); and Hough, *Modern Research for Administrative Decisions* (1970).[10] While these control tools are used in the performance of management control today, none of these books explore at any length the basis of management control theory and principles underlying the development and use of these tools.

Since 1960 there have been a number of books on management control systems, an important new management control tool. These include: Forrester, *Industrial Dynamics* (1961); Anthony, Dearden and Vancil, *Management Control Systems* (1965); Young, *Management: A System Analysis* (1966); Glans *et al.*, *Management Systems* (1968); Cleland and King, *Systems Analysis and Profit Management* (1968); Rudwick, *Systems Analysis for Effective Planning* (1969); and Symonds, *A Design for Business Intelligence* (1971).[11] Although the subject of these studies is business systems, their authors devote some time to discussing management control principles.

Similar books on other control tools in the area of electronic data processing, reporting, organizational behavior and finance, have also touched upon the subject of management control. As Robert N. Anthony points out, however, the field of management control has "scarcely any generally accepted principles, and everyone in the field, therefore, works

[10]Robert Schlaifer, *Probability and Statistics for Business Decisions: An Introduction to Managerial Economics under Uncertainty* (New York: McGraw-Hill Book Company, 1959).

Harold Bierman, Jr. *et al.*, *Quantitative Analysis for Business Decisions* (Rev. ed.; Homewood, Illinois. Richard D. Irwin, Inc., 1965).

Frederick S. Hillier and Gerald J. Lieberman, *Introduction to Operations Research* (San Francisco: Holden-Day, Inc., 1967).

George J. Brabb, *Introduction to Quantitative Management* (New York: Rinehart and Winston, Inc., 1968).

David W. Miller and Martin K. Starr, *Executive Decisions and Operations Research* (Rev. ed.; Englewood Cliffs, New Jersey: Prentice-Hall, Inc., 1969).

Louis Hough, *Modern Research for Administrative Decision* (Englewood Cliffs, New Jersey: Prentice-Hall, 1970).

[11]Jay W. Forrester, *Industrial Dynamics* (Cambridge, Massachusetts: The M.I.T. Press, 1961).

Robert N. Anthony, John Dearden and Richard F. Vancil, *Management Control Systems: Cases and Readings* (Homewood, Illinois: Richard D. Irwin, Inc., 1965).

Stanley Young, *Management: A Systems Analysis* (Glenview, Illinois: Scott, Foresman and Company, 1966).

Thomas B. Glans, Burton Grad, David Holstein, William E. Meyers, Richard N. Schmidt, *Management Systems* (New York: Holt, Rinehart and Winston, Inc., 1968).

David J. Cleland and William R. King, *Systems Analysis and Project Management* (New York: McGraw-Hill Book Company, Inc., 1968).

Bernard H. Rudwick, *Systems Analysis for Effective Planning* (New York: John Wiley & Sons, Inc., 1969).

Curtis W. Symonds, *A Design for Business Intelligence* (New York: American Management Association, 1971).

by intuition and by folklore."[12] In his *Planning and Control Systems: A Framework for Analysis* (1965), Anthony attempted to lay the groundwork upon which a science of management control could be built.

Anthony's *Planning and Control Systems* was a major step forward in the development of management control. His framework for management control is divided into three parts: strategic planning, management control, and operational control. He defines each of these areas as follows:

> *Strategic planning* is the process of deciding on objectives of the organization, on changes in these objectives, on the resources used to attain these objectives, and on the policies that are to govern the acquisition, use, and disposition of these resources.
>
> *Management control* is the process by which managers assure that resources are obtained and used effectively and efficiently in the accomplishment of the organization's objectives.
>
> *Operational control* is the process of assuring that specific tasks are carried out effectively and efficiently.[13]

Within his framework all these areas are related, strategic planning being the basis of management control, and operational control being an extension of management control. He distinguishes the kinds of functions performed in each area in the following chart:

Examples of Activities in a Business Organization Included in Major Framework Headings[14]

Strategic Planning	Management Control	Operational Control
Choosing company objectives	Formulating Budgets	
Planning the organization	Planning staff levels	Controlling hiring
Setting personnel policies	Formulating personnel practices	Implementing policies
Setting financial policies	Working capital planning	Controlling credit extension
Setting marketing policies	Formulating advertising programs	Controlling placement of advertisements
Setting research policies	Deciding on research projects	

[12]Robert N. Anthony, *Planning and Control Systems: A Framework for Analysis* (Boston: Division of Research, Graduate School of Business Administration, Harvard University, 1965), p. vii.

[13]Anthony, *Planning and Control Systems*, pp. 16-18.

[14]Anthony, *Planning and Control Systems*, p. 19.

Choosing new product lines	Choosing product improvements	
Acquiring a new division	Deciding on plant rearrangement	Scheduling production
Deciding on non-routine capital expenditures	Deciding on routine capital expenditures	
	Formulating decision rules for operational control	Controlling inventory
	Measuring, appraising, and improving management performance	Measuring, appraising, and improving workers' efficiency

In his study Anthony goes beyond defining basic control concepts and functions, and gives guidelines for information handling. But he does not discuss all the steps in the control process in any detail. Nor does he deal with specific applications of his control principles to actual business situations, even though he recognizes that management control is an applied science and that, as a result, applications of principles to practice are an inherent part of the science. Anthony did not cover these areas because his objective in writing his study was only to provide an overall framework for the science of management control for use by others in developing the science further.

A few years earlier, in *Executive Control—The Catalyst* (1961), William Travers Jerome III had also begun to break ground for a true science of management control. His book was built on the thesis that control is "a subject area with its own distinctive concepts and precepts."[15] In his study Jerome attempted to develop a scientific framework for management control, and explored at length its theory and principles. Like Anthony's book, Jerome's study also set out to develop "a way of looking at control" and was not designed to be a "how to do it" book. Jerome isolated seven key ideas which permeate every successful system of management control.[16]

1. The purpose of control is *to set the stage for action*, that is, to help managers get the firm's affairs done *in the most profitable way possible*. Such restrictive aspects as may exist in the controls used are only *intended to funnel efforts, not to discourage them*.

[15]Wm. Travers Jerome III, *Executive Control—The Catalyst* (New York: John Wiley and Sons, Inc., 1961), p. 27.
[16]Jerome, *Executive Control*, pp. 30-31.

2. Controls provide the *best "teaching" or educational devices available to executives*. Such controls as budgets, standard costs, and procedure manuals can be used to set the climate within which action takes place. They also serve as a way for management to communicate about the things it wants done, about ways for doing them, and about the success achieved in their doing.

3. Control has positive value because of the way it *facilitates executive self-appraisal*. This point contrasts with the preceding which emphasizes the use of controls for teaching subordinates. The value of self-appraisal arises primarily from the fact that control involves identifying the critical or strategic factors contributing to the firm's overall success. Any attempt to identify such factors and to use these to evaluate progress is bound to have beneficial results.

4. Control is inevitably a *matter of relationships*, of comparisons, of evaluation. To control is to contrast actual or intended performance against some norm or standard. In this sense, control is like measurement which by definition involves a comparison of two or more things.

5. For most managerial purposes, control should be conceived in terms of *trend relationships* rather than in terms of absolute or single figure values. In other words, management interest usually should be triggered whenever current performance shows a disposition to depart from the planned, rather than to await the attainment of any predetermined level of failure (or of success) before taking action. This approach is particularly necessary when evaluating organizational performance.

6. Effective control for managerial purposes requires flexibility rather than steadfast adherence to any given plan of action. It involves identifying and *weighing a great number of possible alternatives* in order not to be caught unprepared should even the most unlikely eventuality occur. This is the true meaning of "unflinching control."

7. Systematic follow-up and *review is fundamental* to any effective system of control. The process of evaluating or of measuring is really that of reviewing. Reviews will be devoid of meaning unless someone is interested in doing something about major performance deviations.

In discussing these key areas, as he does throughout his study, Jerome describes management control in a very positive way, emphasizing the coordination and education benefits of control. He stresses how controls and controlling can be used to improve operations and lead to better solutions to problems. While he recognizes that control has its negative aspects —such as protecting assets, and preventing error—these are secondary to the positive benefits which can come from a more enlightened view of control.

Like other writers in the field, Jerome recognizes the necessity of beginning with the planning base and developing standards based on company planning. He gives five steps for doing this:[17]

1. Asking the question, "What are we trying to do?", is the necessary first step in

17 Jerome, *Executive Control*, pp. 59-64.

THE MANAGEMENT CONTROL PROCESS

spelling out company objectives in order to define success and develop performance measurements. Involved in this initial step is considerable searching self-analysis, nothing more.

2. The second step in this process of establishing performance criteria follows only when satisfactory answers are obtained as a result of the self-analysis described above. This second step calls for top management itself *setting definite objectives* (i.e., the desired results) which can serve as beacons to aid in navigating the firm's course. These objectives should initially contain a statement regarding the kinds of product and service to be offered.

3. The third step in this search for criteria that will enable us both to identify success and to evaluate performance necessitates restating in operational or measurable terms the objectives developed in step two above. In other words, what are the specific activities or accomplishments indicating that satisfactory progress is being made toward meeting the firm's objectives?

4. The fourth step in developing a firm's objectives must include some consideration of the *inevitable inconsistencies* existing among the objectives set. For example, if customer service is a major company objective, the effects upon inventory costs or production scheduling must be duly recognized. Or, if an ambitious research program is desired, the effects upon dividend policy need be weighed, especially if research success leads to a demand for additional plant and equipment.

5. The fifth and last step in the development and use of objectives is clearly basic to the fourth step. This step involves periodic *review of actual results against the projected results*, or, as a minimum, a study of the trends in the measurements used. In other words, once the objectives are defined in terms of measurable activities (step three), it is necessary to find out how we are doing and how we can do better.

The above outline provides a concise review of the steps involved in setting standards. The third step, translating company objectives into measurable terms is, in Jerome's view, the most critical.

Building upon this planning base, Jerome develops guidelines for performing management control. To this end he isolates the following major requirements of an executive control system:[18]

1. A clear perception of the market which the business has been created to serve.
2. A disciplined approach to planning.
3. An organization tailored to the particular job to be done.
4. Effective communication in the somewhat specialized sense of collecting and disseminating information.
5. A climate for control which maintains a balance between compliance and creativity, a climate which simulates use of the control system for coordination and education.
6. Review and analysis.

According to Jerome, therefore, effective management control needs good planning, an organized information communications system, a bal-

18Jerome, *Executive Control*, pp. 69-70, 147ff.

anced viewpoint between compliance and creativity in taking corrective action, and continual review.

Jerome devotes a large part of his study to measuring and evaluating, for, in his words, "management control is mostly an evaluative or measuring process."[19] According to Jerome, effective measurement depends on one's ability to answer the question, "How do you judge business success?" Objective criteria are needed to make this judgment, and these criteria, Jerome feels, are developed through the planning process. Jerome recognizes the difficulties inherent in measuring and evaluating for control, and he reviews a variety of approaches used by such companies as DuPont, Koppers and General Electric.

While Jerome treats many aspects of the subject in much more detail than does Anthony, he does not attempt to develop a complete, systematically organized science of management control. His work is extremely important none the less, and was used extensively in the section of this study concerning the basic principles guiding the exercise of control.

Two additional research studies, which explored the subject of management control in depth, were conducted under Anthony's direction: Robert Deming's *Characteristics of an Effective Management Control System in an Industrial Organization* (1968) and James S. Hekiman's *Management Control in Life Insurance Branch Offices* (1965).[20] Both these studies involve detailed examinations of existing control systems at major corporations, and they both give interesting insights into the various levels of control within a company and the variety of ways control is exercised. These studies, however, were not designed to develop a concept of management control but only to test Anthony's conceptual framework.

Four recent works which study various kinds of control problems are also indicative of the increasing interest in developing a unified concept of a control science. Earl P. Strong and Robert D. Smith, in *Management Control Models* (1968), study the different control tools used in business today as part of a single control discipline. However, while the study has a brief introduction on what control is, like so many earlier works, the focus of the study is on tools and their applications. In contrast, a major part of Marvin Mundel's *A Conceptual Framework for the Management Sciences* (1967) not only deals with the concept of control but also explores at length the ways in which that concept is applied in the production, financial and sales areas. Arnold S. Tannenbaum's book of readings, *Control in Organizations* (1968), also treats control as a unified concept, but he deals only

---

[19]Jerome, *Executive Control*, p. 37.

[20]Robert H. Deming, *Characteristics of an Effective Management Control System in an Industrial Organization* (Boston: Division of Research Graduate School of Business Administration, Harvard University, 1968); James S. Hekimian, *Management Control in Life Insurance Branch Offices* (Boston: Division of Research, Graduate School of Business Administration, Harvard University, 1965).

with the behavioral science aspects of control. Paul M. Stokes' *A Total Systems Approach to Management Control* (1968) gives a concise overview of control for top corporate management, covering the development and use of controls and control standards in eight critical performance areas: finance; operations; productivity; market position; service relations; public, customer, and government relations; employee relations and development; and ownership and member relations.[21]

Two books of readings published in the 1960's attempted to present a unified, comprehensive review of the many areas related to control: B. C. Lemke and James Don Edwards, *Administrative Control and Executive Action* (1961) and Robert J. Mockler, *Readings in Management Control* (1970). While these books were useful in providing a unified focus, no effort was made in them to explain exactly how the individual steps were inter-related within a single scientific discipline of management control.[22]

A number of articles have also explored the subject of management control. In an article written in 1959, Harold Koontz has defined fourteen principles of action for management control which relate very closely to those given in the early chapters of this book:[23]

1. *Principle of Assurance of Objective:* Controls must contribute to the accomplishment of group objectives by detecting deviations from plans in time and in a manner to make corrective action possible.
2. *Principle of Efficiency of Control:* Controls are efficient if they effectively detect deviations from plans and make possible corrective action with the minimum of unsought consequences.
3. *Principle of Control Responsibility:* Control can be exercised only by the manager responsible for the execution of plans.
4. *Principle of Future Controls:* Effective control should be aimed at preventing present and future deviations from plans.
5. *Principle of Direct Control:* The most effective technique of control in an enterprise is to assure the quality of subordinate managers.
6. *Principle of Reflection of Plans:* Controls must be designed so as to reflect the character and structure of plans.
7. *Principle of Organizational Suitability:* Controls must be designed to reflect organization structure.
8. *Principle of Individuality of Controls:* Controls must be designed to meet the personal needs of the individual manager.

[21]Marvin E. Mundel, *A Conceptual Framework for the Management Sciences* (New York: McGraw-Hill Book Company, 1967); Earl P. Strong and Robert D. Smith, *Management Control Models* (New York: Holt, Rinehart and Winston, Inc., 1968); Arnold S. Tannenbaum, *Control in Organizations* (New York: McGraw-Hill Book Company, 1968); Paul M. Stokes, *A Total Systems Approach to Management Control* (New York: American Management Association, 1968).

[22]B. C. Lemke and James Don Edwards, *Administration Control and Executive Action* (Columbus, Ohio: Charles E. Merrill Books, Inc., 1961); Robert J. Mockler, *Readings in Management Control* (New York: Appleton-Century-Crofts, 1970).

[23]Harold Koontz, "Management Control: A Suggested Formulation of Principles," *California Management Review*, Winter, 1959, pp. 50-55.

9. *Principle of Standards:* Effective and efficient control requires objective, accurate, and suitable standards.

10. *Principle of Strategic Point Control:* Effective and efficient control requires that attention be given to those factors which are strategic to the appraisal of performance.

11. *The Exception Principle:* Efficiency in control requires that attention of the manager be given primarily to significant exceptions.

12. *The Principle of Flexibility of Controls:* Controls should incorporate sufficient flexibility to remain effective despite the failure of plans.

13. *Principle of Review:* The control system should be reviewed periodically.

14. *Principle of Action:* Control is only justified if measures are undertaken to correct indicated or experienced deviations from plans through appropriate planning, organizing, staffing, and directing.

Koontz categorizes these principles into three groups. The first five principles deal with the nature and purpose of control, the next three have to do with the structure of control, and the last six deal with the process of conrol. Koontz's principles echo many found in this book. For example, his first states that controls must be based on plans; his third that those using the controls should be involved in their development; the sixth that controls must be tailored to meet the specific individual planning requirements of the operation being controlled; the seventh, that the structure of the control system should be made compatible with that of the company organization; the eighth that the system should be designed to meet the decision-making needs of each operating manager.

Although Koontz developed his principles within a different conceptual framework than that used in this book, they correspond to the basic control principles given in this study. Koontz's principles provide a useful supplement to this study, for they not only reinforce the principles already presented, but they also highlight certain aspects of control, such as "efficiency of control," which are covered only in passing in this study.

Ray Powell, writing in *Financial Executive* in 1966, also gives guidelines for control.[24] According to Powell, effective management control requires the following:

1. Identifying key factors in the business operation which need to be controlled in order to achieve a given overall point.

2. Specifying the basis for establishing standards of performance for each control factor, such as forecasts, budgets, standard costs, turnover ratios, and lead time.

3. Defining the information—accounting and operating data and statistics—that must be accumulated to measure status and performance.

4. Establishing a reporting structure that identifies performance in each control area, relates causes and effects, signals trends, and identifies results by responsibility under the plan of organization.

[24]Ray M. Powell, "Principles of Modern Managerial Control," *Financial Executive*, April 1966, p. 56.

In addition, he believes effective management control will:

1. Control before-the-fact through preplanning.
2. Highlight critical data for managers.
3. Increasingly help monitor events external to the firm, even though in the past they may have been regarded as non-quantifiable.

While Powell's principles are by no means as comprehensive or complete as Koontz's, they are built on the basic principles underlying all earlier discussions of management control. Echoing Koontz' principles, Powell's process begins with examining the control situation and planning factors. He gives greater emphasis, as does this book, to developing the actual information system than have other management theorists. The benefits he sees coming from good control are "preventive maintenance," more effective use of executive time, and better use of external environmental information.

Louis Fried, writing in *Management Services* in 1968, describes the five "functions" which he feels comprise the process of control.[25]

1. Planning, including setting standards and goals, and budgeting.
2. Tracking of actual performance, including most accounting functions.
3. Comparison of standards with actual performance.
4. Reporting of variances.
5. Implementation of corrective action.

Like Powell, Fried emphasizes the preparatory planning needed for effective control, and concentrates on the practical problems associated with developing standards, getting accurate information and measuring results. He cites examples of how the complexity of modern information systems increases errors; how difficult it is to break the accounting orientation of information systems, so that these systems can be designed to suit the needs of the individual decision-makers; how easy it is to automate the comparison of actual against standard and to report deviations; and the ways in which control standards are developed from corporate planning objectives.

Roy A. Lindberg, writing in *Management Services* in 1969, describes what he calls "the unfamiliar art of controlling."[26] His article emphasises the positive aspects of control, argues for selectivity in controls—that is, having them only show large variances at critical points in an operation—and makes the point that most companies spend too much on controls. The four steps he gives for establishing controls are familiar ones: developing effective standards; setting them at strategic points; creating feedback for performance comparison; and setting up the machinery for correcting

[25]Louis Fried, "Executive Controls," *Management Services*, May-June 1968, pp. 17-26.
[26]Roy A. Lindberg, "The Unfamiliar Art of Controlling," *Management Services*, May-June 1969, pp. 15-20.

destructive deviations. So, too, are his practical guidelines for control: control positively; control decisively; dovetail plans and controls; keep controls simple; combine responsibility for execution and control at the operational level; control by comparing; control through variance; control at points; locate controls advantageously; continue control for life of plan. Above all, Lindberg stresses that a manager should never take existing controls for granted, but constantly review them, update them where necessary, and eleminate those no longer needed.

Powell, Fried and Lindberg all attempted to bring greater realism and practicality to the management control process than did many earlier writers. They emphasize the difficulties involved in developing effective information systems, especially in larger companies using computers. Fried and Powell also give greater weight than do many earlier writers to the action steps in the control process. In exercising control, as the earlier chapters of this study have shown, taking corrective action can mean many things, from initiating or recommending to administering the corrective action. And in measuring performance, discovering the significance of deviations is the primary challenge of management control, with the actual measuring being a more or less mechanical process.

Writers today are thus going beyond the old three step control process described in such books as Koontz and O'Donnell's *Principles of Management:*

> The basic control process, wherever found and whatever controller, involves three steps: (1) establishing standards, (2) measuring performance against these standards, and (3) correcting deviations from standards and plans.[27]

Contemporary writers are striving to recognize the true complexities of the control process at work. And they are trying to develop a comprehensive science of management control which takes all these modern-day complexities into account and provides practical guidelines for effective control action.

While Anthony, Jerome and the others cited above have made major contributions to the development of the science of management control, none of these authors claimed to be making any more than a beginning. The state of the science of management control today is similar to the state of the science of corporate long-range planning a decade ago. In 1958 David Ewing put together a book of readings on the subject, a book which was to give focus and impetus to the study of corporate planning.[28] While some work on planning had been done prior to Ewing's book, only after 1960 did major works on the theory and principles of corporate long-range

[27]Harold Koontz and Cyril O'Donnell, *Principles of Management: An Analysis of Managerial Functions* (4th ed.; New York: McGraw-Hill Book Company, 1968), p. 640.

[28]David W. Ewing, ed., *Long-Range Planning for Management* (New York: Harper & Brothers, Publishers, 1958).

planning begin to appear in sufficient numbers to suggest that a science of corporate long-range planning was at last beginning to develop. Hopefully, within the next decade management control will also develop into a well-defined area of management science.

BUILDING A UNIFIED SCIENCE OF MANAGEMENT CONTROL

The work of Koontz, Powell, Fried, Jerome, Anthony, and others provides an interesting perspective within which to review the outline of management control given in this book.

First, there are very few contradictions among the various treatments of the science of management control. Each tends to reinforce and explain the others.

Second, what major differences there are lie in the totality of approach. Koontz attempts to give only overall principles of action, not to develop a unifying conceptual framework for all types of management control. Powell and Fried treat only one aspect of the management control process. Anthony attempts only to develop an overall framework for studying management control, without giving principles for applying management control concepts in practice. Jerome concentrates on—"a way of looking at control"—the concepts, attitudes and atmosphere which should prevail for effective management control. The study presented in this book thus does not contradict or supercede those that went before. Rather, it attempts, by building on these earlier works, to extend them and to outline a more complete science of management control, from conceptual framework to principles of action and tools for doing control.

Third, while this study goes much farther than previous studies, more work still needs to be done before a clearly defined science of management control is fully developed.

The future of the science of management control depends on having a widely accepted systematic definition of the concept and process, and a consistent set of principles for guiding action. Such a systematic organization of concepts and principles is the basis of any science. This study tries to build such a basis. In writing this book an attempt was made both to build upon earlier studies of the subject, since much can be learned from them, and to go beyond them. If those who work on developing a science of management in the future also build from what went before, then I believe we will arrive much more quickly at a single, unified science of management control and avoid much wasted effort.

DISCUSSION QUESTIONS

1. What are the basic differences between the various kinds and levels of management control described in this book? In what ways are they related? In what ways are they distinct?

2. Outline the basic management control process applicable to all these control situations.

3. Name the major areas upon which management control draws for its tools. In what ways are they put to work in the management control process?

4. Discuss the role of economic planning and forecasting techniques in management control.

5. The concept of control given in this study goes far beyond the three step process given in such general studies of management as *Principles of Management*. Discuss the specific aspects of control which are given greater emphasis in this study.

6. Discuss some of the complexities of exercising control and the importance of behavioral science tools in taking effective control action.

7. Why is management control called by many a "developing" science?

8. Why do you think the science of management control is not as fully developed as some of the other management sciences, such as management planning?

9. Look up the definition of "science" in an encyclopedia. Discuss the ways in which management control, as outlined in this book, is or is not truly a science.

10. In what ways do you think the principles of the science of management control, as given in this book, are incomplete and could be expanded?

LIST OF BOOKS CITED

Abramson, Adolph G., and Mack, Russell H. *Business Forecasting in Practice*. New York. John Wiley and Sons, Inc., 1956.

Ackoff, Russell L., and Rivett, Patrick. *A Managers Guide to Operations Research*. New York: John Wiley and Sones, Inc. 1963.

Aguilar, Francis F. *Scanning the Business Environment*. New York: The Macmillan Company, 1968.

Ansoff, H. Igor. *Corporate Strategy*. New York: McGraw-Hill Book Company, Inc., 1965.

Anthony, Robert N. *Management Accounting: Text and Cases*. Third Edition. Homewood, Illinois: Richard D. Irwin, Inc., 1964.

Anthony, Robert N. *Management Accounting Principles*. Homewood, Illinois. Richard D. Irwin, Inc., 1965.

Anthony, Robert N. *Planning and Control Systems: A Framework for Analysis*. Boston: Graduate School of Business Administration, Harvard University, 1965.

Anthony, Robert N., Dearden, John, and Uancil, Richard F. *Management Control Systems: Cases and Readings*. Homewood, Illinois: Richard D. Irwin, Inc., 1965.

Argyris, Chris. *The Impact of Budgets on People*. New York: Controllership Foundation, Inc., 1952.

Argyris, Chris. *Personality and Organization*. New York: Harper and Row, Publishers, 1957.

Backer, Morton, and Jacobsen, Lyle E. *Cost Accounting: A Managerial Approach*. New York: McGraw-Hill Book Company, Inc., 1964.

Barish, Norman N. *Economic Analysis for Engineering and Managerial Decision-Making*. New York: McGraw-Hill Book Company, Inc., 1962.

Bergen, Garret L., and Haney, William V. *Organizational Relations and Management Action: Cases and Issues*. New York: McGraw-Hill Book Company, Inc., 1966.

Beyer, Robert. *Profitability Accounting for Planning and Control*. New York: The Ronald Press Company, 1963.

Bierman, Harold Jr., *et al.*, *Quantitative Analysis for Business Decisions*. Revised edition. Homewood, Illinois: Richard D. Irwin, Inc., 1965.

Black, Homer A., Champion and Brown, R. Gene. *Accounting in Business Decisions: Theory, Method and Use.* Second edition. Englewood Cliffs, N.J.: Prentice-Hall, Inc., 1967.

Bonini, Charles P. *Simulation of Information and Decision Systems in the Firm.* Englewood Cliffs, N.J.: Prentice-Hall, Inc., 1963.

Bonini, Charles P., Jaedicke, Robert K., and Wagner, Harvey M. *Management Controls: New Directions in Basic Research.* New York: McGraw-Hill Book Company, Inc., 1964.

Bowman, Edward H., and Fetter, Robert B. *Analysis for Production Management.* Revised edition. Homewood, Illinois: Richard D. Irwin, Inc., 1961.

Brabb, George J. *Introduction to Quantitative Management.* New York: Holt, Rinehart and Winston, Inc., 1968.

Bratt, Elmer Clark. *Business Cycles and Forecasting.* Fifth edition. Homewood, Illinois: Richard D. Irwin, Inc., 1961.

Brooks, Frederick P. Jr., and Iverson, Kenneth E. *Automatic Data Processing.* Second edition. New York: John Wiley and Sons, Inc., 1963.

Brown, Leland. *Effective Business Report Writing.* Englewood Cliffs, N.J.: Prentice-Hall, Inc., 1963.

Buell, Victor P. *Marketing Management in Action.* New York: McGraw-Hill Book Company, Inc., 1966.

Buffa, Elwood S. *Modern Production Management.* Third edition. New York: John Wiley and Sons, Inc., 1969.

Butler, William F., and Kavish, Robert A. *How Business Economists Forecast.* Englewood Cliffs, N.J.: Prentice-Hall, Inc., 1966.

Childs, William H. *Accounting for Management Control.* New York: Simmons-Boardman, 1960.

Cleland, David J., and King, William R. *Systems Analysis and Project Management.* New York: McGraw-Hill Book Company, Inc., 1968.

Costello, Timothy W., and Zalkind, Sheldon S. *Psychology in Administration.* Englewood Cliffs, N.J.: Prentice-Hall, Inc., 1963.

Croxton, Frederick E., and Conden, Dudley J. *Applied General Statistics.* Englewood Cliffs, N.J.: Prentice-Hall, Inc., 1965.

Dale, Ernest. *Management: Theory and Practice.* New York: McGraw-Hill Book Company, Inc., 1965.

Dauten, Carl A. *Business Cycles and Forecasting.* Second edition. Cincinnati: South-Western Publishing, 1961.

Davis, Gordon B. *An Introduction to Electronic Computers.* New York: McGraw-Hill Book Company, Inc., 1965.

Davis, Keith. *Human Relations at Work.* New York: McGraw-Hill Book Company, Inc., 1967.

Dearden, John. *Computers in Business Management.* Homewood, Illinois: Dow Jones-Irwin, Inc., 1966.

Dearden, John and McFarlan, F. Warren. *Management Information Systems: Text and Cases.* Homewood, Illinois: Richard D. Irwin, Inc., 1966.

Deming, Robert H. *Characteristics of an Effective Management Control System in an Industrial Organization.* Cambridge, Mass.: Harvard University, 1968.

Dietz, Peter O. *Measurement of Return on Investment in Pension Funds.* New York: Financial Executives Research Foundation, 1968.

Dommasch, Daniel O., and Laudeman, Charles W. *Principles Underlying Systems Engineering.* New York: Pitman Publishing Corp., 1962.

Drucker, Peter F. *The Practice of Management.* New York: Harper and Row, 1954.

Elliott, C. Orville, and Wasley, Robert S. *Business Information Processing Systems.* Homewood, Illinois: Richard D. Irwin, Inc., 1965.

Emory, C. William and Wiland, Powell. *Making Management Decisions:* Boston: Houghton Mifflin Company, 1968.

Ewing, David W. *Long-Range Planning for Management.* Revised edition. New York: Harper and Row, Publishers, 1964.

Fayol, Henri. *General and Industrial Management.* New York: Pitman Corp., 1949.

Flink, Solomon J., Gronewald, Donald. *Managerial Finance.* New York: John Wiley and Sons, Inc., 1969.

Forrester, Jay W. *Industrial Dynamics.* Cambridge, Mass.: The M.I.T. Press, 1961.

Fremgen, James M. *Managerial Cost Analysis.* Homewood, Illinois: Richard D. Irwin, Inc., 1966.

Glans, Thomas B., Grad, Burton, Holstein, David, Meyers, William E., and Schmidt, Richard N., 1966.

Goetz, Billy E. *Quantitative Methods: A Survey and Guide for Managers.* New York: McGraw-Hill Book Company, Inc., 1965.

Greenlaw, Paul S., Herron, Lowell W., and Randon, Richard H. *Business Simulation in Industrial and University Education.* Englewood Cliffs, N.J.: Prentice-Hall, Inc., 1962.

Greenwood, James. *EDP: The Feasibility Study—Analysis and Improvement of Data Processing.* Washington, D.C.: Systems and Procedures Association, 1962.

Hall, John F. *Psychology of Motivation.* Chicago, Illinois: J.B. Lippincott Company, 1961.

Hardwick, C. T., and Landuyt, B. F. *Administrative Strategy and Decision-Making.* Second edition. Cincinnati: South-Western Publishing Company, 1966.

Hargrove, Merwin M. *Behavioral Science Implications.* Revised edition. Homewood, Illinois: Richard D. Irwin, Inc., 1966.

Heckert, J. Brooks and Willson, James D. *Business Budgeting and Control.* Third edition. New York: The Ronald Press Company, 1967.

Heckert, J. Brooks and Willson, James D. *Controllership.* Second edition. New York: The Ronald Company, 1962.

Heiser, Herman C. *Budgeting: Principles and Practice.* New York: The Ronald Press Company, 1959.

Hekimian, James S. *Management Control in Life Insurance Branch Offices.* Boston: Graduate School of Business Administration, Harvard University, 1965.

Hillier, Frederick S., and Lieberman, Gerald J. *Introduction to Operations Research.* San Francisco: Holden-Day, Inc., 1967.

Holden, Paul E., Fish, Lounsbury S., and Smith, Hubert L. *Top Management Organization and Control: A Research Study of the Management Policies and Practices of Thirty-one Leading Industrial Corporations.* New York: McGraw-Hill Book Company, Inc., 1951.

Hopeman, Richard J. *Production Concepts and Controls.* Columbus, Ohio: Charles E. Merrill Books, Inc., 1965.

Louis Hough. *Modern Research for Administrative Decisions.* Englewood Cliffs, N.J.: Prentice-Hall Inc., 1970.

Hunt, Pearson, Williams, Charles M., and Donaldson, George. *Basic Business Finance: Text and Cases.* Third edition. Homewood, Illinois: Richard D. Irwin, Inc., 1966.

Jerome, William Travers III. *Executive Control—the Catalyst.* New York: John Wiley and Sons, Inc., 1961.

Jones, Manley Howe, *Executive Decision-Making.* Revised edition. Homewood, Illinois: Richard D. Irwin, Inc., 1962.

Johnson, Richard A., Kast, Fremont E., and Rosenzweig, James E. *The Theory and Management of Systems.* New York: McGraw-Hill Book Company, Inc., 1963.

Julius, Michael J. *Personnel Management.* Sixth edition. Homewood, Illinois: Richard D. Irwin, Inc., 1971.

Keller, I. Wayne, Ferrara, William L. *Management Accounting for Profit Control.* Second edition. New York: McGraw-Hill Book Company, Inc., 1966.

Kepner, Charles H., and Tregoe, Benjamin B. *The Rational Manager: A Systematic Approach to Problem Solving and Decision-Making.* New York: McGraw-Hill Book Company, Inc., 1965.

Koontz, Harold and O'Donnell, Cyril. *Principles of Management: An Analysis of Managerial Functions.* Fouth edition. New York: McGraw-Hill Book Company, Inc., 1968.

Korn, S. Winton and Boyd, Thomas. *Accounting for Management Planning and Decision Making.* New York: John Wiley and Sons, Inc., 1969.

Lemke, B. C., and Edwards, James Don. *Administration Control and Executive Action.* Columbus. Ohio: Charles E. Merrill Books, Inc., 1961.

Levin, Richard I., and Kirkpatrick, Charles A. *Planning and Control with PERT / CPM.* New York: McGraw-Hill Book Company, Inc., 1966.

Levin, Richard I., and Kirkpatrick, Charles A. *Quantitative Approach to Management.* New York: McGraw-Hill Book Company, Inc., 1965.

Lewis, Ralph F. *Management Uses of Accounting: Planning and Control for Profit.* New York: Harper and Brothers Publishers, 1961.

Longnecker, Justin G. *Principles of Management and Organization Behavior.* Columbus, Ohio: Charles E. Merrill Books, Inc., 1964.

Lovejoy, Frederick A. *Measuring the Productivity of Organizations.* New York: Financial Executives Research Foundation, 1968.

Malcolm, Donald G., and Rowe, Alan J. *Management Control Systems.* New York: John Wiley and Sons, Inc., 1960.

Martin, E. W. Jr. *Electronic Data Processing: An Introduction.* Revised edition. Homewood, Illinois: Richard D. Irwin, Inc., 1965.

Maslow, Abraham H. *Motivation and Personality.* New York: Harper and Row, Publishers, 1954.

Mautz, Robert K. *Financial Reporting by Conglomerate and Concentric Companies.* New York: Financial Executives Research Foundation, 1968.

McCarthy, E. Jerome, McCarthy, J. A., and Hermes, Durward. *Integrated Data Processing.* New York: John Wiley and Sons, Inc., 1966.

McDonough, Adrian M., and Garrett, Leonard J. *Management Systems: Working Concepts and Practices.* Homewood, Illinois: Richard D. Irwin, Inc., 1965.

McGregor, Douglas. *The Human Side of the Enterprise.* New York: McGraw-Hill Book Company, Inc., 1960.

Miller, David W., and Starr, Martin K. *Executive Decisions and Operations Research.* Revised edition. Englewood Cliffs, N.J.: Prentice-Hall, Inc., 1969.

Mockler, Robert J. *Business Planning and Policy Development.* New York: Appleton-Century-Crofts, 1971.

Mockler, Robert J. *Circulation Planning and Development for the National Observer: A Research Study on Business Applications of Management Planning and Control Principles.* Atlanta, Georgia: Georgia State College, 1967.

Mockler, Robert J. *Readings in Management Control.* New York: Appleton-Century-Crofts, 1970.

Mockler, Robert J. *Putting Computers to Work More Efficiently in Business Publishing.* New York: American Business Press Association, 1969.

Moore, Franklin G. *Manufacturing Management.* Homewood, Illinois: Richard D. Irwin, Inc., 1964.

Moore, Geoffrey H. *Business Cycles Indicators.* Princeton, N.J.: Princeton University Press, 1960.

Murphy, John S. *Basics of Digital Computer Programming.* New York: John F. Rider, Publisher, Inc., 1964.

Neuner, John J. W. *Cost Accounting: Principles and Practice.* Sixth edition. Homewood, Illinois: Richard D. Irwin, Inc., 1962.

Newman, William H. *Administrative Action: The Techniques of Organization and Management.* Second edition. Englewood Cliffs, N.J.: Prentice-Hall, Inc., 1963.

Newman, William H., Summer, Charles E., and Warren, E. Kirby. *The Process of Management: Concepts, Behavior and Practice.* Second edition. Englewood Cliffs, N.J.: Prentice-Hall, Inc., 1967.

Norbeck, Edward F. *et al. Operational Auditing for Management Control.* New York: American Management Association, 1969.

Osborn, Alex F. *Applied Imagination.* New York: Charles Scribner's Sons, 1953.

Paynter, Henry M. *Analysis and Design of Engineering Systems.* Cambridge, Mass.: The M.I.T. Press, 1961.

Pigors, Paul and Meyers, Charles A. *Personnel Administration.* New York: McGraw-Hill Book Company, Inc., 1964.

Pigors, Paul, Meyers, Charles A., and Malon, F. T. *Management of Human Resources.* New York: McGraw-Hill Book Company, Inc., 1964.

Postley, John A. *Computers and People.* New York: McGraw-Hill Book Company, Inc., 1960.

Prince, Thomas R. *Information Systems for Management Planning and Control.* Homewood, Illinois: Richard D. Irwin, Inc., 1966.

Richards, May D., and Greenlaw, Paul S. *Management Decision-Making.* Homewood, Illinois: Richard D. Irwin, Inc., 1966.

Rose, T. G., and Farr Donald E. *Higher Management Control.* New York: McGraw-Hill Book Company, 1957.

Rudwick, Bernard H. *Systems Analysis for Effective Planning.* New York: John Wiley and Sons, Inc., 1969.

Schiff, Michael and Mellman, Martin. *Financial Management of the Marketing Function*. New York: Financial Executives Research Foundation, 1962.

Schlaifer, Robert. *Probability and Statistics for Business Decisions*. New York: McGraw-Hill Book Company, Inc., 1959.

Schmidt, Richard N., and Meyers, William E. *Introduction to Computer Science and Data Processing*. New York: Holt, Rinehart and Winston, Inc., 1966.

Schneller, Kenneth E. *Case Analysis and Business Problem Solving*. New York: McGraw-Hill Book Company, Inc., 1967.

Simon, Herbert A. *The New Science of Management Decision*. New York: Harper and Row, Publishers, Inc., 1960.

Solomons, David. *Divisional Performance: Measurement and Control*. New York: Financial Executives Research Foundation, 1965.

Solomon, Irving I., and Weingart, Laurence O. *Management Uses of the Computer*. New York: Harper and Row, Publishers, 1966.

Steiner, George A. *Managerial Long-Range Planning*. New York: McGraw-Hill Book Company, Inc., 1963.

Stokes, Paul M. *A Total Systems Approach to Management Control*. New York: American Management Association, 1968.

Strong, Earl P., and Smith, Robert D. *Management Control*. New York: American Management Association, 1968.

Strong, Earl P., and Smith, Robert D. *Management Control Models*. New York: Holt, Rinehart and Winston, Inc., 1968.

Summer, Charles E. Jr., and O'Connell, Jeremiah J. *The Managerial Mind: Science and Theory in Policy Decisions*. Homewood, Illinois: Richard D. Irwin, Inc., 1964.

Symonds, Curtis W. *A Design for Business Intelligence*. New York: American Management Association, 1971.

Tannenbaum, Arnold S. *Control in Organization*. New York: McGraw-Hill Book Company, Inc., 1968.

Tannenbaum, Robert, Weschler, Irving R., and Massarik, Fred. *Leadership Science Approach*. New York: McGraw-Hill Book Company, Inc., 1961.

Terry, George R. *Principles of Management*. Fourth edition. Homewood, Illinois: Richard D. Irwin, Inc., 1964.

Vance, Lawrence L., and Taussig, Russell. *Accounting Principles for Control*. Revised edition. New York: Holt, Rinehart and Winston, 1966.

Vazsonyi, A. *Scientific Programming in Business and Industry*. New York: John Wiley and Sons, Inc., 1958.

Villers, Raymond. *Research and Development Planning and Control*. Financial Executives Research Foundation, 1964.

Wadia, Maneck S. *Management and the Behavioral Sciences: Text and Readings*. Boston: Allyn and Bacon, Inc., 1968.

Welsch, Glenn A., and Surd, Burward H. *Management Planning and Control*. New York: Financial Executives Research Foundation, 1968.

Weston, J. Fred, and Brigham, Eugene F. *Managerial Finance*. Second edition. New York: Holt, Rinehart and Winston, 1962.

Wiener, Norbert. *The Human Use of Human Beings: Cybernetics and Society*. Boston: Houghton Mifflin Company, 1950.

Withington, Frederick. *The Use of Computers in Business Organizations.* Reading, Mass.: Addison-Wesley Publishing Company, 1966.

Wolfe, Harry Deane. *Business Forecasting Methods.* New York: Holt, Rinehart and Winston, 1966.

Young, Stanley. *Management: A Systems Analysis.* Glenview, Illinois: Scott, Foresman and Company, 1966.

INDEX